New Directions in M

D0370685

The field of media and politics is quickly changing as society transforms and new technologies develop continuously. Academic research in the area is rapidly breaking new ground to keep pace with the prolific media developments. This innovative, up-to-date text moves beyond rudimentary concepts and definitions to consider the exciting scholarly research that addresses the monumental recent changes in the media system of the United States and the world. This carefully crafted volume addresses the big questions that academic researchers are asking, exposing students to the rigorous scholarship in the field but making it readily understandable by undergraduate students.

Each chapter starts with a "big question" about the impact of the news media, provides an overview of the more general topic, and answers that question by appealing to the best, most-up-to-date research in the field. The volume as a whole is held together by an exploration of the rapidly changing media environment and the influence these changes have on individual political behavior and governments as a whole.

New Directions in Media and Politics will make an ideal book for courses as it digs deeper into the questions that standard textbooks only hint at—and presents scholarly evidence to support the arguments made.

Travis N. Ridout is Associate Professor and Thomas S. Foley Distinguished Professor of Government and Public Policy in the School of Politics, Philosophy and Public Affairs at Washington State University. He is co-author of *The Persuasive Power of Campaign Advertising* (2011) and *Campaign Advertising and American Democracy* (2007).

New Directions in American Politics

The Routledge series *New Directions in American Politics* is composed of contributed volumes covering key areas of study in the field of American politics and government. Each title provides a state-of-the-art overview of current trends in its respective subfield, with an eye toward cutting edge research accessible to advanced undergraduate and beginning graduate students. While the volumes touch on the main topics of relevant study, they are not meant to cover the "nuts and bolts" of the subject. Rather, they engage readers in the most recent scholarship, real-world controversies, and theoretical debates with the aim of getting students excited about the same issues that animate scholars.

New Directions in Media and Politics

Edited by
Travis N. Ridout

Routledge
Taylor & Francis Group

NEW YORK AND LONDON

First published 2013
by Routledge
711 Third Avenue, New York, NY 10017

Simultaneously published in the UK
by Routledge
2 Park Square, Milton Park, Abingdon, Oxon OX14 4RN

Routledge is an imprint of the Taylor & Francis Group, an informa business

Library of Congress Cataloging in Publication Data
   New directions in media and politics / Travis N. Ridout, editor.
   p. cm. – (New directions in American politics)
   1. Communication in politics–United States. 2. Mass media–Political
aspects–United States. 3. Mass media–United States. I. Ridout, Travis N.,
1974–
   JA85.2.U6N48 2012
   320.97301'4–dc23
   2012027032

ISBN: 978–0–415–53732–2 (hbk)
ISBN: 978–0–415–53733–9 (pbk)
ISBN: 978–0–203–10905–2 (ebk)

Typeset in Gill Sans & Minion
by Swales & Willis Ltd, Exeter, Devon

Printed and bound in the United States of America by
Edwards Brothers Malloy

To my children, Lorelei, Julianne and Isaac

Contents

Figures

Tables

Preface

Those of us who study media and politics struggle at times to keep up with the massive changes that the American media system has undergone in recent years. The decline of print newspapers, consolidation in the media industry, the rise of a more partisan media, the migration of news to the Internet, changing definitions of what a journalist is, increased audience choices—what does all of this mean for the American people and American democracy? It is a challenge to address the impact of such changes, and yet these challenges are what make the field so exciting. We are not—or at least we hope that we are not—studying the same things we were two decades ago and in the same way. Instead, we are finding new ways to address new questions.

One thing I appreciate about the collection of chapters assembled here is that they represent a diversity of points of view and methodological approaches. Some chapters are based on the collection of original data, some are based on sophisticated statistical modeling techniques (simplified for your reading ease), some chapters provide an overview of others' research, and some chapters, like the final one, spin a good yarn. Many chapters are focused on the elite news media, but others discuss the non-elite media, and one even pays attention to "everyday citizens" in the form of political bloggers, though, admittedly, there is probably not enough discussion of these everyday voices—a lament heard whenever scholars of political communication gather together. Almost all chapters pay attention to both traditional media and the new media. Indeed, I find it almost impossible to separate the two in this day and age. In short, while the volume does not cover everything, it provides a good taste of what is the state of the art in the study of media and politics in the United States.

I could not have chosen a better group of authors for the chapters in this volume. Each chapter is written by people who ask really fascinating questions and arrive at interesting conclusions. Moreover, in contrast to the experience of most editors, the contributors to this volume actually met most deadlines—and when they did not, they kept me apprised of their schedule for completion. I cannot thank them enough for making the experience of editing this book a pleasure rather than drudgery. As a result of their conscientiousness, I will be able to turn in this manuscript on time!

I also want to thank Michael Kerns at Routledge for guiding me through this process in a way that resulted in low stress levels for me. He convinced me that editing this book would be the right thing to do, and so far, he has been correct.

Travis N. Ridout
Pullman, Washington
July 2012

Contributors

Leticia Bode (Ph.D., University of Wisconsin–Madison) is an Assistant Professor in the Department of Communication, Culture, and Technology at Georgetown University. Her research interests include political communication, public opinion, and political behavior, with an emphasis on how innovations in technology affect the political process for both elites and the public.

James N. Druckman is the Payson S. Wild Professor of Political Science and a Faculty Fellow at the Institute for Policy Research at Northwestern University. His work focuses on preference formation and political communication.

Beth C. Easter is a Ph.D. candidate in the Department of Political Science at Indiana University. She holds a Juris Doctorate from Emory Law School and is a licensed member of the Michigan Bar. Her research interests include judicial politics, elections, political parties, and interest groups. Her dissertation examines the participation of political parties and organized interests in state Supreme Court elections. A grant from the National Science Foundation Law and Social Sciences Program has funded this project, which helped Easter to conduct a national survey of political parties and organized interests.

Stephanie Edgerly (Ph.D., University of Wisconsin–Madison) is an Assistant Professor in the Medill School of Journalism and Integrated Marketing Management at Northwestern University. Her research explores how changes in the media landscape provide citizens with new opportunities for political engagement. She is particularly interested in the interplay between psychology and environment on political understanding and decision-making.

Michael M. Franz is Associate Professor of Government and Legal Studies at Bowdoin College. His research interests include campaign finance and political advertising. He is the author or co-author of four books, including *Choices and Changes: Interest Groups in the Electoral Process* (2008) and *The Persuasive Power of Campaign Advertising* (2011). He is co-director of the Wesleyan Media Project, which tracks and codes political ads on television.

Erika Franklin Fowler is Assistant Professor of Government at Wesleyan University and co-director of the Wesleyan Media Project, which tracks and analyzes all political ads aired on broadcast television in real-time during elections. She specializes in political communication and has published extensively on topics relating to local media coverage and political advertising. Prior to arriving at Wesleyan, she spent two years as a Robert Wood Johnson Scholar in Health Policy Research at the University of Michigan and five years as the Research Director of the University of Wisconsin NewsLab, one of the largest and most systematic local television election tracking projects ever conducted. Fowler holds a Ph.D. from the University of Wisconsin–Madison.

Roderick P. Hart is Dean of the College of Communication at the University of Texas at Austin and holds the Shivers Chair in Communication and Government. He is the author or editor of twelve books including *Political Tone: What Leaders Say and Why*, forthcoming from the University Of Chicago Press. He also serves as executive director of the Annette Strauss Institute for Civic Participation.

Danny Hayes is Assistant Professor of Political Science at George Washington University. His research focuses on political communication and political behavior. He is the co-author of *Influence from Abroad: Foreign Voices, the Media, and U.S. Public Opinion* (forthcoming, Cambridge University Press) and has published numerous articles in the *American Journal of Political Science, Political Research Quarterly, Political Behavior,* and *Political Communication,* among others.

Young Mie Kim (Ph.D., University of Illinois at Urbana—Champaign) is an Assistant Professor in the School of Journalism and Mass Communication and Donovan Wright Faculty Fellow of the College of Letters and Science at the University of Wisconsin–Madison. Kim's research program centers on how the "new" media environment—characterized as the development of digital communication technologies and the adoption of entertainment-oriented media formats—contributes to the changing foundation of political communication. Kim's research has developed a theoretical framework that explains the facilitation of issue publics in the age of digital media.

Samara Klar is a Ph.D. candidate in the Department of Political Science at Northwestern University. Her work focuses on the influence of personal identities on political preferences and political behavior.

Yanna Krupnikov is an Assistant Professor of Political Science at Northwestern University. Her research focuses on the way campaign communication affects individual behavior. Her work has been published in the *Journal of Politics,* the *American Journal of Political Science* and *Political Communication.*

Jonathan M. Ladd is Associate Professor of Public Policy and Government at Georgetown University. He is the author of *Why Americans Hate the Media* *and How it Matters* (2012) as well as several articles about the news media, public opinion and voting.

Matthew Lang is a Ph.D. candidate in Political Science at the University of Houston. His research interests include presidential party building, presidential leadership, and state politics.

Regina G. Lawrence (Ph.D. Political Science, University of Washington, 1997) holds the Jesse H. Jones Centennial Chair in School of Journalism at the University of Texas at Austin. She is the author of *The Politics of Force: Media and the Construction of Police Brutality* (2000) and co-author (with W. Lance Bennett and Steven Livingston) of *When the Press Fails: Political Power and the News Media from Iraq to Katrina* (2007). Her latest book is *Hillary Clinton's Run for the White House: Media, Gender Strategy, and Campaign Politics* (2009, co-authored with Melody Rose), which won an honorable mention Carrie Chapman Catt Prize for Research.

Ashley Muddiman is a Ph.D. candidate in the Communication Studies Department at the University of Texas at Austin and has worked as a research assistant at the Annette Strauss Institute for Civic Participation. Her research interests include political incivility and media effects.

Travis N. Ridout is Associate Professor and the Thomas S. Foley Distinguished Professor of Government and Public Policy in the School of Politics, Philosophy and Public Affairs at Washington State University. He specializes in the study of political communication, with a focus on campaigns and political advertising. He is co-author of *The Persuasive Power of Campaign Advertising* (2011). He also serves as co-director of the Wesleyan Media Project.

Piers Robinson is Senior Lecturer in International Politics at the University of Manchester. He specializes in media, communications and international politics and is lead author of *Pockets of Resistance: British News Media, War and Theory in the 2003 Invasion of Iraq* (2010) and author of *The CNN Effect: the Myth of News, Foreign Policy and Intervention* (2002).

Joshua Robison is a Ph.D. candidate in the Department of Political Science at Northwestern University. His work focuses on the influence of value orientations on political behavior.

Brandon Rottinghaus is Associate Professor and the Senator Don Henderson Scholar in the Department of Political Science at the University of Houston. His research interests include the presidency, executive-legislative relations and public opinion. He is author of *The Provisional Pulpit: Modern Presidential Leadership of Public Opinion* (2010). He is also the co-director of the Presidential Proclamations Project.

Dhavan V. Shah (Ph.D., University of Minnesota–Twin Cities) is Louis A. & Mary E. Maier-Bascom Professor at the University of Wisconsin, where he is also Director of the Mass Communication Research Center. His research concerns the social psychology of communication influence, especially effects of information and communication technologies (ICT), on community engagement, electoral participation, and youth socialization. He has authored numerous articles in leading communication and political science journals.

Natalie (Talia) Jomini Stroud is an Assistant Professor in the Department of Communication Studies and Assistant Director of Research at the Annette Strauss Institute for Civic Participation at the University of Texas at Austin. Her book, *Niche News: The Politics of News Choice* (2011), explores the prevalence, antecedents, and consequences of partisan selective exposure.

C. Danielle Vinson is a Professor of Political Science at Furman University. She is the author of *Local Media Coverage of Congress and Its Members* (2003) and has written articles on political parties and the media, religion and politics in the media, and communication and spending in political campaigns.

Chapter 1

Introduction

Travis N. Ridout

A textbook on Media and Politics from 20 years ago would look dramatically different from a textbook on that topic today. We cannot necessarily say that about the other fields of study in American politics, such as Congress or judicial politics. For while there have certainly been recent changes in, say, committee structures in Congress, I would argue that the changes in the American media system in recent years have been much more dramatic.

As I write this, the one daily newspaper serving New Orleans publishes its print version only three days a week.[1] How times have changed. That a metropolitan area of over 1.1 million people can no longer support a daily print newspaper would have been unthinkable a decade ago. In making the move to thrice-weekly publication, the *Times Picayune* cut by half the number of reporters in the newsroom as the organization shifts its focus to its website.[2] Of course, the turmoil at the *Times Picayune* should not be all that surprising, given the rapid pace with which readership of printed newspapers has plummeted. One big change to the American media system, then, is the decline in the American newspaper.

That has been accompanied by the rise of blatantly partisan and ideological news organizations. From the 1920s through the 1970s, most news organizations sought to provide news that was fair, objective and balanced.[3] But as the news media moved toward a more interpretative style of reporting in the 1980s, that political neutrality began to wane. This was perhaps first seen in the rise of conservative talk radio in the late 1980s, when Rush Limbaugh started broadcasting nationally. In 1996, Fox News—an unabashedly conservative cable news network—went on the air. Since then, a variety of websites, both on the left and the right of the political spectrum, have been established. Instead of providing a balanced, mainstream recitation of the day's events in order to appeal to the largest possible audience, many news organizations nowadays provide a point of view, something that many news consumers applaud.

Maybe the biggest change of the past two decades is the movement of news and its consumers to an online environment. By early 2010, more people reported that they sought out news online than read a print newspaper or listened to news on the radio.[4] Online-only websites, such as Huffington Post, Salon and ProPublica are now generating news instead of just redistributing stories written by reporters at traditional news organizations. And, of course, everyday citizens—armed with their camera phones and Twitter accounts—are helping to make the news, too, resulting in what has been called "distributed journalism."[5] This has led to a blurring between who is a journalist and who is not.

These are just a few of the changes to the American (and global) media environment that the authors of the chapters in this book talk about. Suffice it to say, *the media environment in the United States and around the world is undergoing rapid change.* This serves as the first main theme of this volume. Those who study political communication are struggling—though making vast strides—to keep up with these changes and their impact. Thus, the second theme of this volume is that *changes in the media environment have the potential to influence the political behavior of individuals and the functioning of governments and democracy.* The authors in this volume address the many ways in which changes to the media system have had an impact on how citizens think about politics and interact with their governments. These range from how voters respond to being contacted by a politician through Facebook to whether people learn more from political blogs than they do from newspapers.

Yet when I recently reviewed all of the contributions in this book, I noticed that almost every chapter referred to one consequence in particular. Namely, today's media environment has made it easy—and maybe even encouraged—people to expose themselves to news sources whose politics they agree with. The presence nowadays of so many news organizations that are upfront about their own political ideologies or partisanship means that people can easily seek out news sources that reinforce their beliefs rather than challenging them. Because of the prevalence of this idea, I placed at the front of this volume Talia Stroud and Ashley Muddiman's chapter, which explores how people choose the media sources they use. Their chapter discusses the concept of selective exposure. As the authors show, choosing to use like-minded media has consequences for how easily people make political decisions, how much people participate politically and even how much they know about politics. Yet today's media environment not only facilitates choosing like-minded media sources, it also facilitates the avoidance of politics. People's entertainment preferences are easily satisfied in this era of 200 channels and billions of websites, and thus one need not engage with politics at all.

In chapter 3, Jonathan Ladd talks about another change in the media environment over the past decades: the dramatic decline in how much trust and confidence that people have in the news media. He shows that a lack of trust leads people to choose like-minded media sources. This selection helps to shape people's opinions about political matters, leading Republicans and Democrats to starkly different perceptions of politics and political issues.

Of course, as Erika Franklin Fowler rightly points out in chapter 4, not all people turn to a partisan media source. In fact, many still consume a traditional, mainstream news source: local television news. A common criticism of local television news is *not* that it's providing one-sided political coverage but that it's providing virtually no coverage at all of elections and government; you might as well be watching ESPN or MTV. Yet Fowler shows that this stereotype is not completely true. Local news broadcasts do provide a fair amount of political coverage, especially during the heat of an electoral campaign.

Piers Robinson takes us outside the United States in chapter 5. His focus is on how the media cover war and conflict around the globe, though he pays particular attention to how the American and British press covers those events. In doing so, he addresses an important question: in its coverage of war, do the news media serve to drum up war, or do they act as agents of peace? Robinson's answer to this question is careful and nuanced, but he ultimately finds considerable support for the warmonger label.

No book on media and politics today should ignore the role of social media, such as Twitter, Facebook and YouTube. Indeed, when I conceptualized this book, I wanted the role of social media in politics today to be something that was addressed not just in a single chapter but by a multitude of authors. And I believe the book succeeds in that: you can find Facebook mentioned in six chapters and the verb "tweet" used in three. Still, while I wanted to show the importance of social media in a variety of contexts, I wanted one chapter that focused on that topic alone. That chapter is chapter 6. Stephanie Edgerly, Leticia Bode, Young Mie Kim and Dhavan Shah are doing cutting-edge research to try to figure out how social media influence the conduct of political campaigns and how the introduction of these new technologies has had an impact on the voter. Although the authors find that the use of social media in a campaign context can encourage political participation, they worry that many "digitally disengaged" Americans are not benefitting from the mobilizing potential of social media.

Chapter 7, by Yanna Krupnikov and Beth Easter, focuses on a debate that has received much attention recently: are negative campaigns bad or good for the American voter and for American democracy more generally? But instead of staking out one position, the authors carefully consider the circumstances under which negativity may inspire participation—and when it may impede participation. And so "it depends" is the appropriate answer to the question of whether campaign negativity depresses political participation.

In chapter 8, Michael Franz takes us inside the world of the political strategist. He shows how technological change has enabled campaigns to better target their messages to an intended audience. He explains how campaigns place their advertising not just in specific media markets but on specific television stations and even during specific programs in order to better reach the audiences they want to speak to. But while this may be "efficient" for campaigners, it creates a situation in which some voters are not hearing from politicians on both sides, a development that is decidedly not good for American democracy, in the view of Franz.

Regina Lawrence considers media coverage of one particular type of candidate in chapter 9: women running for office. She asks whether women candidates get a fair shake from the news media. While pointing out hurdles that women candidates still may face—and illustrating that with a discussion of Hillary Clinton's 2008 campaign for the White House—Lawrence remains fairly optimistic that the hurdles facing women candidates are now fewer than those they faced in the past.

Most media and politics textbooks devote considerable attention to the relationship between the news media and the branches of government, and this book is no exception. In chapter 10, C. Danielle Vinson examines the relationship between Congress and the news media—and which actor has the upper hand. Although Vinson argues that the news media ultimately get to determine what is newsworthy, she notes an impressive array of techniques that Members of Congress have adopted in their (often successful) attempts to steer the coverage that they receive. In chapter 11, Brandon Rottinghaus and Matthew Lang take us down Pennsylvania Avenue to the White House. They consider whether the president even has the ability to lead the American public anymore in this era of a fragmented—and increasingly critical—news media. But while modern presidential communication may be difficult, presidents do have various means of communication at their disposal, and the environment is sometimes ripe for presidential leadership and persuasion.

Chapter 12 shifts our focus to the more subtle ways by which the media send messages. This chapter, by Samara Klar, Josh Robison, and James Druckman, focuses on framing and makes an important distinction between frames in communication (the words, images and style that a presenter uses to relay information) and frames in thought (how individuals perceive a situation). The authors discuss how both types of frames are established and then go on to note the situations under which frames can—and cannot—have an influence on people's opinions.

Danny Hayes ponders a highly relevant question in chapter 13: whether or not the new media do a better job than traditional media sources in providing citizens with information about policy debates. To answer this question, Hayes compares coverage of the 2011 crisis in Libya within traditional news sources, represented by network news broadcasts and elite newspapers, with coverage by the new media, represented by two prominent blogs and cable news. Surprisingly, Hayes finds very few differences in coverage across the old and new media outlets, suggesting that the promise and potential of these new media sources is not being fulfilled.

Rod Hart ends this volume with a "big picture" look at politics in the digital age. He addresses the staggering failure of journalism's economic model in this Internet era and points out the dangers of a citizenry that may be too "wired." He also bemoans a lack of courage among those scholars who study media and politics, warning that they must set aside their fascination with numbers in order to study real people using their everyday voices.

Final Words

In thinking about what this textbook should look like, I wanted to avoid some of the artificial boundaries that often define the study of media and politics. I did not want to assign some authors to write about the old media and others to write about the new media. I did not want to have some authors write about how news organizations make the news, while others wrote about the consequences of how the news is constructed. Instead, I wanted the contributors to this volume to have a lot of freedom to address the most interesting questions confronting the field of media and politics and, almost invariably, answering those questions requires stepping across boundaries.

Because of this, some topics traditionally covered in a media and politics textbook are not found here, such as the routines of the newsroom or how the news media cover the court system. But covering everything was never my goal. Instead, I hope that this book, by introducing you to some of the best scholars doing the most interesting research in the field, will make you want to learn more about the intersection of media and politics in the United States, a topic that is constantly changing.

Notes

1 John Pope, "Times-Picayune to Cut Back to Publishing Three Days a Week," *Washington Post*, May 26, 2012. http://www.washingtonpost.com/politics/times-picayune-to-cut-back-to-publishing-three-days-a-week/2012/05/26/gJQAyltisU_story.html

2 Kevin McGill, "Times-Picayune Cuts Half of Newsroom Staff," *Bloomberg Businessweek*, June 12, 2012. http://www.businessweek.com/ap/2012-06-12/times-picayune-cutting-half-of-newsroom-staff

3 Darrell M. West, *The Rise and Fall of the Media Establishment* (Boston: Bedford/St. Martin's, 2001).

4 Doug Gross, "Survey: More Americans Get News from Internet than Newspapers or Radio," CNN, March 1, 2010. http://articles.cnn.com/2010-03-01/tech/social.network.news_1_social-networking-sites-social-media-social-experience?_s=PM:TECH

5 Jeremy D. Mayer and Michael Cornfield, "The Internet and the Future of Media Politics," in *Media Power, Media Politics*, 2nd ed., ed. Mark J. Rozell and Jeremy D. Mayer (Lanham, Md.: Rowman and Littlefield, 2008), 319–338.

Chapter 2

The American Media System Today

Is the Public Fragmenting?

Natalie (Talia) Jomini Stroud and Ashley Muddiman

How do people navigate the many, many media choices they have at their disposal? More specifically, which sources do we choose when looking for news and information about public affairs? And what are the effects of all of these choices? This chapter explores what we know—and what we don't know—about our media selections and their consequences. A media environment with so many choices not only facilitates our ability to choose whatever we prefer—it *requires* us to choose. If you have a cable television package, it isn't possible to flip through all of your available television channels without dedicating a good bit of time. And the Internet requires us to actively select the content that we see. So how do we choose? Why do some gravitate toward Fox News and others toward MSNBC? This chapter explores the extent to which our political beliefs govern our choices, a behavior known as selective exposure. We examine whether selective exposure occurs and why we might prefer like-minded information. We then turn to the consequences of using like-minded news. The final section of this chapter describes other factors that influence which sources garner our time and attention, including negativity, issue interests, and entertainment preferences.

Selective Exposure

Selective exposure is the motivated selection of pro-attitudinal messages and the motivated avoidance of counter-attitudinal messages. There has been extensive debate over the occurrence of selective exposure – does it actually occur with any frequency? A brief overview of two research studies will give you a preliminary feel for the debate. Consider the following scenario, developed by Jonathan Freedman: you've been asked to listen to an interview of a fellow student who is applying to participate in a conference overseas.[1] As you listen, it becomes clear that the interview is going extremely well. This student seems well qualified for the conference. After you've listened to the interview in its entirety, you are asked: "Should the applicant be accepted to participate in the conference?" Thinking through what you just heard, you feel confident in saying "Yes." Then you learn that two more pieces of information about this applicant are available—one piece of information is a positive review of the applicant and the second is a negative review of the applicant. Which do you pick? In this study, people overwhelmingly chose the *negative* review.

In this same study, some participants were asked to listen to a negative interview, where the student applicant seemed notably unqualified for the conference. Guess what – when asked to pick between the positive and negative reviews afterward, these participants tended to pick the *positive* review after hearing the *negative* interview.

Notice that this is exactly the opposite of what selective exposure would predict! If we prefer information that matches our beliefs, we would expect that those hearing the positive interview would choose the *positive* information and those hearing the negative interview would choose the *negative* information. Why did this happen? Should we rid books, like this one, of the concept of selective exposure as a result? Before we do so, consider the next study.

Imagine that you're a member of a partisan group on campus—either the Young Democrats, or the College Republicans. After a day of attending classes, you grab your mail as you head into your home. It's political season, so you're not surprised to see a political letter included among the bills, magazines, and product advertisements. When you look closely at the letter, you see that it is an offer to sign up for some brochures with information favoring your preferred political candidate. The brochures look as if they will be interesting and will contain strong, valid, and persuasive arguments. Do you sign up for the brochures?

Now imagine that instead, the letter offered you the opportunity to obtain brochures that favored the opposition. Now what? The results of Aaron Lowin's research showed that college-age Democrats and Republicans were more likely to request brochures containing strong arguments *when the brochure favored their preferred candidate.*

The story is more complicated, however. The previous results were for brochures containing *strong arguments.* What if the arguments were rather weak, though? What if they were the sorts of arguments that you could refute easily? Would you want to read these easily refutable arguments about your own candidate or about the opposition? Here, the pattern reverses. Respondents preferred to read weak arguments favoring the opposition, as opposed to weak arguments favoring their preferred candidate.

These studies tell us a lot about selective exposure. First, they tell us that selective exposure doesn't always occur. Different contexts can affect the extent to which selective exposure occurs. Interview situations may motivate different information selection patterns in comparison to political brochures. Strong arguments may motivate different selection patterns in comparison to weak arguments. Second, when comparing the first and second studies, it appears that politics may inspire a greater degree of selective exposure in comparison to other topics. This observation is echoed by several others who find something particularly potent about selective exposure tendencies in political contexts.[2]

Why might politics inspire the selection of like-minded information? Politics can spark strong emotions and feelings of self-identity—just the sort of circumstances that may lead people to prefer information matching their beliefs. For this reason, we focus on the selection of like-minded *political* information, known as partisan selective exposure, in the subsequent pages.

Partisan Selective Exposure in the Modern Media Environment

The modern media environment has become a particularly fruitful ground for examining the selective exposure hypothesis. One facet that has garnered much recent attention is the outlets on which citizens rely for news. Do citizens turn to media outlets matching their political predispositions? Although not all citizens do so, evidence clearly suggests that some do.

The correlation between political beliefs and where citizens turn for news today is striking. If someone who is well informed about politics tells us a few places where she turns regularly for news, we're willing to bet that we can make a pretty good guess about her partisanship. For example, as shown in Figure 2.1, Republicans are more likely to name Fox News as their main television source, while Democrats are more likely to name CNN or MSNBC. In fact, research suggests that political leanings help to predict which newspapers people read, which talk radio programs they select, which cable news outlets they prefer, and which Internet websites they visit.[3]

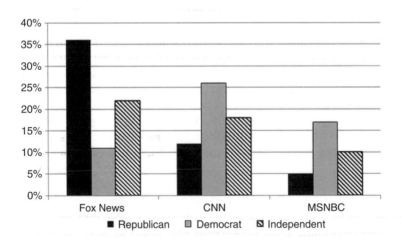

Figure 2.1 Main television source by partisanship

Source: Data from the Pew Research Center, January 4–8, 2012.

Experimental evidence confirms that news sources send ideological cues. Consider the following two studies. First, Shanto Iyengar and Kyu Hahn randomly assigned news stories to various media sources.[4] Imagine that you saw a political news article and that the source was Fox News—would you read it? What if instead the same article was attributed to National Public Radio, or CNN, or the BBC? Iyengar and Hahn found that the source made a difference. Conservatives were drawn to Fox News and liberals were repelled by this source attribution.

Another study examined which magazines people would select in a waiting room and which they would select for a free subscription.[5] In this study, we secretly observed which magazines people selected while they were waiting to participate in another research study. The political magazines were purposefully displayed in the waiting room to facilitate browsing. Nearly an hour later, after actually participating in another unrelated study, participants were offered a free subscription to one of the magazines they had seen in the waiting room. Political leanings were related both to which magazines people browsed in the waiting room and which magazines they selected for a free subscription. People seem to be drawn to like-minded political content.

One vexing question is whether the Internet facilitates or depresses selective exposure. The Internet permits ample opportunities to explore diverse views. And some undoubtedly take advantage; when Jennifer Stromer-Galley interviewed people who discuss politics online, several of them mentioned that they enjoyed hearing views unlike their own![6] One study that tracked where people surf online found that those looking at left-leaning websites also look at right-leaning sites.[7] Yet the Internet also provides ready access to like-minded information. Several studies looking at how Internet users behave have found that citizens gravitate toward like-minded political information.[8]

Social networking sites (SNS) are similarly complicated in terms of whether we connect with diverse or mainly like-minded others. Scholars have uncovered some evidence of ideological clustering on college students' Facebook pages.[9] And there is evidence that ideology affects our SNS behavior; according to recent research by the Pew Research Center, "9% of [adults participating in social networking sites (SNS)] have blocked, unfriended, or hidden someone on the site because they posted something about politics or issues that they disagreed with or found offensive."[10] It seems that new media technologies have not completely absolved people of preferring views echoing their own.

There seems to be ample evidence that people are drawn toward like-minded content. Not all people and not in all circumstances, to be sure, but there is something compelling about information with which we agree. Why would people display a preference for like-minded political information? The next section reviews various reasons why we may seek congenial messages.

Psychological Reasons that Selective Exposure Occurs

A number of psychological theories have been proposed to explain selective exposure. Here, we'll focus on three: cognitive dissonance, cognitive misers, and information quality.

First, Leon Festinger proposed that selective exposure may occur as a result of cognitive dissonance.[11] According to Festinger, people can experience discomfort when they hold two ideas that conflict. Say, for example, that you strongly identify with a particular political party. You've voted consistently for this party—you even have a bumper sticker on your car supporting the party's presidential candidate. When listening to a presidential debate, however, you are completely surprised to find that you agree more with the opposing candidate on a particular issue. Learning this, you are shocked—are there other such issues where you disagree with your party? Did you perhaps misunderstand what the candidates said on the issue? We've all experienced cognitive dissonance at one point or another, so even if you aren't strongly partisan, it is likely that you can recall an instance in which you've learned something that does not square well with other ideas that you hold to be true. This feeling is known as cognitive dissonance. When people experience cognitive dissonance, they typically are motivated to reduce this feeling. One strategy for reducing cognitive dissonance, Festinger proposed, is selective exposure. By looking at like-minded information and avoiding contradictory information, a state of cognitive harmony can be restored. Reading more about your candidate's stance on the issue in question may reveal that you really are more in alignment than you originally thought. Or looking at all of the other issues on which you agree with your candidate may confirm that even though on this one issue you might hold a different belief, on many other issues your party choice makes good sense. Although cognitive dissonance is a compelling explanation for selective exposure, it isn't clear that it operates in all instances. Is cognitive dissonance the best explanation for why someone might habitually turn to the same outlets for news? Other explanations, reviewed below, provide alternate reasons that we may prefer like-minded sources.

Second, selective exposure may be the result of a desire to minimize use of our cognitive resources.[12] Humans, it seems, like to conserve their cognitive energy. The label "cognitive misers" isn't completely out of place. Indeed, this seems to be the case for many when it comes to politics. Learning about politics takes an investment of time, resources, and energy. Not everyone does this—indeed, we would guess that nearly everyone takes some shortcuts when it comes to politics. Instead of thoroughly researching where each candidate stands on all of the issues to find a best match, some rely on partisan labels, some on polling data, others on endorsements. Selective exposure may be another form of this behavior. Engaging with counter-attitudinal information is mentally taxing. The arguments are more challenging to process and the act of coming up with counter-arguments requires careful thinking. Like-minded information, on the other hand, fits well with our existing thought processes. There's no need for counter-argument. Put simply, selective exposure is easier. This may be a primary reason for why we engage in the behavior. This explanation, however, may not be entirely satisfying. Surely we aren't always this lazy!

A third argument is that selective exposure occurs because we would like to pick the highest-quality information sources.[13] In an environment filled with media choices, we have to select something if we want to learn about news and politics. Perhaps we rationally survey the available options in search of the best source. Isn't this a refreshing way to think about our choices? It isn't as rational as it might seem, however. Think about it—why don't we agree on which sources are the best, the highest in quality, and the most truthful? Something else must be at play. It turns out that partisanship relates to which sources we find to be of the highest quality. Like-minded sources seem to fit much better with our current understanding of the world. Since the information seems more correct, we infer that these sources are higher quality.

This coheres with what we know about how citizens think about media bias. The public perceives bias in the news. According to non-partisan survey research conducted by the Pew Research Center, "37% of Americans say there is a great deal of bias in news coverage and 30% say there is a fair amount of bias."[14] Even news articles that seem balanced and objective to an audience un-invested in the news topic can seem extremely biased to individuals who have an opinion on the topic.[15] Exposure to news with a partisan slant also is affected by our political beliefs.[16] Instead of assuming that all news is slanted against their opinions, people who view like-minded news see it as less biased than news that counters their partisan beliefs. Thus, when asked to evaluate the media bias of television channels and shows, such as CNN and Fox News, conservatives tend to perceive more bias in CNN than Fox News and liberals see the opposite.[17] Partisan viewers also think the *hosts* of programs are biased when those viewers disagree with the opinions expressed in a story.[18] One person's reasonable, fair, and high-quality outlet is another person's nightmare of bias, deception, and distortion.

A fragmented political media environment allows citizens to select political information based on their partisanship. But what are the *consequences* of these choices? We now turn to the effects of partisan selective exposure.

Outcomes of Partisan Selective Exposure

How does the use of like-minded media affect our attitudes, beliefs, and behavior? In this section, we discuss the consequences of partisan selective exposure. As an attentive reader will readily note, some of these consequences seem, on balance, rather positive. Wouldn't it be great if we could inspire more citizens to participate in politics, for example? Other consequences of partisan selective exposure, however, could be read more negatively. Might partisan selective exposure result in a more polarized, less tolerant electorate? Although one may label participation as a benefit and polarization as a detriment, we are fully conscious—and you should be as well—that a strong argument could be made that these normative labels should be reversed. In reading the next section, we encourage you to think through where you stand. On balance, do you think that partisan selective exposure is a good thing or a bad thing?

Political Participation, Partisan Identities, and Partisan Selective Exposure

The use of like-minded political media may affect our partisan identities and the extent to which we participate in politics. First, using partisan media that matches one's political dispositions can reinforce citizens' partisan self-concepts. Silvia Knobloch-Westerwick and Jingbo Meng demonstrated this in a clever experiment. Participants viewed the headlines of a number of news articles and picked some of these news articles to read. Afterward, they were timed to see how quickly they said a series of political characteristics applied (or did not apply) to them. How long did it take participants to say that they were Democrats or Republicans; liberals or conservatives? People who chose like-minded news articles identified their partisanship and political ideology more quickly than people who read articles that countered their political views.[19] These faster response times suggest that those who get their information from like-minded sources are reminded that they identify with a liberal or conservative point of view on a particular issue. Though more research is necessary to support this finding, reinforcing political self-concepts may help people make political decisions more easily because they can rely more readily on what like-minded partisans believe.

Second, like-minded media use may influence *when* people make a decision to vote for a certain political candidate. In both the 2004 and 2008 presidential elections, voters who received their political information from like-minded sources decided on their candidate choice earlier in the election cycle.[20] People who choose to read or watch political information that opposes their views tend to take longer to make a voting decision.[21] Thus Republicans who watch Fox News and Democrats who watch MSNBC will feel more committed to their partisan candidates earlier in a campaign cycle than partisans who do not use like-minded news sources.

Third, partisan selective exposure is related to high levels of political participation. Citizen participation is imperative in a representative democracy. Participation involves getting citizens to enact the self-rule necessary for a democracy and ensures that the government represents different interest groups found in the country.[22] Strong political parties have been linked to high participation in the past. In the middle of the 19th century, when political parties were strong in the United States, voting, political parades, and other engaging activities were widespread.[23] Voting day was like a party, rather than a drab activity to squeeze into a busy Tuesday. In much the same way that high levels of participation coincided with high levels of partisanship in times past, partisan selective exposure may be related to political participation today.

Research confirms this relationship; people who use like-minded political media also tend to be active politically. Liberal Democrats, for instance, who watch CNN or MSNBC or read newspapers endorsing a Democratic presidential candidate are more likely to participate in campaign activities than liberal Democrats who do not get political information from those sources. Conservative Republicans are more likely to participate if they watch Fox News or read newspapers endorsing a Republican presidential candidate. These relationships do not show whether using like-minded media *causes* participation, but they do demonstrate that those using pro-attitudinal partisan media also tend to participate in politics.[24]

Susanna Dilliplane's study of the 2008 presidential election gives us some evidence that selective exposure comes before higher levels of participation.[25] By measuring the amount of like-minded media people consumed at *multiple* times during the campaign, as well as their participation in activities such as wearing campaign buttons and telling people why they should vote for a certain candidate, Dilliplane was able to see how participation changed during the course of the election. Individuals who watched like-minded news rather than news that conflicted with their political opinions increased their political campaign involvement during the months of the 2008 campaign. Conversely, people who watched news that contradicted their political beliefs participated in *fewer* campaign activities over time.

It is challenging to figure out whether selective exposure *causes* earlier vote choices and more participation in campaign activities. It may be, for instance, that people make a decision about their vote choice and participate in a campaign *before* they begin to watch like-minded news. There is some evidence for both perspectives, and more research is necessary to determine whether selective exposure causes people to participate and make a voting commitment. In either case, the evidence shows a strong relationship between partisan selective exposure, early vote choice, and high political participation.

Information and Partisan Selective Exposure

Choice of media outlet also may influence what people believe and know about politics. Many political theories assume that citizens need a stable base of knowledge so that they can discuss politics together, weigh the benefits and consequences of political issues, and vote for the candidate that best represents their issue positions. Citizens do not always meet this high standard of political knowledge, however.[26] This raises the question: Does using like-minded news facilitate or hamper citizens' learning about politics?

One study investigating the link between selective exposure and political knowledge found little reason to fear a drop in knowledge when people choose like-minded media sources. Conducted during the 2004 election, the National

Annenberg Election Survey asked survey respondents factual questions about the presidential candidates at multiple times during the campaign. Which candidate wanted to make additional stem cell lines from human embryos available for federally funded research? Which candidate was a former prosecutor? Those individuals who used like-minded media sources knew just as much about the candidates as people who did not use like-minded sources. In fact, in one instance, like-minded media use seemed to prompt more—not less—learning about the candidates.[27] These findings suggest that factual political knowledge about the presidential candidates may not be at risk when people use like-minded media.

Although general information about presidential candidates can be found in media sources of all political leanings, these facts are only one form of political information. And concluding that partisan media use does not affect any of our beliefs about politics would be premature. Others have examined forms of political information that arguably are less clear-cut and more closely tied to partisanship. Scholars interested in political misinformation, for instance, have found differences in what people *think* they know based on the news sources that they use. Misinformation research focuses on "facts" that citizens believe to be true but that are actually false. This may include believing that the United States spends more money on foreign aid than on law enforcement, or that President Barack Obama was not born in the United States. C. Richard Hofstetter and his colleagues found that San Diego residents who listened to conservative talk radio believed more false information about issues such as teen pregnancy, unemployment, and illegal immigration than those who listened to moderate talk radio.[28] A similar pattern emerged with respect to the Iraq War. On the one hand, Fox News viewers were more likely to believe that Iraq had weapons of mass destruction and close links to al Qaeda before the Iraq war. People who listened to National Public Radio (NPR) and watched PBS, on the other hand, were more likely to believe that Iraq was *not* linked to al Qaeda.[29] Thus there is some evidence that people who use different news sources believe that different political facts are true.

Adding more complexity to the relationship between like-minded media use and knowledge are circumstances in which facts are contested. Kathleen Hall Jamieson and Joseph Cappella write: "Did the Bush administration gain more jobs than it lost? The Democrats cited the payroll survey to say no; the Republicans cited the household survey to say yes."[30] When looking at contested facts, the media people use are related to what they believe. Again drawing from Jamieson and Cappella: "Even though self-identified conservatives or self-identified Republicans drew inferences consistent with their partisan views, Fox viewers and Limbaugh listeners were even more likely to do so. [The] analyses indicate an opposite pattern for Democrats and those who listen to NPR and watch CNN."[31] Ample evidence indicates that patterns of belief differ, depending on which information source one uses.

Once again, the cause of these differences is in question. We do not know, for example, whether watching cable news or listening to opinionated talk radio leads to differences in knowledge. It could be, instead, that people who believe that Iraq had ties to al Qaeda gravitate toward Fox News. More research is needed to determine whether partisan selective exposure causes these differences. At this point in time, the evidence suggests that partisan selective exposure does not make citizens less likely to know basic political facts about candidates. Yet partisan media use does seem to be related to misinformation and different views on contested facts.

Fragmentation, Polarization, and Partisan Selective Exposure

Partisan selective exposure relates not only to political participation and held beliefs about the world, but it also seems to affect our attitudes about politics. It does so by leading us to different impressions of which issues facing the nation are important and by affecting our attitudes toward political figures.

Like-minded media use influences which issues people nominate as the most important problems facing the United States. This is based on the idea of agenda setting—essentially, the issues emphasized in media coverage of politics become the issues considered to be most important by the public. If the media emphasize a troubled economy, then citizens are more likely to say that the economy is an important issue. The seminal article on agenda setting, by Maxwell McCombs and Donald Shaw, was written about the 1968 presidential campaign.[32] McCombs and Shaw suggested that irrespective of which media outlet people used, they still would believe that the same issues, be they the economy, terrorism, or a specific war, were important. In the 1960s, an era characterized by fewer media options, this makes sense.

Fast-forward to today, however, and things have changed. If media outlets like Fox News and MSNBC emphasize different issues, then people who get their political information from these channels may think different issues are important. During the 2004 presidential election, for instance, conservative Republicans who got their political information from conservative news outlets were particularly likely to say that terrorism was the most important problem facing the U.S. Liberal Democrats using liberal media were, instead, more inclined than others to say that the most important problem facing the United States was the War in Iraq. If, as this evidence suggests, like-minded media use encourages Republicans and Democrats to perceive different issues as important, it may become difficult to bring citizens together to solve the nation's problems.[33]

Also important is the degree to which like-minded media use strengthens and polarizes political attitudes. Polarization of political attitudes occurs when individuals' attitudes become more extreme. Take, for instance, the effects of viewing *Fahrenheit 9/11*, the liberal Michael Moore film critical of President George W. Bush's response to the September 11, 2001, terrorist attacks. People who watched the film had lower opinions of President Bush than people who *intended* to watch the film, but did not.[34] Attitudes toward presidential candidates also polarize during campaigns. Liberal Democrats using like-minded media during the 2004 election liked Democratic candidate John Kerry more and Republican candidate George W. Bush less as the campaign progressed. Conservative Republicans who got their information from conservative media moved in the opposite direction; they rated Democratic candidate Kerry less favorably and Republican candidate Bush more favorably over the course of the campaign.[35] Watching like-minded media, it seems, strengthens partisan attitudes rather than encouraging voters to think graciously about opponents of their political party.

As we have explained, partisan selective exposure affects citizens in a number of ways. When people use like-minded media, their partisan identities become strengthened and they are likely to be highly involved in politics. They also may learn more about political candidates than people who do not use sources that match their partisanship, though it is possible some of the information they receive may not be factually true. Perhaps most troubling, it is likely that they will strengthen their partisan attitudes toward political figures and think that different issues are most important for the United States to address. We leave to you the question of whether partisan selective exposure worries you or not.

Outcomes of Encountering Counter-Attitudinal Information

Although we may prefer pro-attitudinal information, this does not mean that we isolate ourselves completely from views with which we disagree. To this point, we've been describing selective exposure as a single behavior. Selective exposure can be seen as consisting of two separate behaviors, however: (1) selective avoidance, where people avoid contradictory messages; and (2) selective approach, where people seek confirmatory messages. It is possible that our desire for like-minded information is much stronger than our desire to avoid information that contradicts our beliefs.[36]

Even though we might prefer like-minded information, we might sometimes look to contradictory information nonetheless. Why? The reasons here are multiple. Perhaps we think that the information is easily refutable—think about the weak arguments from the opposition in the Lowin study of requesting political brochures described earlier. Why not look at the other side if we can easily dismiss their arguments and confirm our own views? It's also possible that we might just be curious! Ever flipped to different cable news channels after a political event? [If you haven't done this, we highly recommend it!] It is interesting to see how different channels cover exactly the same event.

Thinking about how we react to counter-attitudinal information is worth our time. Indeed, exposure to such information is often suggested as a solution to the potentially problematic consequences of partisan selective exposure. Don't like the idea of a polarized citizenry that looks to media outlets that confirm their closely held beliefs? Have people look at the other side! Fox viewers, flip to MSNBC! MSNBC viewers, flip to Fox! Before starting our campaign, however, we need a strong understanding of how people react to hearing the other side.

Encouraging people to read political information that contradicts their partisan views may not always be helpful. Citizens who strongly identify with a political party may process political facts in a biased way, especially when encountering information that contradicts their beliefs. After all, political beliefs relate to the amount of *incorrect* political information a person believes to be true in some instances.[37] People who hold the most inaccurate beliefs about welfare, for example, and are the most confident in those inaccurate beliefs, *also* tend to be strong partisans.[38]

In fact, encouraging exposure to alternative viewpoints can lead to a boomerang effect, in which individuals' original beliefs are *strengthened* by exposure to information counter to their beliefs. In a series of experiments, researchers Brendan Nyhan and Jason Reifler asked people to read news articles about political topics such as the Iraq War and stem cell research. All of these news articles included incorrect information, such as suggesting that Iraq had weapons of mass destruction, and some of the articles included corrections to the incorrect statements. Unfortunately, viewing news articles with corrective information did little to decrease partisans' misperceptions. When liberals read that President George W. Bush did *not* ban stem cell research, they still believed that he did. When conservatives read that Iraq did *not* have weapons of mass destruction, they were *more likely* to believe that these weapons were hidden in the country.[39] Simply exposing people to information with which they disagree *does not* mean that those people will change their political beliefs. We need to be more mindful about figuring out how to counter any potentially problematic aspects of partisan selective exposure. And, as the next section shows, we need to recognize that people sometimes select news for reasons other than partisanship.

Other Forms of Selection

Partisanship is not the only factor that influences which messages people select. In the sections below, we explore three other factors that affect information selection. First, we explore our preference for negative information. Then we turn to understanding how our interest in various issues affects news selection. Third, we explore how our news and entertainment preferences play a role in determining whether or not we'll even look at the news in the first place.

Negativity, Incivility, and News Selection

Another type of selection bias occurs when individuals are choosing political information: negativity bias. People seem to gravitate toward negative, more than positive, information. Essentially, bad news is more appealing than good news. Psychological studies consistently find that negative information stands out from positive information.[40] Our brains are more active both when we process negative information and when we first form negative impressions about images or people.[41] Not only are people attracted to the negative, they recall details about negative information better than about positive information.[42]

The political implications are clear. Both campaigns and media coverage of politics have been studied (and criticized) for their focus on negative messages, events, and news stories. Even though voters report disliking political negativity and even though negative campaigns may have detrimental effects on citizens, it also is possible that negativity may attract citizen attention and increase voter turnout, at least when candidates' attacks are based on political issues.[43]

There are many reasons to believe that a negativity bias exists when selecting political messages. Negative political information may gain attention because it is physiologically arousing, as measured through skin conductance tests.[44] It also may influence political behavior because negative messages stand out compared to the widespread positive information in voters' daily lives. Intensely impolite and uncivil political messages also can increase individuals' physical arousal levels, perceptions that a message is entertaining, and, at times, interest in politics.[45] There is something quite compelling about negative information. We just can't seem to look away.

Studies confirm that negativity plays a role in readers' choices. In an experiment set up to mimic an online campaign setting, Michael Meffert and his colleagues found that voters selected more negative news stories about candidates than positive articles.[46] Moreover, people chose negative stories even when those stories didn't favor their preferred candidate. When making article choices, in fact, the negativity bias *overrode* patterns of partisan selective exposure. In addition to partisanship, therefore, we should be attuned to the human inclination to select negative information.

Issue Preferences and Selection

Not only do like-minded news sources and negative news tone motivate exposure, but political issues also can affect exposure patterns. Not surprisingly, we're drawn to information about issues that are meaningful to us. If you're passionate about foreign affairs, for example, you'll be far more likely to look at information on this topic.[47] Within the domain of examining political issues, however, people still seem drawn toward like-minded information. Whether the issue is abortion or gun control, or health care, people prefer to select messages matching their beliefs as opposed to contradictory messages.[48]

Online, people may have even more opportunities to pursue their issue interests. News websites, for example, organize information into issue categories that facilitate users' selection based on issues. For those who are interested in local or national politics, or business, information is easy to find. Just look at the menus atop most news sites. One study compared the information that college students select when using a hard copy of the *New York Times* to their information selection when using the online version of the newspaper.[49] Students using the online version were less likely to learn about politics and public affairs, compared to those using the hard copy. Researchers Scott Althaus and David Tewksbury attributed this finding to the differences in how information is presented online versus in a hard-copy newspaper. A hard-copy newspaper gives clear visual cues about which stories are most important—headline size and placement in the newspaper guide readers' selections. And to get to any particular story or selection, hard-copy newspaper readers must browse past other stories that may catch their attention. Online, however, only a few stories are prioritized and the rest are organized based on interest. Online readers can narrowly target their interest areas and avoid issues that they find less compelling. Those uninterested in politics and public affairs can skip over these issues online more readily than when reading a hard copy. In sum, research documents that our issue preferences affect our news selections.

Prime-Time Programming Is More Fun . . . Or Is It?

A related form of selectivity is whether or not citizens look at the news at all. Some who read through this chapter may think: "But I rarely look at the news! This doesn't apply to me!" Not so fast. In fact, by opting out of the news, you may be using the media environment in a way that is not terribly dissimilar to those who select news matching what they believe. Instead of choosing from left- and right-leaning media, people can choose news or entertainment.

Honing in on the 2012 campaign, young people in particular are unlikely to follow election news very closely. In January of 2012, 20 percent of 18–29 year olds said that they followed election news closely in contrast to 40 percent of those aged 65 and above.[50] Some citizens would prefer to look at entertainment media in contrast to news. In many ways, the media environment facilitates this choice. If you don't want to see the news, you can flip the channel or browse another website.

We see this in practice. Presidential prime-time addresses once attracted a greater percentage of the television audience than they do today. As Matthew Baum and Samuel Kernell write, "cable (and, more recently, satellite) technology has allowed the public to become strategically discriminating in its viewing decisions."[51] Why watch the president if you're not interested, especially when you easily can switch to a reality show marathon on MTV or Bravo?

The consequences of this ability to select entertainment programming are startling. Markus Prior has shown that cable and Internet access can exacerbate gaps between those who prefer entertainment and those who prefer news.[52] As choices increase, those preferring entertainment can obtain more entertaining fare and those preferring news can become news junkies. What's the consequence? Those who prefer entertainment and who have more opportunity to select entertainment via cable television and the Internet not only know less about politics, they also participate in politics less frequently than those who have fewer choices. Essentially, the number of media choices allows some people to opt out—opt out of news, opt out of knowing about politics, and opt out of participating in politics.

One related explanation for this result is that incidental exposure has declined. Incidental exposure is the idea that sometimes people are exposed to news even when they aren't seeking news content. In years past, when television viewers had to either watch the president or turn off the television, some may have watched the president even if they were completely uninterested simply because they had nothing else to watch. In many ways, it is easier for us to tune out of politics altogether today—change the channel, switch to a different media source, or browse to another website. How much incidental exposure happens today is an interesting question. Are there places where you encounter news and politics inadvertently? If so, where does that happen? Is it via Facebook, or a political advertisement? Or in a chat room, where the main topic was something other than politics?[53] If incidental exposure is occurring less frequently, then we may be forming more coherent and distinct media clusters, such as an entertainment cluster and a partisan news cluster. This would produce two very different publics based on the media selections that each group made.

Conclusion

This chapter aimed to provide you with some insight into what we know about the choices people make in a complicated and fragmented media environment. Many things govern our choices, but our political affiliations and preferences are important in understanding why we make the choices that we do. When a strong partisan looks for news, congenial news outlets seem compelling. When someone who doesn't really enjoy the news looks for a mediated experience, a myriad of entertainment outlets will fit the bill. What we choose, however, has important consequences for our democratic system. We hope that as a result of reading this chapter, you'll carefully consider your own media diet. Think about the effects of the media that you choose to use—and the sources that you might not elect to use. And if you think any of the findings in this chapter are troubling, we encourage you to think about how you might work to fix it.

Notes

1 This example is from Jonathan L. Freedman, "Preference for Dissonant Information," *Journal of Personality and Social Psychology* 2 (1965): 287–289.
2 See, for example, William Hart, Dolores Albarracín, Alice Eagly, Inge Brechan, Matthew J. Lindberg, and Lisa Merrill, "Feeling Validated Versus Being Correct: A Meta-Analysis of Selective Exposure to Information," *Psychological Bulletin* 135 (2009): 555–588.
3 Natalie Jomini Stroud, *Niche News: The Politics of News Choice* (New York: Oxford University Press, 2011).

4 Shanto Iyengar and Kyu S. Hahn, "Red Media, Blue Media: Evidence of Ideological Selectivity in Media Use," *Journal of Communication* 59 (2009): 19–39.

5 Stroud, *Niche News.*

6 Jennifer Stromer-Galley, "Diversity of Political Conversation on the Internet," *Journal of Computer-Mediated Communication* 8 (2003).

7 Matthew Gentzkow and Jesse M. Shapiro, "Ideological Segregation Online and Offline," *The Quarterly Journal of Economics* 126 (2011): 1799–1839.

8 Bruce A. Bimber and Richard Davis, *Campaigning Online: The Internet in U.S. Elections* (New York: Oxford University Press, 2003); Silvia Knobloch-Westerwick and Jingbo Meng, "Looking the Other Way: Selective Exposure to Attitude-Consistent and Counterattitudinal Political Information," *Communication Research* 36 (2009): 426–448.

9 Brian J. Gaines and Jeffery J. Mondak, "Typing Together? Clustering of Ideological Types in Online Social Networks," *Journal of Information Technology & Politics* 6 (2009): 216–231.

10 Pew Research Center, *Social Networking Sites and Politics* (2012), http://pewinternet. org/~/media//Files/Reports/2012/PIP_SNS_and_politics.pdf.

11 Leon Festinger, *A Theory of Cognitive Dissonance* (Stanford: Stanford University Press, 1957).

12 Dean A. Ziemke, "Selective Exposure in a Presidential Campaign Contingent on Certainty and Salience," in *Communication Yearbook 4*, ed. Dan Nimmo (New Brunswick, NJ: Transaction Books, 1980): 497–511.

13 Peter Fischer, Stefan Schulz-Hardt, and Dieter Frey, "Selective Exposure and Information Quantity: How Different Information Quantities Moderate Decision Makers' Preference for Consistent and Inconsistent Information," *Journal of Personality and Social Psychology* 94 (2008): 231–244; Peter Fischer, Eva Jonas, Dieter Frey, and Stefan Schulz-Hardt, "Selective Exposure to Information: The Impact of Information Limits," *European Journal of Social Psychology* 35 (2005): 469–492.

14 Pew Research Center, *Cable Leads the Pack as Campaign News Source* (2012), http:// www.people-press.org/files/legacy-pdf/2012%20Communicating%20Release.pdf, 4.

15 Albert C. Gunther and Kathleen Schmitt, "Mapping Boundaries of the Hostile Media Effect," *Journal of Communication* 54 (2004): 55–70; Glenn J. Hansen and Hyunjung Kim, "Is the Media Biased against Me? A Meta-Analysis of the Hostile Media Effect Research," *Communication Research Reports* 28 (2011): 169–179; Robert P. Vallone, Lee Ross and Mark R. Lepper, "The Hostile Media Phenomenon: Biased Perception and Perceptions of Media Bias in Coverage of the Beirut Massacre," *Journal of Personality and Social Psychology* 49 (1985): 577–585.

16 Kevin Arceneaux, Martin Johnson and Chad Murphy. "Polarized Political Communication, Oppositional Media Hostility, and Selective Exposure." *Journal of Politics* 74 (2011): 174–186.

17 Kevin Coe, David Tewksbury, Bradley J. Bond, Kristin L. Drogos, et al., "Hostile News: Partisan Use and Perceptions of Cable News Programming," *Journal of Communication* 58 (2008): 201–219.

18 Lauren Feldman, "Partisan Differences in Opinionated News Perceptions: A Test of the Hostile Media Effect," *Political Behavior* 33 (2011): 407–432.

19 Silvia Knobloch-Westerwick, and Jingbo Meng, "Reinforcement of the Political Self through Selective Exposure to Political Messages," *Journal of Communication* 61 (2011): 349–368.

20 Stroud, *Niche News*; Susanna Dilliplane, "All the News You Want to Hear: The Impact of Partisan News Exposure on Political Participation," *Public Opinion Quarterly* 75 (2011): 287–316.

21 Ibid.
22 Stephen Macedo, *Democracy at Risk: How Political Choices Undermine Citizen Participation, and What We Can Do About It* (Washington, DC: Brookings Institution Press, 2005); Stephen J. Rosenstone and John Mark Hansen, *Mobilization, Participation, and Democracy in America* (New York: Pearson Education, 2003).
23 Michael Schudson, *The Good Citizen: A History of American Civic Life* (New York: The Free Press, 1998).
24 Stroud, *Niche News.*
25 Dilliplane, "All the News You Want to Hear."
26 Michael Delli Carpini and Scott Keeter, *What Americans Know About Politics and Why It Matters* (New Haven, CT: Yale University Press, 1996).
27 Stroud, *Niche News.*
28 C. Richard Hofstetter, David Barker, James T. Smith, Gina M. Zari, and Thomas A. Ingrassia, "Information, Misinformation, and Political Talk Radio," *Political Research Quarterly* 52 (1999): 353–369.
29 Steven Kull, Clay Ramsay and Evan Lewis, "Misperceptions, the Media, and the Iraq War," *Political Science Quarterly* 118 (2003): 569–98.
30 Kathleen Hall Jamieson and Joseph N. Cappella, *Echo Chamber: Rush Limbaugh and the Conservative Media Establishment* (New York: Oxford University Press, 2008), 233.
31 Ibid, 232.
32 Maxwell E. McCombs and Donald L. Shaw, "The Agenda-Setting Function of Mass Media," *Public Opinion Quarterly* 36 (1972): 176–187.
33 Stroud, *Niche News.*
34 Natalie Jomini Stroud, "Media Effects, Selective Exposure, and Fahrenheit 9/11," *Political Communication* 24 (2007): 415–32.
35 Stroud, *Niche News.*
36 R. Kelly Garrett, "Politically Motivated Reinforcement Seeking: Reframing the Selective Exposure Debate," *Journal of Communication* 59 (2009): 676–699; R. Kelly Garrett, "Echo Chambers Online?: Politically Motivated Selective Exposure among Internet News Users," *Journal of Computer-Mediated Communication* 14 (2009): 265–285.
37 Chris Wells, Justin Reedy, John Gastil, and Carolyn Lee, "Information Distortion and Voting Choices: The Origins and Effects of Factual Beliefs in Initiative Elections," *Political Psychology* 30 (2009): 953–969; Kull, Ramsay and Lewis, "Misperceptions, the Media, and the Iraq War"; Barry A. Hollander, "Persistence in the Perception of Barack Obama as a Muslim in the 2008 Presidential Campaign," *Journal of Media & Religion* 9 (2010): 55–66.
38 James H. Kuklinski, Paul J. Quirk, Jennifer Jerit, David Schwieder, and Robert F. Rich, "Misinformation and the Currency of Democratic Citizenship," *Journal of Politics* 62 (2000): 790–816.
39 Brendan Nyhan and Jason Reifler, "When Corrections Fail: The Persistence of Political Misperceptions," *Political Behavior* 32 (2010): 303–330.
40 Roy F. Baumeister, Ellen Bratslavsky, Catrin Finkenauer and Kathleen D. Vohs, "Bad Is Stronger Than Good," *Review of General Psychology* 5 (2001): 323–370; Tiffany A. Ito, Jeff T. Larsen, N. Kyle Smith, and John T. Cacioppo, "Negative Information Weighs More Heavily on the Brain: The Negativity Bias in Evaluative Categorizations," *Journal of Personality and Social Psychology* 75 (1998): 887–900.
41 Ibid.
42 Ito et al., "Negative Information Weighs More Heavily on the Brain"; Gregory L. Robinson-Riegler and Ward M. Winton, "The Role of Conscious Recollection in Recognition of Affective Material: Evidence for Positive-Negative Asymmetry," *Journal of General Psychology* 123 (1996): 93–104; Benjamin E. Hilbig, "Sad, Thus

True: Negativity Bias in Judgments of Truth," *Journal of Experimental Social Psychology* 45 (2009): 983–986.

43 Stephen Ansolabehere and Shanto Iyengar, *Going Negative: How Attack Ads Shrink and Polarize the Public* (New York: The Free Press, 1995); Diana C. Mutz and Byron Reeves, "The New Videomalaise: Effects of Televised Incivility on Political Trust," *American Political Science Review* 99 (2005): 1–15; Daniel Stevens, "Elements of Negativity: Volume and Proportion in Exposure to Negative Advertising," *Political Behavior* 31 (2009): 429–454; Kim F. Kahn and Patrick J. Kenney, "Do Negative Campaigns Mobilize or Suppress Turnout? Clarifying the Relationship between Negativity and Participation," *American Political Science Review* 93 (1999): 877–889.

44 Stuart Soroka and Stephen McAdams, "An Experimental Study of the Differential Effects of Positive Versus Negative News Content" (paper presented at the Elections, Public Opinion and Parties Annual Conference, Colchester, United Kingdom, September 10–12, 2010).

45 Mutz and Reeves, "The New Videomalaise"; Ashley Muddiman, "Something about Incivility: Impact of Uncivil Mediated Messages on Political Trust and Perceived Entertainment Value" (paper presented at the International Communication Association annual conference, Boston, May 26–30, 2011); Deborah J. Brooks and John G. Geer, "Beyond Negativity: The Effects of Incivility on the Electorate," *American Journal of Political Science* 51 (2007): 1–16.

46 Michael F. Meffert, Sungeun Chung, Amber J. Joiner, Leah Waks and Jennifer Garst, "The Effects of Negativity and Motivated Information Processing During a Political Campaign," *Journal of Communication* 56 (2006): 27–51.

47 Shanto Iyengar, Kyu S. Hahn, Jon A. Krosnick and John Walker, "Selective Exposure to Campaign Communication: The Role of Anticipated Agreement and Issue Public Membership," *Journal of Politics* 70 (2008): 186–200; Young Mie Kim, "Issue Publics in the New Information Environment: Selectivity, Domain Specificity, and Extremity," *Communication Research* 36 (2009): 254–284.

48 Knobloch-Westerwick and Meng, "Looking the Other Way"; Charles S. Taber and Milton Lodge, "Motivated Skepticism in the Evaluation of Political Beliefs," *American Journal of Political Science* 50 (2006): 755–769.

49 David Tewksbury and Scott Althaus, "Differences in Knowledge Acquisition among Readers of the Paper and Online Versions of a National Newspaper," *Journalism & Mass Communication Quarterly* 77 (2000): 457–479.

50 Pew Research Center, *Cable Leads the Pack*, 6.

51 Matthew A. Baum and Samuel Kernell, "How Cable Ended the Golden Age of Presidential Television: From 1969 to 2006," in *Principles and Practice of American Politics: Classic and Contemporary Readings*, ed. Samuel Kernell and Steven S. Smith (Washington, DC: CQ Press, 2010), 323.

52 Markus Prior, *Post-Broadcast Democracy: How Media Choice Increases Inequality in Political Involvement and Polarizes Elections* (New York: Cambridge University Press, 2007).

53 See, for example, Magdalena E. Wojcieszak and Diana C. Mutz, "Online Groups and Political Discourse: Do Online Discussion Spaces Facilitate Exposure to Political Disagreement?" *Journal of Communication* 59 (2009): 40–56.

Chapter 3

The Era of Media Distrust and Its Consequences for Perceptions of Political Reality

Jonathan M. Ladd

Americans have a long tradition of satirizing their political leaders, institutions, and issues of the day. Political cartoons have depicted politicians and political controversies from the fight over the Stamp Acts of the mid-1700s to the present day.[1] Since it debuted in 1975, skits depicting politicians have been a regular feature of the popular NBC comedy show *Saturday Night Live*.[2] The show's parodies of presidents and the quadrennial presidential debates have become cultural traditions, almost rivaling actual election debates and presidential press conferences. Politicians have also long been targets of humor from late-night talk-show hosts. One study of the 2000 presidential campaign found that late-night comedians made 771 jokes lampooning then-Governor George W. Bush and 494 at the expense of Vice President Al Gore.[3]

However, in the 2000s, a comedy show became popular whose content differed in an interesting way from most previous American political satire. In 1999, Jon Stewart became host of *The Daily Show*, an evening talk show on the Comedy Central cable channel. He changed the show from one that focused mostly on general comedy to one emphasizing more political topics. The show received relatively (for cable) high ratings and was praised by television critics. By 2004, it was featured in positive cover stories in *Newsweek* and *Entertainment Weekly* magazines. Jon Stewart became such a celebrity that he was invited to host the Oscars in 2006 and 2008.

In a significant departure, most of the biting satire on *The Daily Show* focuses on the political news media, rather than directly on politicians. While *Saturday Night Live* has usually featured impersonations of politicians, *The Daily Show* predominantly impersonates television news anchors, reporters, and pundits. It depicts these journalists as clueless, self-important buffoons.[4] Why did the most influential political comedy show in the last decade aim its fire largely at the press? What changed in American political culture that made this type of political satire so popular and critically praised?

The Daily Show's anti-media tone is not an aberration. When listening to political discourse in the United States, it can seem as if no one has anything good to say about the news media. During the 2012 Republican presidential primaries, the frontrunner and eventual nominee Mitt Romney was challenged for months by two candidates, Rick Santorum and Newt Gingrich, who had very little Republican institutional support. One of the strategies these candidates used to appeal to Republican voters and prolong the race despite their relative lack of funds and organization was to regularly criticize the news media.

During Republican presidential debates in late 2011 and early 2012, Gingrich made attacking the media the centerpiece of his rhetorical strategy. In a September 2011 debate, he responded to a question from *Politico*'s John Harris by proclaiming, "I for one, and I hope that all of my friends up here, are going to repudiate every effort of the news media to get Republicans to fight each other, to protect Barack Obama who deserves to be defeated."[5] Similarly, in a November 2011 debate focusing on economic issues and sponsored by CNBC, he responded to a question about the national economy by lamenting, "It is sad that the news media doesn't report accurately how the economy works."[6] Later, he responded to a health care policy question by Maria Bartiromo of CNBC by saying, "My colleagues have done a terrific job answering an absurd question."[7] Even Fox News reporters were not safe. In a Fox-sponsored debate, he angrily told moderator Chris Wallace, "I wish you would put aside the gotcha questions . . . I would love to see the rest of tonight's debate [involve] asking us about what we would do to lead an America whose president has failed to lead instead of playing Mickey Mouse games."[8] In a January 2012 debate, when CNN's John King asked Gingrich about his alleged past marital infidelity, Gingrich responded by saying, "I think the destructive, vicious negative nature of much of the news media makes it harder to govern this country, harder to attract decent people to run for public office. I'm appalled you would begin a presidential debate on a topic like that."[9]

While attacks on the press were not as central to Santorum's campaign, he unequivocally endorsed the sentiment that the media were enemies and deserving of attack. After criticizing a *New York Times*' reporter's question as "bull[expletive]" while campaigning in Wisconsin, he defended his words on the morning television program *Fox and Friends* by claiming, "If you haven't cursed out a *New York Times* reporter during the course of a campaign, you're not really a real Republican is the way I look at it."[10] The reporter who was on the receiving end of the expletive, Jeff Zeleny, was circumspect about the political benefits of media attacks, observing that, "It is a very common tactic for Republican presidential candidates, or even Democratic presidential candidates, to try and use the media as foil here. We've seen Newt Gingrich do it throughout the campaign season. So he clearly knew the cameras were rolling here."[11]

There is evidence that Zeleny is correct that both sides of the American partisan divide see benefits to attacking the media. The Obama administration has had a number of rhetorical clashes with Fox News. In 2009, less than a year into the administration, Obama Senior Advisor David Axelrod said on ABC's *This Week* program, "Mr. [Rupert] Murdoch has a talent for making money, and I understand that their programming is geared toward making money . . . [but]

they're not really a news station." White House Chief of Staff Rahm Emmanuel echoed this, saying in an interview with CNN that Fox News is "not a news organization so much as it has a perspective."[12] Several months later, interim White House Communications Director Anita Dunn went on CNN to attack the Fox News channel, saying,

> The reality of it is that Fox News often operates almost as either the research arm or the communications arm of the Republican Party. And it is not ideological . . . what I think is fair to say about Fox, and the way we view it, is that it is more of a wing of the Republican Party.[13]

This type of rhetoric is not completely new, yet has become increasingly common in the past several decades. During the Nixon administration, Vice President Spiro Agnew attacked the national news media, saying:

> . . . this little group of men who not only enjoy a right of instant rebuttal to every presidential address, but more importantly, wield a free hand in selecting, presenting, and interpreting the great issues of our nation . . . What do Americans know of the men who wield this power? . . . Little other than that they reflect an urbane and assured presence, seemingly well informed on every important matter . . . To a man, these commentators and producers live and work in the geographic and intellectual confines of Washington, DC, or New York City . . . They talk constantly to one another, thereby providing artificial reinforcement to their shared viewpoints . . . Is it not fair or relevant to question [this power's] concentration in the hands of a tiny and closed fraternity of privileged men, elected by no one, and enjoying a monopoly sanctioned and licensed by government? The views of the fraternity do not represent the views of America.[14]

In the past several decades, this theme has been echoed by many prominent politicians and activists. For instance, in the 1992 presidential campaign, a popular bumper sticker read, "Annoy the Media, Re-Elect Bush."[15] In 1996, Republican presidential nominee Bob Dole attacked the press on the campaign trail, saying,

> We've got to stop the liberal bias in this country. Don't read the stuff. Don't watch television. You make up your own mind. Don't let them make up your mind for you. We are not going to let the media steal this election. The country belongs to the people, not the *New York Times*.[16]

In 2002, President George W. Bush endorsed Bernard Goldberg's book, *Bias: A C.B.S. Insider Exposes How the Media Distort the News* by prominently displaying a copy under his arm in front of photographers when leaving for a trip to Maine.[17]

All these attacks on the press have led some journalists to lament over how they are treated. In his postmortem on the 2004 presidential election, Dean of the Columbia University Graduate School of Journalism Nicholas Lemann wrote in the *New Yorker* that, ". . . 2004 was such a bad-karma campaign year for the mainstream media, which collectively felt both more harshly attacked and less important—a pair of misfortunes that rarely occur at the same time." Former Editor-in-Chief of *The Hotline* and current *Congressional Quarterly* blogger Craig Crawford wrote in his 2006 book, *Attack the Messenger: How Politicians Turn You against the Media*, that "Today's media is as bullied as ever" and that "Public distrust of the news media is one of the most hazardous political challenges now facing Americans."[18] The evidence suggests that there is at least some basis for these journalists' concerns. This change in public discourse about the media has been accompanied by a large decline in the public's trust in the media.

The Decline in Media Trust

Over the past 40 years, there has been incredible growth in the number of media options. While in the 1950s and 1960s people had relatively few choices for news and entertainment, now they have much more discretion. They can watch as much (or as little) news and entertainment as they prefer. And in the realm of news, they can choose sources that focus on all varieties of information, including topics such as celebrity and entertainment, business, sports, as well as politics.[19] Finally, even among the political news options, there are different styles from which to choose. One can select information presented in a style similar to that which predominated in the mid-twentieth century, in which the journalist attempts to present the facts from a neutral perspective, or one can choose a source that mixes information with opinion and analysis. Sometime the latter format features debate, where competing sides argue about a political issue. But more often different sources occupy their own ideological niches on different news outlets and present the news from either a liberal or conservative perspective.[20]

Yet ironically, despite each person's ability to craft her media diet to suit her preferences, satisfaction with the media has not increased. In fact, it is much lower than in the mid-twentieth century, when people had a comparatively meager selection of new sources. Figure 3.1 shows the percentage of the public that believed newspapers were fair, as measured in the 1956 American National Election Studies (ANES), a nationally representative survey conducted at the time of the presidential election. The figure separates respondents by party identification and political knowledge. In the mid-1950s, both parties had substantial faith in the press's fairness. Overall, 78 percent of Republicans and 64 percent of Democrats saw newspapers as fair. Political knowledge had only a small relationship to these attitudes. The only exception is a small decline in

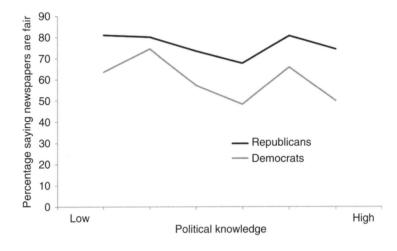

Figure 3.1 Belief in newspaper fairness in 1956

Source: 1956 American National Election Studies Time Series Survey.

beliefs in fairness as Democrats became more knowledgeable. In the third and fifth knowledge categories (out of five), only 48 and 50 percent believed newspapers were fair, while in the first and second categories, 64 percent and 74 percent believed that they were fair. But overall, a much greater proportion of people had trust in the media than would have in subsequent decades, across all party and knowledge categories.

The General Social Survey (GSS), a nationally representative survey of social attitudes conducted approximately every 2 years, has included a question battery probing trust in a variety of social institutions in every survey since 1973. The press is one of these institutions. Figure 3.2 graphs average confidence in the press among GSS respondents from 1973 to 2008. As a point of comparison, it also shows average confidence across all other institutions in the GSS battery.[21] The figure shows that confidence in the press declined during the 1970s, leveled off for a while in the mid-1980s, dropped sharply in the early 1990s, and then settled into a slow gradual decline throughout the 2000s. This all adds up to a substantial reduction in press confidence since the early 1970s. This drop is much larger than the modest decline in average confidence in all other institutions.

The pattern is not confined to Republicans, as some people suspect. Figure 3.3 presents the same GSS data separated into Democratic and Republican groups.[22] Democrats have consistently had more confidence in the press than Republicans have had, but this does not obscure the secular trend. The partisan gap grew in the mid-1970s, before shrinking and remaining relatively small

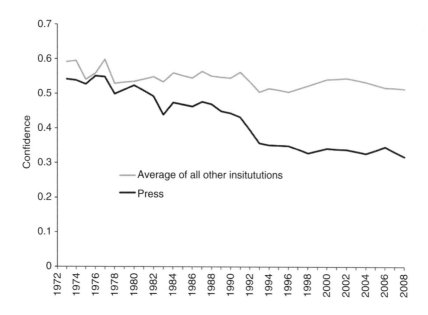

Figure 3.2 Confidence in the press compared to other institutions, 1973–2008

Source: 1973–2008 General Social Surveys.

Note: Figure graphs average confidence across all respondents in the given GSS survey. Responses are coded so that I indicates "a great deal," 0.5 indicates "only some," and 0 indicates "hardly any" trust. Institutions included in the average calculation are all institutions, other than the press, where confidence was probed in every GSS survey from 1973 to 2008.

through the 1980s and early to mid-1990s. The only survey in which the gap entirely disappeared was conducted in 1998, not long after the Monica Lewinsky scandal broke. The gap then grew during George W. Bush's presidency. But among both parties, confidence in the press has declined substantially over the past 40 years.

This pattern is not only in the GSS. Since 1985, the Pew Center for the People and the Press has every year asked a national sample of Americans whether they think news organizations "get the facts straight" or "their stories and reports are often inaccurate." Figure 3.4 shows the trend over time. From 1985 to 2011, the percentage of Americans saying new organizations "get the facts straight" declined from 55 percent to 25 percent, while those saying "their stories and reports are often inaccurate" increased from 34 percent to 66 percent. In summary, over the past 40 years the public has become less trusting that the national news media will provide them with accurate information. This decline in media trust is steeper than the decline in institutional trust overall and has occurred among both parties.

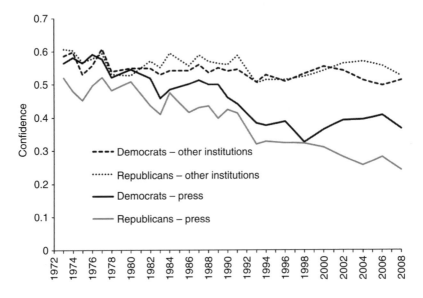

Figure 3.3 Confidence in the press compared to confidence in other institutions among Democrats and Republicans, 1973–2008

Source: 1973–2008 General Social Surveys.
From Jonathan M. Ladd, *Why Americans Hate the Media and How it Matters* (Princeton: Princeton University Press, 2012), Figure 4.4, by permission of Princeton University Press.

Note: Figure graphs average confidence across all respondents in the given GSS survey. Responses are coded so that 1 indicates "a great deal," .5 indicates "only some," and 0 indicates "hardly any" trust. Institutions included in the average calculation are all institutions, other than the press, where confidence was probed in every GSS survey from 1973 to 2008.

Media Distrust Polarizes Media Choices

Does this growing media-distrust change how people learn about the political world? There is substantial evidence that it does.[23] Those who distrust the media are less influenced by new messages they encounter. Instead, they rely more on their prior beliefs and partisan predispositions to form their current political perceptions. This happens for two reasons. First, even when someone who distrusts the press confronts the exact same message as someone who trusts the press, the former will be less accepting of the message. But that is not all. Those who distrust the media are also exposed to different messages because they tend to select the media outlets they use based on their partisanship, choosing those that reinforce their predispositions. This partisan media sorting is increasing over time among the entire American public, but media distrust is exacerbating it.[24]

To illustrate, Figure 3.5 presents data from "Media Consumption Surveys," conducted by the Pew Center in 2000 and 2010. It shows the percentage of

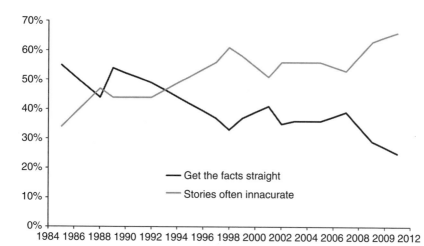

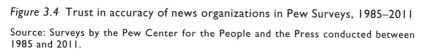

Figure 3.4 Trust in accuracy of news organizations in Pew Surveys, 1985–2011

Source: Surveys by the Pew Center for the People and the Press conducted between 1985 and 2011.

Note: Question asks "In general, do you think news organizations get the facts straight, or do you think that their stories and reports are often inaccurate?"

Democrats and Republicans who report using various prominent news sources "sometimes" or "regularly." In 2000, partisanship plays a relatively small role in source selection. Yet by 2010, things look quite different. A large proportion of these sources are appealing more to one party than the other. Local news and network news both still draw roughly equally from the two parties. However, all of the others draw more from one than the other. A greater percentage of Democrats than Republicans consume news from CNN, NPR, the PBS News Hour, and MSNBC, while a much greater percentage of Republicans rely on Fox News for information. In 2010, 68 percent of Republicans reported watching Fox News, while only 36 percent of Democrats did.

To see the role of media trust in this process, one can separate respondents in each year by that variable. The 2000 Media Consumption Survey also asks respondents: "How satisfied are you with the media's coverage of news about political figures and events in Washington?" Figure 3.6 looks only at 2000, but separates people according to whether or not they are satisfied with media coverage. In Figure 3.6, there continues to be little evidence of partisan selective exposure in 2000. This fact depends very little on attitudes toward the press.[25]

Figure 3.7 also compares partisan media selection patterns among those with more or less media trust, except here the data are from the 2010 Media Consumption Survey. While the exact question probing satisfaction with the media was not asked again in 2010, as a substitute I use a question asking, "How much political

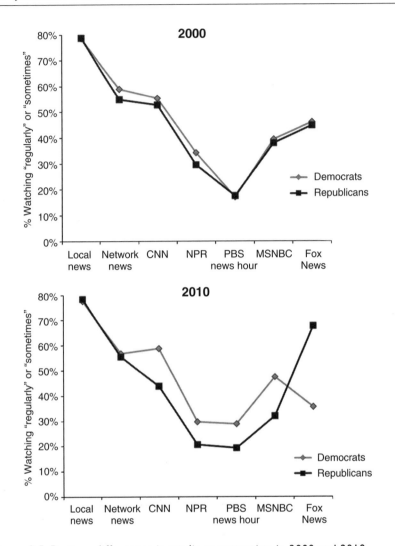

Figure 3.5 Partisan differences in media consumption in 2000 and 2010

Source: 2000 and 2010 Media Consumption Surveys by the Pew Center for the People and the Press.

bias do you see in news coverage?"[26] The bottom portion of Figure 3.7 shows media usage among those who perceive "a lot" of media bias and the top portion shows media usage among those who do not perceive a lot of bias. By 2010, attitudes toward the news media are playing an important role in partisan media selection. Local news, which is subjected to little political criticism, shows no discernable partisan usage pattern. But the other six sources are all the subject of more partisan self-selection when people have less trust in the media's accuracy.

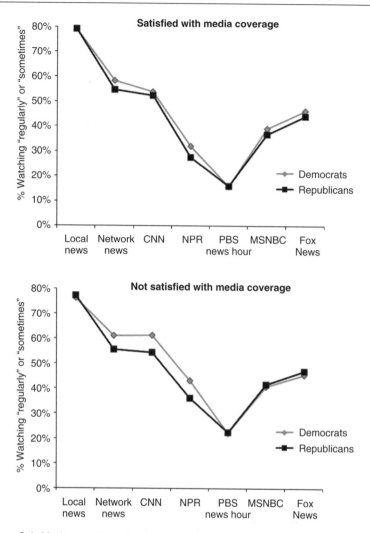

Figure 3.6 Media use by attitudes toward the media in 2000

Source: 2000 Media Consumption Survey by the Pew Center for the People and the Press.

Note: Media evaluation question asks, "How satisfied are you with the media's coverage of news about political figures and events in Washington? Are you very satisfied, fairly satisfied, not too satisfied, or not at all satisfied?"

Media outlets often criticized for having liberal biases are used more frequently by Democrats than Republicans, a gap that increases among those who distrust the media. As one moves from those who do not perceive a lot of media bias to those who do, one moves from Republicans being 9 percentage points more likely to watch network news to Democrats being 9 percentage points

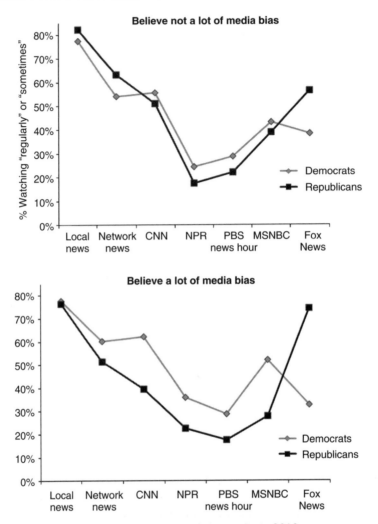

Figure 3.7 Media use by attitudes toward the media in 2010

Source: 2010 Media Consumption Survey by the Pew Center for the People and the Press.

Note: Media evaluation question asks, "How much political bias do you see in news coverage? A lot, some, not much or none at all?"

more likely to watch. The gap between Democrats and Republicans in their CNN viewership grows from 5 to 22 percentage points. The partisan gap in NPR listenership grows from 5 to 13 percentage points. The gap in PBS News Hour viewership grows from 7 to 13 percentage points. And the partisan gap in MSNBC viewership grows from 4 to 24 percentage points.

The one outlet in this table that is often criticized for having a conservative slant is the Fox News channel. In 2010, Republicans were more likely to watch Fox than Democrats. But, in keeping with the pattern, this selectivity was more extreme among those who thought that overall media are biased. Among those who did not perceive a lot of bias, 56 percent of Republicans and 38 percent of Democrats watched Fox at least sometimes, a 19 percentage point gap. But among those who perceived a lot of overall media bias, 75 percent of Republicans and 33 percent of Democrats watched Fox, a 42 percentage point gap.

In summary, in the past several years, as the American people have grown less trusting of the media overall as an institution able to provide them with accurate information, the specific news choices available to the American public have become more diverse. These trends have interacted in an important way. Not only are those who distrust media messages more likely to resist the messages that they do encounter, they encounter different messages because they select media outlets that reinforce their partisan predispositions.

Media Distrust Polarizes Political Perceptions

As media distrust changes the messages that people encounter and absorb, it changes how people learn about the world. Because those who distrust the media are less influenced by new media messages, they instead fall back on their prior beliefs and partisan predispositions to form their current beliefs about the state of the world.

This pattern is evident in survey questions asking for people's perceptions of changes in national problems. The 2000 ANES asked several questions not about people's opinions, but rather their perceptions of how certain national conditions had changed during the 8 years that Bill Clinton had been president. Even though the questions do not ask who should take blame or credit, but simply what changes have taken place, responses differ across parties. Because this was a period when a Democrat was president, Democrats tend to believe that trends in national conditions were better than Republicans believe them to be. This tendency to see objective national conditions through a partisan lens has been documented before.[27] Yet here one can see the role of media distrust in enhancing these partisan differences.

Figure 3.8 shows beliefs about how national conditions changed between 1992 and 2000 in five different areas. In each of these areas, everyone agrees what a good trend would be, regardless of one's ideology or partisanship. For instance, everyone agrees that the economy getting better and the deficit shrinking would be positive outcomes, all else equal.[28] These are the type of questions that tend to produce partisan biases, where people think their party's presidents produce relatively good results and the opposing party's president's relatively poor ones.

Figure 3.8 shows the partisan divide in perceptions of change in these areas among those with less or more trust in the media. In four out of the five areas, partisan divisions in perceptions of national conditions are larger when

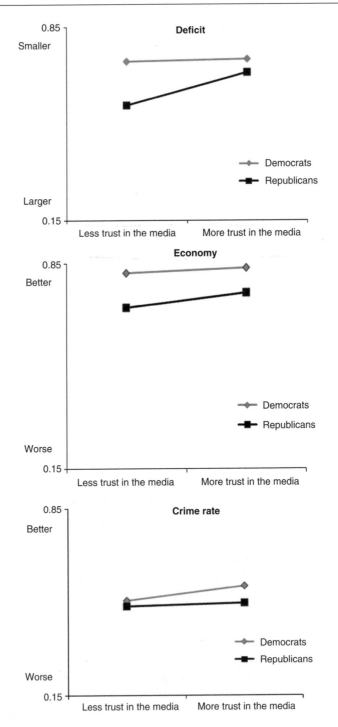

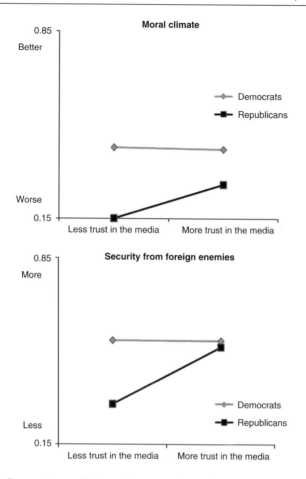

Figure 3.8 Perceptions of change in national conditions from 1992 to 2000

Source: 2000 American National Election Studies Time Series Survey.

Note: Each perception variable is coded to range from 0 to 1, with interior categories equally spaced between those endpoints. For ease of presentation, those saying they trust the media "only some of the time" or "almost never" are grouped here as "Less Trust in the Media." Those who say they trust the media "most of the time" or "just about always" are grouped in the "More Trust in the Media" category. Average perceptions of change in the moral climate among Republicans with "Less Trust in the Media" are exactly 0.15.

people distrust the news media. The only perceptions that are not more polarized when people distrust the media are those of the crime rate.[29] In every other area, we can see the results of distrusting new messages and relying more on partisan sources of information.[30]

Figure 3.9 shows a similar pattern in response to questions in the 2004 ANES.

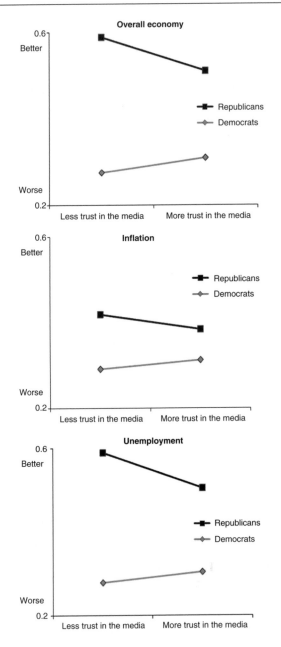

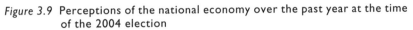

Figure 3.9 Perceptions of the national economy over the past year at the time of the 2004 election

Source: 2004 American National Election Studies Time Series Survey.

Note: Perception and media trust variables are coded as in Figure 3.8.

This survey did not include questions about how people perceived policy to have changed over an 8-year period, but it did include three questions about how national conditions had changed over the past year. These questions asked about the overall national economy, the unemployment rate, and the inflation rate. The pattern in 2004 is the same as in Figure 3.8. Of course, now a Republican was president. So the polarity of the partisan bias is reversed. Republicans now perceive national conditions more positively than Democrats do. But in each of these areas, the amount of partisan polarization is greater among those with less media trust.

Finally, there is an important caveat. This pattern holds in most cases, yet not when the messages about national conditions are so strong and unambiguous that they leave no doubt about the country's direction. In these unusual circumstances, partisan differences in perceptions become much smaller and the media trust effects can disappear.

In 2000, it was clear that many national conditions had improved over the past 8 years. Between 1992 and 2000, the annual growth rate of the U.S. Real Gross Domestic Product (GDP) increased from 3.4 to 4.1 percent,[31] and the unemployment rate declined from 7.5 to 4.0 percent.[32] So there was clearly significant improvement in the economy. The federal budget went from a $290.4 billion deficit in 1992 to a $236.4 billion surplus in 2000.[33] So there was large and unambiguous improvement in the deficit. However, on both of these issues, Figure 3.8 shows that there are substantial partisan differences in perception, which are larger among those who distrust the media.

In the year 2004, the Real U.S. GDP grew by 3.6 percent, the unemployment rate was 5.5 percent, and the inflation rate was 2.7 percent.[34] Overall economic growth and the unemployment rate were both moderately good by historic standards, and the inflation rate was quite low. Yet in Figure 3.9, one can see that people's perceptions in each of these areas exhibit large partisan biases, which are larger when people distrust the media.

National economic conditions at the time the 2008 pre-election ANES survey was conducted were much poorer, as well as more salient. When respondents were asked for their perceptions of unemployment, inflation and the overall economy in the past year, the economy was in the midst of a sudden and well-publicized tailspin that some have called the worse collapse since the Great Depression.[35] Interviews for the pre-election wave of the ANES, when people were asked these three economic perception questions, took place between September 2 and November 3. In 2008, Real GDP shrank by 0.3 percent. But this masks a rapid economic decline in the second half of the year. Real GDP shrank at a -3.7 percent rate in the third quarter and a -8.9 percent rate in the fourth quarter.[36] The unemployment rate grew from 5.0 percent in January 2008, up to 6.1 percent in August and September, 6.5 percent in October, 6.8 percent in November, and 7.1 percent by December. On the other hand, inflation in 2008 was very low. The consumer price index was essentially unchanged from December 2007 to December 2008 (an inflation rate of – 0.02 percent), a decline from the 4.1 percent inflation rate in 2007.[37]

Overall, economic conditions got dramatically worse right when these respondents were being interviewed. Their economic perceptions, displayed in Figure 3.10, reflect this. People believed that performance on all three indicators was very negative (even inflation, which was actually not performing badly).[38] Because all respondents seem to agree that economic conditions are very poor, the partisan differences are much smaller than in 2004, and those differences do not depend on trust in the media.

This illustrates that there is a limit to when trust of media messages and choice of media outlets affect how people learn. At most times, national conditions in most policy areas are at least somewhat ambiguous and politically contested. This allows citizens' partisanship and views about the news media to play an important role in which messages they end up absorbing to form their perceptions. However, there are rare cases when messages in a policy area so strongly and unambiguously point in one direction (such as during a very severe economic crisis), that most people will absorb the dominant message and differences in perception will shrink.

Conclusion

In the last 40 years, levels of trust in the media among the public have significantly declined. While Democrats have consistently had modestly more media trust than Republicans, the long-term decline has occurred among supporters of both parties. This has had important consequences for the American political system.

In recent years, the media environment has become much more fragmented. Yet major media organizations still exist that the public associates with the conventional style of journalism practiced in the mid-twentieth century. But now these organizations must constantly compete with other news sources that provide news in a more ideological and/or entertaining style. In this environment, where people regularly choose which type of news source to use for information, one's level of general media trust is more consequential than ever.

Those who distrust the media in general are more likely to seek out news outlets that reinforce their partisan predispositions. They are also more likely to resist information from the mainstream media. As a result of all this, except in times of national crisis, those who distrust the media have beliefs about national conditions that are more reflective of their partisan predispositions than do those who have more media trust. By leading Americans to not only hold divergent opinions, but also divergent beliefs about the state of the world, media distrust contributes to the growing partisan polarization of the American political system.[39] Whether media trust continues to decline will be an important determinant of the extent to which America's partisan divide grows even wider in the years ahead.

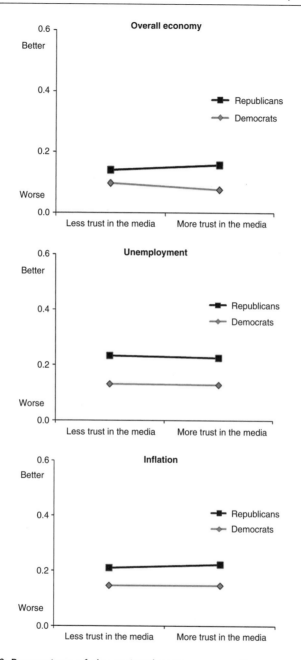

Figure 3.10 Perceptions of the national economy over the past year at the time of the 2008 election

Source: 2008 American National Election Studies Time Series Survey.

Note: Perception and media trust variables are coded as in Figures 3.8 and 3.9.

Notes

1 Stephen Hess and Sandy Northrop, *Drawn & Quartered: The History of American Political Cartoons* (Montgomery, AL: River City Publishing, 1996).

2 Tom Shales and James Andrew Miller, *Live from New York: An Uncensored History of Saturday Night Live* (Boston, MA: Little Brown, 2002).

3 Doris A. Graber, *Mass Media and American Politics*, 6th ed. (Washington, D.C.: CQ Press, 2002), 3–4.

4 Marc Peyser, "Red, White & Funny," *Newsweek*, Jan. 5, 2004; Anthony Wilson-Smith, "Making Fun of the News," *Maclean's*, Feb. 15, 2004.

5 "Gingrich Slams Moderators, Media for Trying to Create Infighting," Real Clear Politics, http://www.realclearpolitics.com/video/2011/09/07/gingrich_slams_moderators_media_for_trying_to_create_infighting.html.

6 Geneva Sands, "Gingrich: News Media Reporting on Economy is 'Sad'," The Hill, http://thehill.com/video/campaign/192793-gingrich-news-media-reporting-on-economy-is-sad.

7 Aaron Blake, "Newt Gingrich's War on Republican Debate Moderators," Washingtonpost.com, http://www.washingtonpost.com/blogs/the-fix/post/newt-gingrichs-war-on-republican-debate-moderators/2011/11/10/gIQAiy558M_blog.html.

8 "Newt Gingrich Blasts Chris Wallace for His 'Gotcha' Questions at IA Debate," YouTube, http://www.youtube.com/watch?v=KxQTp07KS_k.

9 Dylan Byers and Keach Hagey, "CNN's John King Puts Himself on Firing Line," Politico, http://www.politico.com/news/stories/0112/71705.html.

10 David Taintor, "Santorum: Real Conservatives Curse out the New York Times," Talkingpointsmemo.com, http://2012.talkingpointsmemo.com/2012/03/santorum-real-conservatives-criticize-new-york-times.php.

11 "NYT Reporter: Santorum Outburst Was for Cameras," http://www.cbsnews.com/8301-505267_162-57404351/nyt-reporter-santorum-outburst-was-for-cameras/.

12 Mike Allen, "Fox 'Not Really News,' Says Axelrod," Politico, http://www.politico.com/news/stories/1009/28417.html.

13 Sam Stein, "Anita Dunn: Fox News an Outlet for GOP Propaganda," Huffington Post, http://www.huffingtonpost.com/2009/10/11/anita-dunn-fox-news-an-ou_n_316691.html.

14 Spiro Agnew, "Speeches on the Media," in *Killing the Messenger: 100 Years of Media Criticism*, ed. Tom Goldstein (New York, NY: Columbia University Press, 1989), 67–69; John R. Coyne, Jr, *The Impudent Snobs: Agnew vs. the Intellectual Establishment* (New Rochelle, NY: Arlington House, 1972), 267–268.

15 John Dickerson, "The Good News from Iraq: We Can't Hear It—The Bombs are Too Loud," Slate.com, http://www.slate.com/id/2138622/.

16 Darrell M. West, *The Rise and Fall of the Media Establishment* (Boston, MA: Bedford / St. Martin's, 2001), 104.

17 Bernard Goldberg, *Bias: a C.B.S. Insider Exposes How the Media Distort the News* (Washington, DC: Regnery Publishing, 2002); Thomas Streissguth, *Media Bias* (New York, NY: Benchmark Books, 2006), 38.

18 Craig Crawford, *Attack the Messenger: How Politicians Turn You Against the Media* (Lanham, MD: Rowman and Littlefield, 2006), 19, 25.

19 Markus Prior, *Post-Broadcast Democracy: How Media Choice Increases Inequality in Political Involvement and Polarizes Elections* (New York, NY: Cambridge University Press, 2007); Markus Prior, "News Vs. Entertainment: How Increasing Media Choice Widens Gaps in Political Knowledge and Turnout," *American Journal of Political Science* 49 (2005): 577–592.

20 Of course, some news sources, especially web sites, sometimes adopt more idio-

syncratic or extreme ideologies in addition to cotemporary liberalism and conservatism.

21 Institutions included in the average calculation are all institutions, other than the press, where confidence was probed in every GSS survey from 1973 to 2008: major companies, organized religion, education, the executive branch, organized labor, medicine, television, the Supreme Court, the scientific community, Congress, and the military.

22 Independents who lean toward one of the parties are coded as with that party. Those who identify as pure independents are excluded from this figure.

23 For an expanded version of the arguments made here, see Jonathan M. Ladd, *Why Americans Hate the Media and How it Matters* (Princeton, NJ: Princeton University Press, 2012), chap. 6.

24 On partisan selectivity in media exposure, see Natalie Jomini Stroud, "Media Use and Political Predispositions: Revisiting the Concept of Selective Exposure," *Political Behavior* 30 (2008): 341–366; Natalie Jomini Stroud, *Niche News: The Politics of News Choice* (New York: Oxford University Press, 2011); Shanto Iyengar and Kyu S. Hahn, "Red Media, Blue Media: Evidence of Ideological Selectivity in Media Use," *Journal of Communication* 59 (2007): 19–39.

25 The largest effects of media trust are on CNN exposure. The difference between the percentage of Democrats and percentage of Republicans who watch CNN grows from 2 to 6 percentage points when people go from satisfied to not satisfied with media coverage.

26 This question was not asked in 2000. Thus, unfortunately, there is no way to analyze both the 2000 and 2010 surveys using the exact same media trust question. However, elsewhere I find that responses to media trust questions are relatively robust to even fairly large differences in question wording. See Ladd, *Why Americans Hate the Media and How it Matters*, 91–106.

27 Larry M. Bartels, "Beyond the Running Tally: Partisan Bias in Political Perceptions," *Political Behavior* 24 (2002): 117–150; Alan S. Gerber and Gregory A. Huber, "Partisanship, Political Control, and Economic Assessments," *American Journal of Political Science* 54 (2010): 153–173; Alan S. Gerber and Gregory A. Huber, "Partisanship and Economic Behavior: Do Partisan Differences in Economic Forecasts Predict Real Economic Behavior?" *American Political Science Review* 103 (2009): 407–426.

28 Political scientists call these "valence issues." See Donald E. Stokes, "Spatial Models of Party Competition," in *Elections and the Political Order*, ed. Angus Campbell, et al. (New York, NY: Wiley, 1966).

29 Perceptions of the crime rate are notoriously inaccurate. See Martin Gilens, "Political Ignorance and Collective Policy Preferences," *American Political Science Review* 95 (2001): 379–396.

30 Elsewhere, I show that the effect of party identification on each of these perceptions except crime policy is statistically significantly related to trust in the media. This relationship is robust even when controlling for general political knowledge, except in the case of economic conditions, where the interaction coefficient is just as large but no longer statistically significant because the standard error is larger. For details, see Ladd, *Why Americans Hate the Media and How It Matters*: 148–55, 71.

31 Annual Real GDP growth data from 1992 and 2009 are available at the web site of the Bureau of Economic Analysis of the U.S. Department of Commerce: http://www.bea.gov/.

32 United States Census Bureau, *Statistical Abstract of the United States* (Washington, DC: United States Government Printing Office, 2002), 417 and 367.

33 Ibid., p. 305.

34 United States Census Bureau, *Statistical Abstract of the United States* (Washington, DC: United States Government Printing Office, 2012). p. 436; United States Census

Bureau, *Statistical Abstract of the United States* (Washington, DC: United States Government Printing Office, 2006), 411; Inflation data from the web site of the Bureau of Labor Statistics of the U.S. Department of Labor: http://www.bls.gov/data/.

35 David Lightman, "Congressional Budget Office Compares Downturn to Great Depression," McClatchy Newspapers, http://www.mcclatchydc.com/2009/01/27/60822/congressional-budget-office-compares.html; Paul Krugman, "Fighting off Depression," *New York Times*, January 4, 2009.

36 The extent of the economic problem became apparent in the middle of the presidential campaign (and beginning of the ANES interview period) when the Lehman Brothers Financial Services firm collapsed on September 15, followed by Congress debating a $700 billion economic bailout package which was eventually signed into law on October 3. Annual and quarterly Real GDP growth data from 2008 are available at the web site of the Bureau of Economic Analysis (BEA) of the U.S. Department of Commerce: http://www.bea.gov/. The extent of the GDP contraction was not immediately apparent to the BEA. Subsequent revisions to the GDP data over the next few years adjusted the growth numbers downward to their current levels. However, the argument here is not that that people were literally influenced by data coming from the BEA, but rather by the many symptoms of the economic crisis that the GDP data reflect.

37 Monthly unemployment rate and Consumer Price Index data are available at the web site of the Bureau of Labor Statistics of the U.S. Department of Labor: http://www.bls.gov/data/.

38 Note that the right hand scale had to be adjusted to go all the way down to zero in Figure 3.10 because most of the response would be below the bottom of the scale in Figure 3.9, which is 0.2.

39 On party polarization, see for example Nolan McCarty, Keith T. Poole, and Howard Rosenthal, *Polarized America: The Dance of Ideology and Unequal Riches* (Cambridge, MA: MIT Press, 2006); Larry M. Bartels, "Partisanship and Voting Behavior, 1952–1996," *American Journal of Political Science* 44 (2000): 35–50; Marc J. Hetherington, "Resurgent Mass Partisanship: The Role of Elite Polarization," *American Political Science Review* 95 (2001): 619–631.

Chapter 4

Making the News

Is Local Television News Coverage Really That Bad?

Erika Franklin Fowler

Local television has been strongly criticized by a broad cross section of institutional America – academia, the government, public health organizations, citizens' groups, journalists – for presenting an unbalanced and unhealthy diet of information to citizens. Nevertheless, excess violence, trivia, and sensation in local television news, the empty calories of tabloid journalism, have become the standard fare on newscasts.[1]

Whether in Chicago, Sioux Falls, or most any other place in the country, the look of local news is one of form dictating content. At the beginning of broadcasts are the live, local, and late-breaking incidents producers believe will hook people into watching. At the end are the interesting or unusual stories to hold the audience through weather and sports.[2]

It is no secret to those who pay even a marginal amount of attention to news programs that local television news frequently hypes stories about car crashes, fires, violent crime, dangers that are hazardous to your health, and bizarre tricks such as pigs swimming. In short, local television news is notorious for sensationalist coverage of frivolous and serious topics alike. Much of this reputation is earned. For example, a San Diego affiliate ran the following health segment on its late evening newscast in October 2002: "[Anchor]: If you are a gym-aholic, you may want to think about cutting back. New research suggests that working out too much could increase your chance of cancer. That's right." Not only did the station fail to put the report into context by discussing all the known benefits of exercise, medical researchers at the University of Michigan[3] had trouble tracing the origin of the story, suggesting at best that the coverage originated from some researchers' unpublished preliminary findings, which likely did not warrant coverage at all. In another example, in March 2012, a local Philadelphia NBC affiliate devoted at least two stories (more than 4.5 minutes in the first portion of two broadcasts from March 11 and 15) to follow-up coverage of a "coffee attack" in West Philadelphia, where an angry customer allegedly threw "boiling hot coffee on a donut shop worker." The segments featured video of the attack, commentary from police, exclusive interviews with the suspect's sister and former landlord, along with close-up shots of the victim's bandaged arm. These examples provide just a small taste of the type of coverage frequently lamented by critics of local television news who argue that bad journalism is the result of flawed strategies to "dumb down" content and attract larger audiences. Worst still, evidence suggests that these tactics do not even work.[4]

To be sure, one would have difficulty arguing that local television news exemplifies quality journalism or even that local television in general carries large quantities of public affairs programming, which will be discussed at length below. But it is first important to understand why one might care about the content of local television news. In the information age, there are plenty of places to get news about current events, and those who are interested in politics are very unlikely to turn to local television news as the medium of choice for such information. Politics, elections, and public policy are covered much more extensively by many national outlets and even given more lengthy treatment in local newspapers. Certainly increasing the quality of journalism across the board is a noble goal, but if citizens can obtain political information from other sources, why should we be concerned about the lack of substance on one particular medium? The answer lies in part in the popularity of the medium, which led political scientist Markus Prior—in comparing the soft news coverage on local television to soft news formats like *The Today Show*—to conclude that, "local news, not soft news, is the real villain of our story. . . . The major difference between the two formats is that local news is much more popular than soft news. Because of this great popularity, the negative effect of a preference for local news on hard news knowledge is a much more serious obstacle to creating an informed electorate than the various soft news formats."[5]

Indeed, though it is the age of the Internet, more Americans report getting their news from local television news broadcasts than from any other source. And although much has changed over the past two decades in terms of where individuals report getting their information, the prominence of local television news as a regular source to which Americans turn is not a new trend. In fact, according to the Pew Center for the People and the Press, which has tracked media consumption trends since the early 1990s, local television has consistently remained the "go-to" source for most Americans over the past two decades.[6] This is not to say that local television has been immune from the declining audience trends that have plagued newspapers, but local broadcasters have seen much slower declines than other traditional sources and, in fact, a recent 2011 article in the *New York Times* actually reported that the number of local newscasts in many markets was expanding. As advertising revenues have increased, newscasters have innovated, and journalists have become more self-sufficient in the reporting and production of their own pieces.[7]

Evidence for the prominence of local television news in today's fragmented and changing media environment, however, does not come solely from self-reports. Politicians and campaign practitioners on both sides of the aisle regularly discuss the importance of local television news, both as a provider of information to the American electorate, but also as a favored outlet for conveying their message. A *Washington Post* article in 2005 quoted then-President Bush arguing that, in order to influence opinion, one needed to travel around the country talking to local news reporters,[8] and a more recent National Public Radio piece discussed President Obama's strategy of inviting local television newscasters to the White House as one aimed at reaching citizens' living rooms through local stations.[9] Democratic strategist Paul Begala, in discussing former President Clinton's influence in the 2008 presidential primaries, argued that local television was preeminent in audience share and reiterated conventional wisdom that its coverage was far more favorable to politicians than national news media, making it a prime outlet for practitioners to target.[10]

Furthermore, despite the rise of microtargeting in campaign advertising (a tactic examined at length in Chapter 8 of this volume), local television news has consistently been the primary program during which campaigns have placed their ad messages. Although the share of presidential advertising placed on local television has declined from 2000 to 2008, local news commercial breaks featured over a third (35 percent) of all presidential spots aired during 2008. This is a far larger percentage than for the next highest program, *Good Morning America*, which featured just over 2 percent of all ads.[11] Evidence from the Wesleyan Media Project's tracking of political advertising in 2010 found that in a record-breaking year for political advertising, over 40 percent of all advertising aired in the 2010 midterm campaigns was placed on local television news broadcasts, further corroborating the notion that practitioners believe that local news matters.

Despite the attention paid to local television by both Americans and campaign practitioners, scholarly studies of local television news content are relatively rare, especially compared to the wealth of attention paid to national news media, typically print coverage, and political advertising. Studies that have examined the content of local television newscasts, especially election coverage, tend to focus on a small number of stations, markets, or states[12] in part due to the technological difficulties involved in systematically capturing, preserving and analyzing content from stations spanning the nation's 210 media markets.[13] As such, systematic evidence regarding the content *and* effect of local television news across the country is scarce.

The lack of large-scale, systematic evidence on local television election coverage, however, has not prevented speculation about its content, only some of which has been backed by evidence. One primary reason typically given for why local news broadcasters have been able to remain competitive is that they have adapted by "dumbing down" their content, focusing on soft news rather than on politics and governance issues. Others argue that local television newscasts are void of "real" political content and dominated by substance-less coverage of elections. But are the accusations true? And even if local television is less substantive, is the lack of issue focus really a problem?

The few studies that have examined local television news yield important insight into the ways in which content may differ. Perhaps the largest and most systematic study of local television news content outside of elections was a five-year study from the Project for Excellence in Journalism, which analyzed two weeks of content from stations in 20 markets for each year from 1998 to 2002. In particular, the study analyzed the last week of February ("sweeps" week, during which Nielsen computes ratings points for each station and program) and the first week of March (a nonsweeps week for comparison) from every year. The results lend credence to critics' claims. In addition to the surprising uniformity of broadcast structure from dissimilar cities ("mayhem at the top, teasable soft features at the end, and the rest of the day's news in the middle"[14]), the authors argue that "where crime, accidents, and disasters lead the broadcast and soft news concludes the program, what remains is easily lost. Only after the sixth story in an average local news broadcast does civic news (politics/government, social issues, science/technology, etc.) surpass crime, accidents, and disasters and become the most likely topic to appear. And when civics stories are aired, these often complex issues are largely brushed over."[15]

The evidence outside of election season then clearly supports the notion that local newscasters focus primarily on public safety and soft news at the expense of policy and governance. This is far from ideal, and the authors go to great lengths in their analysis to debunk common myths (such as the claim that viewers will not tune in for long stories about issues) in an attempt to help broadcasters improve their coverage, both in style and substance. But do the same patterns hold during the heat of election season, when the availability of civics information is more important in aiding citizen decision-making at the ballot box?

Unlike the Project for Excellence in Journalism's study, the vast majority of research examining local television news coverage of elections is limited by a small number of stations or markets sampled, frequently within the same state,[16] and those that have looked at election coverage in multiple markets are now quite dated.[17] In sum, there is very little systematic evidence speaking to the way in which election content on local television news varies by station, across different types of markets, or with the characteristics of the electoral races covered. This chapter will bring some of the most systematic data to bear on the question of how the election content of local television varies across the country with a specific focus on policy issues, before turning to how such coverage affects citizen knowledge. The evidence suggests that local television's focus may be less problematic than frequently assumed.

Content of Local Television News

Information presented in this chapter comes from the University of Wisconsin NewsLab's tracking of local television news from three election cycles (2002, 2004, and 2006), nearly 10,000 hours of local news programming across multiple markets in each of the three cycles. The 2002 study tracked a representative sample of 122 stations in the 50 largest media markets in the United States, while the 2004 analysis examined a purposive sample of 44 stations in 11 media markets selected based on market size and race competitiveness. The 2006 study only examined the capital city and largest metropolitan market from five states in the Midwest. One additional difference between the three years is noteworthy: the initial 2002 study tracked campaign-related election content only, while both of the 2004 and 2006 studies categorized all broadcast content, enabling comparisons of time devoted to elections in comparison to other topics within a typical newscast. Despite the differing designs across years, by and large there was consistency in terms of the findings across years.[18]

As previously mentioned, local television is frequently charged with being heavy on soft news, both in terms of entertainment broadly conceived (which might include personally engaging scores from local sports teams) and high drama stories (like violent crime, the latest health hazard in medical science journals or natural disaster reports). And large-scale evidence outside of election season supports the charge, but arguably the most crucial time during which citizens need to obtain public affairs information is in the weeks leading up to an election. So how much government and public affairs information is available to citizens via local television news during that time?

Table 4.1 displays the breakdown of the top four topics covered on the average 30-minute local newscast in the final 30 days leading up to Election Day in the 2004 and 2006 cycles. Not surprisingly, given what we know about citizen content preferences, sports and weather coverage dominate the news hole (the amount of time available for news coverage in a 30-minute newscast once advertising time has been subtracted). Indeed between 6 and 7 minutes of the typical 20- to 22-minute newscast are devoted to sports and weather in both years. However, if we combine all government, election, and foreign affairs content into one category, public affairs and current events receive the next highest share of news time, ranging from three minutes, 12 seconds, to 4 minutes, 20 seconds. Collectively, this is more time than is given to the purported staple of local news: crime and injury coverage. Pure local interest stories (those frequently featuring local citizens, businesses or other events) are fourth in line, just shy of 2 minutes of coverage.

What is clear from this evidence is that local television does focus on soft news, with sports, crime and local interest making up the bulk of any given newscast. However, it is also clear that at least during the last 30 days of an election cycle, local broadcasts also contain a non-trivial amount of public affairs

Table 4.1 Average Minutes Devoted to Top Topics in Local Television Newscasts

	Oct–Nov 2004	Oct–Nov 2006
Sports and Weather	6.35	6.97
Gov't/Public Affairs	4.28	3.18
Crime/Injury	3.48	2.47
Local Interest	1.93	1.92

content, a topic second only to sports and weather. Furthermore, when one considers the amount of local news programming available in multiple broadcasts throughout the day and the fact that citizens report tuning into local television regularly for information, the total amount of public affairs and election content citizens encounter over time is likely to be even larger.

What types of coverage comprise the 3 to 4-minute news hole devoted to politics and current events? Table 4.2 demonstrates that election stories garner the largest share of the total, followed by non-electoral coverage of government and public policy stories, and then foreign affairs. During the presidential election cycle of 2004, coverage of the race for the White House constituted the lion's share of coverage, with nearly half (almost two minutes on average) of the public affairs news hole. This suggests that local television coverage may not be very local in focus, unless, of course, the president is campaigning in your state, in which case the national story is also a local story.

The remaining offices on the ballot received an average of 1 minute and 40 seconds of coverage during the 2006 midterm and received an average of 1 minute and 20 seconds of coverage per broadcast during the 2004 presidential campaign. Coverage of governing and public policy was especially compressed during the presidential election year, on average receiving roughly 38 seconds of coverage per broadcast, whereas during the midterm year it received a little over a minute. Foreign affairs received a mere 25 to 30 seconds per broadcast, which is, on the one hand, a very small amount of time but is, on the other hand, perhaps not surprising or unwarranted given the importance local news outlets attach to *local* programming in the public interest.

So if local broadcasters do pay attention to politics and governance during elections in spite of their simultaneous attraction to other soft news topics, should we be concerned? Besides assessing the topical breakdown of local television news coverage, another way to assess critics' concerns about the content of local television is to examine the framing of the political coverage that is provided. A frequently examined metric of election coverage quality includes the extent to which stories focus on the substantive issues of a campaign compared to coverage of the strategy, game or horserace features of the contest.[19] Table 4.3 displays the proportion of coverage devoted to federal and statewide races that focus on strategy compared to issue coverage.[20]

Table 4.2 Average Minutes Devoted to Public Affairs Topics in a Typical 30-Minute Newscast

	Oct–Nov 2004	Oct–Nov 2006
Presidential election	1.95	–
Non-presidential election	1.23	1.68
Gov't (non-election)	0.63	1.07
Foreign affairs	0.47	0.43
Average total minutes	**4.28**	**3.18**

Table 4.3 Proportion of Coverage Devoted to Strategy/Horserace and Issue by Race/Year

	Strategy	Issue
Governor 2002	0.57	0.27
President 2004	0.56	0.34
Governor 2006	0.73	0.18
Senate 2002	0.54	0.16
Senate 2004	0.47	0.38
Senate 2006	0.78	0.17
House 2002	0.46	0.39
House 2004	0.40	0.44
House 2006	0.75	0.17

Note: Numbers do not sum to one due to other types of coverage, including adwatches and coverage of personal characteristics

Numerous scholars have documented the media obsession with coverage of strategy and the horserace at the expense of substance,[21] and Table 4.3 demonstrates that local television news coverage of federal and statewide races is no exception to the rule. In all but one case (U.S. House coverage in 2004), strategy coverage outweighs issue coverage, and in many cases the ratio of strategy to issues exceeds 3:1. Two patterns are noteworthy. First, all of the 2006 contests have the highest ratios (meeting or exceeding 4:1) of strategy to issue coverage, which could indicate something about either the sample—that of stations in Midwestern markets—or something about the competitiveness of the races examined in that year, which we know increases coverage of the horserace.[22] Second, although we know presidential coverage dominated during 2004, leaving less time for coverage of other races like those for U.S. Congress, what is interesting is that issue coverage appears to have been more prominent in the smaller news hole left for both U.S. House and Senate races in 2004, compared to both 2002 and 2006. In other words, local broadcasters may short-change non-presidential federal races during presidential election years, but when they did pay attention to these congressional contests, they were more likely to focus in on the substance of those campaigns.

Determinants of Strategy and Issue Coverage

Understanding local television news coverage of election campaigns, however, requires more than a cursory look at the aggregate numbers. Local news coverage may look remarkably similar overall, but there is also wide variation across different outlets, and the specific amount or focus of coverage on any one station is likely to be affected by the set of circumstances unique to any given station. Specifically, there are at least three broad influences on the way in which broadcasters cover campaigns generally and any given race in particular. The first influence involves political factors associated with the specific elections occurring in the local station's area. The second influence is the characteristics of the station itself, including ownership, network affiliation and editorial-level decision makers. The third set of factors includes structural and regional influences such as the size of the media market and characteristics of the city and region within which a station broadcasts. Drawing on the widespread variation of the 2002 study, which contains a representative (random) sample of 122 of the 200 stations in the 50 largest media markets, I discuss the influence of each of these levels in turn.[23]

Political Factors

Much like the way in which competitiveness drives the volume of advertising and news coverage, increased competition of the election races within a market also drives the extent to which local broadcasters focus on strategy. Figure 4.1 displays the predicted effect of adding a competitive gubernatorial race, a competitive senatorial race and both a competitive gubernatorial and a competitive senatorial race on the expected number of strategy and issue stories aired on an otherwise average station. As shown by the figure, although competition has no effect on the number of substantive issue stories on a local television station, a competitive gubernatorial race increases the predicted number of strategy stories by 8, while a competitive senatorial race increases the predicted count by nearly 11. If both statewide races are competitive, the expected number of strategy stories increases by 13 over the course of the last 30 days of a campaign.

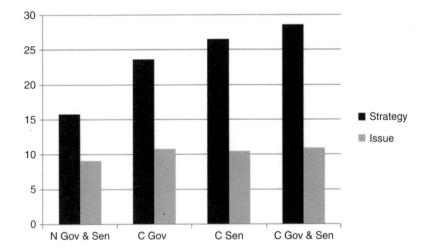

Figure 4.1 Predicted number of strategy and issue stories by competitiveness

Note: Estimates are calculated for stations covering both a senatorial and gubernatorial race, controlling for political, station-level and structural-level characteristics.

Although not as dramatic a change as those for competitive statewide contests, the number of competitive U.S. House races within a given market also has an influence on the number of strategy stories aired. More specifically, for the average local television news station, the addition of one competitive congressional race within the market corresponds with an increase of four strategy stories.

Station Characteristics

There is little doubt that station-level factors play a role in shaping political coverage on the airwaves. Among them, a station's affiliation with a major network is important not only because affiliated stations share video feeds and other resources, but also because network programming can systematically affect election coverage. For example, Fox local television news stations carried coverage of the World Series in October during the time period of the study, and therefore these stations aired fewer election-related stories (both strategy and issue) than they might have, given that baseball preempted many newscasts.

Although people often enter into heated debates about the wisdom of pursuing more government regulation or deregulation of the news media, the Federal Communications Commission and proponents of both arguments frequently lack systematic data on the way in which ownership affects content. A more recent analysis of local news coverage demonstrated that corporate ownership, in contrast to private ownership, corresponds with lower quality election coverage, in part due to the profit maximizing pressures of the former.[24] Another way we might assess the claims of both sides is to compare the quality of news content from stations owned by the ten media conglomerates with the most revenue in 2002 (including big names like Viacom, Disney, Hearst-Argyle, etc.) to the quality of news content from stations owned by those in the mid-tier (those with revenues ranking between 11 and 20), to the rest. Controlling for ownership in the 2002 data, however, reveals no differences in the amount of issue coverage on the airwaves, although stations owned by those in the mid-tier ownership group appear to be less likely to carry strategy stories compared to stations in both the top and bottom tiers. It is important to note, however, that while stations owned by mid-tier owners may be more likely to carry a greater proportion of issue stories compared to strategy ones, they also carry less coverage overall.

One other important station-level characteristic shaping the quantity and quality of news content has to do with the commitments of news teams—journalists, editors, and producers—to providing election-related discussion of the issues.[25] One indicator of such commitment is whether a station pledges to provide candidates themselves with free airtime to speak directly to citizens about the issues of the campaign. Indeed, all else equal, stations that commit themselves to providing free airtime aired an estimated five additional stories focused on substantive issues, compared to those that failed to make the pledge.

Structural and Geographic Factors

Just as political and station-level characteristics shape the content and quality of local television news, so do other external factors. Perhaps the most often cited influence is that of market size. There is wide variation across the nation's 210 media markets in terms of population served. In the top 50 markets alone, which serve two-thirds of the U.S. population, market size ranges from 7.4 million homes in New York City (6 percent of the U.S. population) to just shy of 670,000 in Jacksonville, Florida (0.6 percent of the U.S. population).[26] Scholars have argued that market size shapes election coverage quality in part because "the pressures to abandon journalistic values in pursuit of larger audience share would be greater in bigger markets."[27] In the commercially dominated media environment of the U.S. system, outlets strive to maximize profits, the pursuit of which is affected by the number of competing outlets in search of the same audience. The pressure to abandon quality journalism, some argue, should be especially true for local television news stations, given the increased competition for audience share within larger markets relative to other media such as newspapers in the same market. Figure 4.2 shows the predicted number of strategy and issue stories aired by a local television station, varying the size of the media market within which the station is located.

As demonstrated in Figure 4.2, even after controlling for political competition and other station-level characteristics, not only does the amount of strategy coverage increase as market size increases, but larger markets also tend to

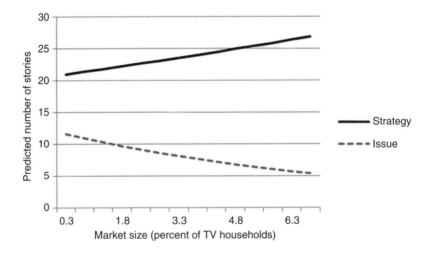

Figure 4.2 Predicted amount of strategy and issue stories by size of media market

Note: Estimates are calculated controlling for political, station and structural level characteristics.

have fewer stories about substantive issues. In other words, the amount of coverage appears impervious to the population size of the market. But increases in strategy stories in larger markets come at the expense of a more substantive focus, a finding that makes sense given that we know coverage of the horserace sells,[28] but also one that may validate the concerns of those who view the influence of market pressure as a race to the bottom.

Survey research has revealed that residents of state capitals are better informed about politics and policy than citizens living elsewhere, perhaps in part due to their proximity to the center of governmental activity.[29] Could an additional explanation for this finding have something to do with the quality of the information environment? The 2002 data reveal no meaningful difference in the amount of issue coverage between capital and non-capital cities, but stations serving capital cities are moderately more likely to air strategy stories.

In sum, the quality of information available on airwaves across the country varies systematically with factors associated with the political characteristics of the elections in each area, station-level affiliations and commitments, and structural and geographic influences regarding where a station is situated. In particular, strategy coverage is less prominent in places with uncompetitive races, on stations owned by mid-tier ownership groups (measured through estimated revenue) and those who do not commit to providing free airtime to candidates. Furthermore, strategy-focused election coverage increases with market size at the expense of substantive issues and to some extent increases in capital cities. All told, while it is clear that local television carries more coverage of the game of politics than of substantive issues, the volume of strategy coverage is related to political factors, station characteristics and market pressures.

Although local television may be a big offender in terms of "dumbing down" its content by focusing more on strategy, it is certainly not the only medium to do so.[30] Moreover, although critics decry the lack of substance on local television, it is unclear that a focus on strategy and the horserace actually detracts from learning about the campaign, especially among the large numbers of low information citizens who tune in. Therefore, I turn next to the question of influence. Is local television's focus on the game aspects of elections really a problem?

The Influence of Local Television Strategy and Horserace Content

Critics of media implicitly assume that increases in the volume of strategy and horserace coverage come at the expense of substantive issue coverage and that such a trade-off affects the quality of public discourse and public knowledge about candidates. The first half of this chapter demonstrated that the balance of strategy and issue coverage is not always zero-sum. As the competitiveness of campaigns within a market increase, stations respond by increasing their coverage of the horserace without appearing to sacrifice their attention to issues (see

Figure 4.3). It is only in the comparison across markets, and specifically comparing large markets to smaller ones, where we find evidence of such a trade-off. Moreover, it is not immediately clear that the increase in strategy coverage of competitive elections is a bad thing. We know that citizens frequently prefer horserace coverage to substantive issue coverage,[31] and such a focus may actually work to excite and engage citizens in the electoral process, creating more attentive viewers who also learn something in the process of getting caught up in the game.

The other important thing to note about local television news is that it not only attracts the largest audiences among media outlets, but its audience, much like audiences of other soft news programming, is comprised of large numbers of low-information citizens,[32] those who would not otherwise choose to tune into politics or elections. In fact, most viewers of local television say that they tune in for tomorrow's weather, meaning that the political information they receive is a by-product of their desire to know whether to bring an umbrella to work tomorrow, rather than a conscious decision to consume political news. Thus, local television news broadcasts are a potentially powerful provider of information to citizens who might otherwise go without. Similar to the argument frequently made about political advertising,[33] local television news may be the earned media equivalent of the campaign spot acting as a multi-vitamin in supplementing the political diet of Americans who do not pay much attention.

So, does the volume of strategy coverage available on local television news influence the extent to which citizens are able to recognize and rate candidates for political office? Figure 4.3 displays the predicted effect of increasing strategy and horserace coverage from one standard deviation below the average amount to one standard deviation above it for citizens with a below average amount of education, a frequently used proxy for the political attentiveness.[34] As demonstrated by the figure, not only does the quantity of strategic information available on local television increase the ability of low-information citizens to rate statewide candidates on a favorability scale, but in all but one case it appears that local television news strategy coverage takes citizens from below a 50 percent chance of being able to rate a given candidate to well over the 50 percent mark.

Given the low information typically held by these citizens, the increase in citizen propensity to rate statewide candidates for office is no small feat. This suggests that local newscasts, while viewed as "dumbed down" by some, may be just the prescription needed for the large percentage of Americans for whom politics is peripheral.

Discussion

While the charge against local broadcasters—namely that they focus on soft news at the expense of important information and on strategy and horserace

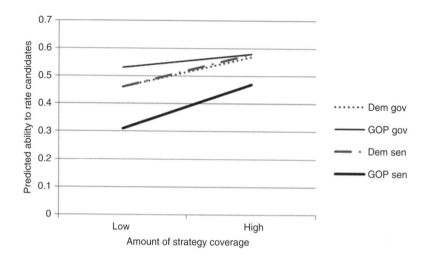

Figure 4.3 Predicted change in ability to rate candidates on a favorability scale based on exposure to strategy and horserace coverage (political novices only)

Note: Estimates are calculated controlling for incumbency, competitiveness, partisanship, partisan strength, age, race, and newspaper use.

rather than on substantive issues—may be true both for the balance of information available on its newscast and for the focus of the election content that actually airs, this chapter provides some push back to the conventional wisdom. Local television coverage of politics and governance ranks second only to sports and weather in volume during the month leading up to November elections, and although sports, weather, crime and injury collectively make up a larger percentage of the broadcast, if one adds up the multiple opportunities for viewing local news along with the number of citizens tuning in, there is a non-trivial amount of election information available on the airwaves that may be democratically beneficial.

Moreover, although the structure of local newscasts may be strikingly similar from city to city, it is also clear that all local television coverage is not alike. In fact, there is systematic variation in the extent to which local television stations focus on strategy and issue coverage. More specifically, stations are responsive to factors such as the competitiveness of the races in their area, the competitive pressures of the size of the market, and the commitments of their organization in determining how elections will be framed. Most importantly, the decision to highlight strategy and horserace elements of a campaign may actually provide a non-trivial benefit to a large proportion of local television audiences. In particular, political novices who pay marginal attention to politics may be particularly aided by increased coverage of strategy and horserace, as such coverage helps them to become more familiar with the candidates in an exciting and more accessible format featuring who is up and who is down. In analyses not shown here, there is evidence that local television news' benefit for low-information voters increases with increased attention to races lower down the ballot. In other words, perhaps critics should be less concerned with the soft news focus of local television and more concerned with its relative lack of *local* content, for which information is not readily available from other sources. Although there are many places to get information on the presidential race (including local television), there are fewer sources that cover one's local U.S. House race. In addition, if strategy coverage is helpful to political novices and is likely to increase with competitive races, then we might also be concerned with the smaller amount of information available to engage politically uninformed citizens in markets with fewer competitive races.

What is clear is that local television news coverage of elections may serve an important role in filling knowledge gaps among the informationally poor. The question then becomes what happens to this democratically desirable effect in the ever-changing media environment that is becoming increasingly user-preference driven.[35] In the golden age of the broadcast era, citizens had little choice over the content to which they were exposed aside from turning off the television. Today, local television newscasts know their audiences primarily tune in for the weather and therefore tease the night's forecast along with the unusual soft news throughout the broadcast to keep viewers tuned in. Although citizens could certainly change the channel, they risk missing the forecast by doing so, and by staying tuned in, they are often unintentionally exposed to the political election information aired on the broadcast, which ends up providing a democratically desirable effect of informing political novices.

Notes

1   Paul Klite, Robert A. Bardwell, and Jason Salzman, "Local TV News: Getting Away with Murder," *The International Journal of Press/Politics* 2 (1997): 102–112.
2   Tom Rosenstiel et al., *We Interrupt This Newscast: How to Improve Local News and Win Ratings, Too* (Cambridge: Cambridge University Press, 2007).
3   Video identified in study by James M. Pribble, et al, "Medical News for the Public to Use: What's on Local TV News?" *The American Journal of Managed Care* 12 (2006): 170–176.
4   Rosenstiel, *We Interrupt This Newscast.*
5   Markus Prior, "Any Good News in Soft News? The Impact of Soft News Preference on Political Knowledge," *Political Communication* 20 (2003): 164.
6   Pew Research Center for the People and the Press, June 2010 Media Consumption Survey.
7   Brian Stetler, "Local TV Newscasts Expanding," *New York Times*, August 21, 2011, B1.
8   Dan Froomkin, "Bush, Deep Throat and the Press," *The Washington Post*, June 3, 2005, accessed April 30, 2012, http://www.washingtonpost.com/wp-dyn/content/blog/2005/06/03/BL2005060300818.html.

9 Mara Liasson, "Obama Grants 4 Local TV Stations Interviews," *National Public Radio*, April 19, 2011, accessed April 30, 2012, http://www.npr.org/2011/04/19/135533892/obama-goes-on-local-tv-with-his-take-on-the-budget.

10 Mark Leibovich, "Vexing Issue for the Clinton Campaign: What to Make of Bill?" *New York Times*, April 29, 2008, A15.

11 Travis N. Ridout, Michael M. Franz and Erika Franklin Fowler, "Advances in the Study of Political Advertising," *The Journal of Political Marketing* (forthcoming).

12 Marion Just, et al., *Crosstalk: Citizens, Candidates, and the Media in a Presidential Campaign*, (Chicago: University of Chicago Press, 1996); Doris A. Graber, *Processing the News: How People Tame the Information Tide*, 2nd ed, (New York: Longman Group, 1988); James Druckman, "Media Matter: How Newspapers and Television News Cover Campaigns and Influence Voters," *Political Communication* 22 (2005): 463–481; Daniel P. Stevens et al, "Local News in a Social Capital Capital: Election 2000 on Minnesota's Local News Stations," *Political Communication* 23 (2006): 61–83.

13 Matthew Hale, Erika Franklin Fowler and Kenneth M. Goldstein, "Capturing Multiple Markets: A New Method for Analyzing Local Television News," *Electronic News* 1 (2007): 227–243.

14 Rosenstiel, *We Interrupt This Newscast*, 33.

15 Rosensteil, *We Interrupt This Newscast*, 34–35.

16 Gene Wyckoff, *The Image Candidates: American Politics in the Age of Television* (New York: The MacMillan Company, 1968); Mary Ellen Leary, *Phantom Politics: Campaigning in California*, (Washington, D.C.: Public Affairs Press, 1977); Sue Carter, Frederick Fico and Jocelyn A. McCabe, "Partisan and Structural Balance in Local Television Election Coverage," *Journalism and Mass Communication Quarterly* 79 (2002): 41–53; Druckman, "Media Matter"; Stevens et al., "Local News."

17 Just, et al., *Crosstalk*; C. Danielle Vinson, *Local Media Coverage of Congress and its Members: Through Local Eyes* (Cresskill, N.J.: Hampton Press, 2003); Johanna Dunaway, "Markets, Ownership, and the Quality of Campaign News," *Journal of Politics* 70 (2008): 1193–1202. Just et al.'s (1996) analysis focuses on four local television stations in the 1992 presidential election, Vinson's (2003) analysis examines eight markets in the 1994 election, and Klite's (1997) study examined 90 stations in 46 markets but only on three Wednesdays prior to the 1996 election. The exception is Johanna Dunaway's (2008) analysis of 16 stations in four markets during the 2004 election, which demonstrates the importance of ownership and market characteristics, but the study examines only two competitive statewide races, which does not enable comparisons across multiple races within a state or to less competitive races.

18 More information is available from the author upon request.

19 See especially, Larry Bartels, *Presidential Primaries and the Dynamics of Public Choice* (Princeton, N.J.: Princeton University Press, 1998); Thomas Patterson, *Out of Order* (New York, Knopf, 1993); also Dunaway, "Markets, Ownership, and Quality."

20 Coders were asked to identify the primary focus of the story from the following options: strategy (primarily discussion of tactics or game of politics), horserace (who is ahead or behind), issue (policy or platform focused), adwatch (assessing the claims made in advertisements), personal characteristics (focuses on aspects of the candidate) or other (specify).

21 Bartels, *Presidential Primaries*; Patterson, *Out of Order*; Doris A. Graber, *Mass Media and American Politics*, 8th ed. (Washington, D.C.: CQ Press, 2010).

22 Danny Hayes, "The Dynamics of Agenda Convergence and the Paradox of Competitiveness in Presidential Campaigns," *Political Research Quarterly* 63 (2010): 594–611.

23 For the technically minded, the results presented in this chapter are from two negative binomial estimations modeling the number of strategy and horserace stories

(model 1) and number of issue stories (model 2) as a function of competitiveness, the presence of statewide races and number of U.S. House toss-up races, the proportion of the U.S. population within the market, an indicator for whether the market covers a capital city, indicators for network affiliation, region, whether a station committed to give candidates free airtime, and whether a station's ownership group is among the top 10 or top 20 earners. More information on specifications and models is available from the author upon request.

24 Dunaway, "Markets, Ownership and Quality."

25 See Laura Roselle, "Local Coverage of the 2000 Election in North Carolina: Does Civic Journalism Make a Difference?" *American Behavioral Scientist* 46 (2003): 600–616.

26 Local television market universe estimates from Nielsen Media for 2011–2012 market ranks. Available online at: http://www.nielsen.com/content/dam/corporate/us/en/public%20factsheets/tv/nielsen-2012-local-DMA-TV-penetration.pdf. Last accessed April 5, 2012.

27 John R. Zaller, *A Theory of Media Politics* (Unpublished manuscript,1999), 41, accessed April 15, 2012, http://www.sscnet.ucla.edu/polisci/faculty/zaller/media%20politics%20book%20.pdf.

28 Shanto Iyengar, Helmut Norpoth and Kyu S. Hahn, "Consumer Demand for Election News: The Horserace Sells," *The Journal of Politics* 66 (2002): 157–175.

29 Michael Delli Carpini and Scott Keeter, *What Americans Know About Politics and Why It Matters* (New Haven: Yale University Press, 1996).

30 Patterson, *Out of Order.*

31 Iyengar, Norpoth, and Hahn, "Consumer Demand for Election News."

32 Erika Franklin Fowler, Ken Goldstein and Dhavan Shah, "The Challenge of Measuring News Consumption," *Political Communication Report* (2008), accessed on April 30, 2012, http://www.jour.unr.edu/pcr/1801_2008_winter/roundtable_fowler.html.

33 Michael M. Franz, Paul B. Freedman, Kenneth M. Goldstein, and Travis N. Ridout, *Campaign Advertising and American Democracy* (Philadelphia, PA: Temple University Press, 2007).

34 Specifics on the model estimated here available from the author upon request.

35 Prior, "Any Good News in Soft News?"

Chapter 5

News Media and War

Warmongers or Peacemakers?[1]

Piers Robinson

War defined the 20th century. World War I and World War II witnessed the birth of contemporary warfare characterized by mechanized militaries and strategies of total war that involved the deliberate targeting of civilian populations and attempts at achieving wholesale death and destruction. The Nazi Holocaust against Jews and Gypsies, the dropping of the nuclear bombs on the Japanese cities of Hiroshima and Nagasaki, and the fire bombing of cities such as Dresden in Germany are the more notable and widely discussed events of this kind. Following World War II, the Cold War stand-off between the Soviet-led East and the U.S.-led West was accompanied by protracted and equally destructive conflicts in countries such as Vietnam and Afghanistan. By the beginning of the 21st century, although the nature of war appears to have changed, political conflict continues to shape the world. The so-called "humanitarian" interventions of the 1990s and the "war on terror" have reshaped, to some extent, the forms of war that now prevail, but violent conflict remains as much a part of the 21st century as it was a part of the 20th. Along with the emergence of contemporary warfare have been exponential advances in communication technology. The late 19th century brought us the ability to communicate instantaneously via the telegraph, which was followed by the emergence of broadcast media and culminated in the profound connectivity of individuals around the world through the Internet.

Throughout this period, governments, military and academics have all come to believe in the enormous power of news media to shape public opinion during war. And yet, there continues to be remarkably divergent views on the role news media and public opinion play in war. For some, news media have traditionally performed a largely propagandistic function, helping to mobilize publics in support of war. For example, Goebbel's masterminding of Nazi propaganda during 1930s Germany is a frequently cited example of the media as a powerful propaganda tool. However, contemporary governments have been no less adept at manipulating public perceptions, as demonstrated by the Bush administration during the run-up to the 2003 invasion of Iraq. In this case, administration officials left the U.S. public with the very clear, and very false, understanding both that Iraq had Weapons of Mass Destruction (WMD) and that Saddam Hussein's regime was linked with the al-Qaida attacks of 9/11.

For other observers, media can present a profound challenge to governments executing war by revealing the misery of warfare to publics and even derailing policy away from war and toward peace. A good example of this was the case of media and the Vietnam War where, at least according to popular conception, news media coverage of the violence and suffering turned U.S. citizens against the war. In a similar vein, some have understood news media as a mobilizing force for so-called humanitarian intervention. A prominent example of this was the U.S. decision to deploy 28,000 troops into Somalia during 1992 in order to facilitate the delivery of food aid. For others still, the role of media varies significantly across time and circumstance: at one moment being a cheerleader for belligerent governments, at others highlighting the plight of those suffering in war.

This basic disagreement regarding the role media play during war provides a point of departure for this chapter. Broadly the central questions can be framed as follows: To what extent, and under what conditions, do media act as a cheerleader for governments pursuing war? Alternatively, to what extent and under what conditions do media constrain governments' pursuits of war? In short, when it comes to war, are media warmongers or peacemakers? Following these questions, the chapter explores key debates in the following order: The first section explores the academic orthodoxy, which is built largely upon Daniel Hallin's seminal study of U.S. news media and the Vietnam War.[2] Here I discuss claims about the inadequacy of war reporting and its propensity to reflect uncritically the policy goals of governments. The second section brings into focus contemporary accounts and debates, all of which have sought, in various ways, to explore the role of media as a more independent and active participant in policy making. Here I discuss debates over the *CNN effect*, the arrival of "global" news media and the Internet. In the third section, a range of accounts are highlighted, all of which have sought to develop a more variable and nuanced understanding of the roles media can play during war. Before concluding the chapter, section four assesses the current major issues facing our understanding of the relationship between media, public opinion and war.

Section One: The Orthodoxy: Media as "Warmonger" and "Faithful Servant"[3] to the State

Vietnam became a center point of U.S. foreign policy in the midst of the Cold War. In its attempts to prevent the spread of communist beliefs, the U.S. conducted a lengthy and increasingly bloody war against the majority of the Vietnamese population. During the 1960s and 1970s, the United States became increasingly embroiled in a conflict involving attacks upon, and the forced displacement of, Vietnamese villagers, as well as the strategic bombing of neighboring Laos and Cambodia. For the U.S., the war was understood as a righteous struggle against the evils of Communism. For most of the Vietnamese population (both in North and South Vietnam), the war was a continuation of an anti-colonial struggle that had started with opposition to French rule during the 1950s. By 1974 the United States was defeated, 50,000 U.S. soldiers had died, and millions had lost their lives in South East Asia.[4] In his memoirs, Richard Nixon leaves little doubt that news media coverage of the Vietnam War effectively derailed U.S. attempts to win:

> The Vietnam War was complicated by factors that never before occurred in America's conduct of war . . . More than ever before, television showed the terrible human suffering and sacrifice of war. Whatever the intention behind such relentless and literal reporting of war, the result was a serious demoralization of the home front, raising the question of whether America would ever again be able to fight an enemy abroad with unity and strength of purpose at home.[5]

In line with Nixon's comment, many commentators came to understand U.S. failure in Vietnam largely as a result of media and public opposition to the war.[6] Largely as a consequence of this, the Vietnam War gave birth to the Vietnam Syndrome. This concept refers to the belief that, as casualties mount and critical media coverage increases, public opinion turns increasingly against a war, leading ultimately to military failure due to the lack of support on the home front. The Vietnam Syndrome has become a defining feature of military and political calculations over war and the ability to conduct lengthy military operations when casualties are being taken: it has also provided the impetus behind increasingly sophisticated approaches to managing the media during war time, a subject that will be returned to later in the chapter. At least to an extent, many of those who have bemoaned the impact of media and public opinion on U.S. policy have reflected a realist outlook on international politics. The realist outlook actually perceives public and media influence upon foreign policy as a negative occurrence, largely because publics and journalists do not possess adequate information, judgment and ability to decide what is best for a nation. As a consequence, realists advocate elite (i.e. government officials and foreign policy experts) control over the foreign policy process (See Learning Box 5.1).

Learning Box 5.1: The Realist Perspective on Public Opinion, Media and Foreign Policy

The realist perspective that foreign policy should be immune from public (and also media) influence has a long history. Writing in reference to U.S. public opinion during the early part of the Cold War era, Walter Lippman claimed that "[t]he Unhappy truth is that the prevailing public opinion has been destructively wrong at the critical junctures." In part, the claim underpinning the realist perspective is that foreign-policy elites are best placed to decide what should be done in order to further U.S. national interests and, at the same time, that the U.S. public are largely ignorant and/or ill-informed about international affairs and, therefore, ill-equipped to think about the complexities of foreign policy. But the realist claim is also now underpinned by the *neorealist* position that policy makers react to events in the international system, such as emerging threats and shifts in the balance of power, and not to internal factors such as the desires and wishes of the U.S. public and media pressure. Overall, realism argues that policy makers should remain detached from the pressures of public opinion and media, formulating foreign policy in response to external events in the international system, and not in response to internal domestic politics.

For more information, see Robinson, et al., *Pockets of Resistance*, 39–49.

While belief in the Vietnam Syndrome has persisted among policy makers and the military, political communication scholarship has consistently cast doubt on the claim that U.S. media reporting was central in shifting U.S. political and public attitudes against the Vietnam War. Daniel Hallin's seminal study, The Uncensored War, provided a profound, and highly influential, challenge to claims that U.S. media undermined U.S. war efforts in South East Asia. Drawing upon a detailed and exhaustive analysis of U.S. television news and New York Times coverage of the war, Hallin argues that, contrary to popular perceptions, media coverage was largely supportive of U.S. war aims up until 1968. During this first phase, U.S. news media operated within a sphere of consensus which had been defined by political agreement over the course of the war (see Figure 5.1). However, in 1968, amid a communist uprising throughout South Vietnam, disagreement broke out in public between hawkish members of the U.S. government who sought military victory at all costs, and doves who were arguing that America needed to withdraw from Vietnam. At this point, Hallin argues that media reporting became more critical, but only because U.S. journalists were reporting the viewpoints of those within the political establishment (i.e. the doves) who had started to question the war. At this stage, as Hallin puts it, journalists were operating within a sphere of controversy, a sphere that had been created by the public disagreement of the Washington political establishment. At no point during the war, however, did U.S. journalists operate within a sphere of deviancy in which the morality of the war and the good intentions of the U.S. government were ever questioned. Hallin's simple but profound conclusion is that U.S. media largely followed the contours of elite debate over Vietnam, rather than being the driving force behind elite debate. Another implication of Hallin's analysis is that the media cannot be understood to have played a major role in causing U.S. public support for the war to decline or in the mobilization of the anti-war movement.

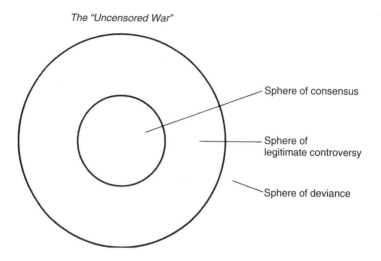

The "Uncensored War"

Sphere of consensus

Sphere of legitimate controversy

Sphere of deviance

Figure 5.1 Hallin's Spheres of Consensus, Controversy and Deviance

Source: From Daniel C. Hallin, *The Uncensored War: The Media and Vietnam*. (Oxford: Oxford University Press, 1986, 117). By permission of Oxford University Press, Inc.

Hallin's analysis is one example of what can be described as the elite-driven model[7] of wartime media state relations, whereby media are understood to largely reflect and reinforce elite viewpoints. Other scholarship, at least that generated during the Cold War, has confirmed Hallin's findings in the context of other wars and other national settings.[8] But what does media coverage that is supportive of government elites look like, and what are the factors that cause journalists to support their governments rather than maintain independence? With respect to the former, descriptions of war-time media coverage have tended to show a mixture of supportive "our boys (and now girls) in battle" coverage that highlights the bravery and professionalism of "our" soldiers while demonizing the "enemy." At its most jingoistic, such coverage barely disguises its enthusiasm and support for troops in battle. For example, during the 2003 invasion of Iraq some presenters on the Fox News Channel wore stars and stripes badge on their lapels. During the 1982 war between Britain and Argentina over the Falklands Islands, the British tabloid newspaper The Sun notoriously published the news of a British submarine attack on the Argentine cruiser the General Belgrano with the headline "Gotcha." Only when it was realized that the cruiser had sunk with heavy loss of life did the newspaper retract the headline (at least in time for later editions). Any criticism that occurs during wartime, according to the elite-driven model, remains confined to procedural-level criticism,[9] where there is argument over issues such as military tactics, troop equipment levels and the relative effectiveness of particular military strategies. Conversely, media criticism rarely reaches substantive-level issues concerning the basic aims, justifications and morality of a war. The overall result of such coverage is that news media play a far bigger role in terms of mobilizing public support in favor of a war, and far less in terms of creating the so-called Vietnam Syndrome. Overall, according to the elite-driven model, most media coverage of conflict does little to advance the cause of peace, but rather encourages further conflict and violence.

With respect to explaining why media coverage of war adopts a support-ive stance, a number of concepts and models have been developed to explain media performance. One explanation focuses upon the close relationship between journalists and official sources. As Bennett explains through his *indexing hypothesis*,[10] journalists tend to index news coverage to the range of view-points that exist among elected officials. This is partly because journalists rely upon government officials as a source of information, especially when it comes to "foreign" affairs. In times of war, this reliance is intensified even further for two main reasons. First, governments devote a large amount of attention to promoting their position through public relations (PR) activities (*perception management*) that are designed to influence journalists. For example, during Gulf War I in 1991, when U.S. forces expelled Saddam Hussein's forces from Kuwait, the U.S. military influenced media reporting through the use of dra-matic imagery of cruise missile and guided missile attacks during press brief-ings. We will return to the issue of PR and *perception management* later in the chapter. Second, the very nature of violent conflict means that information can be hard to come by and, unless journalists are willing to take the risk of walk-ing into a warzone, they can become highly dependent upon military officials as a source of information. There are, however, further reasons why journalists come to use official sources so heavily: as Bennett[11] notes, reporting the views of democratically elected officials is a perfectly reasonable and justifiable thing to do. Focusing news sourcing on government officials ensures journalists are paying attention to the key decision makers who determine the course of events during a crisis. In short, what government officials have to say about a crisis or war is inherently newsworthy. Finally, given the pressures of meeting deadlines and the cost of producing the news, reliance upon the wealth of information disseminated by government officials, which in part flows from the perception management efforts mentioned above, means that official sources become a convenient and cost-effective source of news.[12]

Indexing certainly helps to shape a close relationship between officials and sources, and goes some way to explaining why media can become *faithful ser-vants*[13] both during time of war, as well as in other circumstances. However, there are broader structural dynamics that, according to some scholars, play an equally important role in terms of shaping media output. For some, the *political economy* of the mass media is an important factor. In *Manufacturing Consent*, Herman and Chomsky discuss how the size, concentration of own-ership and profit orientation of the U.S. media influence the range of debate expressed across U.S. news: Because most mainstream news media in the U.S. are owned by major businesses, and because the interests of those businesses overlap with the interests of political elites, the news agenda is broadly compatible with the interests of economic and political elites. For example, the free market ideologue and media mogul Rupert Murdoch was an ardent supporter of the invasion of Iraq, and all of the newspapers owned by his company News Corporation adopted a pro-war stance.[14] More generally, Herman and Chomsky argue that the commitment to opening markets around the world in ways conducive to big business is an interest shared by U.S. political and economic elites. As a result, news media that are a part of a network of corporate conglomerates are unlikely to run news stories that offer a serious challenge to those overlapping and shared interests. In terms of the practicality of how news media reports become tainted by the political views of owners, Herman and Chomsky argue that most of the time editors and journalists either self-censor, knowing in advance the preferred views of their owners, or have simply internalized the values and perspectives of those they work for. Only rarely does this process involve direct strategic interventions from owners. As well as economic interests shaping news output, Herman and Chomsky also note how media reliance upon advertising combines with the controversy-averse sponsors and advertisers: here, a desire not to be seen as too controversial or oppositional is understood to be a powerful disciplining mechanism in terms of constraining the news agenda of mainstream media.

Although arguments over the influence of corporate elite influences on media output have, at times, been dismissed as conspiratorial, the issue of the ownership and concentration of the mass media, especially in the U.S., has persisted for some considerable time. For example, the renowned broadcaster Edward R. Murrow spoke frankly about the commercial pressures on U.S. media in 1958:

> So the question is this: Are the big corporations who pay the freight for radio and television programs wise to use that time exclusively for the sale of goods and services? . . . I refuse to believe that the presidents and chairmen of the boards of these big corporations want their corporate image to consist exclusively of a solemn voice in an echo chamber, or a pretty girl opening the door of a refrigerator, or a horse that talks. They want something better . . . but most of the men whose legal and moral responsibility it is to spend the stockholders' money for advertising are removed from the realities of the mass media by five, six or a dozen contraceptive layers of vice-presidents, public relations counsel and advertising agencies. Their business is to sell goods, and the competition is pretty tough.[15]

Fifty years later, retired CBS anchor Dan Rather, in the midst of a public disagreement with his former employer, chastised the over-commercialization of U.S. news:

> America's biggest, most important news organizations have, over the last 25 years, fallen prey to merger after merger, acquisitions after acquisition

... to the point where they are, now, tiny parts of immeasurably larger corporate entities – entities whose primary business often has nothing to do with news. Entities that may, at any given time, have literally hundreds of regulatory issues before multiple arms of government concerning a vast array of business interests . . . in the current model of corporate news ownership, the incentive to produce good and valuable news is simply not there.[16]

Outside the U.S.-context, recent events surrounding Rupert Murdoch and News Corporation have highlighted just how closely interlinked politicians and media conglomerates can become. For example, the public has learned that former British Prime Minister Tony Blair is godfather to one of Murdoch's daughters,[17] while Andy Coulson (former editor of a Murdoch newspaper) was appointed (without full security clearance) as Chief of Communications for the current Conservative/Liberal Democrat coalition government.[18]

Beyond the economic structuring of the news media industry, a number of authors identify broader ideological constraints that shape news media reporting. For example, Hallin discusses how the ideology of anti-communism helped to unify both policy makers and journalists. In the case of the Vietnam war, this meant that journalists were unable to see the war as anything but a righteous struggle against the evils of communism; alternative frames of reference, for example, seeing the war as an aggressive and imperialistic act, fell so far outside their ideological frame of reference that this interpretation was probably never entertained by most journalists. As we shall see later in the chapter, some scholars argue that the "war on terror" and "humanitarian warfare" perform ideological functions that are not dissimilar to that of anti-communism during the Cold War. Finally, a number of scholars identify patriotism and national identity as the key factor in shaping, through a number of mechanisms, media reporting of war.[19] For example, the appeal to patriotism is a powerful rhetorical tool employed by policy makers in order to silence dissent. At the same time the *rally round the flag* thesis describes how populations tend to instinctively support their leadership at times of national crisis,[20] while commercial news media are vulnerable to the concern that patriotic publics will not welcome critical coverage during war. In addition, the patriotic sentiments of journalists themselves might naturally incline them to support "their" side during a war.

To summarize, there are a number of factors that work together to shape news coverage of war, including reliance upon official sources, the political economy of the mass media, ideological constraints such as anti-communism during the Cold War and patriotism. These factors work to ensure that media coverage of war is, more often than not, supportive of governments and political elites.

Section Two: Media as a Constraint Upon, and a Determinant of, Crisis Policy Making

Other scholars, however, have argued that the story of war, media and public opinion is not one purely of an elite-dominated media and an elite-led public. Moreover, and in contrast to the realist view that media and public influence on foreign policy is not to be welcomed, liberal-democratic viewpoints maintain that media and public opinion certainly should act as an important constraint upon policy makers. This is because public and media scrutiny can help to prevent unnecessary wars and inform better decision making over war (See Learning Box 5.2).

Learning Box 5.2 The Liberal-Democratic Perspective on Public Opinion, Media and Foreign Policy

The idea that public opinion (and media) should influence foreign policy formulation also has a long history. In the early 20th, President Woodrow Wilson articulated the importance of public scrutiny of foreign affairs in his famous "Fourteen Points." Here he called for "Open covenants of peace, openly arrived at, after which there shall be no private international understandings of any kind but diplomacy shall proceed always frankly and in the public view." More specifically, a key component of liberal theory is the *democratic peace thesis*. This thesis maintains that liberal democracies are war-averse because, at least in part, the consent of the public is required. As people generally prefer peace to war, public opinion and media can act as a powerful constraint upon elected leaders and, therefore, the external behaviour of a state. In order for this to occur, public opinion should be able to influence foreign policy and news media must be independent of government. Overall, the liberal-democratic perspective maintains that public opinion and news media can contribute to sound foreign policy, as well as acting as a check against corrupt political elites, and that incorporating public concerns increases the range of opinions and arguments available to policy makers. As a result, more rational and well-thought-out policies can be devised.

For more information, see Robinson, et al., *Pockets of Resistance*, 39–49.

With respect to the influence of public opinion, for example, John Mueller's analysis in War, Presidents and Public Opinion,[21] is that U.S. public support for a war declines over time in inverse proportion to the number of U.S. military casualties. Examining both the Korean War and the Vietnam War, he concludes that the U.S. public responds in a largely rational and informed manner, increasing their opposition to a war the longer it goes on and the more casualties that are taken. For U.S. presidents Harry Truman and Lyndon Johnson, this ultimately led to political damage at the polls. The thesis at work here is a simple but eminently plausible one: as wars become long and protracted and more U.S. soldiers are either killed or injured, all things being equal, fewer and fewer U.S. citizens will support the war. As such, the so-called casualties hypothesis fits within a broader set of arguments regarding how public opinion, in the very broadest terms, serves as a restraint upon policy makers.[22] It is important to note that the kind of media coverage in question here is procedural-level criticism which challenges policy on the basis of whether or not a war is being won, and not so much a substantive-level criticism, which challenge the basic morality and justification for a war.

With respect to the influence of news media, a more radical and determining role has been asserted through debate over the *CNN effect*.[23] Starting in the early 1990s, this debate concerned the apparent ability of news media coverage of suffering people to cause U.S. policy makers to deploy forces in countries such as Somalia (1991–92) and Bosnia (1995) in pursuit of humanitarian objectives. As such, news media were being placed at the heart of a new form of warfare, namely *humanitarian warfare*, whereby Western governments used military force in order to uphold human rights in war-torn countries. In an important sense, the CNN-effect debate represented the start of what was to become a sustained debate over the extent to which technological developments and changing geo-political realities were changing traditional patterns of media deference to government, as theorized by the elite-driven accounts discussed in section one. Broadly speaking, the CNN effect debate was theorized in two ways. First, it was argued that media independence had increased following the end of the Cold War in the late 1980s: with the end of the ideological constraints of anti-communism discussed earlier, journalists were freer to criticize their governments and, in turn, push for humanitarian interventions. Second, the emergence of 24-hours news channels, predicated on live coverage of international events, increased the visibility of crises around the world while the ability to report in real-time (via portable satellite communication equipment) meant that news organizations were able to bypass official channels. As such, news technology appeared to be disrupting the traditional patterns of indexing and reliance upon official sources discussed in section one.

In fact, rather than confirming the impression of an all-powerful media, a large body of research into the CNN effect suggested a far more circumscribed and conditional role for the media, at least in the realm of humanitarian warfare. For example, Livingston and Eachus[24] argued that, in the case of U.S. intervention in Somalia (Operation Restore Hope, 1992), it was government officials who were drawing the attention of journalists to the humanitarian disaster there, not the other way round. Accordingly, they conclude that in the case of Operation Restore Hope the U.S. media demonstrated a familiar pattern of media indexing. Later, Livingston[25] argued that, rather than determining foreign policy decisions, media were having a more subtle range of effects, including *agenda setting, accelerant* and *impediment effects*. With the agenda-setting effect, media place a conflict on the foreign policy agenda thereby demanding attention from policy makers, but the media do not ultimately determine what action is finally taken. With the accelerant effect, the process of policy making is speeded up in response to the "24–7" news environment, with policy makers being forced to act quicker than in earlier eras. Finally, the impediment effect refers to the concern policy makers' have about future negative coverage of U.S. casualties and how this might act as a block to policy makers intervening during a humanitarian crisis.[26] Other research has found that media influence on policy is most likely to occur only when political elites are divided over policy[27] and with respect to particular policy types. For example, Robinson argues that media can trigger the use of air power during a humanitarian crisis but not the deployment of ground troops,[28] while Livingston argues that media can play a far greater role with respect to low-cost humanitarian responses where troops are not at risk, such as helping aid agencies deliver food aid.[29]

Whatever the reality was regarding media impact on foreign policy post-Cold War, the CNN-effect debate of the 1990s ran in tandem with a variety of theoretical developments that sought to describe a more variable and nuanced understanding of media-state relations, both in conditions of war and foreign policy more generally. It is to these accounts that we now turn.

Section Three: Theorizing Variability in Media-State Relations; Neopluralist Models

Most attempts to develop a variable understanding of the media-foreign-policy-public-opinion nexus have not rejected entirely the elite-driven theories discussed in section one, but instead have explored the conditions under which media play a more independent and influential role. For example, Gadi Wolfsfeld's political contest model[30] conceptualizes the mass media as a central arena in which the struggle between authorities (political elites) and challengers (non-elite groups) are played out. In this contest, authorities have considerable power to set the news agenda and, most of the time, they succeed in promoting their agendas and frames to the media, as described by elite-driven accounts. However, as Wolfsfeld describes, control over the political environment is never total and, when challengers are able to a) initiate events, b) regulate the flow of information and c) mobilize elite support, they can be successful at setting the media agenda. By way of example, Wolfsfeld analyses the case of the first Palestinian Intifada (1987–1993) when Palestinians were able to initiate an uprising, prevent Israeli authorities from controlling the movement of journalists throughout the occupied territories and, finally, draw support from the Israeli political left. As a result, Palestinians were successful at promoting a frame[31] of injustice and defiance, which helped to promote their cause and to pave the way for the Oslo Accords in 1993. As such, Wolfsfeld's model allows for the possibility of significant non-elite influence upon media coverage.

Also theorizing variability, but more restrictive with regard to the extent to which media can become an advocate for non-elite groups, are Robinson's policy-media interaction model and Entman's cascading activation model.[32] The former focuses on theorizing the CNN effect as a function of both media framing and levels of policy uncertainty in government: specifically, when policy makers are uncertain over what to do, a window is provided through which critically framed media reports can start to influence and shape policy. Exploring events surrounding the fall of the UN "safe area" Srebrenica and the defence of Gorazde "safe area" during the 1992–1995 Bosnian War, Robinson shows how, amid policy uncertainty in the White House, critically framed and emotive coverage of civilians suffering during these events served to influence a policy decision in Washington to use greater force against Bosnian Serb nationalists.[33] Finally, Entman's model theorizes independent and oppositional news media as occurring when (1) dissensus exists among officials at the top level of government, (2) mid-level officials promote challenges to existing policy and (3) events occur that are culturally ambiguous and open to contestation. For example, Entman analyzes how the images emerging from the Abu Ghraib prison in Iraq, showing acts of abuse and torture by U.S. troops against Iraqi detainees, created a significant degree of media coverage that was critical of the U.S. government. This emerged because the events in question were culturally incongruous for Americans and, as such, the appalling images were difficult for the U.S. administration to explain away; at the same time, the existence of elite dissensus coupled with the emergence of some mid-level officials who became critical of the White House provided journalists with a source of political challenges to the White House.

More recently, researchers have attempted to develop a better sense of both chronological (changes over time) and spacial (e.g. variations across national contexts) dimensions. For example, Baum and Groeling's *War Stories*[34] theorizes how media and publics are supportive of U.S. governments in the early stages of a conflict. However, as a war drags on, more and more information gradually comes to light (casualties, military errors, stories of abuse and so on) that enable the public to develop a more independent view of events. At the same time, the propensity of journalists to focus on those who criticize and challenge the government means news media play an increasingly important role in terms of shaping public opinion and constraining policy makers. In short, Baum and Groeling argue that, while the story of media-state dynamics is one of media and public subservience to the government in the opening stages of a war, this does not hold true at the later stages of a conflict when a more informed public and an intrinsically critical media start to place significant constraints upon policy makers. Finally, in analyzing British news media coverage of the 2003 invasion of Iraq, Robinson and colleagues document significant variations in media independence across different British television news broadcasters and national newspapers.[35] Although they find that most U.K. media coverage conformed to the predictions of the elite-driven model, a minority of media outlets were able to attain higher levels of independence with several U.K. papers adopting an anti-war stance. One of their main conclusions is that the different *media systems* and *journalistic cultures* found across different national contexts can have an important impact upon the levels of media independence, with U.K. media demonstrating somewhat higher levels of independence than the U.S. media, at least with respect to the 2003 Iraq War.

To summarize the key points from sections two and three, not all scholars focus on how media and public opinion function to support governments and political elites. For some, public opinion can act as a broad constraint on policy makers, especially during long and protracted wars where rising casualty counts can serve to erode public support for the war. At the same time, some scholars have described how news media coverage of humanitarian crises can be a factor in persuading policy makers to actually intervene in order to protect civilians and uphold human rights. Reflecting an awareness of the variability of media-state-public opinion dynamics, a number of scholars have sought to develop in recent years what can be described as neo-pluralist accounts of media-state relations.

Section Four: The "New Media Environment," Perception Management and Ideology

Whatever models and theories political communication scholars have developed in the past, the last 15 years have witnessed political and technological developments that have presented profound challenges to existing knowledge. On the one hand, the events of 9/11 have ushered in a new era of war and conflict, dominated by U.S.-led military operations in Iraq and Afghanistan. Both of these wars have become protracted and deeply controversial conflicts accompanied by heavy loss of life. At the same time, the media environment has witnessed dramatic changes with the emergence of the Internet as the key platform for news dissemination and interpersonal communication. The array of communication formats such as Twitter and Facebook, the presence of all mainstream news media on the Internet, and online Citizen Journalism aided by the proliferation of digital cameras and mobile phones, have all created the impression of a radically pluralized media sphere. In this pluralized sphere, traditional patterns of elite-dominated media have been radically undermined, at least according to some.[36] Various claims have been made about the transformative power of new communication technology, ranging from arguments about the role of the Internet during the Arab Spring[37] to claims that Internet-based communication has created a new paradigm of diffuse war[38] in which "nobody knows who will see an event, where and when they will see it, or how they will interpret it." These claims are labeled here as the media empowerment thesis.

But how true are such claims? In this final section, we explore arguments that suggest significant change has taken place in the relationship among media, governments and war. But we also map out alternative arguments related to new ideological imperatives and perception management strategies, which suggest that there is far greater continuity than change.

The Power of New Technology

In the first instance, it is important to differentiate between arguments about the power of new communication technology and politics in general, and arguments about how this technology influences our experience of war. Many commentators talk in very general terms about the empowering and mobilizing potential of new media[39] but, in doing so, fail to appreciate that not all policy areas and issues areas are influenced in the same way. So for example, it may well be the case that social media, the Internet and Arab-based global media such as Al Jazeera, were factors in enabling and sustaining the recent Arab Spring. On the other hand, such technology may be having a far more circumscribed role in relation to how U.S. citizens understand the on-going U.S.-led war in Afghanistan.

With this caveat in mind, a theme in the media empowerment thesis is that 1) the proliferation of diverse news media outlets, including global media such as BBC World, CNN and Al Jazeera, 2) the ability of people to record and disseminate information via the Internet and 3) real-time communication enabled by lightweight digital equipment all combine to effectively disrupt the monopoly of governments as information providers. In short, patterns of indexing (i.e. reliance upon official sources) discussed earlier are understood to have been undermined in the new media environment. For some, these developments have caused incremental changes with the number of non-official voices increasing relative to official voices but not overtaking them. As such, the new media environment can be understood to have shifted, if not fundamentally altered, patterns of wartime media-state relations, making the neo-pluralist accounts described earlier more relevant. For others, changes due to the new media environment are more profound. For example, Hoskins and O'Loughlin[40] highlight the radically unpredictable nature of the current information environment. Because of the way in which the Internet enables anyone to upload and disseminate information, and with an entirely unpredictable audience, there is no way of knowing when and where decisive impacts might occur. As a result, reality takes on a seemingly chaotic form with events in one part of the world being communicated and reframed in ways that generate challenges to militaries and governments. So, a NATO airstrike in Afghanistan that kills civilians might be recorded by a mobile phone camera. As Western news media ask NATO officials for answers and explanations, the mobile phone footage is already circulating on websites around the world, with non-Western media criticizing the NATO action. Extremist websites draw upon the incident to exploit its propaganda value, encouraging attacks against Western targets in retaliation while authorities in Afghanistan are confronted by widespread public protests at the presence of foreign troops on Afghan soil. Ultimately, violence occurs in parts of the world seemingly unconnected to the war in Afghanistan, while public support in Western countries is further eroded by the ensuing negative coverage generated in mainstream news media. In a similar vein, BBC journalist and scholar Nik Gowing[41] argues that the information environment today has radically undermined the ability of governments to influence and shape public perceptions.

As tempting as it is to draw such dramatic inferences from the major changes that we have witnessed with the arrival of the Internet, there are grounds for a more cautious assessment. On the one hand, for all the attention to social networking and alternative media on the web, the majority of Internet users continue to use the websites of existing mainstream news media as their primary sources of news information. To an extent, therefore, news consumers are simply accessing the online version of what they would have, in the past, obtained by watching television news or reading a newspaper. There is also the problem of information overload, whereby Internet users are simply left dazed and confused by the multitude of alternative and contradictory pieces of information available on the web. The end result of this is that individuals may be increasingly turned off from watching the news or, alternatively, end up possessing a superficial understanding of a wide range of issues; here, the tendency to skip over Internet news sites, combined with continuous news headline feeds to mobile phones, may lead individuals to *see more* but *know less*. More broadly, with the rise of digital television, the proliferation of multiple channels and the increasing specialization or narrowcasting of news information, there is a very real danger that publics will become increasingly fragmented. What this means is that, rather than a large proportion of the public consuming news from similar or overlapping sources (e.g., the evening news or a national newspaper), audiences are becoming increasingly specialized with channels emerging that are dedicated to international news and politically-orientated current affairs programming. The consequences of this are two-fold. First, people may increasingly choose news programs that reflect their political bias, with the result that their political views become polarized. In a democracy where consensus building and dialogue between competing views is often considered to be essential, this polarization may have a very negative effect. Second, if news consumers are increasingly divided among those interested in specific issues, audiences become fragmented and smaller and less able to generate political influence. For example, debates over the CNN effect, discussed earlier, work with an assumption that enough of an audience is watching or reading the news to create sufficient political pressure to force politicians to pay attention. In a world in which there are many news programs, all with relatively small and unique audiences, it is not clear if such pressure could actually be created. In short, rather than empowering publics, the Internet may be helping to generate a *fragmented public sphere.*[42] In sum, there remain plenty of arguments both for and against the ability of Internet-based news and information media to radically transform the ways in which people understand the world. This brings us to two final issues, both of which point toward important dynamics that may serve to undermine the potential of the Internet to fundamentally transform wartime media-state relations.

The Power of "Perception Management"

Even if new technology has considerable potential to broaden and deepen public understanding of, and engagement with, war and conflict, it is also the case that governments have devoted increasing resources and time to attempts to shape and influence public perceptions in ways conducive to their preferred policies. Referred to variously as perception management, strategic communication, public diplomacy and, recently, global engagement, these activities involve the promotion of policy through carefully crafted public relations campaigns, exploitation of links with journalists and media outlets and, most generally, taking advantage of the considerable resources at the disposal of governments in order to attempt to dominate the information environment with their preferred frames. Some scholars argue that such activities amount to nothing less than propaganda.[43] The preeminent example of such activities in recent years was the campaign by the U.S. and British governments to persuade the world that Saddam Hussein posed a serious threat due to his possession of WMD and his alleged relationship with terrorism. In the U.S., the White House Information Group was set up in August 2002 to coordinate a "systematic media campaign"[44] that would reveal to the American public details of the threat posed by Iraq's alleged WMD activities. By September 2002, administration officials were publicly discussing the possibility of a nuclear attack, either from Iraq or terrorists armed by Iraq, with the chilling sound bite, "We don't want the smoking gun to be a mushroom cloud" used by Secretary of State Condoleeza Rice on CNN.[45] In the U.K., at the same time as the perception management campaign got underway in the U.S., a dossier based on intelligence about Iraq was published in September 2002, written by the Joint Intelligence Committee but with substantial involvement from the Prime Minister's office and from Alistair Campbell, Blair's Communications Director. In what has become a controversial and frequently discredited process (Doig and Pythian, 2005; Morrison, 2011), the dossier created an exaggerated sense of the threat from Iraq, suggesting in particular that Iraq could fire strategic weapons of mass destruction within 45 minutes of an order to do so. The news media's reports on the dossier gave particular attention to the claim that Iraqi WMD could be ready "within 45 minutes of an order to use them" (Prime Minister's Office, 2002); "Brits 45 minutes from doom" was one newspaper's headline.[46]

The key point to be taken here is that, while the new media environment has the potential to empower non-elites, publics and pressure groups to challenge those with political power, governments themselves are not simply passive and impotent: As Wolfsfeld's political contest model describes, there is a continual struggle, with governments devoting considerable resources and time to managing and influencing the information environment. Even in the era of the Internet, governments have considerable, if not total, influence over how issues are framed and what issues are on the agenda. In the case outlined above, despite the Iraq conflict receiving global scrutiny, the presence of the Internet, and many skeptical voices, the U.S. and British governments were remarkably successful at persuading most of their citizens that Iraq possessed weapons of mass destruction and that Saddam Hussein was linked with Islamic fundamentalist terrorists. In this case, ultimately, the British and American governments were able to get themselves heard, loud and clear, despite the new media environment. This leads to a final issue concerning the power of political narratives such as "the war on terror" and the ideological effects that they can have.

The Power of Political and Ideological Narratives

As discussed in section one, one of the arguments used to explain media deference during the Cold War era was the ideology of anti-communism. A central question for today concerns the extent to which new ideological narratives, such as the "war on terror," have come to shape the contemporary information environment. Ideological narratives such as "anti-communism" and the "war on terror" are important because they structure the way policy-makers, journalists and the public perceive the world. As such, ideology can play an important and a priori role in terms of establishing frames that are then absorbed and communicated by journalists to the public at large. The medium of communication, whether it is the Internet or a newspaper, is secondary to this process. To put another way, if ideological narratives are firmly established, then the availability of communication technology may have little impact other than to act as a transmitter of that ideology.

To what extent are ideological imperatives in play today? The case of both the Iraq War and the on-going conflict in Afghanistan are instructive here. On the one hand, both have been justified as part of the "war on terror" and rationalized accordingly as justified and necessary actions designed to defend against Islamic fundamentalist terrorism.[47] At the same time, many critics have argued that this representation has disguised the true reasons for launching the war, including broader geo-strategic imperatives and material interests. For example, Afghanistan lies in Central Asia, which is a key oil-producing region that stands at the crossroads between U.S., Russian and Chinese interests. The projection of U.S. influence in the region is a plausible and likely subtext to the war there. In Iraq, many critical voices have asserted that the U.S. invasion was driven, not by fear of WMD or terrorism, but the desire to project U.S. power in the Middle East, at least in part because of its importance in terms of oil resources. But because of the dominance of the "war on terror," relatively few citizens in the U.S. and the U.K. understood, and understand, these wars as anything other than part of a struggle against terrorism. Other ideological constraints that have been identified by some scholars include the ideology of humanitarian warfare, whereby Western action against Iraq and Afghanistan has been framed in terms of morally upstanding battles against dictatorship and extremism and in pursuit of human rights and freedom.[48] Also, and of particular relevance to cases of war, nationalism and patriotism can also be seen as ideological constraints, as noted in section one. Here, as with the "war on terror" and "humanitarian warfare" ideologies, nationalism still remains a potent force that shapes how both journalists and publics perceive wars. Even during long-running and controversial wars, such as those in Afghanistan and Iraq, most journalists and the majority of publics feel obligated on some level to support "their boys and girls" who are fighting on the frontline.[49]

Overall, the presence of ideological imperatives, whether they are relatively weak or strong, can counteract the empowering potential of new technology.

Section Five: Conclusions

This chapter has outlined contrasting visions regarding the relationship between media, public opinion and war. From one perspective, elite-driven theories and models emphasize the role of the media as a reinforcement of a state's war policy, with public opinion being molded so as to support troops in battle. Such analyses, which are widely supported by much of the research into media, war and public opinion, strongly suggest that the media act largely as a "war monger." Other accounts have cast media and public opinion in a more favorable light, highlighting how public opinion can mobilize against costly wars and how media might even be a force for influencing policy makers to come to the aid of suffering people in war-torn countries. Such analyses, although less prominent than the elite-driven accounts, suggest that, at least to some extent, media can at times perform a role more akin to that of a peacemaker. Developments over the last 20 years, including the emergence of a new media environment, increasingly sophisticated approaches to perception management and the omnipresent "war on terror," have raised debate over the extent to which media and the public now relate to war in a different way. However, it is important to keep in mind the influential consequences of the "war on terror" and overlapping strategies employed by governments to maintain and shore up support for military endeavors such as those witnessed over the last ten years in Iraq and Afghanistan. Overall, and given the various contrasting claims, the development of neo-pluralist models are of particular use to scholars of media and war because they allow us to start to make sense of the elite-driven-pluralist dichotomy. By attempting to theorize how media and public opinion can, at different times and under different circumstances, come to influence political elites, neo-pluralist accounts offer productive moves forward.

All of this accepted, when dealing with the subject of media and war, it is important to recall that debate over the adequacy of most war reporting persists to this day. Despite being divided by 20 years, the Vietnam and Afghan wars show remarkable similarity: both have been long and protracted with rising casualty counts and declining public support, both have become electoral issues for those governments involved and have come to be perceived by many as failed wars. But throughout both conflicts media have, at least initially, played a largely supportive role in terms of these wars being started, the enemy in both cases has been demonized and, most importantly, the fatal consequences of these wars for civilians have largely been ignored by Western politicians, journalists and publics.[50] As such, it is important to recognize that media coverage of war still leaves an awful lot to be desired. For realists who wish to see elite control over foreign policy preserved (see Learning Box 5.1), such a state of affairs is perhaps acceptable. But from a more liberal viewpoint (see Learning Box 5.2), and certainly for those who wish to see less violent conflict, the ability of media and publics to adequately scrutinize their governments and act as a check on unnecessary or erroneous wars is a vital feature of a democratic state. Accordingly, the failure of so much of media coverage of war to achieve this function should be a cause of continuing concern.

Notes

1 Thanks to Stefanie Haueis for comments on earlier drafts of this manuscript.
2 Daniel Hallin, *The Uncensored War: The Media and Vietnam* (Berkeley, CA: University of California Press, 1989).
3 The phrase "faithful servant" is borrowed from Gadi Wolfsfeld, *The Media and Political Conflict: News from the Middle East* (Cambridge and New York: Cambridge University Press, 1997).
4 John Tirman, *The Deaths of Others: The Fate of Civilians in America's Wars* (Oxford: Oxford University Press, 2011).
5 Richard Nixon, *Memoirs* (New York: Grossett and Dunlop, 1978), 350.
6 For example, Peter Braestrup, *Big Story: How the American Press and Televison Reported and Interpreted the Crisis of Tet 1968 in Vietnam and Washington* (Novato, CA: Presidio, 1994) and William C. Westmoreland, "Vietnam in Perspective," *Military Review* 59 (1979): 34–43.
7 Piers Robinson, Peter Goddard, Katy Parry and Craig Murray, "Testing Models of Media Performance in War: U.K. TV News and the 2003 Invasion of Iraq," *Journal of Communication* 52 (2009): 678–688.
8 For example Glasgow University Media Group, *War and Peace News* (Milton Keynes: Open University Press, 1985); W. Lance Bennett and David L. Paletz, ed. *Taken by Storm: The Media, Public Opinion, and U.S. Foreign Policy in the Gulf War* (Chicago, IL: University of Chicago Press, 1994); Tamar Liebes, *Reporting the Arab-Israeli Conflict: How Hegemony Works* (London: Routledge, 1994).
9 For recent discussion of the procedural vs. substantive distinction see Scott Althaus, "When News Norms Collide, Follow the Lead: New Evidence for Press Independence," *Political Communication* 20 (2003): 386; and Piers Robinson, Peter Goddard, Katy Parry, Craig Murray and Phil Taylor, *Pockets of Resistance: British News Media, War and Theory in the 2003 Invasion of Iraq.* (Manchester: Manchester University Press, 2010), 11–33.
10 W. Lance Bennett, "Toward a Theory of Press-State Relations in the United States," *Journal of Communication* 40 (1990): 103–127.
11 Ibid.

12 Ibid. See also Edward Herman and Noam Chomsky, *Manufacturing Consent: The Political Economy of the Mass Media* (New York: Pantheon, 1988).
13 Wolfsfeld, *The Media and Political Conflict*.
14 Daya Thussu, *News as Entertainment: The Rise of Global Infotainment*, 2nd ed. (London: Sage, 1997), 118–122.
15 Edward R Murrow, October 15, 1958, RTNDA Convention, Chicago. Available online at www. Turnoffyourtv.com/commentary/hiddenagenda/nurrow.html: Download date March 14, 2012.
16 Dan Rather speech at the "National Conference for Media Reform," June 8, 2008; available at www.sanders.senate.gov/newsroom/news/?id=4a19a38e-0017-4aa8-bc1d-d9fe5a9eb22f. Download date March 14, 2012.
17 See "Tony Blair Godfather to Rupert Murdoch's Daughter," September 5, 2011, accessed March 29, 2012, www.bbc.co.uk/news/uk-politics-14785501.
18 See "Downing Street 'Did Not Record Who Knew' about Andy Coulson," by Robert Booth *The Guardian*, October 5, 2011.
19 Op Cit. See note 8.
20 John Mueller, *War, Presidents and Public Opinion* (New York: John Wiley, 1978).
21 Ibid.
22 Michael Margolis and Gary A. Mauser, ed., *Manipulating Public Opinion* (Belmont CA: Brooks Cole, 1989).
23 Piers Robinson, "The CNN Effect: Can the News Media Drive Foreign Policy," *Review of International Studies* 25 (1999): 301–309.
24 Steven Livingston and Todd Eachus, "Humanitarian Crises and U.S. Foreign Policy," *Political Communication* 12 (1995): 413–429.
25 Steven Livingston, "Clarifying the CNN Effect: An Examination of Media Effects According to Type of Military Intervention," *Research Paper R-18* (Cambridge, MA: The Joan Shorenstein Center, 1997).
26 For a more detailed discussion of various types of media influence see Piers Robinson, *The CNN Effect: The Myth of News, Foreign Policy and Intervention* (London and New York: Routledge, 2002): 37–41.
27 Robinson, *The CNN Effect*: 117–132.
28 Ibid.
29 For recent debate over the CNN effect, see Special Issue "The CNN Effect Revisited," *Media,War and Conflict* 4 (2011): 3–95.
30 Gadi Wolfsfeld, *The Media and Political Conflict* (Cambridge: Cambridge University Press, 1997).
31 For a full discussion of the concept of framing, see Chapter 12 in this volume.
32 Robinson, *The CNN Effect*; Robert Entman, *Projections of Power: Framing News, Public Opinion and U.S. Foreign Policy* (Chicago: University of Chicago Press, 2004).
33 Robinson, *The CNN Effect*.
34 Matthew Baum and Tim Groeling, *War Stories: The Causes and Consequences of Public Views of War* (Princeton: Princeton University Press, 2010).
35 Robinson, et al., *Pockets of Resistance*.
36 Manuel Castells, *Information Power* (Oxford: Oxford University Press, 2009).
37 Nik Gowing, "Time to Move On: New Media Realities, New Vulnerabilities of Power," *Media, War and Conflict* 4 (2011): 13–19.
38 Andrew Hoskins and Ben O'Loughlin, *Media and War: The Emergence of Diffused War* (Cambridge: Polity, 2010).
39 For example, Manuel Castells, *Information Power*; Gowing, "Time to Move on."
40 Hoskins and O'Loughlin, *Media and War*.
41 Gowing, "Time to Move On."
42 Zizi Papacharissi, "The Virtual Sphere: The Internet as a Public Sphere," *New Media and Society* 1 (2002): 9–27.

43 Philip M. Taylor, "Perception Management and the `War' Against Terror," *Journal of Information Warfare* 1 (2002): 16–29; David Miller and Rizwaan Sabir, "Propaganda and Terrorism" in *Media and Terrorism: Global Perspectives*, ed. Daya Thussu and Des Freedman (Thousand Oaks: Sage Publications, 2011).

44 W. Lance Bennett, Steven Livingston and Regina Lawrence, *When the Press Fails: Political Power and the News Media From Katrina to Iraq* (Chicago: Chicago University Press, 2007), 18.

45 Ibid., 22–23.

46 For more on the U.S. and U.K. perception management campaigns see Paul Pillar, *Intelligence and U.S. Foreign Policy; Iraq, 9/11 and Misguided Reform* (New York: Columbia University Press, 2010); Brian Jones, *Failing Intelligence: The True Story of How We Were Fooled into Going to War in Iraq* (London: Biteback, 2010).

47 David Domke, *God Willing? Political Fundamentalism in the White House, the "War on Terror" and the Echoing Press* (London: Pluto Press, 2004); Richard Jackson, *Writing the War on Terrorism: Language, Politics and Counter-Terrorism* (Manchester: Manchester University Press, 2006).

48 David Chandler, *From Kosovo to Kabul and Beyond: Human Rights and International Intervention* (London: Pluto Press, 2005); Philip Hammond, *Framing Post-Cold War Conflicts: The Media and International Intervention* (Manchester: Manchester University Press, 2007); Robinson, et al., *Pockets of Resistance*: 170–172.

49 Robinson, et al., *Pockets of Resistance*.

50 Tirman, *The Deaths of Others*.

Chapter 6

Campaigns Go Social

Are Facebook, YouTube and Twitter Changing Elections?

Stephanie Edgerly, Leticia Bode,
Young Mie Kim, and Dhavan V. Shah

> Were it not for the Internet, Barack Obama would not be president. Were it
> not for the Internet, Barack Obama would not have been the nominee.
> – Arianna Huffington, editor in chief of Huffington Post,
> in the *New York Times* (11/7/08)

Over the past decades, the landscape of politics has drastically changed with mass adoption of digital technology. The terms "campaigning online," "digital election campaigns," "Facebook election," "digital politics," "e-democracy," and the like have frequently appeared in public discourse to describe the transformation that contemporary politics has undergone. Central to this transformation is the active use of digital media by election campaigns.

Modern elections present a unique arena in which campaigns can test the viability of digital media. Elections are major political events that draw significant media attention, from both news media and entertainment media, and motivate citizens to pay more attention to politics and ultimately to play a role in the political process.[1] This communication-rich environment creates fertile ground for campaigns to test the utility of digital media to connect voters with campaigns in new and different ways. Tools that work are embraced widely; tools that don't work fall to the wayside. In many respects, election campaigns can be understood through a social Darwinist lens, with survival of the fittest media. The wide adoption of digital and mobile media platforms, and with them the rise of social media such as Facebook, YouTube, and Twitter, has set the stage for these new campaign practices directed at voters.

Campaigns Go Digital: "New" Campaign Practices

Since the first candidate website, built for California Senator Diane Feinstein's re-election campaign in 1994, digital campaign sites have become a visible part of election campaigning.[2] During the 1996 presidential campaign, both major-party candidates developed websites, though the promotion of such sites was still in its infancy. During the midterm elections of 1998, more than half of Senate candidates had websites for their campaign, while 35 percent of House candidates did.[3] By the 2000 election, candidate websites had become a common tool of presidential, congressional, and gubernatorial campaigns.[4] They were used to inform voters about the candidate, volunteering opportunities and to collect donations. A standard website contained a candidate biography, issue statements, contact information, and campaign schedule. Websites also tended to include photos of the candidate and the option to make online donations with a credit card. However, the pre-social media campaigns were little more than creating an online presence. Websites were similar to "brochureware," offering official talking points and infrequently updated.[5] And fearing a loss of information control, candidates avoided informational exchanges, let alone genuine dialogue with voters on their websites.[6] Nonetheless, the popularity of email and messaging systems foreshadowed the emergence of social media platforms, with early evidence of the political potential of online interactions with family, friends, and co-workers.[7]

Social Media Campaigns

As campaigns realized the connective potential of the Internet, the simple information brochure model gave way to a new model in which candidates actively reach out to traditionally alienated voters (e.g., young voters), interact with potential supporters, and provide supporters with a venue for becoming a part of the campaigns. This perspective shift in campaign practices has been enabled and accelerated by the adoption of social media, including but not limited to Facebook, YouTube, and Twitter.

Candidates' adoption of Facebook started when the company developed a feature called "Election Pulse 2006," which allowed candidates to create profile pages for congressional and gubernatorial campaigns.[8] The feature was designed to help Facebook users learn about different candidates. Users were able to view candidate profiles and could register their support for specific candidates. Profiles displayed the number of supporters each candidate had, and users were then notified if any of their Facebook friends also supported the same candidate.

Since that time, Facebook has transitioned toward candidate pages (rather than profiles) that allow campaigns the ability to post a variety of information (e.g., website links, YouTube videos, announcements, and photos). The development of the Facebook "news feed" also created a connection between candidates and users.[9] The news feed is a homepage of sorts, which displays the most recent updates posted by friends and "liked" Facebook pages. If a user "likes" a campaign Facebook page, his or her network would be notified, and the user would see future updates relating to that candidate on his or her news feed. This technological feature provides candidates with another point of contact with supporters and their connections, making supporters' engagement much more visible than ever before.

Similarly, during the 2006 election, YouTube allowed candidates to create "channels," where they could upload video content, and let users comment on videos. Over the years, YouTube has developed a more integrated interface, with candidate channels adorned with campaign logos, slogans, links to campaign websites, and most recently, streaming live updates from Twitter and Facebook feeds. Fueled by advancements in video production and upload technology, YouTube has become a hub for original video content (generated by both campaigns and citizens).[10] Many videos about political candidates have gone "viral," receiving millions of views and mainstream media attention.

Twitter, another social media outlet that began to play a significant role since the 2008 election, is a microblogging service that allows users to send and read short messages of up to 140 characters (known as "tweets"). On Twitter, users "follow" other users, resulting in a profile page displaying the most recent tweets from followed accounts. For campaigns, this means that they choose which Twitter accounts to follow (i.e., which accounts they wish to receive updates from), while also allowing Twitter users to follow the campaign account. Campaigns can tweet to followers about events and respond to messages that are directed at the campaign. This allows campaigns unique access to users that choose to follow them—generally strong supporters. When these strong supporters "retweet" campaign information to their followers, the campaign reaches a more removed level of potential supporters. Additionally, Twitter users often include hash tags (#) in their tweets. A search function allows users to look for tweets of interest under a specific hash tag, and view the most popular "trending" hash tags circulating worldwide, nationally, or locally. Ultimately, Twitter allows for direct communication between candidates and voters (even if such potential is not always realized), and can be an effective platform for information dissemination. Facebook, YouTube, and Twitter stand among the most prominent tools in modern digital campaigning.

New Campaign Practices in a Digital Media Age

Despite the different technical features of Facebook, YouTube, and Twitter, the adoption of such social media has significantly contributed to the evolution of election campaign practices. New campaign practices have been greatly influenced by marketing tactics that address patterns of social fragmentation and the declining viewership of broadcast media. Additionally, the potential of the Internet to connect both urban and suburban communities in various forms of social activism and volunteerism coincides with the growth of the political blogosphere, and bloggers' calls for protest and collective action, both of which predated the integration of social media tools into campaigns.[11] In synthesizing these developments, we identify four distinctive patterns of emergent campaign practices that have been facilitated by digital and social media: microtargeting, personalization, interactivity, and sustained engagement.

The first aspect involves the **microtargeting** of voters. Fueled by advances in communication and database technology, campaigns can now target certain voters with specific information. By doing this, campaigns have a better chance of appealing to the specific issues that are most important to different voters.[12] For example, campaigns have created targeted websites that focus on a certain voter demographic (e.g., college students, the elderly, Catholics). Additionally, campaigns construct data profiles of possible supporters based on where people live, their job, purchasing behavior, credit scores, search patterns and history, and more.[13] Information disclosed on social media websites is also prime data for these profiles. For example, specific campaign ads are displayed to Facebook users based on their self-reported political views or the content of their recent posts. YouTube ads can be customized based on a user's geographic location. And campaigns track specific Twitter hashtags and contact the people who use them, at times encouraging interaction. It is believed that marketing companies have profiles (based on an average of 1,500 pieces of data) for around 96 percent of Americans.[14]

The second trend of modern campaigns involves the **personalization** of politics. There is a growing trend in political campaigns to depoliticize politics.[15] Kim and colleagues find an upward trend in presidential candidates using "niche" media, such as biographies, comedy talk shows, and other "soft" media, to promote information about the candidate's personality.[16] This trend can be extended to the types of information disclosed via social media. What a candidate likes to do for fun, or a picture of the candidate eating a hamburger at a diner becomes integral to the style of an election campaign. By doing so, the candidate becomes a person, not just an institutional figure running for office. This connection between voters and the candidate can lead to increased support and participation.

The third aspect campaigns are embracing is increased **interactivity**. Network-based technological advances, especially the advent of social media, enable voters to communicate directly with the campaigns and gain more control over their experiences. Initially, this interactivity took the form of asynchronous messaging between voters and campaign staff (e.g., voters emailing a campaign or posting on a campaign website, and staff responding at a later point in time). In this period, candidates often avoided online interaction with voters for fear of losing control over campaign messaging.[17] However, voters now have the opportunity to communicate in real time with the campaign and its supporters (e.g., via Twitter, Google + Hangouts, etc.) and have grown to expect this as a norm. By allowing voters to express themselves to the campaign and to interact with others, the campaign takes on a deeper level of meaning. No longer is the candidate just a face on the television, but a person with whom voters have an expectation of interaction. When done successfully, supporters will develop a sense of community and connectedness with the candidate and with fellow supporters. Online networks allow campaigns to move beyond a fundraising orientation and toward the building of a relationship-based community of supporters. As Sam Graham-Felsen, Obama's chief blogger said, "If you can figure out how to leverage the power of friendship, that opens up incredible possibilities."[18]

The fourth aspect of new campaigning facilitated by digital media is the idea of **sustained engagement**. The goal of many political campaigns is to secure votes, to mobilize supporters to show up at voting precincts. Modern campaigns, however, sustain a level of engagement with voters for months (even years) before Election Day. In explaining the virtues of ongoing engagement, Wael Ghonim, author of *Revolution 2.0*, makes the distinction between this form of ongoing engagement (which Ghonim refers to as "engagism") and activism.[19] Because activism is based on "membership" and characterized by more aggressive and confrontational tones, it promotes a disconnect between those who are highly involved (e.g., activists) and the general public. Sustained engagement, on the other hand, is about inviting people to a campaign, letting them set the tone, and sustaining a connection over time. Ghonim argues that social media campaigns accomplish sustained engagement through a series on incremental steps: having people connect with or "like" your cause, comment on your cause, become active in online activities, and finally, in offline activities. Successful election campaigns provide several points of entry for supporters to participate in the campaign. These opportunities involve information about offline participation (e.g., canvassing, rallies, and meetings) as well as ways to participate online (e.g., donations, forwarding campaign messages, uploading videos, commenting, or creating a poster). Ultimately, the involvement of supporters throughout the campaign increases the likelihood they will vote.

As digital technology develops, campaigns are becoming more sophisticated in how they connect with voters. Candidates and staff increasingly base their communication strategies around microtargeting, personalization, interactivity, and sustained engagement. The development of these core strategies can be seen across the short history of digital media advancements.

From Dean to Obama: Advances in Digital Campaigning

The 2004 election, and specifically, the primary campaign of Howard Dean, marked a turning point in how campaigns utilize digital technology. Dean, the former Governor of Vermont, was vying to be the Democrat nominee for president. He was considered a long shot with little national name recognition prior to his campaign. However, through a series of strategic campaign decisions, he was able to become a front-runner for the nomination.

The Dean campaign embraced blogging as a way to get supporters involved in the day-to-day happenings of the campaign and as a way to connect supporters with each other.[20] The campaign's "Blog for America" was updated daily by staff members (something other campaigns did not prioritize), with posts concerning campaign events, Dean's responses to campaign topics, and links to news stories about the campaign. But what made the Dean blog so successful was sustained engagement with supporters—the ability to involve supporters in creating content for the blog. For example, in a single twenty-four hour period, the Dean campaign posted 400 blog messages, spurring over 4,000 comments.[21] It was estimated that around 2,000 comments a day were posted to the Dean blog.[22] The campaign also held contests where supporters could be a "guest blogger" for a day. Campaign staff even used the blog to ask for suggestions about speeches or campaign events. According to campaign manager, Joe Trippi, "We didn't just monitor these blogs. We listened. We took the feedback seriously. There were times that we altered Dean's stump speech based on a suggestion from a blog, or improved our campaign strategy."[23]

The Dean campaign website also used features from Meetup.com, a website where members could form digital communities around common interests and to plan "Meetups" offline. The Dean campaign used the infrastructure of Meetup to connect supporters and facilitate discussions—online and off. For example, people could enter their zip codes and find the closest Dean Meetup taking place.[24] The ability to link individual supporters together created a deeper connection among supporters and the campaign. At one point, the Dean group on Meetup had over 140,000 members and in one month had over 800 Meetups scheduled.[25] Taken together, both the Dean blog and Meetups illustrate the effectiveness of networks—of taking advantage of offline and online networks, combined with digital technology, to circulate messages and organize events.

Last, the Dean campaign altered the structure of campaign donations. Before the Internet, campaigns survived by orchestrating elaborate fundraisers (e.g., dinners, concerts) that targeted a few, large donations. Candidate websites, however, provide a space for supporters to donate money without the large overhead costs for campaigns of organizing an offline fundraising event, and associated costs for supporters to attend. The result is a change in the composition of campaign donations—large sums of money can be raised from the small donations of a lot of supporters. This was the model that enabled Dean to move from an unknown to a contender for the Democratic Party's nominee. During his primary campaign, Dean raised over $40 million in small donations, with an average contribution amount of only $143.[26] A great exemplar of personalization and interactivity was the "Lunch with Dean" event (an idea proposed by a Dean blogger). The Dean campaign posted a photo of Dean eating a $3 turkey sandwich and encouraged supporters to donate $50 in exchange for having lunch with Dean online. The campaign raised $500,000 in small donations—doubling the money raised at the Bush–Cheney dinner that was holding a $2,000 a plate fundraising event.[27] Although Dean's bid to be the Democratic nominee was unsuccessful, his model had a lasting effect. Moving forward, campaigns saw the power of online mobilization, resulting in new organizational and communication structures.

The 2006 Midterm Elections: A Social Media Test Run

The 2006 midterm election was the first election in which social media websites were embraced by campaigns. Although still in its discovery phase, campaign activity on Facebook and YouTube received significant attention from voters and from the mainstream media. Furthermore, Democrats seemed to have the upper hand in utilizing social media for campaign purposes.[28] Facebook emailed all major party candidates for Congress with the opportunity to add content to a Facebook profile page. This invitation, however, received a lukewarm reception. Only 32 percent of candidates running for Senate and 13 percent of those running for the House posted content to their profile.[29] Hillary Clinton, Senate candidate in New York, had the most supporters with over 12,000. Nine of the ten profiles with the most supporters belonged to Democrats.

In 2006, campaigns mostly used YouTube as an advertising tool, a complement to television and radio. Campaign staff uploaded favorable videos to YouTube while also posting less-than-flattering videos of opponents.[30] The Montana Democratic Party, for example, posted several videos of Conrad Burns, a Republican senator from Montana, dozing off during a bill hearing. Similarly, the defeat of Connecticut Senator Joseph Liebermann was partly attributed to unfavorable interview content uploaded to YouTube. Election outcomes in Minnesota and Missouri were also credited to the influence of YouTube. However, campaign adoption rates of social media were still low. Only 10 percent of candidates for Senate used YouTube, and none of the 1,102 House candidates had their own channel.[31]

The 2008 Presidential Election: The "Social Media Election"

The 2008 presidential election marked the coordination of digital technology and social media practices. Campaigns featured more targeted messaging strategies and more fully embraced user-generated content. Nicknamed the "Social Media Election," 2008 became an election cycle in which campaigns embraced more sophisticated use of Facebook, YouTube, and Twitter. It was now standard procedure for campaign websites to feature a variety of social media icons that linked to their campaign pages. Barack Obama, in particular, was coined the "King of Social Media" for his campaign's ability to engage voters across a variety of social media.[32]

No longer were election bloggers limited to campaign staff. By 2008, voters could become bloggers. Campaign websites provided the technological infrastructure for voters to start their own blogs about candidates and campaigns, deepening their engagement with other voters as well as candidates. The Obama campaign, for example, had a feature called MyBO.com that facilitated the creation of supporters' blogs, and Republican Rudy Giuliani had a similar feature called "Rudy on your blog." Campaign websites were no longer just a space for potential supporters to learn about candidates, they now provided a space for expression and to develop a deeper connection with the candidate and friends.

Campaigns also made even greater use of microtargeting via listservs and databases. The Obama campaign compiled an impressive email list of over 13 million addresses.[33] Additionally, it developed a sophisticated database of information about potential voters. Not only did the campaign collect information through its website and social media pages, but also merged this information with demographic, neighborhood, and lifestyle data available through marketing and census reports. In essence, the Obama campaign created portraits of the issue priorities for different voters and devised unique communication strategies for each one. Over the course of the election, the Obama campaign sent out more than 7,000 different messages targeting specific voters. When factoring in their large listserv, this resulted in over 1 billion emails sent from the campaign.[34] How does this type of targeting influence campaign messages? For the Obama campaign, this meant that if you were in a demographic that made you statistically more likely to have children, the campaign sent you an email about education policy and not one about taxes.[35]

The 2008 election was also a landmark for distinctive fundraising efforts. During the primary election, Republican candidate Ron Paul set a single-day record, raising $6 million online. And over the course of the 21-month election campaign, the Obama campaign raised a record-shattering half a billion dollars online, with the average online donation of $80.[36] It is no coincidence that candidates who were big fundraisers were also highly interactive. Paul led Republican candidates with the most Facebook supporters (though he did not win the Republican nomination) and by the end of the 2008 election, the Obama Facebook page had more than 2 million supporters (while his Republican rival McCain had just over 600,000).[37] Much of Obama's fundraising ability was attributed to his campaign's understanding about the type of personalized information users wanted to see on social media. Obama's Facebook page, for example, included his favorite musicians (Miles Davis, Stevie Wonder, and Bob Dylan) and listed his love for basketball, writing, and "loafing w/kids."[38] By doing so, he became more relatable; voters felt like they understood who Obama was as a person, not just as a politician. In comparison, McCain's Facebook page listed fishing as a favorite activity, and *Letters from Iwo Jima* as his favorite movie, information that many younger Facebook users may have found less relatable.

The 2008 presidential election also accelerated interactivity on YouTube. Both the McCain and Obama campaigns maintained official YouTube channels, uploading videos ranging from elongated television commercials, to personal addresses, and event speeches.[39] Videos tended to exemplify a great deal of personalization, with an emphasis on personal traits of the candidates over political experience.[40] Yet some of the most widely viewed videos did not come from the campaign. The most popular was the "Yes We Can" viral video from will.i.am, which was produced independent of the campaign and based on

Obama's New Hampshire presidential primary concession speech. The video received over 17 million views within 2 months of its release, and ultimately accumulated over 30 million viewings.[41] Wallsten found that political bloggers and campaign emails and posts played crucial roles in getting people to watch the video.[42] Ultimately, the Obama campaign was more successful than opponents in using YouTube as a campaign tool. The Obama channel attracted more than 97 million video views across 18 million channel visits, whereas the McCain channel attracted only 25 million video views across 2 million visits.[43]

Twitter also entered the political scene in 2008. Completing its domination of social media, the Obama campaign netted over 125,000 followers, compared to McCain's 5,300.[44] But the candidates in 2008 were just beginning to use Twitter, as were voters (only 4 percent of U.S. Internet users were on Twitter in 2008). Over the next year Twitter users grew by 200 percent, illustrating just how quickly social media are adopted. This growth can also be seen in Obama's Twitter page, which now boasts over 20 million followers.

Twitter and the 2010 Midterm Elections: Shifting Momentum?

During the 2010 elections, a different pattern emerged for social media use by campaigns. Up to this point, it had been Democrats who led the way with social media adoption. However, in 2010, it was Republicans who more readily adopted Twitter as a campaign tool.[45] Additionally, candidates who were young, running for Senate, and better financed were more likely to use Twitter in their campaigns.[46] Compared to Facebook and YouTube, campaigns are still in the discovery stage of using Twitter. Recent research suggests that Twitter provides an additional platform for incumbent candidates more than challengers.[47] It can be helpful in maintaining enthusiasm and awareness, but unknown candidates are not yet using Twitter as a meaningful campaign tool. One study based on tweets from Senate candidates during the 2010 election found that tweets were mainly positive in tone, with very few negative tweets directed at other candidates.[48] Twitter, and how candidates will use it to connect with voters, remains in flux.

It is certain, however, that across different elections, the adoption of digital media, especially social media such as Facebook, YouTube, and Twitter, has set a stage for new campaign practices. Microtargeting, personalization, interactivity, and sustained engagement have been found across different elections and appear to set a new norm for election campaigns.

Are the "New" Campaign Practices Changing Voters?

New campaign practices have brought about great potential to bring voters into the foreground of election campaigns and to provide opportunities to engage in "bottom-up" politics. Empirical evidence supports this case, indicating that online social networks offer voters, and especially young people, a new space where they may share diverse political views, discuss politics, and weigh-in on various political issues.[49] Although only a small portion of American youth engaged in such behaviors in the 2008 campaign, it is generally expected that the numbers will grow as new campaign practices continue to catch on with candidates and become more deeply integrated into election campaigns, providing more confirmation that new digital campaign practices foster sustained engagement among voters.

Social media spaces are distinct from other online arenas such as email, chat rooms, and the like. Those who engage with politics via social media do not necessarily do so in other venues, and their behaviors in social media can be unrelated to behaviors in other online environments.[50] College undergraduates, for example, tend to engage in various political behaviors on Facebook, suggesting this is becoming a normal activity, at least for younger generations.[51] This norm has not yet translated to older Facebook users. Moreover, citizen-driven campaign models (as opposed to elite-driven) are making use of various social media to further their cause. In 2008, for example, both sides of the Proposition 8 campaign in California used YouTube extensively to recruit, mobilize, and persuade voters.[52] When used with sophistication, this process also allows campaigns to selectively target individual voters for engagement, fundraising, and mobilization efforts. However, are Facebook, YouTube, and Twitter really changing everything? To what extent do these new election campaign practices influence voters, their political behavior, and ultimately our democracy?

Voting

Given that election campaigns are strategic communication activities designed to increase voting and influence vote choice, the ultimate question involves the ability of social media to alter citizen voting. The evidence for effects of social media on voting turnout is somewhat mixed. Although 2008 and 2010 were touted as "social media" elections and campaigns specifically made an effort to mobilize young people, turnout among young adults remained relatively low. There was a slight increase in voting among those aged 18 to 24 in 2008, but turnout among the same cohort in 2010 was actually lower than typical for a midterm election.[53] On the other hand, early research testing the effects of social media use on turnout suggests a positive indirect impact. That is, use of Facebook for political purposes did not impact voting directly but did influence the factors that predict voting. For instance, one study shows that young adults' engagement with the community was a very important precondition for the likelihood of voting—simply spending time on social media, absent such community engagement, was actually negatively related to one's likelihood of voting.[54] The potential is certainly there and may only be realized under certain circumstances, but there is not necessarily a blanket effect of social media that is likely to increase electoral turnout across the board.

It is also unclear yet what effect social media may have on vote choice. Some scholars have argued that the use of social media for election campaigns greatly influences vote choice. For example, the number of Facebook fans a politician has can sometimes function as a rough indicator of how well he or she would do in the election.[55] During the 2008 presidential primaries, Facebook support was found to be a significant indicator of candidate vote share, even when controlling for more traditional measures of fundraising, media coverage, and campaign events. And for House candidates running in open-seat districts, those who updated their profile had a 3.8 percent higher vote share compared to candidates who did not.[56] This support, however, does not necessarily translate into securing the party's nomination. Again, Republican Ron Paul had a large community of Facebook supporters, yet failed to secure the Republican Party's nomination, while the eventual Republican nominee, John McCain, was largely absent on Facebook during the primaries. This suggests that traditional resources are still an important factor in political campaigning. Facebook campaigning is likely to be most effective when coupled with traditional resources such as campaign events, television advertising, and mainstream media attention. During the 2008 general election, young adults who were most politically active in social media were more likely to be Obama supporters than McCain supporters, but that could be an artifact of a single election.[57] The Obama campaign actively targeted young people, and specifically did so using social media, so this particular election is not generalizable to the broader electoral context.

There is no denying that social media has enhanced the "socialness" of voting. On Election Day 2008, Facebook developed an "I Voted" button that users could click to let their Facebook friends know that they made it to the polls. More than 5.4 million users displayed to their social network that they participated in the political process that day.[58]

Political Information and Discussion

Elections not only offer an increase in the volume of political information, but also motivate voters to learn about politics and become involved.[59] As a result, another important way that new campaign practices influence voters is through political information acquisition and discussion. From a normative perspective, various scholars have been concerned that all the "choice" provided by digital media would allow citizens to "opt out" of political information entirely. That is, digital media can facilitate users' ability to actively seek out only information that interests them. For some sectors of the population (e.g., politically interested) this would actually allow greater exposure to political information, but for others (e.g., those preferring non-political, and/or entertainment-oriented content), digital media would facilitate the avoidance of political information all together.[60] The concern of such scholars is that citizens who avoid political information may do so at the cost of political knowledge, discussion, and democracy in general.[61] The customizability of social media was expected to continue along those lines, giving additional opportunities for users to tailor the information they received to their own preferences, and thus allowing them to avoid political information almost entirely. If you choose not to "follow" a politician, she won't appear on your Twitter feed. If you don't "like" your friends' posts about politics, Facebook will quickly filter them out of your news feed entirely.[62]

Mixed empirical evidence exists as to whether new campaign practices increase the potential for selective information consumption. Because online information provides higher levels of interactivity and topic specialization, users are able to pick and choose the types of information to which they are exposed. Sunstein forewarned an "echo chamber effect"—where users only see information that confirms their previous opinions, thus resulting in reinforcement and polarization rather than tolerance and understanding which is associated with exposure to a wide range of opinions.[63] One line of research argues that users seek out like-minded information, and opt out of disagreeable or uninteresting information.[64] Political partisans, for example, tend to avoid disagreeable information online.[65] Also individuals who feel deeply about a particular issue also tend to selectively focus on learning more about the issue, and even use the issue as the primary criterion for their voting decisions. For these people, selectivity is less about the agreeableness of the content, and more about their passion for a specific issue.[66]

A second line of research, however, suggests that social media are spaces where Internet users encounter agreeable and disagreeable information. Studies have shown that youths engage in political dialogue in social media settings, posting divergent comments about political issues that spur additional discussion.[67] In certain circumstances, this exchange of ideas even resembles deliberation (i.e., civility, reason-giving, evidence).[68] Moreover, evidence from the Netherlands suggests that social network sites even provide an unusual opportunity to reach those who are less interested politics.[69] New research also confirms that those exposed to political information via Facebook and Twitter remember this information and learn from it.[70] Political content on social media sites can even roughly parallel public opinion, at least around certain topics.[71] Moreover, because social media networks tend to be relatively politically heterogeneous, the information to which users are exposed is likely to also be relatively diverse.[72] Taken together, these studies suggest that social media lower the barriers to accepting disagreeable information and increase the likelihood that users will be exposed to and learn from divergent points of view.[73]

Political Participation

Election campaigns also provide opportunities for political participation, which is essential for sustaining a strong and healthy democracy. As a result, researchers pay special attention to the ability of social media to translate online engagement into conventional, offline political participation, such as volunteering, donating money, and wearing campaign buttons.

Early research on social media campaigns suggested an overall negative impact on participation. The major concern raised was that social media made participation too easy—with just a click, users could "sign" an online petition, voice support for a cause, send an email to a politician and more. The argument made was that these "easy" behaviors would replace, rather than complement, the more traditional activities that are necessary ingredients for the democratic ideal. This tendency to replace "hard" offline political behaviors with "easy" social media substitutes was deemed "slacktivism."[74]

While some scholars still consider this to be a major concern, most research suggests that online activities (including social media activities) complement, supplement, or even encourage traditional behaviors, rather than replacing them, especially among youth.[75] Scholars have found no evidence of the "substitution thesis," but rather suggest social media participation "is at worst harmless fun and can at best help invigorate citizens."[76] Engaging in political behavior in social media also tends to have a positive effect on classic means of political participation.[77] For example, over the course of the 2008 election, adolescents who engaged in political activities on social networking sites were more likely to participate in offline political activities, and politically oriented social media use even predicted growth in offline participation over the course of the election cycle.[78] Even activities as simple as viewing the pages of political candidates have been shown to boost political efficacy and engagement.[79] While there are some notable exceptions,[80] generally research has found positive implications of social media use on political participation. Online activity in some circumstances is actually a precondition for offline political behavior (echoing the importance of sustained engagement and incremental steps in participation).[81] Research has consistently determined that engagement—even non-political engagement—in social media positively predict behaviors like political participation and decreases cynicism.[82] Social media have also been documented as facilitating political participation via mobilization efforts. This includes helping to communicate the existence, time, and location of political protests and elections, or encouraging users to engage in sustainable, environmentally friendly behaviors.[83] However, that engagement cannot be superficial—users must be actively participating with their online networks in order to realize the positive effects on political participation.[84] From research thus far, it is clear that the information, connections, and closeness that social media offer are key elements in encouraging citizens to participate in politics.

Conclusion: Strong Democracy?

Election campaigns have gone digital. The past decade clearly demonstrated that digital media, especially online social networks, have become a crucial part of election campaign practices. The wide adoption of social media has enabled and facilitated "new" election campaign practices like microtargeting, personalization, interactivity, and sustained engagement. These new practices are dramatically changing the landscape of contemporary politics. The question campaign practitioners now ask is no longer *whether* they should utilize social media for election campaigns, but *how* they should use social media to increase their ability to reach voters and increase their electoral margins. Future elections will further test the potential of digital and social media to serve as a complement to more conventional campaign efforts.

Do the new digital campaign practices bode well for a strong future democracy? The answer is not yet conclusive. Empirical evidence supports the idea that new campaign practices enable citizens to actively engage in political processes, from learning about politics to participating in and even developing bottom-up, grassroots-oriented, campaigns. The new campaign practices and their democratic potential, however, do not necessarily guarantee a strong democracy. Without long-term institutional-level resources, interactions, and support, the potential, energy, and momentum digital campaign practices facilitate and their corresponding potential for strong democracy might soon dissipate. Given that a sizable portion of the U.S. population does not have high-speed Internet access and limited facility with social media, another question must be asked: Who is being left behind by the movement of campaigns into the digital realm?

Notes

1 Dhavan V. Shah, Jaeho Cho, Seungahn Nah, Melissa R. Gotlieb, Hyunseo Hwang, Nam-Jin Lee, Rosanne M. Scholl and Douglas M. McLeod, "Campaign Ads, Online Messaging, and Participation: Extending the Communication Mediation Model," *Journal of Communication* 57 (2007): 676–703; Young Mie Kim, Bryan Wang, Melissa Gotlieb, Itay Gabay, and Stephanie Edgerly, "Ambivalence Reduction and Polarization in the Campaign Information Environment: The Interaction Between Individual-level and Contextual-level Influences," *Communication Research* (Forthcoming); James E. Campbell, *The American Campaign: U.S. Presidential Campaigns and the National Vote* (College Station, TX: Texas A&M University Press, 1996).

2 Jody C. Baumgartner and Peter L. Francia, *Conventional Wisdom and American Elections: Exploding Myths, Exploring Misconceptions* (New York: Rowman & Littlefield Publishers, 2008).

3 Girish J. Gulati and Christine B. Williams, "Closing the Gap, Raising the Bar: Candidate Web Sites Communication in the 2006 Campaigns for Congress," *Social Science Computer Review* 24 (2007): 448.

4 Richard Davis, Jody C. Baumgartner, Peter L. Francia, and Jonathan S. Morris, "The Internet in U.S. Election Campaigns," in *The Routledge Handbook of Internet Politics*, ed. Andrew Chadwick and Philip N. Howard (New York: Routledge Taylor and Francis Group, 2009), 13.

5 Bruce Bimber and Richard Davis, *Campaigning Online: The Internet in U.S. Elections* (New York: Oxford University Press, 2003), 24.

6 Jennifer Stromer-Galley, "On-line Interaction and Why Candidates Avoid It," *Journal of Communication* 50 (2000): 111–132.

7 Dhavan V. Shah, Jack M. McLeod and So-Hyang Yoon, "Communication, Context, and Community: An Exploration of Print, Broadcast, and Internet Influences," *Communication Research* 28 (2001): 464–506; Dhavan V. Shah, Nojin Kwak and R. Lance Holbert, "'Connecting' and 'Disconnecting' with Civic Life: Patterns of Internet Use and the Production of Social Capital," *Political Communication* 18 (2001): 141–162; Norman Nie, "Sociability, Interpersonal Relations, and the Internet: Reconciling Conflicting Findings," *American Behavioral Scientist* 45 (2001): 420–435.

8 Christine B. Williams and Girish J. Gulati, "Social Networks in Political Campaigns: Facebook and the 2006 Midterm Election," (paper presented at the annual meeting of the American Political Science Association, Chicago, Illinois, August 30-September 2, 2007).

9 "Facebook Gets a Facelift," The Facebook Blog, accessed February 26, 2012, https://blog.facebook.com/blog.php?post=2207967130

10 Kjerstin Thorson, Brian Ekdale, Porismita Borah, Kang Namkoong and Chirag Shah, "YouTube and Proposition 8: A Case Study in Video Activism," *Information, Communication & Society* 13 (2010): 325–349.

11 Keith Hampton and Barry Wellman, "Neighboring in Netville: How the Internet Supports Community and Social Capital in a Wired Suburb," *City & Community* 2 (2003): 277–311; Soren Matei and Sandra Ball-Rokeach, "Real and Virtual Social Ties: Connections in the Everyday Lives of Seven Ethnic Neighborhoods," *American Behavioral Scientist* 45 (2001): 550–564.

12 Young Mie Kim, "Issue Publics in the New Information Environment: Selectivity, Domain-specificity, and Extremity," *Communication Research* 36 (2009): 254–284.

13 Philip N. Howard, *New Media Campaigns and the Managed Citizen* (New York: Cambridge University Press, 2005).

14 Eli Pariser, *The Filer Bubble: What the Internet is Hiding from You* (New York: The Penguin Press, 2011), 7.

15 Christina Holtz-Bacha, "Professionalization of Political Communication," *Journal of Political Marketing* 1 (2002): 23–37; Paolo Mancini, "Leader, President, Person: Lexical Ambiguities and Interpretive Implications," *European Journal of Communication* 26 (2011): 48–63.

16 Young Mie Kim, Fei Shen, and Ivan Dylko, "Now Going into the Public: Development of Presidential Candidates' Leadership Strategies from 1980 to 2008" (paper presented at the annual meeting of the American Political Science Association, Boston, August 28–31, 2008).

17 Jennifer Stromer-Galley, "On-line Interaction and Why Candidates Avoid It."

18 Ed Pilkington and Amanda Michel, "Obama, Facebook and the Power of Friendship: The 2012 Data Election," *The Guardian*, February 17, 2012, accessed February 17, 2012 http://www.guardian.co.uk/world/2012/feb/17/obama-digital-data-machine-facebook-election

19 Wael Ghonim, *Revolution 2.0: The Power of the People is Greater Than the People in Power: A Memoir* (New York: Houghton Mifflin Harcourt, 2012).

20 Joe Trippi, *The Revolution Will Not Be Televised: Democracy, the Internet, and the Overthrow of Everything* (New York: William Morrow, 2004), 148; Matthew R. Kerbel and Joel D. Bloom, "Blog for America and Civic Involvement," *Harvard International Journal of Press/Politics* 10 (2005): 3–27.

21 Jennifer Stromer-Galley and Andrea B. Baker, "Joy and Sorrow of Interactivity on the Campaign Trail: Blogs in the Primary Campaign of Howard Dean," in *The Internet Election: Perspectives on the Web in Campaign 2004*, ed. Andrew Paul Williams and John C. Tedesco (Lanham, Maryland: Rowman & Littlefield, 2006), 111–131.

22 Dan Gillmor, *We the Media: Grassroots Journalism, By the People, for the People* (Cambridge: O'Reilly, 2004), 97.

23 Trippi, *The Revolution Will Not Be Televised*, 146.

24 Trippi, *The Revolution Will Not Be Televised*, 146.
25 Gary Wolf, "How the Internet Invented Howard Dean," *Wired*, January 2004, accessed March 22, 2012, http://www.wired.com/wired/archive/12.01/dean.html
26 Ryan Singel, "Net Politics Down but Not Out," *Wired*, February 2, 2004, accessed March 22, 2012 http://www.wired.com/politics/law/news/2004/02/62123?currentPage=all
27 Trippi, *The Revolution Will Not Be Televised*, 148.
28 Williams and Gulati, "Social Networks in Political Campaigns."
29 Williams and Gulati, "Social Networks in Political Campaigns."
30 Vassia Gueorguieva, "Voters, MySpace, and YouTube: The Impact of Alternative Communication Channels on the 2006 Election Cycle and Beyond," *Social Science Computer Review* 26 (2008): 288–300.
31 Williams and Gulati, "Social Networks in Political Campaigns," 7.
32 Jose Antonio Vargas, "Barack Obama, Social Networking King," *The Washington Post*, October 6, 2007, accessed March 23, 2012, http://voices.washingtonpost.com/44/2007/10/barack-obama-social-networking.html
33 Jose Antonio Vargas, "Obama Raised Half a Billion Online," *The Washington Post*, November 20, 2008, accessed March 4, 2012, http://voices.washingtonpost.com/44/2008/11/obama-raised-half-a-billion-on.html
34 Vargas, "Obama Raised Half a Billion Online."
35 Mike Madden, "Barack Obama's Super Marketing Machine," *Salon*, July 16, 2008, accessed March 4, 2012, http://www.salon.com/2008/07/16/obama_data/
36 Vargas, "Obama Raised Half a Billion Online."
37 Matthew Fraser and Soumitra Dutta, "Barack Obama and the Facebook Election," *US News and World Report*, November 19, 2008, accessed March 4, 2012, http://www.usnews.com/opinion/articles/2008/11/19/barack-obama-and-the-facebook-election.
38 "Barack Obama and the Facebook Election," *US News and World* Report.
39 Juliann Cortese and Jennifer M. Proffitt, "Political Messages in the First Presidential YouTube Election: A Content Analysis of the 2008 Presidential Candidates' YouTube Sites" (paper presented at the annual conference of the Association for Education in Journalism and Mass Communication, Boston, Massachusetts, August 5–8, 2009).
40 Scott H. Church, "YouTube Politics: YouChoose and Leadership Rhetoric During the 2008 Election," *Journal of Information Technology & Politics* 7 (2010): 124–142.
41 Brian Stelter, "Finding Political News Online, the Young Pass It On," *New York Times*, accessed March 23, 2012, http://www.nytimes.com/2008/03/27/us/politics/27voters.html
42 Kevin Wallsten, "'Yes We Can': How Online Viewership, Blog Discussion, Campaign Statements, and Mainstream Media Coverage Produced a Viral Video Phenomenon," *Journal of Information Technology & Politics* 7 (2010): 163–181.
43 Fraser and Dutta, "Barack Obama and the Facebook Election."
44 Andrew Rasiej and Micah L. Sifry, "The Web: 2008's Winning Ticket," *Politico*, November 12, 2008, accessed March 4, 2012, http://www.politico.com/news/stories/1108/15520.html
45 Christine B. Williams and Girish J. Gulati, "Communicating with Constituents in 140 Characters or Less: Twitter and the Diffusion of Technology Innovation in the United States Congress," *Social Science Research Network Working Paper Series*, Paper 43 (2010).
46 David S. Lassen and Adam R. Brown, "Twitter: The Electoral Connection?" *Social Science Computer Review* 29 (2010): 419–436.
47 Williams and Gulati, "Communicating with Constituents."
48 Leticia Bode, David Lassen, Young Mie Kim, Travis N. Ridout, Erika Franklin Fowler, Michael Franz and Dhavan Shah, "Putting New Media in Old Strategies: Candidate Use of Twitter during the 2010 Midterm Elections" (paper presented at

the annual meeting of the American Political Science Association, Seattle, September 1–4, 2011).

49 CIRCLE. (2010). "Youth Voting." Center for Information and Research on Civic Learning and Engagement. Available at http://www.civicyouth.org/quick-facts/youth-voting/ . Accessed on July 1, 2012.

50 CIRCLE. (2010). "Youth Voting."

51 CIRCLE. (2010). "Youth Voting."

52 Thorson, et al., "YouTube and Proposition 8."

53 CIRCLE. (2010). "Youth Voting."

54 Leticia Bode, "Facebooking it to the Polls: A Study in Online Social Networking and Political Behavior," Journal of Information, Technology, and Politics (forthcoming).

55 Christine B. Williams and Girish J. Gulati, "Social Networks in Political Campaigns: Facebook and the Congressional Elections of 2006 and 2008," New Media & Society (forthcoming).

56 Williams and Gulati, "Social Networks in Political Campaigns."

57 Leticia Bode, Emily K. Vraga, Porismita Borah and Dhavan V. Shah, "A New Space for Political Behavior: Political Social Networking and Its Democratic Consequences," Journal of Computer-Mediated Communication (forthcoming).

58 Vargas, "Obama Raised Half a Billion Online."

59 Kim et al., "Ambivalence Reduction and Polarization in the Campaign Information Environment."

60 Markus Prior, Post-Broadcast Democracy: How Media Choice Increases Inequality in Political Involvement and Polarizes Elections (Cambridge: Cambridge University Press, 2007).

61 Cass R. Sunstein, Republic.com 2.0. (Princeton: Princeton University Press, 2007).

62 Pariser, The Filter Bubble.

63 Eric Gilbert, Tony Bergstrom, and Karrie Karahalios, "Blogs Are Echo Chambers" (paper presented at the Hawaii International Conference on System Sciences, January 5–8, 2009).

64 See David O. Sears and Jonathan L. Freedman, "Selective Exposure to Information: A Critical Review," Public Opinion Quarterly 31 (1967): 194–213, for an overview. See Sunstein, Republic.Com 2.0 for an update related to online selective exposure.

65 Shanto Iyengar, Kyu S. Hahn, Jon A. Krosnick, and John Walker, "Selective Exposure to Campaign Communication: The Role of Anticipated Agreement and Issue Public Membership," Journal of Politics 70 (2008): 186–200; Natalie Jomini Stroud, Niche News: The Politics of News Choice (New York: Oxford University Press, 2011).

66 Kim, "Issue Publics in the New Information Environment"; Young Mie Kim, "Where Is My Issue? The Influence of News Coverage on Subsequent Information Selection on the Web," Journal of Broadcasting and Electronic Media 52 (2008): 600–621; Young Mie Kim, "How Intrinsic and Extrinsic Motivations Interact in Selectivity: Investigating the Moderating Effects of Situational Information Processing Goals in Issue Publics' Web Behavior," Communication Research 34 (2007): 185–211.

67 Juliana Fernandes, Magda Giurcanu, Kevin W. Bowers and Jeffrey C. Neely, "The Writing on the Wall: A Content Analysis of College Students' Facebook Groups for the 2008 Election," Mass Communication and Society 13 (2010): 65–675.

68 Christopher M. Mascaro and Sean P. Goggins, "Brewing up Citizen Engagement: The Coffee Party on Facebook," Proceedings of the 5th International Conference on Communities and Technologies (2011).

69 Sonja Utz, "The (Potential) Benefits of Campaigning Via Social Network Sites," Journal of Computer-Mediated Communication 14 (2009): 221–243.

70 Leticia Bode, "Political Information 2.0: A Study in Political Learning Via Social Media" (PhD diss., University of Wisconsin, 2012).

71 Brendan O'Connor, Ramnath Balasubramanyan, Bryan R. Routledge, and Noah

A. Smith. "From Tweets to Polls: Linking Text Sentiment to Public Opinion Time Series." (Tepper School of Business, Paper 559, 2010). http://repository.cmu.edu/tepper/559

72 Bode, "Political Information 2.0."

73 Bode, "Political Information 2.0."

74 Evgeny Morozov, "The Brave New World of Slacktivism," *Foreign Policy*, May 19, 2009.

75 Nam-jin Lee, Dhavan V. Shah and Jack M. McLeod, "Processes of Political Socialization: A Communication Mediation Approach to Youth Civic Engagement," *Communication Research* (forthcoming).

76 Henrik S. Christensen, "Political Activities on the Internet: Slacktivism or Political Participation by Other Means?" *First Monday* 16 (2011). See also Dana Rotman, Sarah Vieweg, Sarita Yardi, Ed Chi, Jenny Preece, Ben Shneiderman, Peter Pirolli, and Tom Glaisyer, "From Slacktivism to Activism: Participatory Culture in the Age of Social Media" (paper presented at the conference on Human Factors in Computing Systems, Vancouver, British Columbia, May 7–12, 2011) for a discussion of theory related to the absence of Slacktivism.

77 Jessica Vitak, Paul Zube, Andrew Smock, Caleb T. Carr, Nicole Ellison, and Cliff Lampe, "It's Complicated: Facebook Users' Political Participation in the 2008 Election," *Cyberpsychology, Behavior, and Social Networking 14* (2011): 107–114.

78 Bode, et al., "A New Space for Political Behavior."

79 Terri L. *Towner and David Dulio, "The Web 2.0 Election: Does the Online Medium Matter?" The Journal of Political Marketing 10* (2011): 165–188.

80 Jody C. Baumgartner and Jonathan S. Morris, "MyFaceTube Politics: Social Networking Websites and Political Engagement of Young Adults," *Social Science Computer Review* 28 (2011): 24–44; Weiwu Zhang, Thomas J. Johnson, Trent Seltzer and Shannon L. Bichard, "The Revolution Will Be Networked: The Influence of Social Networking Sites on Political Attitudes and Behavior," *Social Science Computer Review* 28 (2010): 75–92; Matthew J. Kushin and Masahiro Yamamoto, "Did Social Media Really Matter? College Students' Use of Online Media and Political Decision Making in the 2008 Election," *Mass Communication and Society 13* (2010): 608–630; Panagiotis Panagiotopoulos, Steven Sams, Tony Elliman, and Guy Fitzgerald, "Do Social Networking Groups Support Online Petitions?" *Transforming Government: People, Process and Policy* 5 (2010): 20–31.

81 Christina Neumayer and Judith Schossboeck, "Political Lurkers? Young People in Austria and Their Political Life Worlds Online," Proceedings of the International Conference for E-Democracy and Open Government. Krems, Austria, May 2011; Ghonim, Revolution 2.0.

82 Josh *Pasek, Eian More, and Daniel Romer, "Realizing the Social Internet: Online Social Networking Meets Offline Civic Engagement," Journal of Information Technology and Politics 6* (2009): 197–215: *Gary* Hanson, Paul Michael Haridakis, Audrey Wagstaff Cunningham, Rekha Sharma and J. D. Ponder, "The 2008 Presidential Campaign: Political Cynicism in the Age of Facebook, MySpace and YouTube," *Mass Communication & Society* 13 (2010): 584–607.

83 Bode, "Facebooking it to the Polls."

84 Bode, "Facebooking it to the Polls."

Chapter 7

Negative Campaigns

Are They Good for American Democracy?

Yanna Krupnikov and Beth C. Easter

Over the past 30 years, there has been a tremendous increase in the number of negative ads broadcast during American campaigns. While in the 1960 Presidential election fewer than 10 percent of all ads could be classified as "negative," by 2000 that number hovered closer to 40 percent.[1] Congressional elections have also become increasingly negative. In both 2008 and 2010, more than half of all the ads aired by candidates for Congress contained negativity.[2]

It would be an understatement to suggest that people—be they voters, journalists or politicians—do not like negativity. Former Senator Tom Daschle, for example, once described negativity as "the crack cocaine of politics."[3] During the 2008 primary campaign, the *New York Times*, which initially endorsed Hillary Clinton, later published a harsh editorial criticizing Clinton's negative ads, noting that negativity is doing "harm to her, her opponent, her party and the 2008 election."[4] Meanwhile, former President Jimmy Carter argued that "the spending of a lot of that money on a negative campaign to destroy the reputation and character of . . . opponents is what has divided our country."[5]

Political candidates, too, treat negativity as a problematic component of a campaign. During a 2008 presidential debate, for example, both candidates commented on negativity. "Your ads, 100 percent of them have been negative," Democrat Barack Obama told Republican John McCain. In turn, McCain argued "Senator Obama has spent more money on negative ads than any political campaign in history."[6]

In survey after survey, ordinary Americans routinely report that they do not like negative ads. In a recent survey, 71 percent reported that negativity has no place in politics. In an additional poll, 84 percent reported that negative campaigns bothered them.[7] And, Americans believe that each election is even more overwhelmingly negative than the last. While 55 percent believed that the 2008 campaign was too negative, 67 percent reported that the 2010 campaign was too negative. By January 2012, before the general election campaign for president had even begun, more than half of voters had reported that the campaign had already been too negative.[8]

Given media coverage of negativity and given the fact that ordinary Americans routinely report that they do not like negative ads, it is easy to imagine that negative ads have serious, troubling consequences for American politics and for representative democracy. Indeed, as John Geer writes, "worries about negativity lie at the very center of concerns about the health of our electoral system and whether that system promotes a process that can be thought of as democratic."[9]

The key component of negative ads is that they are, in a word, negative, and it is easy to envision that something negative might have a harmful effect. It is reasonable to suspect, for example, that negativity might lead people to be disillusioned with politics, to disapprove of candidates who run negative ads, and, eventually, to turn away from political participation all together.

Responding to these concerns about the role of negativity in the political process, over the last three decades scholars in a variety of disciplines including political science, communication and psychology, have amassed a large and diverse body of literature about the effect of negativity on voter behavior. This work has considered whether negative ads, in particular, change the way people respond to politics and the way they participate in the political process. This work has relied on numerous methodologies and has considered many national elections.

Surprisingly, however, the effects of negative advertising have turned out to be quite elusive. After decades of research, scholars have found conflicting results. Sometimes negativity—as one might have initially predicted—does have negative consequences for the political process. Other times, however, negativity has no effect on people and, even more strikingly, sometimes negativity can actually increase voters' interest in the political process, leading them to be more knowledgeable and involved in elections.

So which is it? Are negative ads as harmful and divisive as the media (and former President Jimmy Carter) suggest? Or are negative ads actually a helpful component of a campaign? And, as campaigns work to incorporate more Internet-based advertising, are the effects of negative campaign ads likely to change in the future? In this chapter we consider these questions. First, we define negativity. Second, we present the various effects negativity has on the political process. Third, we consider why scholars have found such conflicting results. Next, we turn to the digital future of negativity and consider whether the increased use of the Internet for campaigning will change the way negativity affects the political process.

Defining Negativity

In order to understand the effects of negativity, it is first important to define what we mean by a "negative ad." At its most basic definition, a negative ad is one in which a candidate critiques another.[10] Conversely, a positive ad is one in which a candidate promotes himself. In between a purely negative ad and positive ad is a contrast ad, which includes both a criticism of the opponent and positive information about the sponsor of the ad.

Each of these types of ads—negative, positive or contrast—can have different types of content. An ad may have issue content, which focuses on the issue positions, beliefs and past votes of either the candidate or the opponent. For example, in his 1992 ad "Read My Lips," Democrat Bill Clinton criticized his opponent, Republican George H.W. Bush, on tax policies. Alternatively, an ad may be focused on image, or the biography, personal characteristics or character traits of either the candidate or the opponent. In 2008, for example, McCain sponsored an ad that compared his opponent, Obama, to a socialite and a celebrity, and questioned Obama's ability to be a leader.

Lee Sigelman and Mark Kugler have suggested that voters are more likely to identify negative image ads as being truly negative and are much more likely to believe that negative image ads are problematic.[11] In contrast, voters are more likely to forgive negative issue ads. Further, scholars suggest that voters are more likely to judge negative issue ads as being more "fair" than negative image ads. Freedman, Wood, and Lawton report that while 81 percent of voters believe that it is fair for an ad to criticize a candidate for "talking one way and voting another," only 28 percent believe that it is fair for an ad to criticize a candidate for extra-marital affairs.[12]

Generally, negative issue ads have been more prevalent than negative image ads. In 2008, for example, only 21 percent of all ads sponsored by the Democratic candidates for Congress and 23 percent of all ads sponsored by the Republican candidates for Congress focused solely on the image attributes of the opponent.[13]

The Many Effects of Campaign Negativity

Relying on these definitions of negativity, scholars have identified a number of ways in which negativity can affect the political process. These effects range from very troubling to highly encouraging to completely minimal. It is these variations that have made the effect of negative campaigning one of the most enduring and interesting puzzles in political science. Below, we consider three possible broad effects of negativity.

Effect 1: Decrease in Voter Turnout

Given the criticisms of negativity, it is quite reasonable to expect that this form of advertising could be harmful to the political process. In fact, Ansolabehere and Iyengar show just such an effect: in a series of experiments they find that people who see negative ads reported that they were much less likely to turn out to vote than people who see positive ads.[14] This argument hinges on the way voters respond to negativity. Ansolabehere and Iyengar show that negativity makes voters feel less efficacious, or less like they have any power over the political process. When individuals no longer believe they have any power over the political process, they are much less likely to turn out to vote.

Another possibility is that negativity leads to a "plague-on-both-your-houses."[15] While the general goal of a negative ad is to criticize the opponent, it is possible that negative ads may have an additional, unintended effect. Since voters routinely report that they dislike negativity, it is possible that they may also express some dissatisfaction with the candidate who *sponsored* the ad. This effect is known as the *boomerang* effect.

The boomerang effect occurs when a negative ad creates not only negative feelings toward the candidate being criticized by the ad, but also toward the candidate who sponsored the ad.[16] Kahn and Kenney show that this happens to both challengers and incumbents: after the candidates sponsored negativity, voters gave them lower evaluations.[17] Notably, however, individuals are much more forgiving when negativity is sponsored by a candidate of their own party.[18]

This boomerang effect may be responsible for the "plague-on-both-your-houses" effect. A voter may form negative perceptions of one candidate due to the information conveyed in a negative ad, but the same voter may also be frustrated with the other candidate for simply sponsoring negativity. This leaves the voter dissatisfied with both of his candidate options. In turn, this form of dissatisfaction may lead voters to lose interest and withdraw from the political process.

The idea that negative ads can turn voters away from the polls certainly fits the image of negativity as a "problematic" component of a campaign. If individuals dislike negativity, and if negativity produces not only lower evaluations of the candidate being criticized, but also of the sponsor, then it stands to reason that negativity could have a harmful effect on American democracy. And, the possibility that individuals are systematically less likely to vote as a result of negative ads is as harmful of an effect as any. Yet, additional research on the effects of negativity has led to very different results.

Effect 2: Increase in Interest and Participation

While Ansolabehere and Iyengar find that negativity leads people away from the polls, Freedman and Goldstein find that negativity does just the opposite—it increases the chance that individuals will turn out to vote.[19] How can negative advertising—something that so many voters actively report disliking—lead to such a positive outcome? There are a number of possibilities.

First, as we already mentioned, negative ads are more likely to focus on issues rather than candidate personalities. Conversely, positive ads often are more likely to discuss candidate biographies and background.[20] This focus on issue content makes negative ads more informative and, in turn, may offer citizens more helpful political information. Koch summarizes this as follows:

> . . . Scholars maintain that at least in presidential campaigns negative ads are characterized by a higher level of issue content than positive ads

... Positive ads frequently aim to promote the personal qualities of the candidate and thus are viewed as fluff pieces that fail to provide citizens with information necessary for influencing the direction of government policy.[21]

In sum, negativity may provide individuals with more helpful information, and this increase in helpful information may translate to voting.

Another possibility is that negativity is simply more interesting than positivity. Psychologists have long shown that people are drawn to negativity; people find negativity more helpful in making decisions and more helpful in organizing information.[22] People's tendency to be drawn to negative information is termed the "negativity bias," and this bias has been documented in numerous political situations.[23] This negativity bias may lead individuals to focus on negative ads, thus increasing people's interest in the campaign, and an increase in interest may lead to a higher chance of voting.

The negativity bias may also have an additional effect. Because people are drawn to negativity, increases in exposure to negative ads may suggest to voters that they have all the necessary information they need to make political choices. Indeed, research has shown that higher exposure to negative ads leads people to make candidate choices more quickly and to have more certainty in their choice.[24] If people are more certain in their choices, they are more likely to turn out to vote.

In sum, despite the fact that individuals report dissatisfaction with negativity, these ads may actually be quite helpful for democracy. By providing more information, increasing voter interest, and helping individuals make choices, negative ads may help voters who would otherwise retreat from the political process to make it to the polls.

Effect 3: Null Effect

It is also possible, however, that negativity has no effect on political behavior at all. Finkel and Geer find no evidence that negativity changes the way individuals behave during a campaign, and Lau and Geer reach a similar conclusion.[25] In fact, Lau and Rovner conclude that there is "no general support for the hypothesis that negative political campaigning depresses voter turnout," though they note there is a bit more support for the possibility that negativity increases voter turnout.

Again, there are a number of reasonable explanations for such an outcome. While it is possible that, as Ansolabehere and Iyengar show, individuals may feel less efficacious as a result of negativity; negative ads are just one part of a larger campaign process. It is possible that other parts of the campaign—talking to friends and neighbors, getting visits from campaign staff—may lead individuals to feel some connection to politics and overcome the effects of negativity.

Further, while the negativity bias is powerful, it is possible that campaigns are so highly saturated by various forms of media that people simply pay little attention to ads. In other words, again, the other factors in a campaign are simply more important for people than the advertising.

Explaining Conflicting Results

The fact that scholarship on campaign negativity leads to three very different results is, at first glance, unsatisfying. Negativity is a large part of any given national campaign; negative ads generally receive a great deal of scrutiny, both from the mainstream media and from the candidates themselves. Moreover, scholars have spent a great deal of effort to identify how negativity affects the political process. Over the last 30 years, there have been more than 110 separate analyses devoted to analyzing the effects of negativity.[26] So why have these studies produced such different results?

It is possible that at least part of the reason for these differing results is the methods scholars have used to conduct analyses. Analyzing whether or not a person has seen a particular negative ad is inherently a difficult process, and measures of exposure to negativity are generally imperfect.[27] Further, the effects of ads are fleeting—while a negative ad can have a strong immediate effect, its power may fade after several weeks, or even after several hours.[28] Finally, there is some reason to believe that scholars who conduct experimental research on negativity and scholars who rely on survey and campaign ad counts often reach different conclusions, because people are more likely to focus on ads when they are in an experimental laboratory.[29]

Yet methodological differences cannot explain the full extent of the disagreement. Rather, the difference in findings hints at the possibility that the relationship between negativity and political outcomes is much more complex than scholars originally suspected. In other words, it is possible that there are additional factors that influence whether negativity affects voters, factors that can change whether negativity leads voters to or away from the polls.

First, it is possible that different people respond differently to campaign ads. For example, it is possible that people who are strong partisans are much less responsive to negativity than weak partisans. Also, it is possible that women are much more responsive to negativity than men.[30] While we may not observe the effects of negativity over the entire population, we may see that negativity is particularly likely to lead certain voters away from the polls.

Second, it is possible that negative ads have different effects when they are *targeted,* or deliberately designed to appeal to certain, specific voter groups. Advertisements that are targeted may discuss issues that are of specific interest to a specific voter group, while untargeted advertisements may consider issues that are of general interest to the public but may not be uniquely interesting to a specific voter. For example, an advertisement targeted toward voters with children may focus on issues of education, child health and other parental issues. To ensure that such an ad reaches its intended audience, campaigns may deliberately air this ad during programs that parents of young children are more likely to watch.[31] In contrast, campaigns may air ads that do not have specific group targets during television programs that have a more varied audience. This is a reasonable proposition; though studies show little evidence that targeting ads to specific groups changes the effect of negativity.[32]

Third, individuals may treat negative ads sponsored by certain types of candidates differently. Specifically, it is possible that voters respond differently to negative ads sponsored by female or black candidates than to negative ads sponsored by white male candidates. While recent scholarship has attempted to trace the different responses to negativity due to the gender of the sponsor,[33] there has been considerably less work on the differential response to negativity by the race of the sponsor. Nonetheless, existing research on candidate race does suggest the possibility that individuals will be less forgiving of when black candidates go negative.[34]

A fourth option lies in the packaging of negative advertisements. Ted Brader shows that some negative ads have a great deal more emotional content than others. For example, some ads rely on music and images to convey a message and thus lead voters to experience certain emotions. In turn, feeling emotions such as anger and fear can change the way people behave. Brader's work suggests that it is not simply negativity that can have an effect on the political process, but the emotional components of negativity.[35]

Next, it is also possible that voters are not quite as dissatisfied with negativity as they claim. Kyle Mattes and David Redlawsk, for example, find that survey respondents tend to overstate their dislike of negativity, simply because they believe it is appropriate to do so. In other words, it is not that individuals mind negativity when it appears on their television screen, but rather that they think they *should* mind negativity. This leads people to report a strong dislike for negative ads, when in reality the effect of these ads may be inconsequential.[36]

Finally, it is possible that the timing of negativity can change the way people respond. Negativity early in the campaign, for example, may help people to make choices among candidates. In contrast, negativity after a person has already made a candidate choice can suggest to individuals that they have selected a poor candidate and lead them away from the polls.[37]

In sum, while it is surprising that scholars have reached conflicting findings about the role of negativity in politics, this does not in itself suggest that negativity has no effect. Rather, it is likely that the effect of negativity is highly nuanced, meaning that we cannot expect that negative ads have a uniform effect. Negativity, it seems, has a different effect under different political conditions.

Negativity in the Digital Age

To this point, we have focused on televised negativity as much of the existing scholarly research is based on these types of negative ads. Yet, the face of negativity continues to change with every election. More and more negative ads are now being transmitted via the Internet. Since campaign websites first appeared in 1994, online campaigning has grown exponentially.[38] It is not only that candidate websites are now ubiquitous, but candidates have taken advantage of several new web technologies. Candidates now rely on blogs, Twitter, Facebook, web ads, and YouTube videos to translate their traditional campaign strategies to the web. Broadly speaking, this approach can be classified as "web campaigning" or "those activities with political objectives that are manifested in, inscribed on, and enabled through the World Wide Web."[39]

The Internet provides campaigns with several advantages over traditional campaign techniques. First, the Internet provides virtually limitless space to attack without having to sacrifice other parts of a candidate's message.[40] Second, campaigns can reach voters at a lower cost.[41] Third, the Internet provides an interactive forum in that voters are able to respond to the candidate.[42] Finally, the Internet allows candidates to respond quickly to claims made by their opponents.[43]

As with traditional campaigns, the development of online campaigning has raised additional concerns about negativity. How will this type of negativity affect the political process? Can we simply translate what we know about televised negativity to this very new medium of advertising? We consider existing research on both of these questions below.

Candidate Strategy

In order to trace the effects of campaign negativity online it is first important to consider whether candidates treat web and television ads in a similar manner. Here, much like with televised negativity, scholars again disagree. On the one hand, some have proposed the *innovation hypothesis,* which states that there will be significant differences between online negative campaigning and traditional negative campaigning because of the distinct types of media features.[44] As a result of these media differences, we should expect a fundamental change in political campaigns.

On the other hand, scholars have also suggested the *normalization hypothesis,* which states that negative online campaigning should closely resemble traditional negative campaigning.[45] In other words, if the normalization hypothesis is true, candidates should extend traditional negative campaign techniques to online campaigning.

Studies provide two types of support for the normalization hypothesis. First, research shows that both presidential candidates and congressional candidates go negative at similar rates on the web as on television.[46] For example, Druckman and colleagues conducted one of the most systematic studies comparing when congressional candidates go negative on their websites with when they go negative on television advertising. Forty-eight percent of congressional candidates went negative on their websites, while 55 percent of congressional candidates ran negative television advertisements.[47]

The second type of support for the normalization hypothesis is that candidates go negative under similar conditions in both online campaigning and televised campaigning.[48] Much as they do with television ads, challengers are more likely than incumbents to go negative online.[49] Candidates, including incumbents, are also more likely to go negative online as competition increases, a finding that is echoed in research on televised campaign ads.[50] Other factors that have been shown to increase campaign negativity include open-seat races and having more campaign resources.[51] In other words, candidates go negative online under the same circumstances that they go negative on television.

Further supporting the normalization hypothesis, evidence shows that even as online campaigning continues to grow, candidates have not abandoned traditional negative campaign techniques. Rather, candidates have extended traditional negative campaigning to online campaigning. While in 2008 Barack Obama focused on web-based strategies, he also set a record for the amount of money spent on televised ads.

Effects of Online Negativity

A second consideration is whether negative campaigning online has a similar impact on voters as negative campaigning on television. Even though online campaigning has substantially expanded, few systematic studies have examined the impact of negative campaigning online on citizens.[52]

It is not clear to what extent findings from traditional negative campaigning will apply to negative online campaigning. For example, will negative online campaigning stimulate individuals to seek out additional political information, change political attitudes, or influence political behavior such as voting? Do the unique media features of the Internet have an impact on people's perceptions of politics or how they process information? This is an area of research that needs to be further studied.

This is an important area of research because individuals are increasingly using the Internet to get political information. The percentage of individuals who reported getting most of their election news from the Internet increased from 7 percent in 2002 to 24 percent in 2010.[53] However, all individuals are not equally likely to access political information on the Internet. Rather, individuals who are better educated, more affluent, younger, and more partisan than the general population are more likely to access political information on the Internet and to visit candidate websites.[54] Research indicates that people who pay attention to campaigns through the Internet are also paying attention through traditional media.[55] In other words, the Internet supplements traditional media for the majority of individuals, but it is unclear whether it has an additional, unique effect on citizens.

The Future of Negativity

In January 2012, before the 2012 presidential general election campaign had begun, before the Republican voters had even selected a nominee for president, *New York Magazine* pronounced that the coming Presidential campaign was to be a "tsunami of slime." "It's going to get ugly—it always does, and this year, it already has," the article noted.[56] As most recent campaigns have shown, campaign negativity has become a tradition in American politics.

Indeed, following the January 2010 Supreme Court ruling in *Citizens United v FEC*, corporations and unions can now sponsor ads to promote candidates during political campaigns. This ruling has led to the rise of "Super PACs" or political action committees that gather funds from corporations, unions, interest groups and even ordinary citizens and spend this money on the sponsorship of campaign activity—most notably, campaign advertising. The creation of these Super PACs has led to a tremendous increase in ads sponsored by outside groups. A comparison of a similar time-period in the 2008 and 2012 Republican primaries, for example, shows a 1627 percent increase in the number of ads sponsored by outside groups.[57] The ads sponsored by these external groups are overwhelmingly negative, suggesting continuing increases in campaign negativity.

Moreover, the introduction of the Internet has further altered the campaign process. Negative ads are becoming more targeted and are taking on a different shape for the online audience. While only time will tell if the effects of online negativity are different than the effects of televised negativity, it is quite likely that, at the very least, increased reliance on web-based sources means that voters will see even greater numbers of negative ads.

So what do these ads mean for democracy? A recurring argument in media coverage of campaigns is that candidate negativity is so ubiquitous because "it works." Indeed, the ads that have garnered the most media attention during campaigns have generally been negative. While anecdotal descriptions of negativity in a campaign setting may suggest its ultimate effectiveness, decades of scholarly research suggest a different story. The effects of negativity are too nuanced, too conditional, and too complicated to ever be summed up as either "it works" or "it doesn't work."

Notes

1 John Geer, *In Defense of Negativity: Attack Ads in Presidential Campaigns* (Chicago: University of Chicago Press, 2006) Figure 5.1, 86.
2 Information about 2008 from Kantar Media/CMAG with analysis by the Wesleyan Media Project; 2010 information from Erika Franklin Fowler and Travis N. Ridout, "Advertising Trends in 2010," *The Forum* 8 (2010): 1–15.
3 Geer, *In Defense of Negativity*, 1.
4 Editorial, "The Low Road to Victory," *New York Times*, April 23, 2008.
5 Karen Farabaugh, "Jimmy Carter: Negative Political Ads are Dividing the Nation," *Voices of America*, January 25, 2012.

6 Jim Rutenberg, "Nearing Record, Obama's Ad Effort Swamps McCain." *New York Times*, October 17, 2008.
7 Geer, *In Defense of Negativity*, 2
8 All data from the Pew Weekly Interest Poll
9 Geer, *In Defense of Negativity*, 2
10 Geer, *In Defense of Negativity*, 23
11 Lee Sigelman and Mark Kugler, "Why Is Research on the Effects of Negative Campaigning So Inconclusive? Understanding Citizens' Perceptions of Negativity," *Journal of Politics* 65 (2003): 142–60.
12 Paul Freedman, William Wood, and Dale Lawton, "Do's and Don't's of Negative Ads: What Voters Say," *Campaigns & Elections* 20 (1999): 20–25.
13 Kantar Media/CMAG with analysis by the Wesleyan Media Project
14 Stephen Ansolabehere and Shanto Iyengar, *Going Negative: How Attack Ads Shrink and Polarize the Public* (New York: Free Press, 1995).
15 Michael Basil, Caroline Schooler and Byron Reeves, "Positive and Negative Political Advertising: Effectiveness of Advertisements and Perceptions of Candidates," in *Television and Political Advertising*, ed. Frank Biocca (Hillsdale, New Jersey: Earlbaum, 1991). Also discussed in Stephen Ansolabehere, Shanto Iyengar, Adam Simon and Nicholas Valentino, "Does Attack Advertising Demobilize the Electorate?" *American Political Science Review* 88 (1994): 829–838.
16 Gina Garramone, "Voter Response to Negative Political Ads," *Journalism Quarterly* 61 (1984): 250–259.
17 Kim Kahn and Patrick Kenney, *No Holds Barred: Negativity in U.S. Senate Campaigns* (Upper Saddle River, NJ: Pearson Education, 2004).
18 Douglas Matthews and Beth Dietz-Uhler, "The Black-Sheep Effect: How Positive and Negative Advertisements Affect Voters' Perceptions of the Sponsor of the Advertisement," *Journal of Applied Social Psychology* 28 (1998): 1903–1915.
19 Ken Goldstein and Paul Freedman, "Campaign Advertising and Voter Turnout: New Evidence for a Stimulation Effect," *Journal of Politics* 64 (2002): 721–740.
20 Geer, *In Defense of Negativity*.
21 Jeffrey Koch, "Campaign Advertisements' Impact on Voter Certainty and Knowledge of House Candidates' Ideological Positions," *Political Research Quarterly* 61 (2008): 609–621, p. 610.
22 Karen E. James and Paul J. Hensel, "Negative Advertising: The Malicious Strain of Comparative Advertising," *Journal of Advertising* 20 (1991): 53–69.
23 Richard Lau, "Negativity in Political Perception," *Political Behavior* 4 (1982): 353–377. Daron Shaw, "A Study of Presidential Campaign Event Effects from 1952 to 1992," *Journal of Politics* 61 (1999): 387–422.
24 Yanna Krupnikov, "Negative Advertising and Voter Choice: The Role of Ads in Candidate Selection," *Political Communication*, forthcoming.
25 Steven Finkel and John G. Geer, "A Spot Check: Casting Doubt on the Demobilizing Effect of Attack Advertising," *American Journal of Political Science* 42 (1998): 573–595; John Geer and Richard Lau, "A New Approach for Estimating Campaign Effects," *British Journal of Political Science* 35 (2006): 269–290.
26 Richard Lau, Lee Sigelman and Ivy Brown Rovner, "The Effects of Negative Political Campaigns: A Meta-Analytic Reassessment," *Journal of Politics* 69 (2007): 1176–1209.
27 Paul Freedman and Ken Goldstein, "Measuring Media Exposure and the Effects of Negative Campaign Ads," *American Journal of Political Science* 43 (1999): 1189–1208.
28 Seth Hill, James Lo, Lynn Vavreck and John Zaller, "The Duration of Advertising Effects in the 2000 Presidential Campaign" (paper presented at the annual meeting of the American Political Science Association, Boston, August 28–31, 2008).

29 Joshua Clinton and John Lapinski, "'Targeted' Advertising and Voter Turnout: An Experimental Study of the 2000 Presidential Election," *Journal of Politics* 66 (2004): 69–96.

30 James King and Jason McConnell, "The Effect of Negative Campaign Advertising on Vote Choice: The Mediating Influence of Gender," *Social Science Quarterly* 84 (2003): 843–857.

31 Travis N. Ridout, Michael Franz, Kenneth Goldstein and William Feltus, "Separation by Television Program: Understanding the Targeting of Political Advertising in Presidential Elections," *Political Communication* 29 (2012): 1–23.

32 Clinton and Lapinski " 'Targeted' Advertising and Voter Turnout."

33 Kim L. Fridkin and Patrick Kenney, "Variability in Citizen Reactions to Different Types of Negative Campaigns," *American Journal of Political Science* 55 (2011): 307–325; Kim L. Fridkin, Patrick J. Kenney and Gina Serignese Woodall, "Bad for Men, Better for Women: The Impact of Stereotypes during Political Campaigns," *Political Behavior* 31 (2009): 53–77.

34 Spencer Piston, "How Explicit Racial Prejudice Hurt Obama in the 2008 Election," *Political Behavior* 32 (2010): 431–451.

35 Ted Brader, *Campaigning for Hearts and Minds* (Chicago: University of Chicago Press, 2006).

36 Kyle Mattes and David Redlawsk, "Negative about Negativity: Public Opinion and the Framing of Negative Campaigning" (paper presented at the annual meeting of the American Political Science Association, Seattle, September 1–4, 2011).

37 Yanna Krupnikov, "When Does Negativity Demobilize? Tracing the Conditional Effect of Negative Campaigning on Voter Turnout," *American Journal of Political Science* 55 (2011): 796–812.

38 Bruce Bimber and Richard Davis, *Campaigning Online: The Internet in U.S. Elections* (New York: Oxford University Press, 2003); Kristen A. Foot and Steven M. Schneider, *Web Campaigning* (Cambridge, MA: The MIT Press, 2006).

39 Foot and Schneider, *Web Campaigning.*

40 James N. Druckman, Martin J. Kifer and Michael Parkin, "Timeless Strategy Meets New Medium: Going Negative on Congressional Campaign Web Sites, 2002–2006," *Political Communication* 27 (2010): 88–103.

41 Lynda Lee Kaid, "Political Web Wars: The Use of the Internet for Political Advertising," in *The Internet Election*, ed. Andrew Paul Williams and John C. Tedesco (Lanham, MD: Rowman & Littlefield, 2006), 67–82.

42 Lynda Lee Kaid, "Political Advertising and Information Seeking: Comparing Exposure via Traditional and Internet Channels," *Journal of Advertising* 31 (2002): 27–35.

43 Kaid, "Political Web Wars."

44 Jay G. Blumler and Michael Gurevitch, "The New Media and Our Political Communication Discontents: Democratizing Cyberspace," *Information, Communication & Society* 4 (2001): 1–13; Robert Klotz, "Virtual Criticism: Negative Advertising on the Internet in the 1996 Senate Races," *Political Communication* 15 (1998): 347–365; Robert Klotz, *The Politics of Internet Communication* (Lanham, MD: Rowman & Littlefield, 2003).

45 Michael Margolis and David Resnick. *Politics as Usual: The Cyberspace "Revolution"* (Thousand Oaks, CA: Sage, 2000); Eva Johanna Schweitzer, "Innovation or Normalization in E-campaigning," *European Journal of Communication* 23 (2008): 449–470.

46 For studies on congressional candidates see: Druckman et al. "Timeless Strategy Meets New Medium" and James N. Druckman, Martin J. Kifer and Michael Parkin. "Campaign Communications in U.S. Congressional Elections." *American Political Science Review* 103 (2009): 343–366; for studies on presidential candidates see:

Boubacar Souley and Robert H. Wicks, "Tracking the 2004 Presidential Campaign Web Sites: Similarities and Differences," *American Behavioral Scientist* 49 (2005): 535–547; and Robert H. Wicks and Boubacar Souley, "Going Negative: Candidate Usage of Internet Web Sites during the 2000 Presidential Campaign," *Journalism and Mass Communication Quarterly* 80 (2003): 128–144.

47 Druckman et al., "Timeless Strategy Meets New Medium."

48 Druckman et al., "Campaign Communications"; Druckman et al. "Timeless Strategy Meets New Medium"; Foot and Schneider, "Web Campaigning"; Christopher P. Latimer, "Utilizing the Internet as a Campaign Tool: The Relationship Between Incumbency, Political Party Affiliation, Election Outcomes, and the Quality of Campaign Web Sites in the United States," *Journal of Information Technology & Politics* 4 (2008): 81–95; and Margolis and Resnick, "Politics as Usual."

49 Druckman et al. "Campaign Communications"; Druckman et al., "Timeless Strategy Meets New Medium"; Kim Fridkin Kahn and Patrick J. Kenney, *No Holds Barred: Negativity in U.S. Senate Campaigns* (Upper Saddle River, NJ: Pearson Prentice Hall, 2004); Souley and Wicks, "Tracking the 2004 Presidential Campaign Web Sites"; Wicks and Souley, "Going Negative."

50 Druckman et al., "Timeless Strategy Meets New Medium"; Souley and Wicks, "Tracking the 2004 Presidential Campaign Web Sites"; Wicks and Souley "Going Negative"; Kahn and Kenney, *No Holds Barred.*

51 Druckman et al., "Timeless Strategy Meets New Medium."

52 Lynda Lee Kaid and Monica Postelnicu, "Political Advertising in the 2004 Election: Comparison of Traditional Television and Internet Message," *American Behavioral Scientist* 49 (2005): 265–278; H. Denis Wu and Nicole S. Dahmen, "Web Sponsorship and Campaign Effects: Assessing the Difference between Positive and Negative Web Sites," *Journal of Political Marketing* 9 (2010): 314–329.

53 Aaron Smith, "The Internet and Campaign 2010," Pew Research Center. 2011. http://www.pewinternet.org/~/media//Files/Reports/2011/Internet%20and%20Campaign%202010.pdf

54 Smith, "The Internet and Campaign 2010"; Bimber and Davis, *Campaigning Online*; Druckman et al., "Timeless Strategy Meets New Medium."

55 Bimber and Davis, *Campaigning Online.*

56 Joe Hagan, "The Coming Tsunami of Slime," *New York Magazine*, January 22, 2012.

57 Wesleyan Media Project, "Outside Group Involvement in GOP Contest Skyrockets Compared to 2008," January 30, 2012, accessed on July 1, 2012, http://mediaproject.wesleyan.edu/2012/01/30/group-involvement-skyrockets/

Chapter 8

Targeting Campaign Messages

Good for Campaigns but Bad for America?

Michael M. Franz

In contemporary American politics, data on voters has become a valuable asset. Candidates ask sophisticated questions about their constituencies: where are the voters needed to build a winning coalition? How many voters are "persuadable" in the sense that they are dissatisfied with their own party and willing to vote for candidates of the competing party? Are core supporters in need of a "nudge" to help stay with the team, and where are these voters in the district or state? In an age of expanding technological options, candidates are turning to an army of data experts to mine the available lists of voters to find every possible vote. It is this development in American elections that is the focus of this chapter.

Think of it this way: the groups you contribute money to, or the magazines you subscribe to, might help candidates determine what political positions you care about. Whether you like dark beer or light beer, for example, what clothing store you frequent, and what car you drive might be related to your support for the wars in Afghanistan and Iraq. Whether you watch sports or mysteries might be relevant as well, and whether you like CBS over NBC for your favorite comedy shows could act as a "tell" of what position you take on health-care reform. Indeed, our consumer habits and entertainment preferences match well with many other preferences in our daily life, including our political ones. Because of this, candidates, parties, and interest groups can determine quite a bit about voters by looking to their behavior as consumers and citizens. Because candidates cannot ask every voter for support, they sort constituents into categories that allow for an efficient targeting of their resources.

Is this good or bad for American democracy? What are the advantages and disadvantages of this new reliance on data? This chapter begins with a discussion of how campaigns target voters in various ways, from broadly targeting general groups to geo-targeting areas based on how they voted in the past. The chapter then turns from a discussion of these long-standing approaches to finding potential votes to a discussion of more recent techniques that involve more finely grained targeting of specific individuals based on extensive data analysis. The chapter then reviews how campaigns use data on viewer characteristics of certain television programs, or show genres to target more precisely a desired audience with their 30-second ads. All of these advances in the use of technology by campaigns are attempts to allocate resources more efficiently, and there is much to like about these developments from the standpoint of campaigns. The chapter concludes, however, by raising some concerns about these developments, asking the reader to speculate further on what harm can come from such extensive data mining.

Microtargeting

Campaigns are strategic. When a candidate and her staff meet to discuss tactics for winning an election, a lot of factors are on the table. Whom should we target? What should we say? How should we say it? In general, campaigns use three major approaches to engage the electorate: mobilizing one's base or a set of likely supporters to turn out on Election Day, priming a set of issues so as to focus the campaign on policies that advantage the candidate, and persuading swing voters that you are the better candidate.[1] Mobilization and persuasion usually mean talking to specific audiences, while priming concerns what you say in those conversations.

Whatever the goal, a campaign can take a number of different approaches. First, whether for purposes of mobilization or persuasion, candidates can target broadly. For example, if presidential candidates want to target young people, they could appear on MTV or campaign with a popularity celebrity. If candidates want to target African American voters, they could appear on BET, speak at the NAACP annual convention, or give a Sunday lecture in a predominately black church. These types of appearances will always be covered by the national media, easily reaching a targeted demographic group. State-level candidates can take generally the same approach, but on a smaller scale. To reach younger voters, the candidate might schedule stops at local colleges or universities. Or to reach older voters, she might speak at retirement communities or advertise in newspapers. None of this requires much more than a strategy session and some common sense.

A second, and more finely grained approach, is to use precinct data to identify neighborhoods that are particularly balanced in their vote for Republican or Democratic candidates (swing precincts, with persuasion as the goal) or to find precincts that more consistently benefit one's own party (if mobilization is the goal), thereby ignoring neighborhoods that disproportionately favor the other party. Such geographic targeting is a traditional approach for reaching specific voters, and it is generally costless—all one needs is the ability to download past election tallies from the state elections office and sort precincts by election outcomes. An experienced intern can provide a list of target precincts with a few hours of work in an Excel spreadsheet.

This type of targeting, however, potentially leaves a lot of voters living in safe precincts ignored by the campaigns, even though these voters might be open to persuasion. A disaffected Republican in a deep blue precinct, for example, may never be contacted by a Republican candidate. In simple terms, while the geo-targeting is easy and quite precise, it leaves lots of voters on the table. Of course, some recent research has highlighted the tendency of Americans to "sort" themselves into locales with political preferences that match their own.[2] Think of the liberal who refuses a new job in the Deep South because of a fear of living in a red state. This should mean that geo-targeting may reach a more homogenous set of voters than in years' past. Subsequent research has demonstrated, though, that within counties there is much variation in the political preferences of voters, and employment and economic opportunities often prevent or dissuade voters from sorting more aggressively into red or blue neighborhoods. In short, there is ample partisan diversity within neighborhoods across the country.[3]

Microtargeting is one approach that looks for voters across the district or state, regardless (or in spite of) their residence. Consider the most simplistic method. Using the voter registration files in a state, which has one entry for every registered voter, a campaign can contact registered Independents (for persuasion) or like-partisans (for mobilization). One can even use turnout history as a proxy for engagement, where a Democrat who only occasionally votes might be a persuasion target for a Republican campaign, and vice versa. A Democrat who always votes in his party's primary, by contrast, is unlikely to be persuaded by a Republican's message. With this approach, every voter in the state or district is identified and categorized. This helps not only with mobilization and persuasion but priming, as a campaign can approximate what types of campaign appeals are most likely to "work" on different audiences.

One complication is that not every state records a voter's party identification. In fact, only twenty-eight states and Washington, D.C., do so. Another eleven states track which primary a voter participated in, and this can help a campaign approximate the partisan preference of the voter (i.e., a consistent voter in Democratic primaries vs. a voter who over time moves back and forth across party primaries). In states with no party registration or tracked primary participation, only turnout history ends up helping candidates figure out which voters to approach, but it gives no help in identifying the voter's party leaning.

All told, this form of micro (read individual-level) targeting is quite precise, but it also still leaves some voters untouched. A regular-voting Republican might be disaffected by the issue positions of the Republican candidate in a given election and thus might make a good persuasion target for the Democratic candidate. But the voter registration file does very little to identify such voters. Enter a much more bulked-up approach that relies on leveraging an extensive amount of data. The process looks something like this:

Step 1: Conduct a large survey in the state that is being targeted. For presidential campaigns, this might be a set of battleground states, and for Senate campaigns it could be the entire state or part of the state. Ask a series of questions about political attitudes and consumer habits. What party does the respondent identify with, and how often does she vote in presidential and midterm elections? What types of policies does the respondent support? What types of magazines or hobbies does the respondent have? The goal here is to link the non-political attitudes and behaviors to the political positions of the respondent, establishing a connection that can be generalized. One can then predict the probability that a respondent will head to the polls on Election Day, vote for the Democratic or Republican candidate, or support particular issue positions. Most importantly, the predictors could be a set of behaviors unconnected to politics—for example, people who shop at Target in preference to Wal-Mart tend to support greater investments in education; regular runners are more likely to support health-care reform and a single-payer system.

Step 2: Obtain the list of registered voters in the state. As noted above, these data are already available to campaigns who want a less precise form of targeting based only on party identification or turnout history. Ten to fifteen years ago, however, the parties tried to be the keepers of these large datasets, using them to help presidential candidates target across the fifty states. The Democrats under the direction of their party chairman, Howard Dean, created a voter file called Vote Builder that housed the voter registration records of over 150 million Americans. Dean's predecessor, Terry McAufflife, had invested resources in an earlier iteration known as Demzilla. The Republicans had their own voter list called the Voter Vault.

For both parties, however, maintaining the list proved unwieldy and too costly. Since 2002, the parties have been unable to raise large contributions called "soft money," so they were forced to maintain the voter databases with their regulated contributions. Moreover, campaign finance laws prevent the party committees from coordinating extensively with allied interest groups (like unions for Democrats or business associations for Republicans). As a consequence, Democrats after the 2004 elections helped to create a for-profit company called Catalist, and Republicans in 2011 formed a similar group, the DataTrust. (The Democrats still house their own file called the Voter Activation Network, and Republicans have worked to create DataTrust in a way that gives some power to Republican Party leaders in how the data are accessed.) Both companies act as holders of the data, which they update regularly, and candidates and other groups can purchase the data for a fee, without the added hassle of transforming the data into a workable and readable format.

Step 3: With the polling data and the list of registered voters in hand, the next step is to purchase the consumer histories of voters in files maintained by credit card companies. These are purchased from commercial marketing firms like Experian Americas and InfoUSA. If you have ever obtained your own credit report, you know that these vendors hold an extensive amount of data on what credit cards we have and how much debt we owe. Catalist and the DataTrust, along with others, purchase the information and merge it with the voter lists. This produces a large file with voters' party registration status and voter turnout history, along with information obtained from the consumer and marketing data.[4]

Step 4: Using the merged database and the links established in Step 1, create profiles of voters that might be the focus of a persuasion or mobilization target.

This is essentially a data-driven exercise in which you look for strong relationships that allow you to segment the electorate into useful categories. For example, if Social Security is a key issue for the campaign, the analysis might identify the types of voters who are most open to persuasion on a particular Social Security reform. The survey analysis is critical in this regard. For example, if the analysis of the survey data showed that subscribing to hunting and fishing magazines raised the probability of supporting cap-and-trade policies, one could identify the voters in the registration file with such magazine subscriptions. Or Democratic candidates might find Republicans most amenable to a specific policy appeal about education or the War on Terror. The "segments" produced will vary across elections and years, but in general the goal is the same: locate any voter who might be a persuadable. Additionally, locate disaffected partisans who need reassurance from their own candidate to stick with their party.

There are some important caveats, however. First, the consumer database is not a deterministic predictor of political behavior. Some data on voters' consumer patterns or organizational memberships might be outdated, for example. Moreover, all of this work is meant to label a voter as "probably" supporting a candidate or issue positions. A voter might be labeled as having a 70 percent chance of voting for the Republican or a 76 percent chance of opposing Obama's health care law. Thus, the goal with analysis is to improve the odds of finding and reaching voters with effective appeals, but you are not guaranteed of having success.

A second caveat is related, in that a lot of this work is time-consuming, and it certainly is not cost free. The voter registration list, which can usually be obtained from the party or the state elections office for a small fee or for free, has explicitly political information that might be sufficient, as noted above. In states that record party registration or primary election turnout, knowing whether a voter is a Democrat or Republican, and the number of elections he has voted in, might tell you all you want to know. In other words, a Republican might target a registered Democrat who did not vote in an election year where the nominee was considered too liberal. This might suggest a swing voter turned off by the behavior of his own party. Indeed, this particular—and more simple—approach is probably the more common one, as the increased gain in information useful for persuasion and mobilization from consumer-based microtargeting is still not known.

At the end of the day, the goal of microtargeting is to improve on targeting strategies of the past, with the understanding that persuadable Democrats can be located even in neighborhoods largely populated by strong Republicans. The analysis helps instruct whom to call on the phone, what to put in your mailed literature, and what types of appeals will work when knocking on doors. Sunshine Hillygus and Todd Shields looked for evidence of different policy appeals in the 2004 presidential election, and found considerable diversity. They argue that candidates can use certain issues—what they call "wedge" issues—to appeal to a certain segment of the opposing party. Perhaps a Republican is in favor of federally-funded stem cell research, in opposition to her party's stance; and she may hold this position in spite of supporting the party on most other issues. If a Democratic candidate can isolate Republicans who fit this profile—using the steps outlined above—he can send targeted mailings about his support for stem cell research, with the hopes of convincing the recipients to vote Democratic. Indeed, Hillygus and Shields found that "mail sent to persuadable voters [in 2004] was more likely to contain wedge issues than that received by the partisan base. . . . Persuadable voters—Independents and weak partisans—received the highest percentage of divisive-issue content."[5]

Such targeting, more broadly, can be seen as both good and bad. On the plus side, this is a process in which many voters are actively sought after and not assumed obvious supporters or opponents. This has the effect of encouraging campaigns to be more engaged with the voting electorate. Indeed, in recent years, political consultants have adopted a whole host of new strategies that put the emphasis back on direct contacts with voters—strategies inspired, in part, by research in political science—under the presumption that a direct connection is far more impactful than a massive and impersonal media blitz on television.[6]

Targeting Television Messages

The above discussion has focused on what campaigns are doing in their peer-to-peer contacts in the home, with mailed literature, and through phone calls. But targeting also occurs with television advertising, and such targeting can be enhanced with the kind of data noted above. There are, however, real limits to the level of precision that can come with targeting television buys. Because television targeting is a bit blunter—we know the "types" of people that watch certain program genres as opposed to individual viewing habits—we can term this type of targeting "macrotargeting."[7]

Indeed, macrotargeting is almost a requirement in contemporary politics, given the changes in Americans' viewing habits. Let's review the evidence step-by-step. First off, Americans are watching more television than ever before. Nielsen estimated that in 2009, the typical household watched television each day for over 8 hours and 20 minutes, and the average person watched just under 5 hours. These were the highest levels of television viewing since Nielsen began collecting data. Figure 8.1 shows these numbers by year for the available data back to 1950. In that year the typical household watched just over 4 hours and 30 minutes a day. To be sure, the advent of DVR as reflected in Nielsen's estimates since 2005 amplifies these numbers, but even when excluding the 2005–2009 period, the number of household viewing hours was still on the rise in recent decades.

Increased exposure to television, however, is important particularly in light of the declining viewing of political news on television. The logic here is simple. As cable diffused into almost every American home, viewing options diversified. This created the opportunity for people to choose explicitly non-political entertainment, and many have. One piece of evidence in this regard

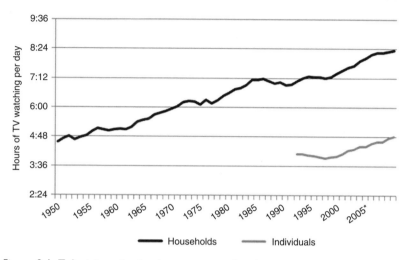

Figure 8.1 Television viewing hours are on the rise

Source: Nielsen Media Research.

Note: 2005–2009 includes live viewing plus 7-day playback on a DVR device.

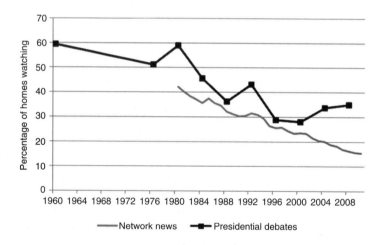

Figure 8.2 Viewing of news and debates declines

Source: Nielsen Media Research.

is the decline in viewership of national network news and presidential debates. The percentage of homes tuned into these sources of political information is shown in Figure 8.2.

In 1980, 40 percent of America homes watched the nightly national news on ABC, NBC, or CBS. There has been an almost unabated decline in these numbers; in 2010 only 15 percent of American homes watched the national news. This represents about 23 million people. (The 40 percent share in 1980 translates into over 52 million viewers.) Of course, some viewers in recent years have switched to cable news, but this explains only part of the lost audience for the network news, as the decline in viewing pre-dated the launch of Fox News and MSNBC in the mid-1990s. Moreover, the average number of Americans watching Fox, MSNBC and CNN on any night during primetime in 2011 was about 3.4 million total, not a particularly high number.[8]

The decline is reflected also in the number of homes that tune into presidential debates on the three major networks. An average of 60 percent of American homes watched the four Kennedy–Nixon debates in 1960. This represented about 28 million homes. In the highly contentious Gore–Bush contest in 2000, which featured three debates, about the same number of households tuned in, but this now represented—forty years later—only 28 percent of American households. Even viewership of the Obama–McCain debates in 2008 was lower than viewership of every other debate between 1960 and 1992.

These declines in the consumption of explicitly political information are reflected in more comprehensive analyses of Americans' exposure to news. In 2010, the Pew Research Center for the People and the Press published a report based on their extensive polling of Americans.[9] Their report showed a decline in consumption of local news broadcasts, radio, and print newspapers. For example, 56 percent of Americans reported reading a newspaper in 1991, but the percentage dropped to 31 percent in 2010. Fifty-four percent reported listening to the radio for news in 1991, but only 34 percent did so in 2010. Pew did report, however, a sharp increase in the number of Americans who get their news online, which has increased from 24 percent in 2002 to 34 percent in 2010. Forty-four percent reported getting news online or through a mobile device in 2010, the first year mobile-application use was asked about.

These trends have direct consequences for campaigns that have traditionally aired lots of ads on broadcast television stations. More viewing hours across a wider range of television programming has forced candidates to buy more ads in the hopes of reaching potential voters. Whereas ten years ago 100 ads on local news could reach a certain percentage of the electorate in the final week of the campaign, it might take 150 or 200 ads (or more) to reach that same threshold now. Viewers are simply harder to reach as they spread out across more television channels. Moreover, while viewing hours are higher than in years past, many people watching recorded television programs on a DVR are likely to skip past commercials, making the ad a wasted appeal.

This can be seen clearly with some comparable advertising data across the last ten years. Figure 8.3 plots pairs of states and media markets for Senate races between 2000 and 2010. Because Senate terms are six years, we can best compare advertising trends by looking at the average number of ads in a media

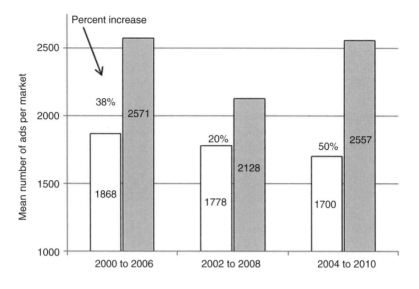

Figure 8.3 Ads by candidates in Senate races increase

Source: Wisconsin Advertising Project and Wesleyan Media Project.

market for Senate candidates in 2000 and 2006; 2002 and 2008; and 2004 and 2010. The figure shows paired markets for ads aired by candidates between September 1 and Election Day.[10] The results show increases in all three pairs of Senate elections. In 2000, for example, candidates aired an average 1,868 ads, but by 2006 the number of ads grew to 2,571—a 38 percent increase. The 2008 Senate campaigns saw a 20 percent increase in ads over 2002, and the 2010 Senate campaigns saw a 50 percent increase in ads over 2004.

All told, the evidence points to candidates airing more ads. This may seem counter-intuitive given the spread of the Internet and the potential to reach voters through social media. Indeed, these technological advances would seem to make buying ads on television less important. But consider again Figure 8.1. Television is a critical part of Americans' daily lives, now more than ever, and because viewership is so high, campaigns are able to reach many voters quickly. Of course, viewers' diffusion across a wide number of channels has forced candidates to invest even more in television ads. This is an incredibly important trend in American politics. As much as journalists and citizens talk about Twitter, Facebook, YouTube, and other social media platforms, television is still king.

Indeed, the move from broadcasting to narrowcasting[11]—that is, the increased viewing options for Americans—brings with it the challenge of a greater ad budget, but also the opportunity to target specific audiences. As noted above, the data on television viewing is not as precise as the voter targeting data that the parties own. For example, candidates do not know the viewing habits of specific voters like they know their consumer buying patterns. Nonetheless, there are powerful survey data that capture the viewing profile of either specific shows or program genres. Scarborough Research, for example, surveys over 100,000 Americans in election years, asking them which television programs they watch. The company can describe the viewers of over two dozen program types, ranging from soap operas to science fiction. This level of detail can tell a campaign quite a bit about the type of show to target if a particular type of viewer is the intended audience.

For example, Figure 8.4 plots the percentage of male respondents between the ages of 18 and 44 and female respondents over the age of 44 who reported regularly watching twenty-three different television genres in 2008. Indeed, the type of message that might appeal to younger men (say, for example, lower taxes) might be different than the type of message that might appeal to older women (i.e., investments in education). As might be expected, younger men were least likely to report watching daytime soap operas or talk shows, but these were the genres with the highest female viewing. Young men were much more likely to watch music videos, science fiction, and sports programming, all of which had considerably fewer older female viewers. Tailoring different ads to

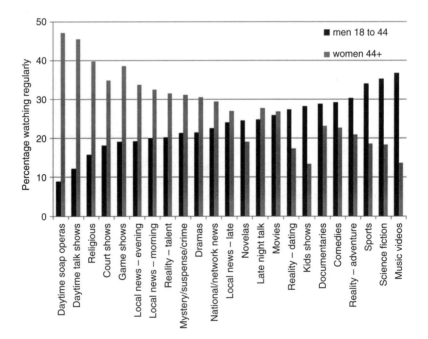

Figure 8.4 Different audiences watch different types of television

Source: Scarborough Research.

different genres of programming is a good way to reach varied audiences. And those tailored messages are consequently less likely to reach an audience not meant to see them.

Although the data shown in Figure 8.4 are intuitive, they nonetheless illustrate the potential usefulness of having data on television viewing patterns. Campaigns can learn, among other things, which programs Democrats tend to watch in disproportionate numbers over Republicans (such as daytime talk shows like Dr. Oz and court shows like Judge Judy). And across all of the genres asked about in the Scarborough data, Democrats watch more television than Republicans, a gap that diminishes on the weekends. This implies overall that Republicans will have a harder time finding television shows with large percentages of likeminded partisan viewers.

Indeed, this was an insight first noted by Bush advisors in the 2004 election.[12] Bush's team identified the times of day during which Republicans watched in greater numbers, along with the types of shows with a greater Republican audience. The survey data also reveal considerable variation across media markets and states, allowing campaigns to find shows with a particular audience in a particular state, at a cost far less than blanketing a battleground state with ads. To borrow a war metaphor, think of this strategy as one using smart bombs over carpet bombs. Moreover, Hillygus and Shields argue that "candidates [in 2004] focused on consensual policy issues when communicating with a broad-based audience in television ads, but were willing to make wedge appeals in narrowly targeted campaign messages [off the air]."[13] However, with a richer set of data on who is watching which shows, candidates are free to highlight wedge-issues on television as well.

Of course, these differences in the audiences for particular programs are not overwhelming—a lot of self-reported Democrats and Republicans show up in the audiences of all programs genres—and the genre categories themselves are often too broad (e.g., dramas, comedies, and movies) to be able to target very distinct audiences. Nonetheless, the Scarborough data also ask about a cross-section of specific shows (e.g., *How I Met Your Mother, CSI, The Office*), meaning candidates can work with the available data to establish a genre or program list that becomes the focus of a particular ad buy. And other surveys are available from different sources that can supplement these data or provide a finer grain of detail. Nielsen collects data on viewer characteristics, for example, and Lovett and Peress used data from the Simmons National Consumer Survey to estimate the partisanship of viewers of over 700 programs.[14]

The availability of data is quite empowering to campaigns who want to more efficiently allocate their advertising dollars. But as with microtargeting, these tactics are still somewhat new, and not all campaigns employ these macrotargeting techniques. Indeed, while presidential campaigns have moved to adopt such strategies, as noted with the Bush campaign in 2004 (and as will be described with more evidence below), congressional campaigns writ large have not yet embraced the strategy of precision targeting of political ads.

For one, despite the noted drops in political news consumption on television, it turns out that local news is still preferred by most Americans to other sources of news. In the same Pew Report from 2010 noted above, 58 percent of respondents reported watching news on television, and this percentage is higher than for all other forms of news consumption. While this percentage was down from 68 percent in 1991, campaigns still find it important to buy ads on local news broadcasts.

Moreover, the same Scarborough data reveal the benefits of advertising on local or national news broadcasts. According to the survey results, regular viewers of local and national news have a higher likelihood of turning out to vote in state and presidential elections than do viewers of most other genres. The only other genres with similar turnout numbers are documentaries, religious programs, dramas, mysteries, and sports, and the total viewing audience for many of these genres is considerably lower than for news programs.

Figure 8.5 plots the percentage of all ads aired on news broadcasts between 2000 and 2010. In total, these data categorize over 10 million ad airings in the last six election cycles. For congressional and gubernatorial races in this time period, just under 60 percent of all ads aired appeared on news programs (including local and national), and this percentage has not changed in any appreciable way in the last six elections. There is, indeed, remarkable consistency across years. On the other hand, the percentage of ads aired during news during the presidential campaign of 2000 was much higher (about 64 percent) than in subsequent elections, including the 2008 presidential race, in which just over 50 percent aired during news programming.[15]

In general, presidential, congressional, and gubernatorial candidates air an additional 15–18 percent of their total ads on talk shows (like *The Tonight Show* and *Jimmy Kimmel*) and on game shows, and these percentages have not changed much in the last six elections. (This is not shown on Figure 8.5.) As such, the drop in ads on news from presidential candidates is indicative of a broader ad-buying strategy than was evident in earlier elections. For example, presidential candidates in 2000 bought about 77 percent of all ads on news, games shows, and talk shows. This dropped to 69 percent in 2008. As candidates look elsewhere for a different type of audience, we should expect these investments in traditional programming to continue to drop in 2012 and beyond. That said, the movement toward macrotargeting is not yet evident in congressional and gubernatorial races.

It should be noted, however, that the data used here are imprecise. The over 10 million ads represented in Figure 8.5 are only those aired on broadcast stations in available media markets and on national cable stations. The numbers exclude ads aired on local cable (e.g., the Golf Channel on TimeWarner in Bangor, Maine), and there is some evidence that candidates are using these outlets more frequently. Exactly how much is almost impossible to know, however. The conventional wisdom says that of all political advertising on television, about 5–20 percent is currently bought on local cable channels, and these

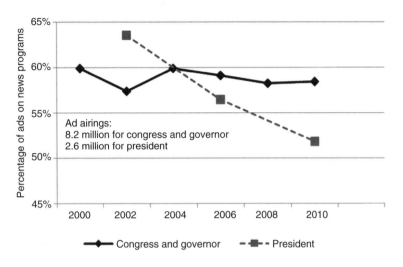

Figure 8.5 Ads on news less prevalent in presidential elections

Source: Wisconsin Advertising Project and Wesleyan Media Project.

percentages are likely to rise in coming years. Local cable is macrotargeting by its very definition, as candidates determine which niche-viewing audience to target in each media market. Because there are no available data to compare across campaigns, there is no way of assessing how Democrats or Republicans are targeting voters on local cable.

Still, the trends reported here at the presidential level point to real changes that are probably much more noticeable at the local cable level. Thus, the numbers reported in Figure 8.5 underestimate the amount of macrotargeting in American politics. It is likely that the lack of trend in the congressional setting means the targeting on local cable has not yet reached the level of presidential campaigns, but it is undoubtedly happening to some extent. And it will continue to accelerate. As campaign strategist Amy Gershkoff has noted:[16]

> [A] broadcast-only strategy no longer works effectively for most campaigns. In 1970, you could buy 1,000 gross rating points per week and reach the average voter 10 times and you could reach 90 percent of voters this way. Today, in some states, if you're up on broadcast TV, your 1,000 points per week might reach less than 40 percent of voters . . . So what's the solution? We have to start thinking about media strategy in a new way. We can't continue to make broadcast TV the centerpiece of campaigns' paid media strategy, have cable TV be the oddball cousin of paid media strategy and treat Web videos as the weird kid at family reunions who sits in the corner and eats paste . . .[17]

In future election cycles, many campaigns will take to heart Gershkoff's message, and we will see the spread of modern ad-targeting strategies, up and down the ticket, fundamentally transforming the way campaigns reach voters.

Discussion

The movement in campaigns towards more precise targeting of voters—whether on television, online, or through peer-to-peer contacts—is seen most often as a triumph of data and a move towards greater efficiency in the allocation of resources. The additional use of Facebook and Twitter to reach voters of a very specific profile—what some call "nano-targeting"—is another development in this direction. Anyone who watches shows on Hulu or the networks' websites will be familiar with the kind of targeting that can happen online; more and more, campaigns are buying ads that appear at the beginning of these videos, though what types of candidate ads we see (those favoring Republicans or Democrats) depends on what we do online. And banner ads appear at the top or on the side of web pages a lot more in recent elections, though the candidates we see in such ads depend, in part, on whether the algorithms think we are liberal or conservative. The use of these techniques is very much a part of what candidates in the 2012 presidential election are doing to find and appeal to voters.[18]

Campaigns in contemporary elections can achieve a lot of precision with fewer resources and can "waste" fewer contacts on voters who will never, under any circumstances, vote for that candidate. One additional appeal of macro-targeting with television ads is more bang for fewer bucks.[19] Advocates of precise local cable buys point specifically to the cost savings over a set number of advertisements on local broadcast shows, though this is not a given in all media markets.

And yet, with all of these advantages for campaigns, there are some important caveats that should inspire some pause. First, microtargeting, and to a lesser extent macrotargeting, has the potential to reinforce voter polarization. The conventional wisdom is that American voters are as polarized politically as the politicians in Washington, but the truth is more complicated. On the one hand, a lot of Americans take middle-of-the-road positions on contentious issues of the day.[20] On the other hand, while self-identified independents make up over 35 percent of the electorate, the vast majority of these voters leans in a liberal or conservative direction and act politically in line with that lean. As such, the percentage of "true" independents is usually less than 10 percent of the electorate.[21] As voters are explicitly targeted based on their political profile, Republicans and Democrats can move potentially farther apart on issues, especially in the absence of a counter-narrative by the other side.

This is largely the story as told by Markus Prior in his book *Post-Broadcast Democracy*.[22] As television channels have spread, and options for entertainment diversified, the less politically engaged encountered less news programming than in years when there were only three television stations. As these citizens encounter politics less often (with their interest in and knowledge of politics declining even more), candidates can more freely ignore them in their contacts. Hillygus and Shields put it this way: "More than ever before, presidential candidates can now ignore large portions of the public—nonvoters, those committed to the opposition, and those living in uncompetitive states."[23] Moreover, engaged partisans can now easily self-select to news shows and commentary that match their political preferences, and campaigns can ignore committed opposition partisans completely. The result is a greater likelihood of either being ignored by both sides or being deemed as not worthy of contacting by one side.

John Zaller notes additionally that campaigns, especially presidential election campaigns, are often balanced efforts with Democratic and Republican candidates spending similar amounts. The presumption here is that voters are exposed to ads from both sides and therefore the impact of a candidate's ads might be small.[24] As candidates more finely target their campaign appeals, though, the overall balance of appeals may be the same (i.e., 2,000 ads aired in a market from both candidates in a race), but who sees those ads is imbalanced, with Republican voters and conservative-leaning Independents seeing only Republican-sponsored ads and Democrats and liberal-leaning Independents seeing only Democratic-sponsored ads. Because imbalances in messaging can move voters in the direction of the imbalance, macrotargeting can have the impact of pulling different voters in opposite directions.

Of course, the evangelists of micro-targeting would argue that it might reduce polarization, as disaffected partisans can be found by campaigns and targeted for persuasion. It should be noted also that if a campaign does not microtarget using consumer data and relies only on party registration and turnout in a state's voter file, it is not possible to know whether a voter is a disaffected partisan or an independent that leans left or right. This can have the effect of increasing the odds that many voters are seen as "in play" by both candidates. On the other hand, the 2008 election generated turnout of only 62 percent of the eligible voters, implying that whole swaths of the electorate simply do not care about elections (or have time to vote), and these are the types of voters who might be left out of the discussion in an electoral environment where microtargeting is on the rise.

Second, and related, microtargeting and macrotargeting can expose voters to different issue appeals, and this can lead voters to have divergent senses of what the campaign is about. One of the virtues of so much advertising on local news is that voters of all stripes get a similar set of appeals from the candidates in a race. If a Democrat airs an ad about health care on local news, Republicans and Independents see the ad also. As such, voters across the political spectrum can correctly perceive campaigns' issue agendas. Some research even demonstrates that Republicans and Democrats often talk about the same set of issues, especially in competitive elections.[25] Additional scholarship notes that candidates often act legislatively in line with what they advertised about in a campaign. That is, candidates who talked a lot of Social Security in their ads make that issue more of a priority when in office. This is seen as good from a democratic perspective—campaigning and policy-making are linked.[26]

With targeted appeals, however, a candidate can focus on selling different issues to different audiences. Republican candidates can prime social and moral issues when contacting households that have been identified as devoutly religious, or when advertising on shows with an audience that attends church. The same candidate can then advertise on economic issues—and with a less polarizing message—when reaching out to moderates and swing voters. This has lots of virtues in terms of the efficient allocation of messages, but it also comes with concerns. Can candidates be different incarnations to different blocs of voters? What if we factor in the role played by interest groups, particularly Super PACs? Can allied groups or party advertising emphasize one message to one audience, while the candidate focuses her efforts on other voters and with a different set of appeals? Does this have the potential to skew what voters think a candidate or campaign was about? In light of this, the outcome of an election can mean different things to different voters. How do candidates understand their victory, then? Might this complicate the ability of candidates to act on the perceived mandate of electoral success?

Finally, there are concerns about privacy. Campaigns are using the data from credit card companies to sort voters into different profiles, and nothing about this is illegal. But how would voters feel knowing that candidates have access to their purchasing history? We expect this at grocery stores and department stores—even if we do not like it—but are voters aware of the level of personal detail held by the candidates? What do the volunteers who knock on doors know about the people they are contacting—their magazine subscriptions, coffee preferences, favorite type of underwear? It is unlikely that this level of detail is loaded onto any iPad volunteers carry around while knocking on doors, of course, but if the data crunchers in a campaign identify a link between a particular consumer pattern and political behavior in a state, you can be sure that this will enter into the contacting decisions of candidates. In a world where Americans are concerned more than ever about privacy and the protection of personal information—what with the rise in identity theft—the fact that politicians and campaign consultants can purchase such personal information about voters might give some people cause for concern.

Consider the strategy of President Obama in his re-election campaign. His campaign team in 2012 pushed supporters accessing the candidate's website for volunteer opportunities or donations to log on using their Facebook username and password. This allowed the campaign, subject to a clickable approval by the Obama supporter, to access one's personal Facebook profile, including birth date, likes/dislikes, and list of friends. Such information was used to help target supporters with specific appeals.

Conclusion

All told, campaigns are moving to take stronger advantage of any and all available data in the pursuit of electoral victory. Many now use lists of voter files appended with personal information to establish a link between what voters buy, or where they contribute money and how they act politically. Candidates then use that information to target voters in commensurate ways. That is, this sophisticated data mining instructs whom campaigns contact and what they say. This is a long way from the campaigns of 20 to 30 years ago, where door knocks or voter contacts were limited to the counties or precincts in which the party had done well in the past.

This sophisticated use of data has moved, in part, to the world of political advertising. We have only suggestive data on this, but it is instructive. As television transforms in the future, with further integration with the Internet, and with greater diffusion of satellite television, candidates will find many opportunities to target more precisely over the airwaves. Indeed, one goal is to obtain cable subscriptions and merge them with voter files, allowing candidates and allied groups to buy local cable spots that are targeted to specific households. The ability to target local cable at the neighborhood level is now possible, but an even finer grain of detail would enhance the efficiency of such ad buys.

And while precision targeting is efficient and perhaps more effective, it does come with certain question marks and concerns. Most of these concerns are normative, or need testing with data, but they are things to look for in future cycles. Does targeting for purposes of mobilizing one's base mean that core Democrats and Republicans lose the opportunity to see ads or hear from candidates of the other side? In the old days, the campaigns broadly targeted and voters saw the efforts of both sides. Even if a voter was never going to vote for a Democrat or Republican, he or she was quite familiar with the content of that candidate's ads and campaign appeals.

Moreover, in a world of microtargeting, can campaigns look differently to different sets of voters? Might the targeting of core supporters merely reinforce the self-selection that happens now in the use of partisan media such as MSNBC or Fox News? And what becomes of the chronic non-voters? They are currently exposed to some campaign messages incidentally when they tune into local news for weather or sports. If campaigns, for reasons of efficient allocation of resources, learn how to ignore non-voters, might this simply reinforce those citizens' sense of disengagement with politics? What will draw them in?

A lot of these concerns might not strike people as worrisome—who cares about non-voters?—but they are worth thinking about and discussing. What are the long-term implications of all of this leveraging of data? As with all changes in technology, the benefits are clear and the advocates are loud. Campaigns are looking to become sleeker and more sophisticated. The ultimate goal is 50 percent of the vote plus 1 voter. There is nothing high and mighty about what a political campaign hopes to accomplish, at least not to the political consultants who value microtargeting. The "public good" component of democracy is more clearly felt at the level of policy-making. Candidates must first win before they can try to change policies to help people. All of this is true. And yet there is nothing wrong with a bit of skepticism here. A lot of good can come from serious conversation about the potential drawbacks of this new era of campaign ad targeting.

Notes

1 John Sides and Jake Haselswerdt, "Campaigns and Elections," in *New Directions in Public Opinion*, ed. Adam Berinsky (New York: Routledge, 2012), 241–257.
2 Bill Bishop, *The Big Sort: Why the Clustering of Like-Minded America Is Tearing Us Apart* (New York: Houghton Mifflin Harcourt, 2008).
3 Wendy Tam-Cho, James Gimpel and Iris Hui, "Voter Migration and the Geographic Sorting of the American Electorate," Working Paper.
4 One challenge for the data crunchers in this step is correctly merging the two files. Voters often have different spellings of names (i.e., Matt or Matthew) and as voters move, even within state, it might be hard to correctly link the files. Imagine a Bill Smith in Boston. There are lots of people with this name, and it takes considerable work to pair the voter registration information with the correct consumer. One approach is match on name and variations of name, along with birthdate.
5 D. Sunshine Hillygus and Todd Shields, *The Persuadable Voter: Wedge Issues in Presidential Campaigns* (Princeton: Princeton University Press, 2008), 175.
6 Alan Gerber and Donald Green, "The Effects of Canvassing, Telephone Calls, and Direct Mail on Voter Turnout: A Field Experiment," *American Political Science Review* 94 (2000): 653–663.
7 Travis Ridout, Michael Franz, Kenneth Goldstein and Will Feltus, "Microtargeting Through Political Advertising," *Political Communication* 29 (2012): 1–23.
8 This figure comes from the same source as the data in Figure 2.
9 The numbers reported for this report are from Pew Research Center, "Americans Spending More Time Following the News," September 12, 2010, accessed March 15, 2012, www.people-press.org/files/legacy-pdf/652.pdf .
10 The graph excludes party and interest group advertising. This may be something to control for if we want a direct comparison across years, and if we think that greater group or party spending would decrease candidate advertising. Interest groups and parties were more aggressive in 2008 and 2010, and so the noted increase in candidate ads that year actually understates the amount of increase across markets.
11 These are terms used to explain the move from three major channels on broadcast networks to the literally hundreds or thousands on cable. See Martin Wattenberg, *Where Have All the Voters Gone?* (Cambridge: Harvard University Press, 2002), 90–91.
12 Douglas Sosnik, Matthew Dowd and Ron Fournier, *Applebee's America: How Successful Political, Business, and Religious Leaders Connect with the New American Community* (New York: Simon and Schuster, 2006), 45–51.
13 Hillygus and Shields, *Persuadable Voter*, 169.
14 Mitchell J. Lovett and Michael Peress, "Targeting Political Advertising on Television," unpublished manuscript (Rochester, NY: University of Rochester, 2010).
15 All of the plotted values in this figure include primary and general election ads.
16 For the quote below, GRPs are a measure of the size of the audience for a television program. One rating point, on average, is equal to 1 percent of the television

household audience in a particular media market. For example, if an ad were aired 40 times, each with an average 10-point rating, that ad would achieve a total 400 GRPs.

17 Amy Gershkoff, "Memo to Democratic Campaign Managers: Times are a'Changin' and So Should Your Paid Media Strategy," *Roll Call*, June 8, 2010, accessed March 29, 2012, http://thehill.com/opinion/op-ed/102023-memo-to-democratic-campaign-managers-times-are-achangin-and-so-should-your-paid-media-strategy-

18 Jeremy Peters, "As TV Viewing Habits Change, Political Ads Follow Would-Be Voters Online," *New York Times*, April 2, 2012, A10

19 Thomas Heath, "Value Added: A Political Junkie's Foray Into the Ad Wars," *Washington Post*, August 24, 2009, accessed March 9, 2012, www.washingtonpost.com/wp-dyn/content/article/2009/08/23/AR2009082302445.html.

20 Morris Fiorina, with Samual Abrams and Jeremy Pope, *Culture War? The Myth of a Polarized America*, 3rd ed. (New York: Longman, 2011)

21 Indeed, in recent elections, partisan-based voting by the electorate is up; presidential coattails are stronger in recent years; and the incumbency effect is lower than in previous years. All of this suggests that voters are not as independent as is commonly assumed. Still, they may be persuadable by the opposing party through wedge appeals, and some research demonstrates that Republicans and Democrats do respond to even television ads from the opposing party. See Travis Ridout and Michael Franz, *The Persuasive Power of Campaign Advertising* (Philadelphia: Temple University Press, 2011).

22 Markus Prior, *Post-Broadcast Democracy: How Media Choices Increase Inequality in Political Involvement and Polarizes Elections* (Cambridge: Cambridge University Press, 2007).

23 Hillygus and Shields, *Persuadable Voter.*

24 John Zaller, "The Myth of Massive Media Impact Revisited," in *Political Persuasion and Attitude Change*, ed. Diana C. Mutz, Paul M. Sniderman, and Richard A. Brody (Ann Arbor: University of Michigan Press, 1996), 17–78.

25 Noah Kaplan, David K. Park and Travis N. Ridout, "Dialogue in American Political Campaigns? An Examination of Issue Engagement in Candidate Television Advertising," *American Journal of Political Science* 50 (2006): 724–736.

26 Tracy Sulkin, *The Legislative Legacy of Congressional Campaigns (Cambridge:* Cambridge University Press, 2011).

Chapter 9

Do the Media Give Women Candidates a Fair Shake?[1]

Regina G. Lawrence

When Hillary Rodham Clinton lost the race for the Democratic presidential nomination to Barack Obama in 2008, many observers were quick to blame media bias and sexism for her loss. The Women's Media Center decried the "pervasive . . . sexism in the media's coverage" of Clinton's campaign and mounted an online petition campaign, urging television viewers to "call on the national broadcast news outlets (CNN, FNC, MSNBC and NBC) to stop treating women as a joke; to stop using inherently gendered language as an insult or criticism; and to ensure that women's voices are present and accounted for in the national political dialogue." The National Organization of Women assembled an online "Media Hall of Shame," a video collection of "the most outrageous moments of sexism from mainstream media's coverage of the 2008 elections," accompanied by a "Misogyny Meter" so viewers could rate each one. The treatment of Clinton on cable news in particular ignited controversy. Most memorably, perhaps, critics decried MSNBC's Chris Matthews claim just after Clinton won the New Hampshire primary that "the reason she may be a front-runner, is her husband messed around" (a reference to her husband's infamous sexual relationship with intern Monica Lewinsky in the 1990s). Matthews later apologized on air for this comment after women's groups organized a letter-writing protest, though he also told the *New York Times* that "I was tonally inaccurate but factually true."[2]

There seems little doubt that Clinton was treated differently than her main competitors in certain respects, particularly on cable news and numerous Internet sites that do not color inside the lines of standard journalistic objectivity.[3] But a careful examination of Hillary Clinton's experience in 2008 sheds a more complex light on the question of how the media cover female candidates for elected office.[4] Indeed, Clinton received, by some measures, fairer treatment in the mainstream press than previous research might have predicted.[5] For example, she received as much or more coverage in leading newspapers and on national evening broadcast news shows than did her male rivals across most months of the nominating contest; previous research, based upon previous (and short-lived) female presidential campaigns, would have predicted that Clinton's campaign would receive short shrift. (That she didn't, reflects both her own considerable name recognition and resources heading into the 2008 election, as well as the pitched contest that ensued between her and then-Senator Barack Obama.)

Beyond the context of that particular campaign, accumulating research reviewed below suggests that while the presidency presents a particularly tough environment for women candidates, media coverage of races for other offices is becoming less skewed against them. In fact, the answer to the question of whether the media give women candidates a fair shake appears to have two parts: "It depends," and "More so today than in the past." That is, the answer depends on which women we are talking about—and the offices for which they are running. But overall, recent research indicates that compared to their predecessors, today's women candidates can expect a fairer (if not a completely fair) shake.

In order to understand this answer, and indeed to think clearly about the question, we need to review:

1   What it means for the media to give candidates "a fair shake."
2   The unique hurdles that women candidates may face in terms of public attitudes and gender stereotypes.
3   What the research suggests about how the media have covered women candidates, and how that coverage appears to be changing.

A Fair Shake: Media Bias and Sexism

A starting point toward defining fairness in media coverage of women running for office is to recognize that "negative" coverage is distinguishable from "sexist" coverage. *Negative* coverage criticizes the candidate or paints her character, her policy positions, or her campaign tactics in an unflattering light.[6] Negative coverage of female candidates that treats them in the same terms and by the same standards as male candidates is not sexist. For example, virtually every serious presidential candidate, particularly the "frontrunners," come in for close media scrutiny of their electoral tactics and strategies, of their personal histories, and of their stated policy positions. Media coverage that subjected Hillary Clinton to this same scrutiny was not necessarily sexist.

Sexist coverage explicitly or implicitly devalues female politicians (and women in general) in comparison to their male counterparts.[7] Sexist coverage can be documented, for example, through a pattern of giving female candidates less coverage than their male opponents, reflecting or implying the presumption that their candidacies are less serious than men's. A study by Kim Kahn found that across a number of races for the Senate, contests that included a woman candidate received less coverage than all-male contests—a difference not attributable to the size of the state or the competitiveness of the race.[8] Sexist coverage can also manifest qualitatively, as when women candidates are criticized with terms alluding to sex and sexuality in ways that are not applied to men.

While outright sexism may be less common in the mainstream media than in the past, more subtle and pernicious is the *gendering* of news, in which stereotypes about male and female attributes shape the content and tone of media coverage.[9] Gendering can be difficult to analyze rigorously because it often involves a perceived or implicit subtext. Given that prevailing gender stereotypes still associate women with traits like empathy, compromise, emotionalism and weakness, gendered media coverage is not helpful to women seeking power—particularly in American presidential politics, with its usual focus on "manly men, doing manly things, in manly ways."[10]

Why Media Coverage Matters for Women

Research has established the importance of news coverage to the success of women's bids for office.[11] Though it is clear that the media are not the lone determinant of election outcomes, evidence clearly indicates that "campaigns serve to activate predispositions and affect how citizens judge candidates,"[12] particularly for voters who lack strong party and issue attachments.

Gender clearly is not an insurmountable barrier to winning office, though gender-related barriers clearly still remain. Evidence of gender bias in electoral politics is offset to some degree by substantial support for women's candidacies in a growing number of electoral contests.[13] The 2008 and 2010 election cycles saw relatively large numbers of women candidates, though overall numbers of women in national-level office stalled, and the 2012 election cycle may see a decrease in national women office-holders. As of early 2012, women held only 17 percent of the seats in Congress and only 22 percent of all statewide elective executive offices.[14]

One explanation for the continuing gender gap in politics is that enduring gendered attitudes pose barriers to women candidates. Women and politics' scholars have argued that the unwritten requirements for holding political office are largely defined in masculine terms.[15] Deeply rooted gender stereotypes hold men as more assertive, decisive, and able to handle crisis[16]—in other words, more leader-like. Similarly, the public often associates women with particular competence in "compassion" issues such as health care, welfare, and education, rather than with more "masculine" issue competencies.[17]

Because women candidates may face greater challenges in establishing their "qualifications" for office,[18] media attention can be particularly pernicious for women candidates when it focuses on candidates' personal traits and/or de-emphasizes their substantive qualifications for office.[19] For example, in the same study described above, Kahn found significantly more paragraphs per day in newspaper coverage of Senate races about male candidates' issue positions than those of female candidates.[20] Similarly, in her study of female presidential candidates throughout American history, Erica Falk found on average 16 percent of paragraphs focused on substantive policy issues in conjunction with women candidates, versus almost twice as many (27 percent) for male candidates.[21] A study of media coverage of Elizabeth Dole's short-lived presidential campaign in 2000 found that while she received more coverage than some of her opponents for the Republican nomination, less coverage focused on issues and more on Dole's personality traits.[22] The same study also found that Dole was directly quoted less often and paraphrased more often than her (male) opponents, a finding echoed in Lawrence and Rose's study of media coverage of Hillary Clinton's presidential campaign.[23] Indeed, Falk's study of women presidential candidates throughout U.S. history finds that "the extra issue coverage garnered by men is mostly converted to character coverage for the women."[24]

Other research has found that women candidates receive more mentions of their personal lives, including their children and marital status. Research is mixed on the question of whether women candidates receive more coverage of their physical appearance, with some finding no significant differences,[25] and others finding more numerous references to their physical attributes.[26]

Developments in Recent Research

So far, this review of research on media coverage of women candidates paints a rather unpromising picture. Indeed, the accumulated evidence of sexist and gendered news—coverage that assumes that women candidates are less newsworthy than men, and that what is most interesting and newsworthy about them is their personal lives and attributes, not their policy issues or substantive qualifications—strongly indicates that women often face a more challenging path to office than men. But recently, research has begun to show some improvements in coverage of women candidates. Bystrom's recent assessment finds that the volume and tone of news about men and women candidates seems to be getting more equitable over time. (She also finds, however, that as recently as 2002 and 2004, women's personal traits garnered more coverage than those of male candidates).[27] And, as the opening paragraphs above explain, media coverage of Hillary Clinton's high-profile presidential campaign overcame at least some obstacles previous female presidential hopefuls had faced.

Along with those apparent real-world improvements has come research exploring new questions, and re-examining seemingly settled questions in new ways. In their recent study of electoral outcomes for women candidates, women and politics scholars Linda Fowler and Jennifer Lawless note the "theoretical and empirical challenges created by the interaction of gender, media, context, and electoral institutions." The landscape in which women compete for office is a complex one, and Fowler and Lawless cite an "emerging consensus" among scholars that "greater focus on the political context is likely to produce bigger scholarly payoffs than is continued attention to observable differences between male and female candidates."[28] In other words, in an era when women are becoming more successful at winning office, the research agenda can expand to consider more nuanced questions about when they are more likely to be successful.

For example, recent studies suggest some key contextual factors that affect the kind of news coverage women candidates receive. Those key variables include the type of office women seek, the party they represent, and whether they are incumbents or challengers, as well as the issues they emphasize in their campaigns and the gender of the opponents they face off against.

The type and level of office women candidates seek may be an important variable because of the phenomenon of "gender-office congruency."[29] The "resonance" model of voting holds that women candidates are generally perceived as more credible on issues stereotypically associated with women's competence in caring, and predicts that women candidates will fare best when they stick to these "compassion" issues rather than venturing into the "male" turf of national security, crime, and economics.[30]

This prior research raises fascinating questions concerning whether this issue advantage operates for some offices more than for others. For example, according to the logic of that literature, governorships should be more attainable for women because state executive offices are generally associated with domestic issues such as education and health care—issues at which women are stereotypically thought to be competent.[31] Yet similar logic suggests, to the contrary, that governorships and other executive offices—particularly the presidency—may be more challenging for women to attain because they are associated in the public's mind with leadership traits more readily attributed to men.[32]

These questions about gender-office congruency in turn raise important questions about media coverage of campaigns that feature female candidates. Put simply, do news outlets pay more attention to women's personality traits (which may put them at a disadvantage for executive offices) or to their issue stands (which may benefit them, depending on the congruence between the office they seek and the issues associated with that office)? Research on that question is in its early stages,[33] and the implications are interesting: If women candidates can benefit from gender-office congruency, then media coverage of their personal traits is potentially *beneficial* if the coverage emphasizes traits the public associates favorably with their gender and the office they seek. Coverage of women's personal traits may therefore not automatically be "bad" for them electorally. By the same token, coverage of issues is not necessarily "good" for a female candidate's chances if the issues covered are associated in the public's mind with stereotypical male competencies—or are not seen as crucial issues to be handled by the office sought. In other words, if the media emphasize counter-stereotypical information, that may condition the influence of gender stereotypes in voter choice.

Another question being pursued in current research is whether incumbency lowers levels of gendered coverage. Consider the example of Dianne Feinstein, the senior Senator from California. Because she has served in the Senate for many years and has an established foreign policy record due to her long service on the Senate Foreign Relations Committee, we would not expect her to be particularly disadvantaged regarding the traditionally male topic of foreign relations—in contrast to challenger and first-term candidates. Levels of electoral competition—how close the voting margins are between candidates—also may affect news coverage of women's campaigns. High competition leads to a higher overall volume of election news and to more horserace coverage and less issue coverage,[34] while increasing the divergence between issues the candidates emphasize and the issues the media emphasize.[35] With regard to gender, these findings suggest that highly competitive races, ironically, may decrease female candidates' ability to get the press to focus on the issues they want to emphasize.

Finally, recent research suggests overlaps of gender with party.[36] Democrats are generally associated with particular traits, such as empathy and compassion, and issues, such as healthcare and education, which overlap with women's stereotypical traits and competencies; Republicans are associated with defense, crime, and economics, all policy areas more readily associated with men.[37] These overlapping considerations may create particular challenges for women of either party. For example, it is possible that because typical Republican issues are not generally seen as "women's" issues, female Republican candidates might not campaign on these issues to avoid sending mixed signals to voters[38]—also creating the possibility for less convergence between the candidate's messaging and the news media's coverage.

The Verdict: Changing Quantity, Changing Quality?

So, overall, opportunities for women in electoral politics have expanded, though clear challenges remain. And as the political landscape for female politicians has evolved, research has evolved as well. Meanwhile, there is much we don't know about how the rapidly changing media landscape is affecting women's bids for office. Note that all of the numerous studies cited above focus on the traditional media (newspapers and television).

Far less is known about how digital and social media may affect women's electoral chances. As one recent paper by journalist Alexis Gelber notes, "there is little research on the political impact of social networking, particularly related to gender."[39] Gelber's paper also offers two hypotheses worth testing. First, she contends, "social networking favors outsiders and newcomers to politics, so it can be an asset for women candidates and activists." Not only do social media allow women to invent or reinvent themselves (as, she argues, both Hillary Clinton and Sarah Palin did after suffering defeat in 2008), a gender advantage online may develop for women candidates because of the emerging majority of women who are active online.[40] Gelber's study concludes that Senate races that involved at least one woman candidate show a positive correlation between the number of a woman politician's female Facebook fans and her electability" (2011, 24). But Gelber also hypothesizes that given the often mean-spirited and divisive rhetoric of online communications, social media can be a mixed blessing for female politicians.

Research on how blogs "cover" (to the degree that term applies) the candidacies of women is also quite limited. Bradley and Wicks examined blog coverage of Sarah Palin's 2008 vice-presidential run, finding that "the blogs did not play to particular gender stereotypes concerning issue coverage, as Palin and Biden received comparable amounts of attention focusing on issue stance."[41] Yet the authors also note that their findings cannot necessarily be generalized to other candidates because Palin's candidacy and persona were in many ways anomalous.

Thus, the answer to whether the media give women candidates a fair shake is somewhat unsettled, and the research agenda for the next generation is evolving. It is safe to say that women are getting a fairer shake than they did in the past. Even in the near term, it is intriguing to imagine that the next women candidate to come within striking distance of the White House may not face the same terrain faced by Hillary Clinton in 2008. The task for future research is to expand the research agenda beyond simplistic binaries (male versus female) and traditional arenas (newspapers and network television) and to better describe the conditions under which women can compete fully as equals with men. In a "post-feminist" era[42] of shifting gender presentations conveyed through numerous social and traditional media, the landscape of constraints and opportunities for women candidates is not yet clearly charted.

Notes

1 The author wishes to thank Johanna Dunaway and Melody Rose for their valuable insights into this subject.
2 Regina G. Lawrence and Melody Rose, *Hillary Clinton's Race for the White House: Gender Politics and the Media on the Campaign Trail* (Boulder, CO: Lynne Reinner Publishers, 2009).
3 Kathleen Hall Jamieson and Jacqueline Dunn, "The 'B' Word in Traditional News and on the Web," *Nieman Reports*, Summer 2008; Lawrence and Rose 2009, chapter 6.
4 I use the terms "female" and "women" more or less interchangeably.
5 Lawrence and Rose, 2009, chapter 5.
6 See for example Stephen J. Farnsworth and S. Robert Lichter, *The Nightly News Nightmare: Television's Coverage of U.S. Presidential Elections, 1988–2004,* 2nd ed. (Lanham, MD: Rowman & Littlefield, 2008), 118.
7 Erika Falk, *Women for President: Media Bias in Eight Campaigns,* 2nd ed. (Urbana, IL: University of Illinois Press, 2010), 155.
8 Kim Fridkin Kahn, *The Political Consequences of Being a Woman: How Stereotypes Influence the Conduct and Consequences of Political Campaigns* (New York: Columbia University Press, 1996).
9 Falk, *Women for President*, 155–156; Elisabeth Gidengil and Joanna Everitt, "Talking Tough: Gender and Reported Speech in Campaign News Coverage," *Political Communication* 20 (2003): 209–232.
10 Georgia Duerst-Lahti, "Masculinity on the Campaign Trail," in *Rethinking Madam President: Are We Ready for a Woman in the White House,* ed. Lori Cox Han and Caroline Heldman (Boulder, CO: Lynne Rienner Publishers, 2007), 87.
11 Dianne G. Bystrom, Terry A. Robertson and Mary Christine Banwart, "Framing the Fight: An Analysis of Media Coverage of Female and Male Candidates in Primary

Races for Governor and US Senate in 2000," *American Behavioral Scientist* 44 (2001): 1999–2012; Kahn, *Political Consequences.*

12 Brian F. Schaffner, "Priming Gender: Campaigning on Women's Issues in U.S. Senate Elections," *American Journal of Political Science* 49 (2005), 805; James N. Druckman, "Media Matter: How Newspapers and Television News Cover Campaigns and Influence Voters," *Political Communication* 22 (2005): 463–481.

13 Barbara C. Burrell, *A Woman's Place is in the House: Campaigning for Congress in the Feminist Era* (Ann Arbor: University of Michigan Press, 1994); Kathleen A. Dolan, *Voting for Women: How the Public Evaluates Women Candidates* (Boulder: Westview Press, 2004); Richard L. Fox, "Congressional Elections: Where Are We on the Road to Gender Parity?" in *Gender and Elections: Shaping the Future of American Politics,* ed. Susan Carroll and Richard Fox. (New York: Cambridge University Press, 2006), 97–116; Kira Sanbonmatsu, *Where Women Run: Gender and Party in the American States* (Ann Arbor: University of Michigan Press, 2006).

14 "Facts on Women Officeholders, Candidates and Voters," Center for American Women in Politics, accessed April 10, 2012, http://www.cawp.rutgers.edu/fast_facts/index.php.

15 Virginia Sapiro, "If U.S. Senator Baker Were a Woman: An Experimental Study of Candidate Images," *Political Psychology* 3 (1982): 61–83; Kira Sanbonmatsu, "Gender Stereotypes and Vote Choice," *American Journal of Political Science* 46 (2002): 20–34; Leonie Huddy and Nayda Terkildsen, "Gender Stereotypes and the Perception of Male and Female Candidates," *American Journal of Political Science* 37 (1993): 119–147.

16 Kathleen A. Dolan, "Is There a 'Gender Affinity Effect' in American Politics?" *Political Research Quarterly* 61 (2008): 79–89.

17 Dianne G. Bystrom, Mary Christine Banwart, Lynda Lee Kaid, and Terry A. Robertson. *Gender and Candidate Communication: VideoStyle, WebStyle, and NewsStyle.* (New York: Routledge, 2004); Kahn, *Political Consequences.*

18 Deborah Alexander and Kristi Andersen, "Gender as a Factor in the Attribution of Leadership Traits," *Political Research Quarterly* 46 (1993): 527–545.

19 Sean Aday and James Devitt, "Style over Substance: Newspaper Coverage of Elizabeth Dole's Presidential Bid," *Harvard International Journal of Press and Politics* 6 (2001): 52–73; Gina Serignese Woodall and Kim L. Fridkin, "Shaping Women's Chances: Stereotypes and the Media," in *Anticipating Madam President,* ed. Robert P. Watson and Ann Gordon (Boulder, CO: Lynne Rienner Publishers, 2003), 69–86.

20 Kahn, *Political Consequences,* 50–51.

21 Falk, *Women for President,* 119.

22 Aday and Devitt, "Style Over Substance"; Woodall and Fridkin, "Shaping Women's Chances," 77.

23 Lawrence and Rose, *Hillary Clinton's Run for the White House.*

24 Falk, *Women for President,* 133.

25 Bystrom et al., "Framing the Fight"; Lawrence and Rose, *Hillary Clinton's Race for the White House.*

26 Aday and Devitt, "Style Over Substance"; James Devitt, "Framing Gender on the Campaign Trail: Female Gubernatorial Candidates and the Press," *Journalism and Mass Communication Quarterly* 79 (2002): 445–463; Diane Heith, "The Lipstick Watch: Media Coverage, Gender, and Presidential Campaigns," in *Anticipating Madam President,* ed. Robert P. Watson and Ann Gordon (Boulder: Lynne Rienner Publishers, 2003), 123–130; Caroline Heldman, Susan Carroll, and Stephanie Olson, "'She Brought Only a Skirt': Print Media Coverage of Elizabeth Dole's Bid for the Republican Presidential Nomination," *Political Communication* 22 (2005), 315–335.

27 Dianne G. Bystrom, "Advertising, Web Sites, and Media Coverage: Gender and Communication along the Campaign Trail," in *Gender and Elections,* 2nd ed., ed.

Susan J. Carroll and Richard L. Fox. (Cambridge: Cambridge University Press, 2010), 239–262.

28 Linda L. Fowler and Jennifer L. Lawless, "Looking for Sex in All the Wrong Places: Press Coverage and the Electoral Fortunes of Gubernatorial Candidates," *Perspectives on Politics* 7 (2009), 518.

29 Johanna Dunaway, Regina G. Lawrence, Melody Rose, and Christopher Weber, "Media Coverage of Female Political Candidates Across Electoral and Institutional Contexts" (paper presented at the annual meeting of the Western Political Science Association, San Antonio, TX, April 22, 2011).

30 Shanto Iyengar, Nicholas A. Valentino, Stephen Ansolabehere, and Adam F. Simon, "Running as a Woman: Gender Stereotyping in Women's Campaigns," in *Women, Media, and Politics*, ed. Pippa Norris, (Oxford: Oxford University Press, 1997), 77–98.

31 Linda Witt, Karen M. Paget, and Glenna Matthews, *Running as a Woman: Gender and Power in American Politics* (New York: The Free Press, 1994); Schaffner, "Priming Gender."

32 Fowler and Lawless, "Looking for Sex In All the Wrong Places"; David Paul and Jessi L. Smith, "Subtle Sexism? Examining Vote Preferences When Women Run Against Men for the Presidency," *Journal of Women, Politics, and Policy* 29 (2008): 451–476; Schaffner, "Priming Gender."

33 Dunaway et al., "Media Coverage of Female Political Candidates."

34 Johanna Dunaway, "Markets, Ownership, and the Quality of Campaign News Coverage," *Journal of Politics* 70 (2008): 1–10.

35 Danny Hayes, "The Dynamics of Agenda Convergence and the Paradox of Competitiveness in Presidential Campaigns," *Political Research Quarterly* 63 (2010): 594–611.

36 Kira Sanbonmatsu and Kathleen Dolan, "Do Gender Stereotypes Transcend Party?" *Political Research Quarterly* 62 (2009): 485–494.

37 Danny Hayes, "Candidate Qualities through a Partisan Lens: A Theory of Trait Ownership," *American Journal of Political Science* 49 (2005): 908–923; Schaffner, "Priming Gender."

38 Jeffrey W. Koch, "Do Citizens Apply Gender Stereotypes to Infer Candidates' Ideological Orientations?" *Journal of Politics* 62 (2000), 414–429.

39 Alexis Gelber, "Digital Divas: Women, Politics and the Social Network," Joan Shorenstein Center on the Press, Politics, and Public Policy, June 2011, 3.

40 Aileen Lee, "Why Women Rule the Internet," *TechCrunch*, March 20, 2011; Aaron Smith, "The Internet's Role in Campaign 2008," Pew Internet Reports, April 15, 2009.

41 Amy M. Bradley and Robert H. Wicks, "A Gendered Blogosphere? Portrayal of Sarah Palin on Political Blogs During the 2008 Presidential Campaign," *Journalism and Mass Communication Quarterly* 88 (2011): 807–820.

42 Rosalind Gill, "Postfeminist Media Culture: Elements of a Sensibility," *European Journal of Cultural Studies*, 10 (2000): 147–166.

Chapter 10

Congress and the Media
Who Has the Upper Hand?

C. Danielle Vinson

In June 2007, Senator Lindsey Graham (R-SC) made multiple media appearances to try to save the immigration reform bill struggling to stay alive in the U.S. Senate. On ABC's *This Week* on June 17, Graham appealed to his Republican colleagues, saying, "This is the best deal we're ever going to get," and he went on to warn lawmakers that scuttling the current bill when there was no viable alternative to replace it would merely prolong current immigration and border security problems. At the same time, Graham's Republican colleague Jim DeMint, South Carolina's other senator, was taking his message to the press to try to kill the legislation. On June 25, DeMint told reporters, "The longer this bill hangs out there, the more opposition grows. Every day that goes by, more and more senators realize this is not the right immigration bill for America. It cannot be adequately fixed, and it must be stopped."[1] Ultimately, DeMint's side prevailed as the public, particularly in Republican-leaning states, turned against the bill and the fragile bipartisan coalition supporting it fell apart. The media campaigns of Graham and DeMint illustrate the new reality that has emerged in Congress: media relations have become a key component of the legislative process as individuals and groups in Congress use the media to communicate with the public and with each other to influence policy debates and legislative outcomes. This chapter looks at the interaction between media and Congress and asks who has the upper hand in this relationship.

Making news is a dynamic, interactive process between reporters and their sources, particularly political actors. Often referred to as the "negotiation of newsworthiness," this relationship involves reporters making decisions about what events and actors to cover and how to report the stories while politicians and others try to influence the reporters' decisions.[2] Most research on this process has focused on the president's interaction with reporters.[3] Scholars have found that the president has substantial influence on coverage because he is inherently newsworthy as the sole representative of the entire country. Other characteristics of the office provide additional advantages over the press. The president can speak with one voice and can control access to himself, avoiding reporters or speaking to them through interviews and press conferences. Thus, presidents often have considerable influence in what is reported about them and how they are covered.

But the advantages enjoyed by the president in dealing with the media do not typically apply to Congress. There are many equal voices in Congress, and no one can claim to speak for the institution or even the entire House or Senate. At best, party leaders may be able to speak for their respective parties, but even that depends on having a consensus within their caucus. Additionally, no one Member of Congress represents more than a sliver of the entire country, making most members of little interest to the national media. And unlike the president, members of Congress cannot maintain physical separation from the press, as reporters hang out in hallways to catch passing members coming from, or going to, meetings. All of this would suggest that Congress has little influence over its coverage and that the negotiation of newsworthiness is heavily slanted in favor of the press.

Because of this assumption, until fairly recently, scholars paid scant attention to media relations in Congress. But as media have become a more important means of communication in Congress, members have put more emphasis on developing media relations and devoting resources to them. The changing nature of the media with the development of the Internet, social networking, Twitter, and blogs has given congressional members a way around mainstream media. And as the opening example of Graham and DeMint suggests, some members, even those with limited formal powers, have found success in making news and framing debates, raising questions about who has the upper hand in the relationship between the media and Congress. That is the question this chapter seeks to answer. And, as we will see, although Congress does not have the same advantages as the president in dealing with the media, it is not without strategies of its own for shaping the news.

To start, we will look briefly at the evolution of the relationship between Members of Congress and the media, paying particular attention to what Members of Congress hope to gain from media coverage. The chapter then examines what studies tell us about the way national and local media cover Congress and the subsequent challenges congressional members face in getting and shaping coverage. We will look at recent developments in how members have responded to these challenges and the determinants of their success. Finally, we will consider the impact of new media on congressional members' ability to gain and influence media attention. The findings suggest that while the media still have the upper hand in determining if and how to cover Congress, the members have become much more adept at playing the hand they are dealt to become more effective in negotiating their newsworthiness.

Why Media Became Important in Congress

The media have not always been considered a useful tool in policymaking. Prior to the 1970s, Members of Congress showed little interest in using the media.

Indeed, members who worked behind the scenes to craft and pass legislation were known as workhorses, while those who sought media attention were derisively labeled showhorses.[4] It was not until the 1970s that members began to recognize the potential symbiosis between news coverage and influence within Congress. In 1977 Senate Republicans chose Howard Baker to be their leader, in part because of his media-relations skills.[5] The Congressional Black Caucus discovered that making the news was a way to force other political actors to pay attention to its concerns, despite its small numbers through the 1970s.[6] By the late 1970s, most members had press secretaries.[7] In the 1990s, scholars began to pay attention to "media entrepreneurs" in Congress, and the distinction between workhorses and showhorses disappeared.[8] Members of Congress had realized the value of making news.

Today, congressional members want to make the news for a variety of reasons. Much like the president, they seek coverage to influence the public agenda.[9] Getting the media to pay attention to an issue makes it more salient to the public, which may force the president to address issues members consider a priority that might not be on his agenda.[10] It can also be a way to compel others in Congress, especially those in positions of power, to take up the issue. If the public is focused on the issue, the cost of inaction is higher for public officials, making it less likely they will ignore the issue.

Once an issue is on the public agenda, members often try to shape coverage in an effort to frame the issue and influence the debate and the interpretation of the policy once it passes Congress.[11] This sort of framing can serve multiple purposes. It can help define the problem and therefore what policy solutions will be considered. It can generate public support or opposition for a policy. If a politician can change the way the media understand and discuss a policy, then the media coverage may direct the public's attention to different aspects of the issue and facilitate shifts in public opinion.[12] Thus, for example, Democrats portrayed the Patient Protection and Affordable Care Act (Obamacare) in 2010 as an extension of health insurance to millions who could not otherwise afford it and as a way to trim long-term healthcare costs. Republicans, in contrast, depicted it as a constitutionally questionable expansion of government power, going so far as to call it a step toward socialized medicine. Each side hoped the media would adopt its frame, which would focus public opinion on the aspect of the legislation that would lead to the most favorable view of that party. Although political pundits often dismissively refer to this as spin, there is a wealth of research that suggests agenda setting and framing have a real impact on public opinion and preferences for specific policies.[13] At the very least, going public in these situations may enable members to increase the traceability or visibility of the actions taken by the majority so the public can hold members accountable for the policy.[14]

In addition to communicating with the public, Members of Congress rely on the media to communicate with other political elites, congressional staff, and each other.[15] As power hierarchies in Congress have given way to more

individualism and independence and formerly closed policymaking iron tri-
angles have opened up to include experts from interest groups, the bureaucracy, think tanks, and Congress, the media have become an important tool for
communicating across these issue networks.[16] Media coverage is a way to signal
opposition or support and to let others know whether a member is available for
bargaining or locked into a position. It can also be used to pressure public officials to change their positions. For example, members of the president's own
party may publicize their opposition to the president in an effort to change his
policy proposals before they reach a vote in Congress.[17]

Finally, members hope to use coverage for their own goals. Many of today's
members are media-savvy individuals, who see going public as one more tool
to influence policy and enhance their own credibility in a policy area. They find
that getting coverage in conjunction with a particular issue is a way "to establish
themselves as 'players.'"[18] If the media view them as credible spokespersons on
an issue, others in Congress may be more likely to involve these members on
that issue to enhance their own credibility. Coverage is also a way to increase
constituent support, as members who make the news appear to be active and
working for constituents.[19]

Clearly, Members of Congress have many good reasons for wanting news
coverage, but how do they make the news? What resources and strategies can
they employ to attract coverage to accomplish their goals and gain the upper
hand with the media? That depends in part on what the media are willing to
cover about Congress.

How Media Cover Congress

How the media cover Congress was the focus of much of the early research on
Congress and the media, with most scholars examining national media and
looking at which members were most likely to get covered. Needing to keep the
interest of a national audience, national media tend to report on members with
power. The national press features members who have authority—primarily
party and committee leaders—and those who have credibility as policy experts.[20]
These members presumably have the most impact on debate or policy. But we
also find that these notions of who has power change over time in response to
changes in Congress. For example, the expanded power of party leaders and the
growing polarization of Congress have increased the percentage of congressional coverage devoted to party leaders compared to committee chairs, who now
find themselves being bypassed by party leaders in the unorthodox lawmaking
processes that have become common in Congress.[21] Additionally, we find the
national media prefer senators to House members and members from large
states or media markets in part because these politicians are expected to be
more widely known that members from small districts and states.[22]

A few other factors also get members noticed by the press. Journalists appear
to be interested in mavericks that buck their party.[23] Indeed recent research

indicates that media are much more interested in covering criticism of a president by congressional members of his own party than praise from his co-partisans.[24] And certain kinds of increased activity in Congress have been linked to more media coverage in recent studies. For women House members, authoring legislation related to women's issues leads to more coverage.[25] Interestingly, the overall number of bills sponsored on all issues has no effect on media coverage of members, men or women, in the House and Senate.[26] Running for president has also been a way for Members of Congress to gain national media attention. And television has added another consideration for getting covered—attractiveness. When controlling for all the factors linked to more coverage of congressional members, one study found that attractiveness increased television coverage of members, but not radio and print coverage.[27]

Once scholars began to figure out which Members of Congress were mostly likely to be covered, they shifted their attention to the substance of that coverage. The findings were not particularly encouraging for congressional members. By the mid-1990s, scholars offered evidence that coverage of Congress was declining, focused on conflict, and often negative. Between 1972 and 1992, national television coverage of Congress had declined by two thirds, going from nearly four stories a day to just over one.[28] Print news has also decreased its coverage of political or public affairs, leaving Congress with a shrinking news hole in traditional media and cable news, which are often more interested in celebrity news and "news you can use."[29] Congressional members are largely relegated to providing reactions to the president or other events the media are covering; journalists rarely expect Congress to lead.[30]

What coverage of Congress exists is overwhelmingly focused on conflict, which is abundant in Congress. Disputes arise between Democrats and Republicans, the House and the Senate, and the Congress and the president. Even when journalists report on issues and policy—which has declined over time but remains the subject of the majority of congressional coverage[31]—they do so in the context of the partisan conflicts over the issue, legislative maneuvering, or the rivalry between the president and Congress.[32] Journalists seem to be committed to providing balance in their stories on politics or at least more than one side of an issue, so they look for Members of Congress offering competing perspectives, which inevitably highlights conflict.[33]

Closely connected to the focus on conflict is the negative tone of congressional coverage. Studies have been nearly unanimous that national media coverage of Congress is negative and often quite cynical.[34] The attention to conflict may be partly responsible for this as coverage opens Congress up to charges of petty bickering among partisans or between the legislative and executive branches. But the negativity also stems from a disproportionate journalistic interest in congressional scandal and cynical assessments of congressional actions. Although scandal does not dominate congressional coverage,[35] it does take up a considerable amount of the news on Congress. Additionally, even when Congress is shown exercising oversight or launching investigations and otherwise doing its job, its efforts are depicted as incompetent, grandstanding, and feeble.[36] Given the limited coverage and its focus on conflict combined with the negative tone, the picture of Congress that emerges from the national media is not particularly flattering.

Some have suggested the local media might provide a more favorable venue at least for individual Members of Congress. Much of what we know about local news coverage of Congress is based on a study by Douglas Arnold and my own study.[37] Both find that local newspaper coverage of Members of Congress happens regularly, though local television coverage is much sparser. However (there's always a however for Congress), coverage varies quite a bit across members and is somewhat less frequent in larger media markets where more members compete for the limited news space. As is the case with national coverage, journalists' news values often dictate much about how Congress is covered locally. Members who do "newsworthy" things—run for higher office, get involved in scandal, or play an important role in the legislative process or debate or in getting things done for the local constituency—are more likely to make the local news. Unlike national news, holding a leadership position in Congress does not automatically translate into more local coverage. In the interest of appealing to their local audience, local news tends to try to find a local angle in its congressional coverage—through the issues it highlights, the sources it uses, or the Members of Congress it spotlights.

Does this lead to a more favorable tone in coverage? The conventional wisdom about local coverage until 2003 was that it was mostly favorable to local Members of Congress, often publishing press releases verbatim.[38] While this turns out not to be true, very little coverage is exclusively negative. In fact, most local coverage of individual members or of Congress more generally is either neutral, or includes both negative and positive evaluations.[39] This does suggest that local media may provide a more hospitable environment than national media for Members of Congress to communicate. But, the audience for local media is limited and not as useful to members trying to influence the national agenda or debate.

Given what we have learned about media coverage of Congress thus far, members must overcome several major challenges to attract and influence coverage. The biggest problem is the shrinking news hole and Congress' lower news value relative to the president. The president has numerous advantages in attracting the limited political coverage available. He is indisputably the head of the executive branch, and because he must be elected nationally, he is familiar to the entire country. Because of his authority and familiarity among the public, he is able to speak with one voice and personalize the institution of the presidency. There is no one member of Congress similarly situated. There is no one face of Congress—and no one in Congress who is as familiar to a national audience as is the president. The president's authority and familiarity make him a better fit for media news values and therefore more newsworthy. The negative tone of congressional coverage and the focus on conflict also make it difficult for Members of Congress to shape coverage in a favorable way. If the president wants to remain positive, the media either cover his positive comments or do without his comments. But if a member of Congress chooses not to go negative, reporters can simply move on to another member who may be more willing to give the media what they want. It would certainly appear that the media have the upper hand when it comes to coverage of Congress.

Coordinating Communication

But Congress is not without resources and strategies to influence its own coverage. Recent research has focused on what members have done to overcome the challenges they face in gaining and shaping coverage. One way for Congress to overcome part of the president's advantage in attracting news coverage is for Congress to learn to speak with one voice. While no individual member of Congress will equal the newsworthiness of the president, many members speaking in unison can provide a counterweight to the president. Together, Members of Congress can have an important impact on legislation and policy, and if they are all saying the same thing, the media have fewer competing messages to select from. It is most likely that the press will report the loudest message. So, the trick for Members of Congress is to figure out how to coordinate their communication. Central to these efforts has been the growing communications role of party leaders in Congress.

Party leaders are expected to help their party members accomplish the party's legislative and electoral goals, and they have discovered that the media can be useful for both. As has already been noted, the media are a valuable resource in pushing issues onto the legislative agenda and focusing the attention of political elites and the public on a small number of issues. If party leaders can attract coverage of their party's legislative priorities, they can shape the agenda. But their interest in media coverage goes beyond policy objectives. The party's ability to accomplish its legislative goals—as well as the way the party is portrayed in the press—may also have electoral repercussions. Take, for example, the case of the minority party in the Senate. Its members have some institutional powers to influence policy, but using holds or filibusters (the refusal to give up the floor and end debate so a bill can be brought to a vote) alone to stop legislation runs the risk of being labeled obstructionist. Therefore, Senate leaders have increasingly combined their threat of filibuster with full-blown public relations campaigns that attempt to explain and justify their procedural strategies.[40] Recognizing the importance of the party's collective reputation, party leaders try to shape the party's brand in the media to ensure it is favorable and thus an asset to its individual members seeking election.[41]

For these reasons, party leaders have added an important communications or public relations element to their jobs. Some have called this "message politics," where leaders figure out what the party wants to communicate and then create strategies for getting that message out to the press.[42] Led by Rep. Newt

Gingrich (R-GA), Republicans began to embrace this idea in the early 1980s as they made television an integral part of their strategy to confront Democrats, rather than trying to cooperate with them.[43] Senate leaders began to act as national party spokespersons on television. It is now standard for party leaders to be charged with promoting the image of the party and its message to help individual members reach their collective goals.

Initially, these communications efforts primarily involved the party leader holding press conferences and being a spokesperson for the party, but leaders realized that they could be more effective if they could coordinate their members. Gary Lee Malecha and Daniel Reagan have studied the evolution of party leaders' media strategies, and they provide several reasons for why coordinated communication is necessary.[44] First, the media will be more interested in a group of members saying the same thing rather than just one talking; coordination raises the likelihood that the media will hear the message. Second, if all a party's members can agree on a message, it helps to clarify the party's brand for the media, the public, and for the party members. Third, coordination expands the possible venues through which the party can communicate, as individual members have their own connections to various media outlets, national and local, and consequently broadens the audience for the party's message. Finally, the need to coordinate goes up as the party's formal or institutional powers to influence policy and political processes decline. For this reason, the House minority party, which has little ability to shape legislation or even stop it if the majority party is united, will have the greatest interest and the most success in coordinating its communication.

As they have realized the importance of using the media to convey the party's message and the necessity of coordinating communication among their party members, leaders have deployed many resources and strategies for media relations. Malecha and Reagan explain how party leaders in the House have concentrated public relations activities in their own hands.[45] The leadership team decides on the party's message and then provides rank and file members with talking points and suggestions for events that will highlight the party's message, both in Washington and when members travel back to their districts. Leaders reiterate their themes by recruiting and organizing members to deliver "one-minute" floor speeches and special order speeches on the House floor that will echo the talking points members are using outside of Congress. To assist members in supporting the party's promotional activities, party leaders have expanded the party's communications bureaucracy to include communications directors, speechwriters, editors for the party websites, and floor debate coordinators. The party's communication staff meets with members' press secretaries to coordinate their activities, and they provide direct assistance to members in the form of technical assistance, media advice, and even help reaching out to media outlets to book members on television or radio shows.

In the Senate, majority and minority leaders have employed similar strategies, but they have been less successful than their House counterparts in centralizing communications. Several factors account for this. Senators have a tradition of independence afforded them by their greater institutional powers. Unlike House members, individual senators do have formal powers that allow them to influence the legislative process and policy outcomes. Also working against coordinated communication are senators' more diverse constituencies that sometimes pull them away from their party's position and message in the interest of the senators' reelection.

Party leaders' efforts to coordinate communication do not focus solely on congressional press relations. They also involve "manipulate[ing] chamber procedures to magnify their message."[46] In one case study of party communications strategies, Malecha and Reagan explain how Democrats timed the release of committee reports and legislation highlighting wasteful spending in the Iraq war with Republicans' efforts to limit expansion of a children's health insurance program in 2007. The Republicans justified their opposition to more spending on the children's program on the grounds of fiscal responsibility. But when that argument was juxtaposed with their willingness to continue pouring money into the Iraq war despite reports of waste, the resulting coverage made them look hypocritical. On the Senate side, party leaders have used filibusters as part of public relations campaigns against the president or the other party.[47] Being able to link the activities going on inside Congress to what members are saying to the media outside Congress is a way to increase media interest in the party's message, though some have noted that this is a strategy much more available to the majority than the minority party because of its greater control over the legislative process. The minority party's success in getting covered depends more on direct promotional efforts than actions in the legislative process.[48]

The real challenge for party leaders is to get their rank and file members to participate in promoting the party's message. In his study on the strategic communication campaigns of congressional parties, Patrick Sellers explains this dilemma and how party leaders attempt to overcome it.[49] Party leaders need many if not all their members to promote the party's message to increase its newsworthiness to the media. Their problem is that *all* their members benefit if the party succeeds in promoting its message, even if some members do not participate in promoting the message. It is a classic collective action problem—members who do not contribute to the effort still reap the benefits, making it likely that some members (possibly many) will choose to free ride on the efforts of the others. But, if too many people do this, the party's message will not meet the media's definition of what is newsworthy. So, how do party leaders insure that members will participate in the party's promotional efforts?

Sellers suggests that one key is in selecting the message. Party leaders need to create a message that will unify their own party and divide the other party. One way to do this is to focus their message on issues the party owns—those on which all members of the party are unified around a particular position that is popular with the public and on which the other party is opposed, or at least divided. Events and the other party do not always make that possible. In those instances in which the party must respond to an issue that might not favor it or would divide it, leaders try to link the issue to others that would be more favorable. For example, environmental issues have typically favored Democrats, but during the recent economic downturn when unemployment rates were high, Republicans have attempted to turn environmental regulations into economic discussions about costly regulations that were hurting business and killing jobs, issues more likely to favor Republicans. By choosing a message that will unify their own party, leaders may improve their chances of getting members to cooperate in the party's promotional efforts and increase their likelihood of news coverage.

Framing

If coordination is an important means of gaining coverage, then framing is an essential component of shaping that coverage. Framing, as used here, is the way we talk about an issue or event that puts it into a context, and it has important implications for public opinion and the alternatives available for addressing the issue. For example, in recent debates over making tax increases on the wealthiest Americans part of a larger plan to reduce budget deficits, Republicans have decried tax increases. Recognizing that increasing taxes is usually unpopular with the public, Democrats have instead tried to reframe the issue as asking the top one percent to pay their fair share, a more popular way of casting the debate. While framing has been most common during the legislative process, at the committee stages and during floor debates, members have begun to employ it more frequently after passage during implementation of major controversial legislation to shape the public's perception of the new law in an effort to gain an advantage for the next election.[50] We see this in the public relations battle to define the healthcare reform bill passed under Obama in 2010. The debate over whether the new law is, as Democrats claim, a necessary extension of healthcare to millions of uninsured people or, as Republicans claim, is a step toward socialized medicine and a violation of the Constitution has raged for nearly two years and figured prominently in two election cycles with no indication yet that the public has been completely convinced of either interpretation.

The language congressional members use to discuss issues is an important part of framing. Members of Congress, particularly party leaders, are increasingly intentional in their choice of language in their public statements. They often use "crafted talk"—words and phrases that have been tested in public opinion polls and focus groups—to frame debates.[51] Thus when Republicans wanted to repeal the inheritance tax, which affected less than 5 percent of Americans, they referred to it as the "death tax," which suggested it affected more people.[52] Those who opposed the repeal preferred the term "estate tax." The logic of the two sides is clear—most people do not own estates, but all of them face death. The language used had the potential to move public opinion on the issue. Because congressional members recognize that they are not operating in a vacuum and that their framing of an issue will often have to compete with the frames of other political elites and the media, the parties test their messages against those of other elites in polls or focus groups before taking their messages to the public.[53]

Catering to Media Values

As party leaders and individual Members of Congress pay more attention to how their language will frame issues, they must also keep in mind the news values of the media. No matter how carefully tested the language, if it does not fit the media's definition of what is news, members will have little success in making or shaping the news. For this reason, members craft their messages to highlight conflict and drama. For the congressional parties and individual members, this often means heightened partisanship and harsh rhetoric.

In his book *When Politicians Attack!*, Tim Groeling suggests that some partisan messages are more interesting to the press than others. Intraparty praise— Republicans praising other Republicans, for example—is not considered very newsworthy. Intraparty criticism is of interest because it is less common or expected in this era of increasing polarization, as parties often attempt to deal with internal strife privately, and those on the losing sides of such disputes may find it better to remain silent if not supportive. Criticism of one party by the other, although expected, is still newsworthy because it highlights conflict and may help to provide reporters with balance in their stories.

How does this affect party leaders' messages? According to Groeling, although they might want to praise their own party, they will find more success in making the news if they can get their members to criticize the opposing party. They certainly do not want their own members criticizing their party. The political context itself may have some impact on how successful leaders will be in getting their members to present a united front. For the minority party, this may be relatively easy, especially during times of unified government; its lack of power provides members with a common purpose—attack the majority in hopes of winning the next election. Thus, minority party members may be quite willing to participate in communication efforts that criticize the majority, and happily for them, the media's interest in balancing different views gives them a reasonable chance of being covered. In contrast, the majority party leaders have a tougher time because their members may be less united in their purpose. Factions within the party may have an incentive to defect from the party leadership's message and publicly criticize their own party to move it in their preferred direction. Such squabbles cater to the media's penchant for drama, and they often spill into the public spotlight, undermining the party leaders' promotional efforts.

To this point, I have focused primarily on party leaders' efforts to gain and shape media coverage. There are, however, others in Congress who have learned the value of coordination and catering to media values to get coverage.

The Congressional Black Caucus (CBC) offers a good example. The CBC was among the early leaders in Congress to use media to try to influence policy-making, going back to the 1970s when the Caucus was first established. With few members and little power over political processes or outcomes, the CBC was adept at using unconventional action to generate media attention to its concerns. Members employed dramatic protests and threats to boycott meetings that fulfilled the media's need for drama and conflict.[54] In more recent years, with a much larger membership and more of its members in positions of power within Congress, the CBC has shifted to more conventional promotional efforts like those of the congressional parties, including coordination of CBC members and well-timed press events.[55]

Likewise, individual Members of Congress have found that catering to the media's definition of news is a way to gain coverage. Senators Jim DeMint and Lindsey Graham, with whom I opened the chapter, provide an excellent example of the different paths members can take to make news. Graham, while not in a formal leadership position, is on committees in the Senate that are often newsworthy because of the issues under their jurisdiction—Judiciary (whose subjects include immigration and judicial appointments) and Armed Services. Graham also has a reputation as a maverick who is not afraid to buck the party establishment on occasion, a trait the media find appealing. Recognizing that the media like the unexpected, Graham is willing to publicly criticize his party and to praise the opposing party from time to time in his quest to push his fellow senators and others in government to work together to solve problems. As I have noted, such messages are newsworthy, and they happen to serve Graham's own goal of creating an image as someone who will work with either party. Graham has also been helped by his folksy style of speaking and seemingly unguarded forthrightness that set him apart from other politicians. During a debate over the health benefits of military reservists, for example, Graham told Chris Wallace, host of *Fox News Sunday* (May 23, 2004), "I love the people in the Pentagon most of the time, but I disagree with them over this."

Senator DeMint's approach to getting news coverage is quite different from Graham's, though it also caters to news values. DeMint uses controversy and heated rhetoric to gain media attention. Unlike Graham, who mixes criticism and praise in his messages, DeMint's messages are usually critiques and are mostly partisan. One of his most famous lines came during the 2009 debate over healthcare reform when he commented, "If Republicans are able to stop Barack Obama on health care, 'it will be his Waterloo, it will break him.'"[56] It certainly raised a ruckus and received extensive coverage. Often he starts his public relations efforts with new media, commenting online via blogs, websites, Twitter, and social media. Then he moves to interviews on conservative talk radio shows, and from there he can begin to attract the attention of television, usually starting with Fox News. He notes that "you have to hit a certain noise threshold" to get the attention of the non-conservative news outlets, but if "you can stir things up enough," the other networks and newspapers will pick up the story and call him for his comments.[57] The examples of Graham and DeMint illustrate that while there are different ways to gain media coverage, all of them require members to fit themselves and their messages to what the media find interesting and newsworthy.

Impact of New Media

Senator DeMint's strategy of using new media to get coverage in mainstream media raises the question of how changes in the media environment have affected congressional communications. Have the developments in technology and social media helped Members of Congress to gain an advantage over mainstream news media? Malecha and Reagan suggest that this is a mixed blessing for Congress. On the positive side, online media allow members more opportunities for unmediated communication with others in government, journalists and pundits, and especially the public. All Members of Congress have a website; over 70 percent now have Twitter, according to tweetcongress.org; more than five hundred members have official Facebook pages;[58] and some even have their own YouTube channels. In addition to the greater number of opportunities to communicate through new media, members are also better able to target their messages to specific audiences. Members can target electronic newsletters to constituents who have expressed an interest in a specific topic. They can post on blogs to target particular ideological or issue-oriented groups. And they can tweet information to their Twitter followers.

There are, however, a few downsides to the new communications environment. While the diverse media provide more points of access, they have also made it more challenging to reach a broad audience and harder to control information.[59] Just as today's media are fragmented, so is the audience. Gone are the days when congressional members could make the local newspaper and reach most of their constituency, or appear on one of the three network evening news programs to reach a national audience. Members need to gain the attention of multiple media outlets, traditional and online, to reach a wide audience today.

And once a story does get out, the multitude of media and the rapid rate at which information and stories can circulate make it harder for political elites to control the story. In 2006, Rep. Mark Foley (R-FL) discovered that personal e-mails can quickly become public when his inappropriate instant messages to House pages found their way into the news. Foley resigned his seat. Sen. Charles Grassley (R-IA) found himself making headlines as he tweeted some rather candid critiques of President Obama,[60] and Rep. Anthony Weiner (D-NY) had to resign after he tweeted inappropriate photos of himself to women who were not his wife. While these examples were mostly self-inflicted, there have been countless cases of politicians making off-the-cuff remarks in small gatherings that were recorded or tweeted by those in attendance and went viral when made public, causing negative media coverage.

Despite the dangers, Members of Congress are trying to harness new media and use it to serve their interests. Malecha and Reagan describe the resulting Cyber Congress. All members have some sort of online office today that includes webpages, e-mail, and social media. Committees and party leaders also have an online presence. Newer members seem to use such resources more heavily. Members use their websites to create an image of themselves and to emphasize party messages and issue positions. Many of the sites also court media coverage by providing information the press would find useful. Following losses in the 2006 midterm elections, House Republican party leaders, who found themselves in the minority, encouraged their members to open Twitter accounts to help them get the party's message out. A Congressional Research Service study on congressional Twitter use found that indeed House GOP members did a majority of the tweeting. The study also found that just under half of the tweets linked to other websites or called attention to members' media events; a quarter referred to legislative or representative duties, and 12 percent announced the member's position on an issue.[61]

Clearly, new media have opened up opportunities for members to communicate directly with the public, but they have not replaced traditional media. Members still need traditional media coverage because it gives them a larger and somewhat less intentional audience than internet and social media. Traditional, independent media also provide a legitimacy or credibility that unmediated sources cannot provide. However, if DeMint's experience is any indication, members have begun to figure out how to use new media both to communicate directly with interested audiences and to pique the interest of mainstream reporters that leads to traditional coverage.

Conclusions

I began the chapter by asking who has the upper hand in the relationship between the media and Congress. The media certainly dictate what is newsworthy, and because Congress has many members with many messages, it does not inherently fit the media's news values. However, congressional members, often led by party leaders, have learned strategies to make themselves and their messages newsworthy. They try to coordinate their messages with other members to present a united front that may rise to the media's standard for importance. They choose language that is interesting and highlights controversy and conflict that not only appeals to the public but also to the media. Essentially, members recognize that they have to design messages that coincide with what the media want to cover, and they have enjoyed success in attracting and shaping coverage as a result. Members may not have the upper hand in dealing with the media, but they are certainly learning to play the hand they are dealt.

Notes

1 Jonathan Weisman, "GOP Backers Offer Immigration Bill Change; Provision Would Require Illegal Residents to Return Home to Gain Legal Status," *Washington Post,* June 26, 2007, A3.

2 Timothy E. Cook, *Governing With The News: The News Media as a Political Institution,* 2nd ed. (Chicago: University of Chicago Press, 2005), 102–109.

3 E.g., George C. Edwards III, *Governing by Campaigning: The Politics of the Bush Presidency* (New York: Pearson Longman, 2007); Samuel Kernell, *Going Public: New Strategies of Presidential Leadership,* 4th ed. (Washington, DC: CQ Press, 2007).

4 Timothy E. Cook, *Making Laws and Making News: Media Strategies in the U.S. House of Representatives* (Washington: Brookings Institution, 1989); Gary Lee Malecha and Daniel J. Reagan, *The Public Congress: Congressional Deliberation in a New Media Age* (New York: Routledge, 2012), 31–35.

5 Richard D. Lyons, "Howard Henry Baker Jr.," *New York Times,* January 5, 1977, A14.

6 Raymond W. Copson, *Congressional Black Caucus and Foreign Policy: 1971–2002* (New York: Novinka Books, 2003).

7 Cook, *Making Laws,* 73.

8 Karen Kedrowski, *Media Entrepreneurs and the Media Enterprise in the U.S. Congress* (Cresskill, NJ: Hampton Press, 1996).

9 Malecha and Reagan, *Public Congress,* 14.

10 Patrick Sellers, *Cycles of Spin: Strategic Communication in the U.S. Congress* (New York: Cambridge University Press, 2010); Barbara Sinclair, *Party Wars: Polarization and the Politics of National Policy Making* (Norman, OK: University of Oklahoma Press, 2006), 255.

11 Malecha and Reagan, *Public Congress,* 14; Barbara Sinclair, "Hostile Partners: The President, Congress, and Lawmaking in the Partisan 1990s," in *Polarized Politics: Congress and the President in a Partisan Era,* ed. Jon R. Bond and Richard Fleisher (Washington, DC: CQ Press, 2000), 144–145.

12 Frank R. Baumgartner and Bryan D. Jones, *Agendas and Instability in American Politics* (Chicago: University of Chicago Press, 1993), 25, 103.

13 For example, John Zaller, "The Myth of Massive Media Impact Revived: New Support for a Discredited Idea," in *Political Persuasion and Attitude Change,* ed. Diana C. Mutz, Paul M. Sniderman, and Richard A. Brody (Ann Arbor, Michigan: University of Michigan Press, 1996); Shanto Iyengar, *Is Anyone Responsible? How Television Frames Political Issues* (Chicago: University of Chicago Press, 1991).

14 R. Douglas Arnold, *The Logic of Congressional Action* (New Haven, CT: Yale University Press, 1990).

15 Kedrowski, *Media Entrepreneurs,* 124–125; Malecha and Reagan, *Public Congress;* Sellers, *Cycles of Spin,* 8.

16 Kedrowski, *Media Entrepreneurs,* 138.

17 Tim Groeling, *When Politicians Attack: Party Cohesion in the Media* (New York: Cambridge University Press, 2010); Tim Groeling and Samuel Kernell, "Congress, the President, and Party Competition via Network News," in *Polarized Politics: Congress and the President in a Partisan Era,* ed. Jon R. Bond and Richard Fleisher (Washington, DC: CQ Press, 2000), 92.

18 Kedrowski, *Media Entrepreneurs,* 5.

19 Malecha and Reagan, *Public Congress,* 16.

20 Cook, *Making Laws,* 44–57; Stephen Hess, *The Ultimate Insiders* (Washington: Brookings Institution, 1986); Stephen Hess, *Live! From Capitol Hill: Studies of Congress and the Media* (Washington, DC: The Brookings Institution, 1991).

21 Malecha and Reagan, *Public Congress*, 68. For a discussion of unorthodox lawmaking, see Barbara Sinclair, *Unorthodox Lawmaking: New Legislative Processes in the U.S. Congress*, 4th ed. (Washington, DC: CQ Press, 2011).

22 Stephanie Greco Larson and Lydia M. Andrade, "Determinants of National Television News Coverage of Women in the House of Representatives, 1987–1998," *Congress & the Presidency* 32 (2005); Israel Waismel-Manor & Yariv Tsfati, "Why Do Better-Looking Members of Congress Receive More Television Coverage?" *Political Communication* 28 (2011).

23 Hess, *Ultimate Insiders*.

24 Groeling, *When Politicians Attack*, 91.

25 Larson and Andrade, "Determinants."

26 Larson and Andrade, "Determinants"; Waismel-Manor and Tsfati, "Why Do Better-Looking Members."

27 Waismel-Manor and Tsfati, "Why Do Better-Looking Members," 452.

28 S. Robert Lichter and Daniel R. Amundson, "Less News is Worse News: Television News Coverage of Congress, 1972–1992," in *Congress, the Press, and the Public*, ed. Thomas E. Mann and Norman J. Ornstein (Washington, DC: The American Enterprise Institute and The Brookings Institution, 1994), 134.

29 Cook, *Governing with the News*, 173.

30 Mark J. Rozell, *In Contempt of Congress: Postwar Press Coverage on Capitol Hill* (Westport, CT: Praeger, 1996), 55.

31 Lichter and Amundson, "Less News," 135.

32 Rozell, *In Contempt of Congress*; Jonathan S. Morris and Rosalee A. Clawson, "Media Coverage of Congress in the 1990s: Scandals, Personalities, and the Prevalence of Policy and Process," *Political Communication* 22 (2005), 306.

33 Sellers, *Cycles of Spin*, 148, 159.

34 Rozell, *In Contempt*; Lichter and Amundson, "Less News."

35 Morris and Clawson, "Media Coverage," 298.

36 Rozell, *In Contempt*, 72.

37 R. Douglas Arnold, *Congress, the Press, and Political Accountability* (New York: Russell Sage Foundation and Princeton University Press, 2004); C. Danielle Vinson, *Local Media Coverage of Congress and Its Members: Through Local Eyes* (Cresskill, NJ: Hampton Press, 2003).

38 Ben H. Bagdikian, "Congress and the Media: Partners in Propaganda," *Columbia Journalism Review* (January/February 1974).

39 Arnold, *Congress, the Press, and Political Accountability*; Vinson, *Local Media Coverage*.

40 Sinclair, "Hostile Partners," 147; Sinclair, *Party Wars*, 255–301.

41 Sellers, *Cycles of Spin*; Groeling, *When Politicians Attack!*

42 C. Lawrence Evans, "Committees, Leaders, and Message Politics," in *Congress Reconsidered*, 7th ed., ed. Lawrence Dodd and Bruce Oppenheimer (Washington, DC: Congressional Quarterly Press, 2001).

43 Nicol C. Rae, "Republican Congressional Leadership in Historical Context," *Extensions* (Spring 2005): 5–9.

44 Malecha and Reagan, *The Public Congress*, 20–22.

45 Ibid., 73–81.

46 Ibid., 106.

47 Sinclair, *Party Wars*.

48 Sellers, *Cycles of Spin*, 171.

49 Sellers, *Cycles of Spin*.

50 Malecha and Reagan, Chapter 6.

51 Douglas B. Harris, "Partisan Framing in Legislative Debates," in *Winning with*

Words: The Origins and Impact of Political Framing, ed. Brian F. Schaffner and Patrick J. Sellers (New York: Routledge, 2010), 45–47.

52 Brian F. Schaffner and Mary Layton Atkinson, "Taxing Death or Estates? When Frames Influence Citizens' Issue Beliefs," in *Winning with Words: The Origins and Impact of Political Framing*, ed. Brian F. Schaffner and Patrick J. Sellers (New York: Routledge, 2010).

53 Harris, "Partisan Framing," 53.

54 Copson, *Congressional Black Caucus*, 9–10.

55 C. Danielle Vinson, "The Congressional Black Caucus Goes Public: How the CBC Uses the Media to Influence Policymaking" (paper presented at the annual meeting of the Midwest Political Science Association, Chicago, Illinois, April 22–24, 2010).

56 Manu Raju, "GOP Leaders Fear Anti-Obama Tone," *Politico*, July 23, 2009. Accessed April 26, 2012.

57 Sen. Jim DeMint, telephone interview with Danielle Vinson, November 4, 2009.

58 Congress on Facebook. *The Social Congress: Key Findings*. http://www.facebook.com/note.php?note_id=10150328408545071 Accessed April 26, 2012.

59 Malecha and Reagan, *The Public Congress*, 25.

60 National Public Radio, "Sen. Grassley's Twitter Broadside at Obama," *All Things Considered*, June 8, 2009, http://www.npr.org/templates/story/story.php?storyId=105128505.

61 Matthew Eric Glassman, Jacob R. Straus, and Colleen J. Shogan, "Social Networking and Constituent Communication: Member Use of Twitter during a Two-Week Period in the 111th Congress," Congressional Research Service Report 7-5700 R40823 (February 3, 2010), www.crs.gov.

ak is to Lead?
onal Modern
ntial Leadership
ui Public Opinion

Brandon Rottinghaus and Matthew Lang

We witness presidents talking all of the time, but what effect does this rhetoric have on the public's policy preferences? All modern presidents spend time attempting to lead public opinion by speaking to groups, giving Saturday radio addresses, holding press conferences, giving speeches from the Oval Office, traveling across the nation to give speeches and more. Given that presidents have an expansive executive office to help shape and control their message, an army of political surrogates to carry out their messages and a cadre of press devoted to their every word, presidents clearly attempt to lead public opinion. Indeed, there is a great deal of pressure on presidents to succeed quickly, and the public has high expectations that presidents will solve domestic and global problems—and quickly. Yet the outdated and inconsistent tools presidents have to accomplish these tasks may not be up to the job.[1] Presidents may be "doomed to failure" because public expectations are out of step with the realities of presidential ability.[2] Presidents may continually seek to lead public opinion but are hampered by a political system that restricts their ability to lead. The tension between these factors (expectations of leadership but a lessened ability to lead) is at the crux of modern presidential leadership.

Reflecting this duality, there is debate about the degree to which presidents can lead public opinion in a modern political environment. Some argue that presidential leadership is a natural phenomenon of presidential skillful persuasion, while others counter by claiming that modern presidential leadership is impossible given a fragmented public, critical media and less attention paid to the president. In addition, there is debate about the successful strategies presidents use, the president's goals in "going public" and the media as an intermediary in this process. In this chapter we explore the current state of the literature on questions about the president's leadership success in an environment of high expectations and lowered ability. We argue that there is more than one way to look at presidential leadership. Presidents do not simply succeed or fail in the abstract; rather presidents' successes at leading the public are conditional on the environments they face. Presidential success at leading public opinion is therefore conditional not only on the constraints of the political world they inhabit, but also on the White House's skills in navigating that environment.

Theories of Presidential Leadership

Most scholars of the modern presidency argue that presidents must be effective leaders to obtain their preferred policies in a system that shares political power among three branches. Underlying opinion leadership is the president's ability to clearly and accurately provide information to the public. For instance, Hargrove argues that presidents can lead public opinion by "teaching" constituents about reality.[3] Neustadt also identifies the phenomenon of "president-as-teacher" (as a resource in the "power to persuade") where "a president concerned for leeway inside government must try to shape the thoughts of men outside.[4] If he would be effective as a guardian of public standing, he must be effective as a teacher to the public."[5] Neustadt acknowledges that this process is difficult but that self-constructed events "create his opportunities to teach."[6] The presence of these "teaching" effects reinforces the argument that presidents are the central player in the political system and, as such, the media centralize him as the protagonist or antagonist in news concerning policy issues.

Samuel Kernell topples Neustadt's logic by suggesting that presidents take their case to the public as a means to indirectly persuade Members of Congress. The theoretical lynchpin of this approach to public leadership is Kernell's "going public" argument, a conceptualization of presidential leadership that supplants traditional institutional political bargaining arrangements and relies instead on active and energetic public leadership of opinion.[7] Kernell argues that presidents do not "go public" to lead public opinion as an end goal—rather, presidents lead public opinion with the hopes of influencing Members of Congress. Kernell notes that:

Political Washington has come to look less like institutionalized pluralism (which is conducive to bargaining) and more like individualized pluralism (which is conducive to going public). Presidents more freely go public nowadays because it is a strategy better adapted to modern politics.[8]

By going "over the heads" of Congress to the root of the representative public, presidents are able to pressure the legislative branch to pursue their agenda.[9] Kernell's two-stage scenario suggests that presidents travel to individual states and cities to communicate their messages to the public. The public, sufficiently mobilized, then communicates their newly formed preferences to their respective Members of Congress. Laracey argues that presidents have long employed this tactic as a way to expand their limited Constitutional power.[10] "Going public" is also a powerful tool to explain presidential behavior and agenda setting. Indeed, Canes-Wrone demonstrates that presidents can obtain influence from not only the act of agenda setting, but also the threat of agenda setting (although presidents do not always have incentives to do so).[11]

Empirical Findings

The theoretical stage set, how often do presidents succeed at leading public opinion? Presidents have not been shy about using the "bully pulpit" to carry their messages to the American public, believing it to be important to their policy success while in office, to their political legacy after they leave office and the future success of their party.[12] Yet, despite lofty expectations for this tactic, some scholars find that presidents are generally unsuccessful at opinion leadership as an instrument to advance their policy agenda.[13] Scholars argue that presidents fail at moving public preferences for a number of reasons, typically in combination with each other, such as shrinking audiences, media message screeners, the political partisanship of citizens and a lack of public attention to the news.[14] Several authors claim that the rise of television (and the rise in the diversity of viewers) challenges the president's ability to lead public opinion.[15] Specifically, the fact that viewers have increased choices nowadays—and that many are exercising this choice by turning to likeminded news sources—means that the president's ability to consistently lead public opinion has been limited.[16] Less attention is paid to presidents, even in venues and on issues that traditionally afforded the president a great deal of coverage, such as foreign policy. Declining trust in government is also to blame.[17]

Given the argument that the presidency (and some individual presidents) is (are) too institutionally weak and situationally disadvantaged to effectively use the bully pulpit,[18] many prominent studies find little success for presidents in moving public opinion to the president's preferred policy outcome. One classic example of failed presidential leadership is Woodrow Wilson's exasperating (and eventually fatal) trip across the nation to drum up support for the League of Nations.[19] Likewise President Carter's efforts at convincing the public to reform the nation's health care system fell short, though he faced several political problems at the time, such as lack of support in Congress and internal White House disorganization.[20] In an analysis of President Clinton's first years in office, Jacobs and Shapiro found the president to be a responsive (but not effective) leader on health care policy and not successful on issues of foreign policy (especially on the Bosnian war).[21]

Perhaps the most significant recent work suggesting presidents cannot lead public opinion is George Edwards's *On Deaf Ears*, which establishes a compelling argument for presidential ineffectiveness in leading public opinion.[22] Edwards examines public approval of a handful of policies that former presidents' Reagan, Bush and Clinton pursued. One of the most important contributions of *On Deaf Ears* is the discussion of the political environment surrounding presidential leadership. Edwards creates a transmission model where he examines the communicator (the president), the message (presidential rhetoric) and the audience (the public). In this model, several variables must be included to justifiably understand presidential leadership. Presidential credibility, popularity and charisma are important. Audience participation, attention and conversion are critical. Not surprisingly, these elements are disconnected at several points, complicating the process of presidential leadership and leaving it largely defunct.[23]

Yet, despite studies indicating less-than-significant public opinion movement after policy speeches, there are many documented instances in which presidents have successfully led public opinion. When and how the president achieves successes is important to study since it is a task where the president himself is central (and perhaps critical to) the success of leadership, allowing scholars to directly examine presidential skill.[24] Previous research has demonstrated that Kennedy,[25] Reagan[26] and Clinton[27] each successfully led the public on specific issues. Neustadt's recommendations about maintaining a positive reputation with those who "share in governing" suggest that popularity can be effective in inducing positive perceptions of the president's actions and may mute disagreements.[28] Indeed, higher popularity can lead to better media coverage.[29] There is also evidence that presidents who are more popular are able to move public opinion in small amounts.[30] Similarly, Canes-Wrone argues that presidents tend to appeal to the public on popular policies and, in doing so, find success in convincing Congress to allocate more funds to the budget items the president requested in his speeches.[31] She continues, "in contrast, by going public about an unpopular domestic proposal, he actually loses legislative influence."[32]

Interestingly, presidents are also successful at motivating positive perceptions of the economy, a potentially powerful tool in bad economic times.[33] Wood argues that presidents attempt to project an image of economic leadership regardless of negative economic news or economic evaluations.[34] Presidents, as stewards of the economy, consistently speak optimistically and positively about the economy. In these cases, the effect of presidential shaping of economic circumstances is indirect: presidential optimism affects news coverage of the economy, which affects economic approval. Likewise, presidential rhetoric operating through these indirect channels can have substantial impacts on U.S. economic growth and unemployment, suggesting that the president (in some ways) has an underappreciated "role as rhetorical leader of the economy."[35] Presidential signals through speeches also influence the market in the short term, including the daily price of oil, the daily yield on the 30 year Treasury bond and monthly measures of the money supply.[36] This "economic leadership" trend also appears to be amplified when presidents are making foreign policy speeches and are more personally popular.[37] This may be a moment where the high expectations of the president meet his ability to effectively meet the challenge (in conjunction with other institutional actors).

In addition, there is consensus that presidents can generally lead public opinion successfully on matters of foreign policy or military intervention.[38] Presidents are more likely to make an appeal on popular foreign policy issues, and when they do they are often successful at leading the public.[39] Findings of presidential leadership of foreign policy on both approval and substantive policy have been consistent over time, partially as a result of the White House's cultivation of this support. For instance, Sigelman found that President Reagan's endorsement of the INF Treaty had a modest impact on support for the treaty among individuals who perceived the Soviets as "relatively nonthreatening," while the endorsement had a much larger impact on treaty support among those who viewed the Soviets as threatening.[40] Individuals exposed to President Reagan's speech committing military personnel to Lebanon and Grenada were more supportive of the policy than those who were not exposed to the speech.[41] Kernell also identified several incidents of foreign policy leadership in *Going Public*, including President Bush on Desert Storm and President Truman on aid to Greece under the Truman Doctrine.[42] President Bush was also successful in leading the public to support his policies in Iraq (such as the "surge") through an Oval Office speech.[43]

Conditional Leadership

As described in the preceding section, several specific political conditions assist presidents in leading public opinion, giving credence to the notion that presidents can *conditionally* lead opinion. As exploiters of moments to lead public opinion, presidents may increase their chances to lead public opinion by successfully framing public opinion, increasing the salience of popular issues, clarifying the public's wishes by revealing how his preferences are consistent with these, defining policies in ways that channel support to his party and exploiting public indifference on issues.[44] The president's leadership ability, however, does not exist in a vacuum. Presidents must operate within the boundary of their political, economic and partisan reality. The greater the number or impact of opposition voices, the less likely that presidents are to lead public opinion. It is the rare moment in which presidents are able to lead public opinion, because there are simply so many different ways in which presidential messages will be obscured; rarely will the message be adequately and completely received by the public. As a result, scholars generally find few moments in which presidents are able to lead public opinion.[45] But, on the other hand, when such contrary voices are more silent or the president's voice is more resonant, the opportunities for presidential leadership will be greater. Thus, leadership is conditional with respect to the political environment.

Looking at public opinion itself, Rottinghaus finds the nature of opinion preferences affects presidential ability to lead public opinion.[46] First, an increase in the percentage of the public registering "don't know" to a policy question assists presidential leadership. This suggests that the more the public learns about a topic or the more certain they become about an issue, the more easily (but modestly) the president is able to lead them. In effect, this is the golden apple of presidential communications. Presidents are teaching and leading—the public hears and understands the president's policy message and alters opinion on that policy accordingly. Second, presidential popularity is a positive factor in opinion movement but only when the issue is a high salience one.[47] However, as a subset of instances of presumed presidential popularity, the results reveal that a president's "honeymoon" is not necessarily a happy one. Although honeymoons are times in which presidents could lead because the criticism of the president would be lower, recent history indicates that presidents have too short a time period in their first years in office in which they are not receiving criticism from the media or opponents. This has had a greater impact on more recent presidents, because of higher expectations and less "friendly" coverage by the media.[48]

Specific communications techniques, often assumed to be an Achilles heel for modern presidents, are also successful. Rottinghaus finds that when presidents made the same argument two days in a row, they were able to move public opinion.[49] Communications tactics involving television also demonstrate success in leading public opinion. Presidents find success at leading public opinion with a "major address." Ostrom and Simon find that President Reagan's major speeches had a modest effect on his short-term popularity, but this effect was generally smaller than the effect of the events taking place in the political and economic environment.[50] This suggests that presentations that are more White House-driven (where the White House has more control over the format and message) are more suitable venues for successful presidential leadership, rather than those events where the president must be reactive to questions, or explain a policy through other kinds of individual speeches. In televised addresses, the White House has the potential to dictate the timing, setting and content—all of which facilitate a greater chance that the president's message will be transmitted in full either directly, or indirectly, through a media "echo" occurring days after these addresses.[51]

Approaching the "conditional" question differently, Wood asks whether or not the president can affect the public's broad ideological preferences with the ideological direction in his public speeches.[52] First, Wood finds that presidents are more likely to lead public opinion during their honeymoon period. Presidents may try to leverage their popularity to lead public opinion, and Wood finds that "when public approval is above average, the public responds more favorably to presidential efforts at persuasion."[53] This is consistent with previous findings that show popular presidents are more likely to lead. Second, the larger the president's support in Congress, and likely to be consistent with the ideological dimension of the public, the more the public is likely to respond favorably to presidential efforts at persuasion. Edwards's notion of presidents "facilitating" opinion is also relevant here presidents sense a broadly supportive opinion environment and act to move public opinion accordingly.

"Going Local"

If presidents find themselves in a political environment in which they are unable to mobilize or persuade the mass public, they may shift tactics. Presidents may "facilitate" leadership of public opinion by reflecting, clarifying or intensifying the opinions of their existing supporters.[54] In this sense, the mass public is less relevant to the president than his partisans (or possible future partisans). Presidents might also seek to mobilize these "special publics" to urge them to pressure Congress.[55] Kernell notes that "the president who rests his leadership on going public will be tempted to travel frequently, in search of sympathetic audiences and 'presidential images.'"[56] To accomplish this strategy, "presidents need to tailor their messages to attract those most predisposed to support them, those with 'special interests,' instead of focusing on building support within broad coalitions."[57] Presidents also have success in leading public preferences of political opponents (at least in personal perceptions of the president), even as they try to rally their base.[58] Modern presidents must balance the needs of their specific constituencies at specific times with the needs of the mass public at other times.[59]

This tactic has grown from presidential prerogative to necessity because the modern media and contemporary political message strategies require sure-handed, direct guidance of the White House's message by the president. The evidence suggests that presidents are taking the cue. More recent presidents have taken more trips per year in their first year in office, and more recent presidents are more likely to travel to larger, more competitive states.[60] Indeed, domestic travel has significantly increased in the past half century to the point where President Clinton was traveling "every fourth day or so during his first three years in office,"[61] which demonstrates the effect of the emergence of "barnstorming" as a consistent communications strategy.

Substantiating this trend, Jeffrey Cohen argues that presidents have modified their public leadership activities by "mobilizing support from their party base, interest groups, and select localities."[62] Instead of going public on a national scale, "presidents now go narrow; that is, they focus their public activities on building support in their party base, some interest groups, and select localities."[63] In 2000, for instance, local Democratic-leaning newspapers were more favorable to the Democratic president (Clinton) and presidential approval in the public had a positive effect on the tone of coverage. There is a window, at least locally, for presidents to buttress and expand local support. Does this positive tone in the local media pay off in more approval for the president? Using the National Annenberg Election Study (NAES), Cohen cleverly matches respondents' approval of the president with the local newspapers they read. Local positive coverage is found to increase approval of the president, especially among those who do not possess strong political predispositions.

Scholars have found that this localized strategy leads to favorable outcomes for presidents. Theoretically, this strategy affords the president with more chances to get his message directly to the public without depending on reporters, who may ask tough questions or provide no news coverage at all. The pay-off for presidents is that coverage of local visits (both by local media and by national media) is more positive toward them than is coverage of their national speeches.[64] Cohen and Powell determine that presidents can attain a modest boost (1–2 percentage points) in their approval at the state-level when using a localized strategy.[65] Domestic political travel (outside of Washington, D.C.) has a modest impact on presidential electoral success and presidential legislative success.[66] Such travel also has a modest impact on state-level presidential approval, although the effect is limited to non-election years and larger states.[67] Ostrom and Simon find that President Reagan's domestic travel did have a small positive effect on his popularity.[68] In addition, presidents can also use the "going local" technique to influence local media outlets, which are generally less critical of presidential policy, more willing to provide extended airtime to the president (and concurrently his message) and more supportive of presidential policy.[69]

To further examine whether or not local media cover the president in a more positive light when he visits, Barrett and Peake analyzed national and local newspaper coverage of President George W. Bush's domestic travel in 2001.[70] Using the *Washington Post* (as a measure of national content) and the highest circulating daily newspaper for each local area, Barrett and Peake find clear differences in the amount and tone of coverage between mediums. For example, on the day following a presidential visit, local outlets printed 214 stories while the *Washington Post* published 45; while nearly 60 percent of all coverage in local outlets was positive, 44 percent of the coverage in the *Washington Post* was positive. When analyzing variation across local coverage, Barrett and Peake conclude that the amount and tone of local coverage regarding George W. Bush's visits was dependent on presidential support in the community. The wider the margin of victory by President Bush in the prior election, the more positive the coverage was, and coverage was greater in those places in which he was more popular.

In an attempt to determine the effectiveness of localized presidential leadership, in which presidents use domestic travel to stump for their policy priorities in hope of creating positive, local news coverage to influence the public's priorities, Eshbaugh-Soha and Peake examine three case studies.[71] They find that when a president has broad public support for a given policy, in addition to high approval, in his first term, a localized strategy was more effective at leading public opinion. For example, President Bush's 60-states-in-60-days tour to stump for Social Security reform produced favorable local coverage.[72] However, an increase in salience does not necessarily equate to an increase in public support when a localized strategy is utilized. Though presidents can lead the agenda of the public and media, when going local, this agenda leadership is dependent on established public support.

The Media and Opinion Leadership

Late 20th and early 21st century presidents face a qualitatively different political environment than their predecessors, making the challenge of leadership of public opinion much more difficult.[73] Although there are several explanations for these differences, one of the most prominent is the emergence of a more aggressive and combative media that is willing to challenge the authority and truth of the president's message. Earlier serving presidents had more cordial relations with the news media and could rely on the media to cooperate with their need to distribute political information.[74] More recent presidents (especially since the Watergate scandal) have faced a more hostile and challenging media that is less willing to provide a "free pass" to the president to use the media as a vehicle for the dissemination of his political messages.[75] The rise of greater polarization and alienation (or outright hostility) between the White House and the media has limited the president's rhetorical reach.[76] The media's power to set the agenda and shape the tone of elections has also grown since parties have declined in power.[77]

Exploring these trends, Farnsworth and Lichter attempt to determine the extent to which news coverage has changed across four recent presidencies: Reagan, H.W. Bush, Clinton, and W. Bush.[78] To accomplish this, they derive data from an expansive content analysis spanning across presidencies, including the traditional television networks (e.g., ABC, CBS, FOX, and NBC) in addition to national, regional, and local newspapers. They find that, irrespective of the issue, the president almost always has the attention of the media, regardless of how hard Congress pushes to mitigate this advantage. In all, presidential coverage outpaces Congressional coverage by nearly three to one. Although presidents continue to dominate news coverage coming out of Washington, this coverage has become increasingly negative, with the media criticizing presidents in nearly every instance, with the exception of when the nation is in a time of war.

Clearly, modern presidents are subjected to a negative connotation of news coverage, but since abstaining from presidential rhetoric is not an option, it is important to understand how presidents manage their communications strategy in a time of fragmented media. To understand this strategy from inside the White House, Kumar interviewed senior staff members and communications officials, in addition to observing White House briefings, over a twenty-five-year period encompassing the four administrations prior to President Obama.[79] Based on her interviews and observations, Kumar gives several suggestions to presidents as they attempt to break through a fragmented media. First, the president should propose and implement policies that have broad public support. No matter how great a president's communications strategy, it will always fail in the face of a public that only weakly supports the president's policies. Second, White House staffers must familiarize themselves with what makes a story newsworthy. Finally, and perhaps most importantly, without a president skilled in public rhetoric, the above suggestions will diminish in impact dramatically.

With the media moving into the era of "24-hour news," presidents can now directly raise public support for their policy agenda in a multitude of ways. In explaining why this phenomenon is occurring, Cohen reveals how coverage of the president has turned increasingly negative, lacked credibility, and reached a substantially smaller audience over time.[80] Though there are few scholars questioning the increasingly negative tone of presidential news coverage, Cohen questions why this has not affected public evaluations of the president as strongly as it has in the past. Cohen believes this relationship has changed immensely in the post-broadcast era, as the public has fractured into "special interest publics." For example, there are groups who have a high interest in politics and listen to, or watch, political news on a daily basis, and those with extremely low interest, who obtain their political information by accident, as a remnant of entertainment programming. Cohen cites two reasons for the public fracturing. First, the growth in media modes has increased the competition among for-profit news-gathering entities, and second, because cable television has increased the amount of options available to viewers, news agencies have changed their reporting styles to better capture the information needs of the public. Due to these factors, Cohen argues that the news media are no longer an institution of "democratic linkage," as they are increasingly covering soft news instead of hard news. As a result, the public is less exposed to the president.

Though Cohen views the media nowadays as being less helpful to the president in leading public opinion, Eshbaugh-Soha and Peake challenge that notion; they examine the reciprocal nature of agenda setting among the president, the media and public by redefining presidential leadership strategies into three categories: focused, sustained, and localized.[81] Regarding a focused strategy, Eshbaugh-Soha and Peake find substantial support for presidents indirectly leading the public through the media, as presidents have the unique ability to act as the gatekeepers of information. Presidents lead the public indirectly through the media when implementing a focused strategy of leadership. When applying a sustained strategy, the findings illustrate that neither the president nor media have direct persuasive power over the public's aggregated economic agenda. However, when parsing out differences between specific policies, presidents have a higher likelihood of leading directly on policies of lower public salience (e.g., deficits and spending), while they are more likely to respond and lead indirectly on issues of higher salience (e.g., unemployment). On the issue of war, presidents indirectly lead the public agenda through increased media coverage of the issue, although this leadership may weaken over time. Specifically, they argue, the George W. Bush administration failed to dictate media coverage as the war in Iraq progressed, and Bush rarely led the public directly.

Conclusion

Townes Van Zandt, the great Texas singer and songwriter, wrote in "To Live is to Fly" (this chapter's title is lightly adapted from his title): "Some fall on you like a storm, / sometimes you dig your own. / The choice is yours to make,/time is yours to take." Linking this allegorically, presidents, like Townes's fictional protagonist, are at times influenced by political events and at times swept up in them. Presidents have choices to make if they want to engage in successful leadership of public opinion—sometimes they choose correctly, sometimes they choose poorly. Partly as a result of this, scholars often understandably mischaracterize the nature of presidential leadership. A president may be trying to lead but will fail because several circumstances are working against him. Alternatively, a president may not be trying to lead but may have success anyway because circumstances favor his message. Context, therefore, is critical. Our intent in this chapter is to analyze presidential leadership of opinion in the proper context and identify the particular conditional moments during which it may succeed.

Recent scholarship has argued that leadership is categorically impossible for presidents as they try to communicate their message to the public. Both George Edwards and Jeffrey Cohen suggest that the concurrent limitations of partisanship, media attention and public attention hamper the president's ability to present his unvarnished message to the American people.[82] Susan Herbst argues that because of these boundaries presidential speech is "hurtling towards its demise."[83] In contrast to these assessments, we argue that these limiting conditions are clearly present for modern presidents, but in instances during which presidents have a clearer window of communication, they have an easier time leading public opinion. The findings presented here make nuanced claims about a president's inability to lead public opinion. Presidents may lead at the margins and only in selected conditions, but they still lead.

In fact, presidents are not always hapless victims of political circumstances, where an unfavorable environment perpetually disadvantages their ability to lead public opinion. Several time periods, conditions and tactics used by presidents serve to advantage the president, especially when it is more likely that the president's message is able to get through with direct, televised communication, through consistently utilizing the "bully pulpit." Leading on the national stage through major addresses, talking about foreign policy or the economy, going "local," converting citizens who are unsure or unaware, and discussing popular issues (especially while popular), all provide a platform for successful leadership. These findings imply that presidents have some control over their own political fortunes and that presidents can strategically lead public opinion, even though this success is conditioned on the degree of public information, the prominence of the issue, the location, the time period and the tactic used. In this context, these findings concur with Edwards' edicts from *The Strategic President* in that presidents are admonished to use their skills to recognize the opportunities for leadership.[84] This chapter has helped to put the president's ability to lead public opinion in context—a critical step to evaluating the impact of presidential rhetoric on the public, Congress and the larger political system.

Presidents must be strategic about when and on which issues they go public. Presidents are more likely to lead public opinion when other leaders or events do not obscure his direct communication with the public. Presidents should succeed at leading public opinion when they make consistent, solid and unwavering attempts to do so.[85] The more the president can avoid the political echo chamber associated with partisan battles, the better the chance the president has to lead public opinion. The ability to lead public opinion is "provisional," with certain factors enhancing leadership success and certain factors detracting from leadership success.[86] Indeed, finding less reliably consistent success with broad national appeals, presidents have increasingly taken their message more directly to their constituents or to more targeted regions or states. This is the new frontier of presidential leadership.

Presidents are consistently pushing to narrow the gap between the high expectations placed on them by the system and the public and their relatively meager ability to persuade the public. The public, as part of the national democratic character associated with the modern presidency, expects presidents to lead.[87] Partisan publics also expect the president to cater to their issues. The political world, however, often gets in their way. Presidents have had mixed success in using public rhetorical leadership to close the gap between their ability to affect their political world (which can be limited) and the expectations placed on them. And, in a real sense, presidents' hands are forced to engage in this "hyper-rhetorical" presidency because the availability of presidential communications creates the opportunities to do so and a crowded media environment creates a de facto requirement to do so.[88] Finding the right moment to pursue their agenda with the public is critical in cutting through the noise of the political system.

Notes

1 Bert A Rockman and Richard W. Waterman, "Two Normative Models of Presidential Leadership," in *Presidential Leadership: The Vortex of Power*, ed. Bert A. Rockman and Richard W. Waterman (New York: Oxford University Press, 2008).
2 Theodore Lowi, *The Personal Presidency: Power Invested Promise Unfulfilled* (Ithaca, NY: Cornell University Press, 1985).
3 Edwin C. Hargrove, *The President as Leader: Appealing to the Better Angels of Our Nature* (Lawrence: University of Kansas Press, 1998).
4 Richard E. Neustadt, *Presidential Power and the Modern Presidents: The Politics of Leadership from Roosevelt to Reagan* (New York: The Free Press, 1990).
5 Neustadt, *Presidential Power and the Modern Presidents*, 84.
6 Neustadt, *Presidential Power and the Modern Presidents*, 89.
7 Samuel Kernell, *Going Public: New Strategies of Presidential Leadership*, (Washington, DC: CQ Press, 2007).
8 Kernell, *Going Public*, x.
9 Kernell, *Going Public*, 2.
10 Melvin Laracey, *Presidents and the People: The Partisan Story of Going Public* (College Station: Texas A&M University Press, 2002).
11 Brandice Canes-Wrone, "The President's Legislative Influence from Public Appeals," *American Journal of Political Science* 45 (2001): 313–29; Brandice Canes-Wrone, *Who Leads Whom? Presidents, Policy and the Public* (Chicago: University of Chicago Press, 2006).

12 George C. Edwards III, *On Deaf Ears: The Limits of the Bully Pulpit* (New Haven: Yale University Press, 2003).
13 Banjamin I. Page, Robert Y. Shapiro and Glenn Dempsey, "What Moves Public Opinion?" *American Political Science Review* 81 (1987): 23–44; Jeffrey E. Cohen, *The Presidency in the Era of 24-Hour News* (Princeton: Princeton University Press, 2008).
14 Joel D. Aberbach and Bert A. Rockman, "Hard Times for Presidential Leadership? (And How Would We Know?)." *Presidential Studies Quarterly* 29 (1999): 757–778.
15 Reed L. Welch, "Presidential Success in Communicating with the Public Through Televised Addresses," *Presidential Studies Quarterly* 33 (2003): 347–365; Reed L. Welch, "Was Reagan Really a Great Communicator? The Influence of Televised Addresses on Public Opinion," *Presidential Studies Quarterly* 33 (2003): 853–76; Garry Young and William B. Perkins, "Presidential Rhetoric, the Public Agenda, and the End of Presidential Television's 'Golden Age,'" *Journal of Politics* 67 (2005): 1190–1205.
16 Samuel Kernell and Laurie L. Rice, "Cable and the Partisan Polarization of the President's Audience," *Presidential Studies Quarterly* 41 (2011): 693–711.
17 Joel D. Aberbach and Bert A. Rockman, "Hard Times for Presidential Leadership?
18 Richard E. Neustadt, "The Weakening White House," *British Journal of Political Science* 31 (2001): 1–11.
19 Kernell, *Going Public.*
20 Robert Finbow, "Presidential Leadership or Structural Constraints? The Failure of President Carter's Health Insurance Proposals," *Presidential Studies Quarterly* 28 (1998): 169–187.
21 Lawrence R. Jacobs and Robert Y. Shapiro, "The Rise of Presidential Polling: The Nixon White House in Historical Perspective," *Public Opinion Quarterly* 59 (1995): 163–195.
22 Edwards III, *On Deaf Ears.*
23 Cohen, *The Presidency in the Era of 24-Hour News.*
24 Bert A. Rockman, "When it Comes to Presidential Leadership, Accentuate the Positive, but Don't Forget the Normative," in *Presidential Leadership: The Vortex of Power,* ed. Bert A. Rockman and Richard W. Waterman (New York: Oxford University Press, 2008).
25 Andreas Wenger and Marcel Gerber, "John F. Kennedy and the Limited Test Ban Treaty: A Case Study of Presidential Leadership," *Presidential Studies Quarterly* 29 (1999): 460–487.
26 John W. Sloan, *The Reagan Effect: Economics and Presidential Leadership* (Lawrence: University of Kansas Press, 1999).
27 Jacobs and Shapiro, "The Rise of Presidential Polling."
28 Neustadt, *Presidential Power and the Modern Presidents.*
29 Buchanan, *The Citizen's Presidency: Standards of Choice and Judgment;* See also Todd M. Schaefer, "Persuading the Persuaders," *Political Communication* 14 (1997): 97–111.
30 Benjamin I. Page, Robert Y. Shapiro and Glenn R. Dempsey, "What Moves Public Opinion?" *American Political Science Review* 81 (1987): 23–44; John Zaller, *The Nature and Origins of Mass Opinion* (New York: Cambridge University Press, 1992).
31 Canes-Wrone, *Who Leads Whom?*
32 Canes-Wrone, *Who Leads Whom?,* 185.
33 B. Dan Wood, *The Politics of Economic Leadership: The Causes and Consequences of Presidential Rhetoric* (Princeton: Princeton University Press, 2007).
34 Wood, *The Politics of Economic Leadership.*

35 B. Dan Wood, Chris T. Owens and Brandy M. Durham, "Presidential Rhetoric and the Economy," *Journal of Politics* 67 (2005): 627–645.
36 Matthew Eshbaugh-Soha, "Presidential Signaling in a Market Economy," *Presidential Studies Quarterly* 35 (2005): 718–735.
37 Jeffrey E. Cohen and John A. Hamman, "The Polls: Can Presidential Rhetoric Affect the Public's Economic Perceptions?" *Presidential Studies Quarterly* 33 (2003): 408–422.
38 Canes-Wrone, *Who Leads Whom?*; Lee Sigelman, "Disarming the Opposition: The President, the Public, and the INF Treaty," *Public Opinion Quarterly* 54 (1990): 37–47; Alan J. Rosenblatt, "Aggressive Foreign Policy Marketing: Public Response to Reagan's 1983 Address on Lebanon and Grenada," *Political Behavior* 20 (1998): 225–240.
39 Canes-Wrone, *Who Leads Whom?*, 101.
40 Lee Sigelman, "Disarming the Opposition."
41 Alan J. Rosenblatt, "Aggressive Foreign Policy Marketing: Public Response to Reagan's 1983 Address on Lebanon and Grenada," *Public Behavior* 20 (1998): 225–240.
42 Kernell, *Going Public.*
43 Kent Tedin, Brandon Rottinghaus and Harrell Rodgers, "When the President Goes Public: The Consequences of Communication Mode for Opinion Change Across Issue Types and Groups," *Political Research Quarterly* 64 (2010): 506–519.
44 George C. Edwards III, *The Strategic Presidency: Persuasion and Opportunity in Presidential Leadership.* (Princeton: Princeton University Press, 2009), 61–62.
45 See Edwards III, *On Deaf Ears: The Limits of the Bully Pulpit*; Cohen, *The Presidency in the Era of 24-Hour News.*
46 Brandon Rottinghaus, *The Provisional Pulpit* (College Station: Texas A&M University Press, 2010).
47 Rottinghaus, *The Provisional Pulpit.*
48 Richard A. Brody, "Is the Honeymoon Over? The American People and President Bush," *The Polling Report* 17 (2001): 5–7.
49 Brandon Rottinghaus, "Strategic Leaders: Identifying Successful Momentary Presidential Leadership of Public Opinion," *Political Communication* 26 (2009): 296–316.
50 Charles W. Ostrom, Jr. and Dennis M. Simon, "The Man in the Teflon Suit? The Environmental Political Drama and Popular Support in the Reagan Presidency," *Public Opinion Quarterly* 53 (1989): 58–82.
51 Welch, "Was Reagan Really a Great Communicator"; Stephen J. Farnsworth and Robert Lichter, *The Mediated Presidency: Television News and Presidential Governance* (Lanham, MD: Rowan and Littlefield, 2006).
52 B. Dan Wood, *The Myth of Presidential Representation* (Cambridge: Cambridge University Press, 2010).
53 Wood, *The Myth of Presidential Representation*, 144–145.
54 Edwards III, *The Strategic Presidency.*
55 Jeffrey E. Cohen and Ken Collier, "Public Opinion: Reconceptualizing Going Public," in *Presidential Policymaking*, ed. Steven A. Shull (Armonk, NY: M.E. Sharpe, 1999).
56 Kernell, *Going Public: New Strategies of Presidential Leadership*, 121.
57 George C. Edwards, III, *Governing by Campaigning: The Politics of the Bush Presidency* (New York: Pearson Longman, 2006), 287.
58 Tedin, Rottinghaus and Rodgers, "When the President Goes Public."
59 Wood, *The Myth of Presidential Representation*, 144–145.
60 Brendan Doherty, "Elections: The Politics of Permanent Campaign: Presidential Travel and the Electoral College, 1977–2004," *Presidential Studies Quarterly* 37 (2007): 749–773.

61 Kernell, *Going Public:*, 121.

62 Jeffrey Cohen, *Going Local* (New York: Cambridge University Press, 2010), 2.

63 Ibid, 3.

64 Andrew W. Barrett and Jeffrey S. Peake, "When the President Comes to Town: Examining Local Newspaper Coverage of Domestic Presidential Travel," *American Politics Research* 35 (2007): 3–31; Matthew Eshbaugh-Soha, "Local Newspaper Coverage of the Presidency," *International Journal of Politics/Press* 13 (2008): 103–119.

65 Jeffrey E. Cohen and Richard J. Powell, "Building Public Support from the Grassroots Up: The Impact of Presidential Travel on State-Level Approval," *Presidential Studies Quarterly* 35 (2005): 11–27.

66 Thomas M. Holbrook, "Did the Whistle-Stop Campaign Matter?" *PS: Political Science* 35 (2002): 59–66; Andrew W. Barrett, "Gone Public: The Impact of Going Public on Presidential Legislative Success," *American Politics Research* 32 (2004): 338–370.

67 Jeffrey E. Cohen and Richard J. Powell, "Building Public Support from the Grassroots Up."

68 Ostrom and Simon, "The Man in the Teflon Suit?"

69 Matthew Eshbaugh-Soha and Jeffrey S. Peake, "'Going Local' to Reform Social Security," *Presidential Studies Quarterly* 36 (2006): 689–704; Barrett and Peake, "When the President Comes to Town."

70 Barrett and Peake, "When the President Comes to Town."

71 Matthew Eshbaugh-Soha and Jeffrey S. Peake, *Breaking Through the Noise: Presidential Leadership, Public Opinion and the News Media* (Palo Alto: Stanford University Press, 2011).

72 Eshbaugh-Soha and Peake, "'Going Local' to Reform Social Security."

73 Rottinghaus, *The Provisional Pulpit*, 64.

74 Martha Joynt Kumar, *Managing the President's Message: The White House Communications Operation* (Baltimore: Johns Hopkins University Press, 2007).

75 Grossman, Michael Baruch and Martha Joynt Kumar, *Portraying the President: The White House and the News Media* (Baltimore: Johns Hopkins University Press, 1981); Steven E. Clayman, Marc N. Elliott, John Heritage and Laurie L. MacDonald, "Historical Trends in Questioning Presidents, 1953–2000," *Presidential Studies Quarterly* 36 (2006): 561–583.

76 Edwards III, *On Deaf Ears*; Cohen, *The Presidency in the Era of 24-Hour News*.

77 Thomas E. Patterson, *Out of Order* (New York: Knopf, 1993).

78 Farnsworth and Lichter, *The Mediated Presidency*.

79 Kumar, *Managing the President's Message*.

80 Cohen, *The Presidency in the Era of 24-Hour News*.

81 Eshbaugh-Soha and Peake, *Breaking Through the Noise*.

82 Edwards III, *On Deaf Ears;* Cohen, *The Presidency in the Era of 24-Hour News*.

83 Susan Herbst, "The Rhetorical Presidency and the Contemporary Media Environment," *Critical Review* 19 (2007), 2–3.

84 Edwards III, *The Strategic President*.

85 Rottinghaus, "Strategic Leaders."

86 Rottinghaus, *The Provisional Pulpit*.

87 Barbara Kellerman, *The Political Presidency: Practice of Presidential Leadership from Kennedy Through Reagan* (New York: Oxford University Press, 1986).

88 John J. Dilulio, "The Hyper-Rhetorical Presidency," *Critical Review* 19 (2007): 315–324.

Chapter 12

Political Dynamics of Framing[1]

Samara Klar, Joshua Robison and James N. Druckman

On March 15, 2012, former Illinois Governor Rod Blagojevich began a four-teen-year prison sentence. This signified the end of the long and painful down-fall of Blagojevich, who had once held presidential aspirations. He became the fourth Illinois governor in recent times to be imprisoned, following in the steps of his predecessor, George Ryan, who was also serving time for corruption. The start of Blagojevich's sentence received national attention due, in part, to allegations that Blagojevich had used his ability to appoint a replacement to President Obama's former Senate seat as an opportunity to sell the seat to the highest bidder. While the media primarily focused upon the corruption angle to the Blagojevich story, others aspects of Blagojevich's reign received much less attention. One of the more interesting, albeit overlooked, comments came from his 2006 gubernatorial campaign foe: Judy Barr Topinka. She stated that the "legacy of Mr. Blagojevich on the state—and its grim financial situation—will last far longer than his 14-year prison term."[2]

Topinka's comment echoed the case she attempted to make six years earlier when she had hoped to upset the Democratic incumbent Blagojevich by fram-ing the campaign as one about the candidates' economic plans for the state. A *Chicago Tribune* editorial, published at the start of the campaign, stated that Topinka "is framing this contest for governor just as it needs to be framed: How can a grossly overcommitted state government bend the financial trend lines that point inexorably toward ruin?"[3] The two candidates had opposing economic approaches, with Topinka proposing the creation of a land-based, state-owned Chicago casino and Blagojevich pushing for the sale or leasing of the state lottery.

Had the campaign frame centered on the economy it may have paved the way for a Topinka upset. Unfortunately for Topinka, this is not what happened. The dominant frame of the campaign, ironically enough, became one of corruption. And neither candidate was spared; for example, the wife of Blagojevich's former campaign treasurer alleged that she received a state job in return for a per-sonal check, and Blagojevich's close advisor Stuart Levine pled guilty to using his position on the state teacher pension and hospital board to extort money. Topinka, for her part, also had connections to Levine, and she had served in the administration of the aforementioned Governor Ryan who was currently on trial for corruption. Voters became disillusioned, with more than half of all voters expressing "little confidence . . . that either Blagojevich or Topinka would clean up corruption."[4] A content analysis of campaign coverage shows that the vast plurality of discussion ended up centering on corruption and having little to do with the failing economy.[5] In the end, voters went with the status quo incumbent—the better known of two "evils."

Would the election have ended differently, with a Topinka victory, had the economy come to define the campaign? Would voters have focused on the economy if the media and the candidates had ultimately spent more time doing so, rather than turning their attention to corruption? These questions can never be directly answered. Yet, what is clear is that how a campaign, an issue, or an event is *framed* can fundamentally change political outcomes by altering how and what people think.

In this chapter, we explore framing research with the goal of demonstrating what we do and do not know about framing. We begin by explaining what a frame is. We provide a number of examples of how elites of various stripes engage in framing. We then turn to a discussion of how frames matter, and perhaps most importantly, *when* frames matter in altering public opinion. We conclude by emphasizing new areas of framing research, as well as some areas where more work is needed.

What Is a Frame?[6]

The term "frame" has varied meanings across disciplines, including cognitive science, economics, sociology, psychology, and more.[7] When it comes to politics, the prototypical approach distinguishes between two uses.[8] First, a frame can refer to the words, images, phrases, and presentation styles a speaker uses to relay information; these are called frames in communication.[9] The frame that the speaker chooses reveals what the speaker believes is most relevant to the topic at hand.[10] For example, a politician who emphasizes economic issues during a political campaign uses an "economy frame," suggesting economic considerations are pertinent (e.g., perhaps more relevant than foreign policy or ethical considerations). Alternatively, a policy advocate who describes universal health care as ensuring equal access for all accentuates egalitarianism rather than, for instance, the costs of coverage.

Second, a frame can refer to an individual's understanding of a given situation, or what can be called *frames in thought*.[11] In this case, a frame is not a property of a communication, but rather describes an individual's perception of a situation; the frame reveals what an individual sees as relevant to understanding a situation. For example, an individual who evaluates candidates based on their economic issue positions is said to be in an economic frame of mind.[12] A person who thinks of universal health care as a basic right for all is in an egalitarian frame of mind.

Frames in communication and frames in thought are similar in that they both are concerned with variations in emphasis or salience. However, they differ in that the former usage focuses on what a speaker says, while the latter usage focuses on what an individual is thinking. When it comes to political framing, one can discuss the framing of an issue (e.g., welfare, affirmative action, energy policy), an event (e.g., a natural disaster, a war), or a campaign.

Frames in communication often play an important role in shaping frames in thought. This process is called a *framing effect*.[13] Framing effects matter because individuals almost always focus only on a subset of possible ways to think about an issue, event, or campaign. Thus, the frame they have in mind determines their opinions and behaviors. A voter's preference between two candidates may vary depending on whether the voter is thinking in an economic or foreign policy frame.[14] In the 2008 U.S. presidential election, a voter might have preferred John McCain to Barack Obama when evaluating them on their foreign policy positions, but preferred Obama to McCain when comparing their economic platforms (or vice versa). So which frame dominates can play a big role in vote choice and ultimately election outcomes. Indeed, consider the aforementioned Illinois gubernatorial campaign. By Election Day, it became fairly clear that an economic frame was not driving most voters' choices—if it had, perhaps Topinka would have been the victor.[15] It is a cruel irony in retrospect that corruption became the dominant frame; as mentioned, we suspect that disillusionment with both candidates led voters to simply opt for the status quo.

Countless examples of framing effects exist: support for universal health care may hinge on whether one thinks of it in terms of egalitarianism or economic costs; an individual's attitude toward welfare recipients may depend on the extent to which one believes their plight is explained by personal failures or by social and economic disadvantages; and one's tolerance for allowing a hate group to publicly rally may hinge on the value one places on defending free speech versus maintaining public safety.[16] In all of these cases, the attitude and/or choices depends on the weights given to the competing frames.

Politicians and policy advocates regularly attempt to frame campaigns and issues to their advantage because they understand that what the public thinks influences election outcomes and public policy.[17] Media outlets also must make choices of which frames to use when covering a story, albeit with a different motivation in mind (e.g. they wish to maximize audience shares rather than win votes). In the next section, we provide examples of elite framing (what Scheufele calls framing building).[18] We then turn to a discussion of how and when these efforts may shape opinions.

Examples of Frames in Communication

Frames come from all types of communicator. Indeed, we all frame topics in our daily conversations: whenever we discuss an issue or an event, we focus on certain aspects. When it comes to politics, a variety of political actors—including politicians, the media, and lobbyists—put forth potentially influential frames.

Politicians spend considerable time determining the frames most advantageous to them.[19,20] One example of a politician's strategic framing choice comes from Druckman and Holmes' study of President Bush's 2002 State of the Union address.[21] Bush faced a fairly divided audience, whose focus had begun to shift from terrorism and homeland security to a lagging economy and the looming threat of recession. Prior to Bush's address, analysts predicted that he would focus equally on terrorism *and* the economy in reaction to this shift in public attention.[22]

The expectation that Bush would shift attention made some superficial sense, but it ignored the strategic considerations facing the President. Bush's issue-specific approval on security (roughly 86 percent) was substantially higher than on the slumping economy (roughly 31 percent).[23] By framing the country's situation in terms of terrorism and homeland security, Bush could potentially induce people to view the administration's performance in terms of its response to terror and its efforts to increase domestic security. By so doing, Bush would then presumably lead citizens to think of him in terms of terrorism, which was to his advantage relative to if voters had focused on his economic performance.

This is exactly what Bush did; an analysis of the frames used by Bush in the State of the Union by Druckman and Holmes demonstrated that 49 percent of the discussion focused on terrorism/homeland security, while only 10 percent of the discussion focused on the economy. This effort to strategically frame the issues of the country in favor of the President's prior approval ratings had an effect on subsequent media coverage. The *New York Times* headline the day after the address stated: "Bush, Focusing on Terrorism, Says Secure U.S. Is Top Priority."[24]

The actions of President Bush in this example are not unique to this specific president or context. Rather, additional evidence suggests that his behavior reflects a general pattern. For example, Druckman, Jacobs, and Ostermeier examine the rhetorical choices of President Nixon during his first term in office (1969–1972).[25] The authors coded Nixon's public statements for the amount of space devoted to distinct issues, such as welfare, crime, and civil rights. Linking this rhetorical data with polling results from Nixon's private archives, Druckman, Jacobs, and Ostermeier find that Nixon chose his frames on domestic issues in strategically favorable ways. For example, if public support for Nixon's position on a particular domestic issue increased by 10 percent, then Nixon increased attention to that issue by an average of 58 percent.[26] Nixon did not, by contrast, significantly respond to changes in issues the public saw as "important" (e.g., he would use a tax frame even if most of the public did not see taxes as an important problem). In short, Nixon framed his addresses so as to induce the public to base their presidential and general evaluations on the criteria that favored him.[27]

Like Presidents, congressional candidates strategically choose their frames. It is well documented that congressional incumbents—those already in office—have an electoral advantage of up to ten percentage points over their challengers.[28] This advantage stems, in part, from their experience of holding office, their familiarity with the district, and the provision of benefits to the district or state that they represent.[29] Incumbents have a strategic incentive to frame their campaigns in terms of experience, familiarity, and benefits, while their challengers will want to frame the campaign in other terms, such as issue positions, partisanship, endorsements, and polls (e.g. to show that the candidate is viable). Druckman, Kifer, and Parkin tested these expectations with data from a representative sample of U.S. House and Senate campaigns from 2002, 2004, and 2006. They did content analyses of candidate websites and coded the terms candidates used to frame the campaign (i.e. the extent to which they emphasize different criteria). As expected, incumbents framed their campaigns in ways that benefit them by emphasizing experience in office, familiarity, and district ties, while challengers framed the campaign in alternative terms. The normative implications are intriguing, since campaign frames that often establish subsequent policy agendas are driven, in no small way, by strategic considerations that may bear little relationship with pressing governmental issues.[30]

The above examples focus on the framing tactics of a single elite actor without taking account of competition between elites or the role of media. There is little doubt that the Democrats emphasized the troubled economy in their public statements following Bush's 2002 State of the Union address; similarly, Nixon's opponents tried to shift the agenda to alternative issues that were less favorable to Nixon. These competing frames often appear when one turns to how the media cover issues and events—unlike politicians intent on winning office, the media (even if driven to increase audience share) often aim to present a more balanced picture of different frames. To explore the extent to which competing frames are represented in news coverage of political issues, Chong and Druckman content analyzed major newspaper coverage of fourteen distinct issues over time, counting the number of frames put forth on each issue (as well as other features of the frames).[31]

Across the fourteen issues studied by Chong and Druckman, the average number of frames employed was 5.09, with the fewest frames employed in the coverage of a 1998 Ku Klux Klan rally in Tennessee and the most on the 2004 Abu Ghraib controversy (when members of the American military were reported to have abused prisoners in the Iraqi prison Abu Ghraib). Importantly, many of the frames employed on each issue came from opposing sides. For example, a frame of individual responsibility concerning Abu Ghraib suggested that fault for the incident lay with the individuals involved, whereas the administration or military commander frames put the bulk of the blame on the culture established by higher-level actors. Opposing sides simultaneously employ contrary frames that often make their way into media coverage. How individuals process these mixes of frames is the topic to which we shortly turn.

Once a set of frames are established, introducing entirely novel ones is not easy. Lobbyists often try to accomplish this in order to change the terms of the debate, but find this task to be quite challenging. For example, Baumgartner, De Boef, and Boydstun explore the rate at which 98 issues, over a nearly two-year period, are re-framed, that is, when a wholly or partially new frame enters the conversation regarding an issue among interest-group lobbyists, media coverage, and other elite level information.[32] They report that "of the 98 issues that fell into our sample, we judged just 4 issues to have undergone some degree of re-framing over the period studied."[33] They point to several challenges of re-framing elite understandings, including limitations in resources, political constraints (e.g., political alignments), and failed lobbyist strategies. The lack of change observed by Baumgartner, et al., is consistent with macro-level studies that show "system-wide definitions of most issues remain relatively constant through time."[34] Research concerning social movements and framing also suggests that re-framing is difficult due to disagreements *within* a particular side over which frame should be adopted in the first place.[35] If an interest group or social movement that seeks to reframe an issue does not possess internal cohesion over what to reframe that issue *as*, then its ability to carry out this change will be curtailed.

The foregoing suggests a series of crucial questions left for further research: when is it advantageous for elites to attempt to re-frame an issue and how often do they have the resources necessary to do so? When elites possess both incentives and resources to re-frame an issue, are they able to accomplish their objective? Answers to these questions would help us to understand why issues are so rarely re-framed, whether because of the absence of elite incentives, shortages of resources to carry out the task, or entrenched public opinion on the issues. With these questions in mind, we next turn to a discussion of when frames do shape the opinions of ordinary citizens.

Framing Effects

Scholars demonstrate framing effects using a variety of methods, including surveys and case studies.[36] The use of experimentation, however, has been critical for developing causal claims concerning the influence of framing on preferences. Experiments provide researchers with the ability to randomly assign participants to receive particular messages at particular points in time. This sidesteps a key limitation of observational studies—the self-selection by participants into messages for reasons that also influence how they interpret the frame. That is, individuals often choose to listen to politicians or read media reports that tend to use frames they already favor. This makes it difficult, if not impossible, to determine if the frames influence their opinions or whether the relationship between frame exposure and opinion is spurious in nature. Experimentation allows researchers to get around this problem because experiments take a group of respondents and randomly assign them to be exposed to one (or multiple) frames instead of another (or others). The random assignment means that, on average, the groups exposed to different communications will be, on average, the same save for being exposed (or not) to the frames in question. Any differences in opinion between groups can then be confidently attributed to the frames to which they were exposed. Experiments also have the advantage because the researcher knows what communications respondents received—they do not have to rely on respondents remembering what they read or heard.[37]

A framing experiment typically begins with participants randomly assigned to receive one of two alternative representations of an issue. The canonical example of this procedure comes from a study conducted by Nelson, Clawson, and Oxley on a potential rally by the Ku Klux Klan (KKK).[38] The researchers randomly provided participants with information that stressed *either* the free speech claims of the KKK, *or* the potential impact on public safety the rally would entail. We can discern a framing effect if opinions toward the rally differed significantly based on the information stressed. Just such an effect occurred; the researchers observed that individuals exposed to the free speech frame were significantly more positive in their support for the proposed rally. In this experiment, and others of similar design, we can conclude that the framing of an issue has great consequence for the opinions individuals express.

The KKK experiment demonstrates that the manner in which elites frame an issue influences public opinion to a significant degree. More evidence for this powerful claim comes from experiments conducted by Iyengar and Kinder.[39] Participants in these experiments were randomly assigned to view edited television newscasts that contained stories on either defense spending, unemployment, or inflation. Iyengar and Kinder found that this simple difference paid great dividends in how participants evaluated the president. Participants ended up evaluating the president based on the issue upon which the newscast focused; someone who viewed a newscast that focused on defense spending, for instance, evaluated the president based on his or her views on defense spending, but not on inflation and unemployment. The content of the newscasts framed politics for participants by stressing the importance of some issues over others.

Early studies on framing provided evidence that even a small change in the framing of an issue could produce quite dramatic shifts in opinion. However, these studies did not explore three crucial aspects of the environment in which framing often occurs: (i) the *competition* between frames, (ii) the *durability* of framing effects and the role of *media choice* on durability, and (iii) the influence of *partisan polarization* on a frame's effectiveness. Recent work in each of these areas has contributed to a more nuanced understanding of framing.

Framing Competition

Citizens typically receive multiple frames concerning an issue from different sides due either to media exposure, or access to general political debate. A critical question is which of these competing frames will win?[40] The initial foray into this question came from Sniderman and Theriault who posited that when exposed to competing frames, neither would win—people would fall back on their values.[41] They state that people are "capable of picking the side of the issue that matches their political principles when they are exposed to a full [competitive] debate."[42] They demonstrated this dynamic by presenting individuals with two competing frames presented together (e.g. an individual receives both a free speech frame and a public safety frame regarding a hate group rally), and found that framing effects largely disappeared; people instead based their decisions on if they generally cared more about free speech or public safety.[43] The authors suggest that competing frames make alternative positions equally accessible, which increases the likelihood that people will be able to identify and choose the side that is consistent with their ideological values.[44]

Not all frames are created equal, however. With this in mind, Druckman and Chong suggest that cancelling out is not the necessary outcome of frame competition.[45] Instead, it is the *stronger* frame that wins. Druckman and Chong define strength as consisting of three elements. The first is availability, which means that the individual needs to make a connection between the consideration/frame and the issue at hand for the frame to matter. In the hate group rally example, an individual must make some connection between free speech and the rally in order for the frame to be influential. The second aspect of strength is accessibility. The frame must actually come to mind as a consideration when thinking about the topic (this often comes from the frame in communication). The final facet of strength is applicability. An individual must view the consideration as compelling or persuasive for it to be considered strong. If free speech comes to mind and is connected to the issue at hand, for instance, but is not seen as an important consideration for the issue of a hate group rally, then the frame will not matter for the individual's opinion. As in much of psychology, availability is assessed by asking people what considerations come to mind, frames are made accessible via communications (e.g., in experiments), and applicability is analyzed by asking different respondents what they think of different frames.[46] For example, how important do individuals rate free speech, public safety, town reputation, possible litter from the rally, and so on, when they think about a hate group rally. Thus, importantly, applicability is perceptual. We will return to the issue of strength in the conclusion.

As shown by a number of studies, the strength of a frame is a key consideration as to how influential it will be on an individual's ultimate opinion. To cite just one example, Druckman conducted a study of support for the aforementioned publicly funded casino during the 2006 Illinois gubernatorial campaign—even though in the end it ended up being a marginal issue.[47] He first pre-tested a variety of frames for strength by asking participants who did not live in Illinois (and thus were not affected by even the marginal coverage given the issue) what considerations came to mind when they thought of a state-owned casino. Then, with a distinct group of non-Illinois participants, he asked them to rate the effectiveness of various considerations in arguing for or against such a casino (he also asked whether these participants viewed each consideration as being in favor or opposed to the casino). In light of these tests, he identified two strong frames (i.e., highly available and applicable): the economic benefits (e.g., for education funds) that would come from a casino and the social costs that casinos generate (e.g., addiction, debt). Obviously the economic frame was a pro frame and the social costs negative. He similarly identified weak frames, including a pro weak frame (i.e., people viewed it as not available and not applicable) of entertainment (i.e., casinos are a source of entertainment) and a weak con frame of morality (e.g., casinos are immoral).

Druckman then conducted a survey of a group of Illinois voters on Election Day, where he randomly exposed individuals to a host of these different mixes of frames (or to no frames whatsoever—this was a control group). Several notable results emanated from this experiment. First, Druckman found that when individuals received a single strong frame, it moved opinions in the expected direction (e.g. those exposed only to the strong pro-economic frame became more supportive of the casino), in line with the results of the single-frame studies described above. Second, weak frames did not influence opinions. Individuals exposed to the weak con morality frame, for instance, were no different than those exposed to no frames when it came to support for the casino. Third, opinions did not change when individuals were exposed to two strong frames from opposite sides of the political spectrum; this outcome was in line with the results reported by Sniderman and Theriault. Finally, and most importantly, frames *did not* cancel out when there was an asymmetry in terms of strength. A strong frame overwhelmed a weak one, even in conditions where respondents received a single strong frame and multiple weak ones, such that opinion moved in the direction of the strong frame. To get a sense of the size of the movement, participants exposed to a strong economic frame were 41 percent more likely to support the casino, even when they received competing weak frames pointing in the opposite direction. While the central lesson of this experiment is that frames only cancel out if both are strong, the results from this study also suggest something else of importance: repetition is not the key to success in framing, contrary to Zaller's claim that citizens "are blown about by whatever current of information manages to develop with the greatest intensity."[48] The key to a successful competitive framing strategy is strength. These results have been replicated with a host of issues including urban sprawl, a hate group rally, a Danish marriage rule, immigration, health care, and the Patriot Act.[49]

In terms of practical consequences, the results are tentatively suggestive that had the economic frame come to dominate the 2006 Illinois gubernatorial campaign, Topinka's proposal may have been supported and perhaps propelled her to victory. More importantly, the key is whether political advocates can figure out which frames are strong—indeed, in some of the aforementioned work, using weak frames is not only ineffective but sometimes backfired and pushed people in the opposite direction.[50]

Framing Durability and Media Choice

One obvious question is whether the types of framing effects we have been discussing endure or whether they are temporary blips in opinion that exist just shortly after exposure to the frame. This question has received some attention with the model being best summed up as: "When competing messages are separated by days or weeks, most individuals give disproportionate weight to the most recent communication because previous effects decay over time."[51] In short, the effects seem short-lived, which means that the frame heard most recently is the one that wins out (as long as it is a strong frame).

Framing effects, generally speaking, do not appear to be durable, and recency bias appears to be the rule. However, there is some conditionality to that finding. First, if an initial strong frame leads an individual to form a strongly held attitude, for example, their attitude toward the casino becomes very important to them, then that initial effect will last.[52] Second, if the first frame is repeated multiple times before the counter-frame is presented, then the first frame can endure.[53] Third, and most importantly, 'media choice' can lead to the endurance of frames.

A reality that we thus far have ignored is that many communications do not simply appear to people from elites (or experimenters). Rather, individuals choose what to watch or read as when they choose to read one story on the Internet rather than another. This is what we mean by "media choice." A recent experiment conducted by Druckman, Fein and Leeper on the subject of universal health care reform was the first to combine information choice and over-time framing within the same experiment.[54] The experiment in question consisted of four sessions that were completed one week apart. During the first session, participants were exposed to either a strong pro frame (i.e., health care will reduce inequalities), a strong con frame (i.e., it will be expensive), both, or no frame at all. The first session thus mimicked the design of prior framing studies. During the fourth session, meanwhile, the participants were exposed either to no additional frame or to a frame opposite of the one they received in the first session; a person who received a strong pro frame (inequalities) in week one, for instance, received a strong con frame (economic costs) in week four. The key methodological innovation occurred during sessions two and three. For these sessions, a selection of participants was randomly allowed to choose from 35 different stories presented on a webpage (they were given fifteen minutes). Eight of the stories were on health care, with four employing a version of the pro frame and four the con frame. The other articles covered alternative political or non-political topics (the topic and direction of coverage was clear in the title that participants clicked when they wanted to read a story). The inclusion of this choice condition enabled Druckman, et al., to observe whether participants selected information based on the frame they received in the first week and, ultimately, the influence of information choice on framing effects.

Druckman and his colleagues found that allowing people to choose did matter. In fact, despite the wide range of available options, people tended to read stories on health care and, more crucially, stories that employed the same pro or con frame to which they were first exposed. Consequently, that first frame was in essence repeated and the initial effect endured—the initial frame effect was stable and the most recent framing effect did not dominate—contrary to the results reported in the Chong and Druckman quote above. The lesson is that the longevity of frames depends on the issue and attitudes formed (e.g., are they strong) and whether people opt to then seek out additional information on the topic. Media choice matters in determining which frames win.

Partisan Polarization and Framing

A final topic of timely importance stems from the reality that most frames come from partisan sources, that is, from Democrats or Republicans. This fact is important to consider as the difference between the two parties has increased over the last quarter century. McCarty states that "by almost all measures of partisan polarization, the divide between Democratic and Republican Members of Congress have widened deeply over the past twenty-five years, reaching levels of partisan conflict not witnessed since the 1920s."[55] How might partisan polarization affect framing?

The question of polarization's influence on framing has been recently taken up in two experiments conducted by Druckman, Peterson, and Slothuus.[56] Two issues were explored: support for oil drilling and support for the DREAM (Development, Relief, and Education for Alien Minors) Act, which would provide a pathway for citizenship for undocumented immigrants who entered the United States before the age of 16, graduate from high school, have good moral character and complete at least two years of college or military service. We will focus on the DREAM Act to illustrate the effects of polarization on framing, as the two experiments used the same design and the results from them were substantially similar.

There were two key dimensions in these experiments. The first dimension concerned the frames received by the experimental subjects. The participants in the study randomly received either (1) a pro strong frame (i.e., the Act will help young people by providing them with new opportunities) and a con strong frame (i.e., the Act encourages illegal immigration and over-burdens the system), (2) the aforementioned pro strong frame and a con weak frame (i.e., the Act is just politics and thus poorly designed), (3) a pro weak frame (i.e., the public supports the Act in polls) and the aforementioned con strong frame, or (4) both the aforementioned pro and strong weak frames. Weak and strong frames were determined via the pre-tests as described above. The second dimension to the experiment, meanwhile, concerned the partisan environment for the issue. In addition to the frames described above, participants randomly received (1) no party endorsements of the frame, (2) a statement that Democrats supported and Republicans opposed the Act but the parties were *not* far apart (*not overly polarized*), or (3), a statement that Democrats supported and Republicans opposed the Act but the parties *were* far apart (very *polarized*). (There also was a control condition that simply asked for support for the Act.)

The researchers found that the presence or absence of party cues, especially in a context of polarization, was an important influence on the nature of the framing effects observed. When party cues were absent, for instance, the resulting framing effects mirrored those observed in the casino study, with (1) strong cues influencing support for the DREAM Act even when pitted against a weak frame, and (2) frames of equal strength cancelling out and having no effect on subsequent opinions. In the conditions with *non-polarized* party cues, the researchers observed two key results. First, when the frames were of unequal strength (e.g., a strong pro frame and a weak con frame), frame strength drove opinions regardless of party cue. For example, when participants were told that the parties were not far apart, their resulting opinion on the issue reflecting the strong frame that they received—becoming more supportive, for instance, when they received the strong pro and weak con frame—regardless of whether they were of the same party as the one endorsing the strong frame. However, party cues did drive opinion when respondents were presented with opposing frames of equal strength. In other words, when the frames were both strong or both weak, people turned to their party for guidance. Perhaps most interesting, however, were the results from the final set of conditions where respondents received polarized party cues. In these conditions, frame strength became irrelevant and people just went along with their party's endorsed frame even if it meant following a weak frame and ignoring a strong one.

The key implication here is that partisan *intensity* matters in competitive framing settings—when parties are polarized (i.e., far apart and homogenous), they drive opinions regardless of the strength of the argument. The results suggest that a polarized political environment may actually lead citizens to hold opinions of a lower quality, ones rooted in arguments that are actually weaker than alternatives offered by the other party. This suggests that the potentially sanguine implications of the elite competition studies described above may be more limited than previously thought.

Conclusion: Unanswered Questions

The study of framing effects has come a long way over the past decade, with various elements of the political environment added to the traditional framing experiment in an effort to produce a more "ecologically" realistic experiment. There remains, however, ample room for future investigation. We review some areas that require more study below.

What is Strength?

These results beg the question of what lies beyond a frame's strength. Why are some frames perceived as strong and others weak? Even the large persuasion literature offers little insight: "Unhappily, this research evidence is not as illuminating as one might suppose . . . It is not yet known what it is about the 'strong arguments' . . . that makes them persuasive."[57] The little research thus far does not paint a particularly flattering portrayal of strength perceptions. For example, Arceneaux finds that "individuals are more likely to be persuaded by political arguments that evoke cognitive biases."[58] Specifically, he reports that messages that highlight averting losses or out-group threats resonate to a greater extent than do other, ostensibly analogous arguments. Druckman and Bolsen report that adding factual information to messages does nothing to enhance their strength.[59] They focus on opinions about new technologies, such as carbon nanotubes (CNTs). Druckman and Bolsen expose experimental participants to different mixes of frames in support and opposed to the technology. For example, a supportive frame for CNTs states: "Most agree that the most important implication of CNTs concerns how they will affect energy cost and availability." An example of an opposed frame is "Most agree that the most important implication of CNTs concerns their unknown long-run implications for human health." Druckman and Bolsen report that each of these two frames shifts opinions in the expected directions. More importantly, when factual information is added to one or both frames (in other conditions)—such as citing a specific study about energy costs (e.g., a study shows CNTS will double the efficiency of solar cells in the coming years), that information does nothing to add to the power of the frame. In short, frames with specific factual evidence are no stronger (in their effects) than analogous frames that include no such evidence. This is troubling insofar as one believes scientific evidence should be accorded greater credibility.

Other work on frame strength suggests it increases in frames that highlight specific emotions, invoke threat against one's own group interests, include multiple, frequently appearing, arguments, and/or have been used in the past.[60] The initial studies on frame strength make clear that one should not confound "strength" with "normative desirability." What exactly is meant by normatively desirable lies outside the purview of this chapter, but is a topic that demands careful consideration.

Continuing Changing Media Environment

Research on framing is far from conclusive thanks to the ever-changing environments in which individuals receive their information. As individuals shifted from receiving political messages from network news to cable television, more programming options became available and viewers who had no interest in watching political news increasingly had the option not to. A result of this growing choice was a widening gap between those with the least political knowledge and those with the most.[61] The implications of an increasing reliance on the Internet for receiving political messages have not yet been fully realized. With the Internet, information consumers can choose exactly when they receive information and they can select their own format, be it in pictures only, in streaming video, from traditional news sources who have an online presence, or from their friends and family in the form of social networking. Furthermore, the Internet allows individuals to respond to messages by commenting on stories or by engaging in dialogue. This interactive element will surely have consequences for how we interpret political messages—once dictated solely by a news source but now subject to viewer interaction.

Where do Frames Come From?

The framing process is typically cast as one in which elite political actors—parties, candidates, and so on—actively formulate frames in competition with each other, which are then communicated to the media and, finally, to the mass public.[62] The public hears what the media reports with the media reporting what is on the government agenda, thereby implying that the process of frame construction occurs on an elite (party/candidate) to elite (media) level. A great deal of attention has been paid to the last portion of this process, the media to public aspect of framing, as evidenced by the research reviewed in this chapter. The first half, however, remains underexplored and appears to actively befuddled researchers.

How do elites choose among frames to communicate to the media? How do the media choose which to use in their coverage of an issue? Some recent work sheds light upon these questions. In a series of studies of elite framing concerning an immigration initative in Switzerland, Hänggli produces evidence that the media are more likely to use frames produced by "powerful" organizations, as measured by the organization's reputation for influence, as well as the degree to which these organizations use the frame in question.[63] Powerful political actors may also have an outsized role in influencing the frames that citizens see, as evidenced by Hänggli's results and by recent work by Entman.[64] These initial results begin to fill in the details of an important part of the framing process by suggesting an interactive process between elites over the construction and transmission of frames, although it still leaves the strategic considerations underlying this process relatively underexplored.

While some strides have been made in understanding the emergence of frames, changes to the media environment suggest that the underlying model, wherein the media largely play a role of frame transmission rather than frame creation, is in need of revision. Hänggli writes, for instance, that journalists in Western democracies abide by a "neutral informational journalistic norm," wherein they attempt to pass along the frames used in competition rather than actively participating in their construction. The evolution of blogging and the (re)emergence of partisan media, however, may very well complicate this argument and raise the specter that political elites have "lost control" over the framing process.[65]

Implications for Accountability

The evolution of research on framing has had powerful implications for notions of representation and accountability. For a long time, the study of representation assumed that mass preferences were exogenous to the activities of elites.[66] The mass public, standing to the side, forms its opinions on its own and then transmits them to elites through the various modes of democratic action available to them. The degree of representation on offer can then be adduced by analyzing how closely aligned the communicated preferences of the mass are with the actions of elites. When this gap is wide, serious problems of representative accountability may occur.[67]

The study of framing effects greatly complicates this picture. Instead of preferences being exogenous to elite activity, elite framing strategies may greatly influence them. And, indeed, it may be the case that our media environment, so resplendent in terms of choice, may very well be fostering this influence. Partisans have an ever-greater ability to select into one-sided, or nearly one-sided, communications, which may then motivate them to seek out only confirming evidence and counterarguments against evidence that they may be wrong. That this occurs within an environment of political polarization may only exacerbate the process insofar as it leads individuals to opt for analytically weaker arguments adopted by their party of choice. In such a world, the question of representation becomes greatly complicated—if the demands of the most active citizens, partisans, are increasingly reliant upon the frames of elites, then where does representation fit into the story?

The possibility that elite frames will come to dominate public opinion, at least for partisans, is a dire proposition, but framing effects need not only be viewed through a pessimistic lens. For one thing, framing effects are not always so threatening, as evidenced by the results from studies showing that equally strong frames on opposite sides of an issue tend to cancel out, thereby leading individuals to form opinions closer to their core values than they otherwise would. On the other hand, framing is immensely important for the formation of public opinion. Framing enables individuals to tame the complexity of public issues and construct meaningful opinions.

In the end, the results reported in the studies here should challenge researchers to revisit some of the standard assumptions of democratic theory and evince a greater flexibility in theory building. In the words of Schattschneider, our task is to "produce a better theory of politics," one that "gets us out of the theoretical trap created by the disparity between the demands made on the public by the common definition of democracy and the capacity of the public to meet these demands."[68]

Notes

1 We thank Heather Madonia for helpful advice and assistance.

2 Monica Davey, "On Eve of Prison, Blagojevich Keeps Talking, but Some Tune Out," *New York Times*, March 14, 2012, A18.

3 The casino plan was not an issue on which voters would directly vote (i.e., an initiative) but initially appeared to be the critical campaign issue (e.g., Rick Pearson, "Topinka Gambling on Casino," *Chicago Tribune*, August 24, 2006.

4 Rick Pearson and John Chase, "Election Shrouded by Levine Guilty Plea," *Chicago Tribune*, October 29, 2006: 1.

5 James N. Druckman, "Competing Frames in the Political Campaign," in *Winning with Words: The Origins and Impact of Political Framing*, ed. Brian F. Schaffner and Patrick J. Sellers (New York: Routledge, 2010: 101–116).

6 Parts of this section come from James N. Druckman, "The Implications of Framing Effects for Citizen Competence," *Political Behavior* 23 (2001): 225–256.

7 James N. Druckman, "What's It All About? Framing in Political Science," in *Perspectives on Framing*, ed. Gideon Keren (New York: Psychology Press, 2011: 279–302).

8 Donald Kinder and Lynn Sanders, *Divided by Color: Racial Politics and Democratic Ideals* (Chicago: University of Chicago Press, 1996); Donald Kinder, "Communication and Opinion," *Annual Review of Political Science* 1 (1998: 173), Dietram Scheufele, "Framing as a Theory of Media Effects," *Journal of Communication* 49 (1999).

9 See, for instance, Joseph N. Cappella and Kathleen Hall Jamieson, *Spiral of Cynicism: The Press and the Public Good* (New York: Oxford University Press, 1997).

10 E.g., William A. Gamson and Andre Modigliani, "The Changing Culture of Affirmative Action," in *Research In Political Sociology,* ed. Richard G. Braungart. (Greenwich: JAI, 1987). 137–177

11 Erving Goffman, *Frame Analysis: An Essay on the Organization of Experience* (Cambridge: Harvard University Press, 1974).

12 See, for instance, William A. Gamson, *Talking Politics* (Cambridge: Cambridge University Press, 1992), Dennis Chong, "How People Think, Reason, and Feel about Rights and Liberties," *American Journal of Political Science* 37 (1993): 867–899.

13 Some scholars draw a distinction between political priming and framing, such that priming focuses explicitly on shaping the criteria on which individuals base evaluations of politicians. We see the two as conceptually indistinguishable and are treating them as such here (see Dennis Chong and James N. Druckman, "Framing Theory," *Annual Review of Political Science* 10 (2007):103–126; James N. Druckman, James H. Kluklinski and Lee Sigelman, "The Unmet Potential of Interdisciplinary Research," *Political Behavior* 31 (2009): 485–510. Additionally, there is a large amount of work on another type of framing effects—called valence or equivalency framing effects. This type of effect refers to how people's preferences change due to different but factually identical descriptions of a topic (e.g., different preferences depending on whether one refers to 5 percent unemployment or 95 percent employment). For an extended treatment, see James Druckman, "What's It All About?"

14 See James N. Enelow and Melvin J. Hinich, *The Spatial Theory of Voting* (Boston: Cambridge University Press, 1984).

15 James Druckman, "Competing Frames in Political Campaigns."

16 Shanto Iyengar, *Is Anyone Responsible? How Television Frames Political Issues* (Chicago: University of Chicago Press, 1991).

17 James N. Druckman and Lawrence Jacobs, "Presidential Responsiveness to Public Opinion," in *The Oxford Handbook of the American Presidency*, ed. George Edwards (Oxford: Oxford University Press, 2010), 160–181).

18 Scheufele, "Framing as a Theory of Media Effects."

19 See, for instance, George Lakoff, *Don't Think of an Elephant!: Know Your Values and Frame the Debate: The Essential Guide for Progressives* (White River Junction: Chelsea Green, 2004); Matt Bai, "The Framing Wars," *New York Times Magazine* (July 17, 2005).

20 There exists a virtual cottage industry in communication studies that traces the evolution of particular frames over time. While there is value in this descriptive enterprise, it provides little insight as to how or why certain frames are chosen.

21 James N. Druckman and Justin W. Holmes, "Does Presidential Rhetoric Matter? Priming and Presidential Approval," *Presidential Studies Quarterly* 34 (2004): 755–778.

22 Druckman and Holmes, "Does Presidential Rhetoric Matter? Priming and Presidential Approval."

23 Lydia Saad, "Bush Soars into State of the Union with Exceptional Public Backing" *The Gallup Organization, Poll Analyses* (January 29, 2002).

24 David E. Sanger, "Bush, Focusing on Terrorism, Says Secure U.S. Top Priority," *New York Times*, January 29, 2002.

25 James N. Druckman, Lawrence Jacobs, Eric Ostermeier, "Candidate Strategies to Prime Issue and Image" *Journal of Politics* 66 (2004): 1180–1202.

26 Druckman, Jacobs, Ostermeier, "Candidate Strategies to Prime Issues and Image."

27 Also see Brandice Canes-Wrone, *Who Leads Whom? Presidents, Policy, and the Public* (Chicago: University of Chicago Press, 2006), who finds that Presidents "go public" on an issue when the public already agrees with them, rather than in an attempt to persuade a disbelieving public of a policy's merits.

28 Stephen Ansolabehere and James M. Snyder, Jr., "Using Term Limits to Estimate Incumbency Advantages When Officeholders Retire Strategically," *Legislative Studies Quarterly* 29 (2004): 487–515.

29 E.g. Gary Jacobson, *The Politics of Congressional Elections* (New York: Longman, 2004).

30 E.g., Kathleen Hall Jamieson, *Everything You Think You Know about Politics and Why You are Wrong* (New York: Basic Books, 2000: 17).

31 Dennis Chong and James N. Druckman, "Identifying Frames in Political News," in *Sourcebook for Political Communication Research: Methods, Measures, and Analytical Techniques*, ed. Erik P. Bucy, R. Lance Holbert (New York: Routledge, 2011). Issues included the Patriot Act, global warming, intelligent design, same-sex marriage in the United States and in Canada, social security at two points in time, the *Bush v. Gore* Supreme Court case, the Abu Ghraib controversy, an immigration initiative, a Nazi rally, two Ku Klux Klan rallies, and a proposal for a state sponsored casino.

32 Frank Baumgartner, Suzanna L. De Boef, and Amber E. Boydstun, *The Decline of the Death Penalty and the Discovery of Innocence* (Cambridge: Cambridge University Press, 2008).

33 Baumgartner, De Boef and Boydstun, *The Decline of the Death Penalty*: 176.

34 Dan B. Wood and Arnold Vedlitz, "Issue Definition, Information Processing, and the Politics of Global Warming," *American Journal of Political Science* 51 (2007): 552–568.

35 For a review, see Robert D. Benford and David A. Snow, "Framing Processes and Social Movements: An Overview and Assessment," *Annual Review of Sociology* 26 (2000): 611–639.

36 See, for instance, William G. Jacoby, "Issue Framing and Public Opinion on Government Spending," *American Journal of Political Science* 44 (2000): 750–767; Paul R. Brewer, Joseph Graf, and Lars Willnat, "Priming or Framing: Media Influence on Attitudes Toward Foreign Countries," *International Journal of Communication Studies* 65 (2003): 493–508; Tobin J. Grant and Thomas J. Rudolph, "Value Conflict, Group Affect, and the Issue of Campaign Finance," *American Journal of Political*

Science 47 (2003): 453–469; Stephen P. Nicholson and Robert M. Howard, "Framing Support for the Supreme Court in the Aftermath of Bush v. Gore," *Journal of Politics* 65 (2003): 676–695.

37 See Thomas E. Nelson, Sarah M. Bryner, and Dustin M. Carnahan, "Media and Politics," in *Cambridge Handbook of Experimental Political Science*, ed. James N. Druckman, Donald P. Green, James H. Kuklinski and Arthur Lupia (New York: Cambridge University Press, 2011), 201–213.

38 Thomas E. Nelson, Rosalee A. Clawson and Zoe M. Oxley, "Media Framing of a Civil Liberties Conflct and Its Effect on Tolerance," *The American Political Science Review* 91 (1997): 567–583.

39 Iyengar and Kinder, *News That Matters*. Many refer to the work in this book as "priming" rather than "framing," but see our prior note regarding their equivalency.

40 On the topic of elite competition and opinion formation, see E. E. Schattschneider, *The Semisovereign People: A Realist's View of Democracy in America* (Holt, Rinehart and Winston, 1960); Robert M. Entman, "Framing: Toward Clarification of a Fractured Paradigm," *Journal of Communication* 43 (1993): 51–58; William H. Riker, *The Strategy of Rhetoric: Campaigning for the American Constitution* (New Haven: Yale University Press, 1996), 33; John Zaller, "The Myth of Massive Media Impact Revived: New Support for a Discredited Idea," in *Political Persuasion and Attitude Change*, ed. Diana Mutz, Richard Brody and Paul Sniderman (Ann Arbor: University of Michigan Press, 1996), 17–79.

41 Paul Sniderman and Sean M. Theriault, "The Structure of Political Argument and the Logic of Issue Framing," in *Studies in Public Opinion*, ed. Willem E. Saris and Paul M. Sniderman (Princeton: Princeton University Press, 2004), 133–165.

42 Sniderman and Theriault, "The Structure of Political Argument."

43 Sniderman and Theriault, "The Structure of Political Argument."

44 Also see Paul R. Brewer and Kimberly Gross, "Values, Framing, and Citizens' Thoughts about Policy Issues: Effects on Content and Quantity," *Political Psychology* 26 (2005): 929–948; and Kasper M. Hansen, "The Sophisticated Public: The Effect of Competing Frames on Public Opinion," *Scandinavian Political Studies* 30 (2007): 377–396.

45 James Druckman and Dennis Chong, "A Theory of Framing and Opinion Formation in Competitive Elite Environments," *Journal of Communication* 57 (2007): 99–118.

46 Daniel O'Keefe, *Persuasion: Theory of Research* (Thousand Oaks: Sage Publications, 2002).

47 James Druckman, "What's It All About?"

48 John Zaller, *The Nature and Origins of Mass Opinion* (Cambridge: Cambridge University Press, 1992), 311. See also: Cappella and Jamieson, *Spirals of Cynicism* and Robin L. Nabi, "Exploring the Framing Effects of Emotion: Do Discrete Emotions Differentially Influence Information Accessibility, Information Seeking and Policy Preference?" *Communication Research* 30 (2003): 225.

49 Dennis Chong and James N Druckman, "Framing Public Opinion in Competitive Democracies," *American Political Science Review* 101 (2007): 637–655; Lene Aarøe, "Investigating Frame Strength: The Case of Episodic and Thematic Frames," *Political Communication* 28 (2011): 207–226; Else Marie Holm, *Emotions as Mediators of Framing Effects* (Arhaus: Politica, 2012); James N. Druckman, Jordan Fein and Thomas Leeper, "A Source of Bias Within Public Opinion Stability" *American Political Science Review* (forthcoming); James Druckman, "Media Effects in Politics," in *Oxford Bibliographies Online: Political Science, ed.* Rick Valelly (New York: Oxford University Press, 2012).

50 James N. Druckman and Kjersten Nelson, "Framing and Deliberation: How Citizens' Conversations Limit Elite Influence," *American Journal of Political Science* 47

(2003): 729–745, state that frames do not necessarily come from elites but can come from within conversations. In their experiment, they provide respondents with one of two conflicting elite frames of an issue. After receiving specific frames from political elites, respondents tend to express preferences in line with these frames. But once respondents hear about conflicting frames from other individuals in the course of a conversation, the effects of the elite frame they were exposed to disappear. Also see James Druckman, "Political Preference Formation: Competition, Deliberation, and the (Ir)relevance of Framing Effects," *American Political Science Review* 98 (2004): 671–686; and Samara Klar, "Partisanship and Preference Formation in a Social Context," working paper (2012).

51 Dennis Chong and James N. Druckman, "Dynamic Public Opinion: Communication Effects Over Time," *American Political Science Review* 104 (2010): 663–680. Also see, David Tewksbury, Jennifer Jones, Matthew W. Peske, Ashlea Raymond, and William Vig, "The Interaction of News and Advocate Frames." *Journalism and Mass Communication Quarterly* 77 (2000): 804–829; Druckman and Nelson, "Framing and Deliberation"; Claes H. de Vreese, "The Effects of Strategic News on Political Cynicism, Issue Evaluations, and Policy Support," *Mass Communication and Society* 7 (2004): 191–214; Diana C. Mutz and Byron Reeves, "The New Videomalaise: Effects of Televised Incivility on Political Trust," *American Political Science Review* 99 (2005): 1–15; Alan S. Gerber, James G. Gimpel, Donald P. Green, and Daron R. Shaw, "How Large and Long Lasting are the Persuasive Effects of Televised Campaign Ads?," *American Political Science Review* 105 (2011): 135–150.

52 Chong and Druckman, "Dynamic Public Opinion."

53 See Druckman, Fein and Leeper, "A Source of Bias."

54 Druckman, Fein, and Leeper, "A Source of Bias."

55 Nolan McCarty, "The Policy Consequences of Partisan Polarization in the United States." Unpublished paper (2012). Also see: Nolan McCarty, Keith Poole, and Howard Rosenthal, *Polarized America: The Dance of Ideology and Unequal Riches* (Cambridge: The MIT Press, 2006); Morris P. Fiorina and Samuel Abrams, "Political Polarization in the American Public," *Annual Review of Political Science* 11 (2008): 563–588.

56 James N. Druckman, Erik Peterson, Rune Slothuus, "How Elite Partisan Polarization Affects Public Opinion Formation" (paper presented at the annual meeting of the Midwest Political Science Association, Chicago, April 12–15, 2012). See also Rune Slothuus and Claes H. de Vreese, "Political Parties, Motivated Reasoning, and Issue Framing Effects," *The Journal of Politics* 72 (2010): 630–645; Rune Slothuus, "When Can Political Parties Lead Public Opinion? Evidence from a Natural Experiment," *Political Communication* 27 (2010): 158–177.

57 O'Keefe, *Persuasion:* 147, 156

58 Kevin Arceneaux, "Cognitive Bias and Strength of Political Arguments," *American Journal of Political Science* 56 (2009): 271–285.

59 James N. Druckman and Toby Bolson, "Framing, Motivated Reasoning, and Opinions about Emerging Technologies," *Journal of Communication* 61 (2011): 659–688.

60 Mark Allen Peterson, "Making Global News: 'Freedom of Speech' and 'Muslim Rage' in U.S. Journalism," *Contemporary Islam* 1 (2007): 247–264. Also see Samara Klar, "The Influence of Competing Identity Primes on Preference" (paper presented at the Annual Meeting of the Midwest Political Science Association, Chicago, March 12–15, 2012); Baumgartner, De Boef and Boydstun, *The Decline of the Death Penalty*; Jill Edy, *News and the Collective Memory of Social Unrest* (Philadelphia: Temple University Press, 2006).

61 Markus Prior, "News vs. Entertainment: How Increasing Media Choice Widens Gap in Political Knowledge and Turnout," *American Journal of Political Science* 49 (2005): 577–592.

62 See, for instance, Iyengar and Kinder, *News that Matters*; Zaller, *The Nature and Origins of Mass Opinion*.

63 Regula Hänggli, "Key Factors in Frame Building How Strategic Political Actors Shape News Media Coverage," *American Behavioral Scientist* 56 (2012): 300–317; Regula Hänggli and Hanspeter Kriesi, "Frame Construction and Frame Promotion (Strategic Framing Choices)," *American Behavioral Scientist* 56 (2012): 260–278.

64 Robert M. Entman, *Projections of Power: Framing News, Public Opinion, and U.S. Foreign Policy* (Chicago: University of Chicago Press, 2004).

65 It may important to ask whether this is a new process or simply a return to an older political equilibrium. As alluded to, the partisanship of the media has waxed and waned over time. This suggests the possibility that the elite-media-public chain may have been different in nature prior to the formulation of objective journalistic norms and that we are currently shifting back to something resembling that state of the world rather than something wholly unique. Meanwhile, work by Hans Noel, "The Coalition Merchants: The Ideological Roots of the Civil Rights Realignment," *The Journal of Politics* 74 (2012): 156–173, suggests that members of the public intellectual class, including the media, have long played a role in influencing party ideology and, through this mechanism, the frames party elites have chosen to use (although Noel does not pitch his work as about framing). The process identified by Noel, however, was of a lagged nature, with the construction of ideology by non-party authors only followed by party adoption a few decades later as young party activists matured and came to institutional power. What may have changed, however, is the *speed* of this process, with the ideology construction and transmission process occurring not over twenty-five years, say, but over five due to the increased rapidity that our modern media environment allows.

66 See Lisa Disch, "The Impurity of Representation and the Vitality of Democracy," *Cultural Studies* 26 (2012): 207–222.

67 For a critique of this model see James H. Kuklinski and Gary M. Segura, "Endogeneity, Exogeneity, Time, and Space in Political Representation," *Legislative Studies Quarterly* 20 (1995): 3–21; Patricia Hurley and Kim Quaile Hill, "Beyond the Demand Input Model: A Theory of Representation Linkages," *The Journal of Politics* 65 (2003): 304–326.

68 Schattschneider, *The Semi-Sovereign People*.

Chapter 13

The News Anew?
Political Coverage in a Transformed Media Age

Danny Hayes

In mid-February 2012, CBS News and the *New York Times* released the results of a survey showing that 67 percent of Americans believed that, in an effort to shrink the federal budget deficit, households that earn more than $1 million a year should pay higher taxes. A month earlier, the Kaiser Family Foundation had conducted a poll on health care. Nearly two years after the passage of the Obama Administration's massive reform bill, 40 percent of Americans wanted either to replace the Patient Protection and Affordable Care Act with a Republican alternative or to scrap health care reform altogether.

Surveys late in 2011 tapped Americans' attitudes toward two foreign policy issues. In a November CBS News poll, 58 percent of the public wanted to reduce the number of U.S. troops in Afghanistan. And in December, as the Iranian government's nuclear program received growing attention during the GOP presidential debates, an NBC News/*Wall Street Journal* survey asked respondents whether they supported military action "if Iran continues with its nuclear research and is close to developing a nuclear weapon." Fifty-four percent said they did.

The vast majority of survey respondents were willing to offer an opinion on these matters. And many of the respondents no doubt held their opinions strongly. But where did these attitudes come from? What did Americans know about the implications of tax policy, health reform, or U.S. foreign policy in the Middle East? What information were respondents basing their responses on?

While the sources of public opinion are numerous, the media are among the key influences on what Americans know and think about politics. The vast majority of us never experience politics directly—everything we know about tax policy, the health care debate, or the military's struggles and successes in Afghanistan comes to us through news outlets. Even when we glean bits of political information from family or friends (Facebook or actual), it is likely that news originated from some television, print, or online outlet. In short, while the media do not dictate our opinions, they do determine the basic information we have at our disposal as we make those judgments.

As the public's main source of political information, the media bear significant responsibilities in the operation of democracy. This raises weighty questions about an institution that receives special First Amendment protections because of its essential role in the democratic process. Do the media provide the public with enough information to make informed political judgments? Does the news contain the kind of information citizens need to arrive at good decisions about government actions? Are citizens exposed to a sufficient diversity of viewpoints to allow them to judge whether the politicians, parties, and candidates are acting in the public's interest?

These questions are central to evaluating the news landscape of the early 21st century. And with the dramatic and ongoing transformation of the media environment, these issues have become especially pressing: Has the dizzying proliferation of new media outlets given citizens access to better information than they had when the news business was monopolized by three broadcast networks and a few national and local newspapers? Is the quality of public affairs information improving? Or is the public simply getting the same kind of news in a different form—old wine in new bottles, as the old saying goes? Or is the news getting worse?

This chapter provides an overview of how scholars have assessed the media's democratic performance in contemporary American politics and considers whether new media are providing citizens with a news diet that is any different than their mainstream predecessors. I then turn to an analysis of media coverage of the debate over U.S. involvement in the 2011 Libyan civil war, using a case study to examine the similarities and differences in the way policy debates are covered in the traditional and new media.

Both the existing literature and the analysis of the Libya debate indicate that the similarities in the coverage of politics in the new and "old" media are much greater than the differences. The information that Americans rely on to judge proposed tax increases, the Obama health care reform, and American military action overseas still is not especially substantive, and not particularly diverse. The information that appears in the new media seems unlikely to help citizens make "better" choices—choices that reflect a range of substantive considerations from a diversity of political actors from inside and out of the government.

The Democratic Responsibilities of the Media

The quality of information that citizens receive from the media is a perennial concern in the practice of democratic politics. Because the media serve as the public's window into the political world, the opinions that citizens hold and the choices they make are strongly influenced by the information that flows to them through the media. A common argument, since the time of the Founding, has been that a responsible, educated media apparatus is a key to producing a responsible, educated electorate. "The press is the best instrument for enlightening the mind of man and improving him as a rational, moral, and social being," Thomas Jefferson is quoted as saying.

Substantive Coverage

But how might we judge whether the media are carrying out their duties? While hallmarks of a well-functioning press are many, two criteria have been used routinely to judge the quality of the information that the press provides to its citizens. First, the media are expected to provide information that helps citizens carry out their basic democratic responsibility of passing judgment on elected officials—and collectively, the government—in regular elections. In order to do this effectively, the argument is, citizens need information about the implications of the policies and positions staked out by candidates and parties. Otherwise, citizens' choices will not be based on an understanding of the actions that politicians have taken or will take while in office, which is the essence of governing.

Research has not graded the U.S. media highly on this count. A common finding in the political communication literature is that the media are far too focused on political gamesmanship and insufficiently concerned with the substance of policy debates.[1] Instead of focusing on the substance of candidate discourse and public policy debates, the media are more inclined to emphasize politicians' strategic considerations, the electoral implications, or the legislative process. As a result, the public is left with an inadequate dose of policy information to judge the actions of their elected officials and the politicians proposing to replace them. For instance, much of the coverage surrounding Barack Obama's sudden announcement in May 2012 that he believes same-sex couples should be able to get married focused not on the possible policy consequences of the president's position, but on the ramifications for his fall reelection bid.

Other examples abound. Studies of one of the major policy episodes of the late 20th century—the 1995–96 debate over the overhaul of the U.S. welfare system—have shown that media coverage was more heavily focused on legislative maneuvering and the political implications of the debate rather than the substance of the law.[2] The new law put time limits on how long Americans could receive welfare benefits from the federal government and imposed conditions for receiving them, changes with significant implications for the social safety net provided by the federal government. Debate over the proposed changes was lengthy and wide-ranging. But coverage was not very substantive.

For instance, a front-page story in *The Los Angeles Times* the day after the landmark bill was signed led with an emphasis on President Clinton's bid for re-election as the main storyline, not the significant changes for America's poor that the law would effect. One study found that about 40 percent of network TV news stories focused on strategy and other "process" frames.[3] Relatively little of the news would have helped news consumers figure out what the bill's passage meant for their lives, the distribution of resources by the government, or the broader implications of the evolution of American social policy. Similarly, 49 percent of Associated Press reports and network television news stories about President Ronald Reagan's 1981 economic plan were framed in terms of political strategy, not policy substance.[4]

The media's tendency to focus on strategy and the political "game" stems in part from the fact that journalists are constantly looking for new developments. Strategy and legislative maneuvering regularly change, but policy positions and the substance of different policy proposals are more static. That means that focusing on what is often referred to as "process" as opposed to policy gives the media convenient new storylines to develop on a regular basis. "That's why they call it 'news,' not olds" is one corny way of emphasizing the centrality of novelty in the production of news. Ultimately, the desire for new developments leads the media to deemphasize substance in favor of process, even if the latter may not be all that useful to citizens who, according to conventional readings of democratic theory, need to determine whether the government is making decisions that represent their interests.

Writing about the game of politics also makes it easier for journalists to maintain objectivity—treating both sides in a policy debate without favor. Stories about policy often raise nettlesome questions about whether the policies will or will not be effective. And on the whole, journalists are uncomfortable making those assessments, for fear of being targeted as biased or unfair. Stories about process tend to be easier to write in a way that avoids controversial policy evaluations.

Independence from Government

A second criterion typically used to assess news quality is the extent to which media coverage is independent from government. That is, rather than serving a conduit for propaganda from elected officials who may have an incentive to mislead the public, the press should provide citizens with a diverse range of perspectives about political issues. Critically, this range of voices should include those that originate outside of government itself. "True democracies," writes Gadi Wolfsfeld, "must have a genuinely independent press who present a wide range of viewpoints for us to consider."[5]

But scholars have concluded that the viewpoints available in mainstream news content tend to be "indexed" to the range of debate occurring within mainstream government circles.[6] This means that coverage often reflects the content of debate within the government itself. But it routinely ignores or marginalizes alternative views from interest groups, citizen protests, or other less powerful actors, such as the recent Occupy Wall Street movement.[7]

This tendency to pay disproportionate attention to government officials stems in part from the professional socialized routines of "beat reporting." Journalists develop relationships with sources, often within the government, who give them information about developing events.[8] That information and the sources' perspectives are valuable to journalists, and they become the material the media rely on in their reporting. Since most political news emanates from within the Beltway, and the halls of Congress, the White House, and the agencies that make up the federal bureaucracy, government officials become major actors in developing news stories.

For instance, network television coverage during debate over Reagan's 1981 tax and budget plan was dominated by officials within the administration and their congressional allies and opponents. More than 88 percent of the source statements aired on network television news programs and in Associated Press reports were attributed to government officials. Just 6.5 percent were attributed to non-governmental groups or social movements. In the debate over welfare reform, 83 percent of sources in *USA Today* and network TV news coverage came from the government.[9] The same dynamic exists in foreign policy as well. Studies of the debates over the U.S.–Libya episode of the mid-1980s and the lead-up to the Iraq War in 2003 found that government sources comprised 80 percent or more of the voices in mainstream news coverage.[10]

To be sure, different government officials have different perspectives about how to solve different policy problems, and these divisions often fall along partisan lines. So the tendency of sources to "index" coverage to the debate occurring within the government itself does not mean that citizens are exposed to a single viewpoint. But it does mean that news coverage itself is heavily influenced by elite divisions or consensus within the government. When elites divide, news coverage reflects the opposing viewpoints.[11] But when there is consensus—for instance, in the U.S. decision to invade Afghanistan following the terrorist attacks of September 11, 2001—news coverage that relies on "official" voices is unlikely to provide citizens with a diversity of viewpoints. Far from being independent of government, media coverage often reflects the perspectives of its inhabitants.

The prominence of government officials in the news isn't all about beat reporting, however. Journalists rely heavily on government sources also because they are highly attuned to power and influence. The media are interested in "shedding light on future developments,"[12] which encourages them to pay disproportionate attention to institutionally influential actors—people like the president and party leaders in Congress.[13] For instance, during the 2002–2003 debate over the Bush Administration's proposal to launch a military invasion of Iraq, White House officials, including President George W. Bush, accounted for 28 percent of all of the statements on broadcast news. This was largely because journalists saw Bush as the key to the resolution of the impasse. Similarly, journalists turned heavily to foreign sources and officials from the United Nations later in the debate when it became clear that the U.N.'s weapons inspections program would be a central issue in how the war debate would end.[14]

In summary, the conclusion of political scientists and communication scholars is that mainstream news coverage rarely lives up to the expectations that many observers set out for it. The content of political news tends to be too heavily focused on non-substantive themes, like political strategy and legislative maneuvering, leaving citizens without access to potentially useful information about the substance of public policy debates. In addition, the media tend to reflect the views inside of government and ignore those outside of it. As a result, a common argument is that the public is not as well-informed as it could be if the media was more substantive and open to a wider diversity of sources.

Perspectives on the New Media

But are these criticisms still applicable? After all, these critiques of the media took root before the new media revolution of the last two decades. The proliferation of cable news outlets and Internet news sites has raised the possibility that the old patterns of media coverage may be less common today.[15] With more political information available to news consumers than ever before, new media outlets may not be driven by the same journalistic conventions and routines that have produced these well-established patterns of coverage. With so many news outlets, there are more opportunities (not to mention space and air time) to devote to policy substance. And because of the Internet's more open environment, it may be the site of more diverse viewpoints. Indeed, pronouncements about the possibilities of the internet's ability to revolutionize political news have been common.[16] "With greater opportunities for individuals to gain access to political information, be it from the internet or 24-hour cable newscasts, the potential is considerable for a well-informed citizenry," write Max McCombs, R. Lance Holbert, Spiro Kiousis, and Wayne Wanta.[17]

Although research that has directly compared the content of news in the traditional and new media is sparse, one fact is clear: the news has grown more ideological and partisan as the number of outlets has expanded.[18] This has made it easier for citizens to seek out information from channels and websites that confirm their existing political beliefs, and has given those outlets an incentive to continue to shape their coverage to cater to their increasingly ideologically motivated audiences. MSNBC and the Daily Kos, for instance, draw audiences made up mostly of liberals and Democrats. On the other side, Fox News and Hot Air, for example, have audiences disproportionately comprised of conservatives and Republicans. If one of the media's main democratic responsibilities is to provide citizens with a diversity of viewpoints that will lead them to political judgments that reflect a relatively comprehensive consideration of different perspectives, then the rise of opinionated and ideological media does not augur well for the fulfillment of this goal. To be sure, citizens could encounter a wide variety of news sources by attending to a number of different news sources. But to the extent that people's news consumption habits tend to reflect their political preferences,[19] they will not benefit from the ideological diversity available in the wider information environment. Instead, whether citizens are exposed to a diversity of views depends on whether any individual outlet (or a few outlets) that they watch or read provides those perspectives.

But while cable and online news is more partisan than its older counterpart, there is much less evidence about whether it is more or less likely than traditional media to focus on the substance of political debates rather than political process. And there has been almost no consideration of how much attention new outlets devote to "official" versus "non-official" sources in their reporting of public policy. If we are to judge the quality of news in the new media environment, these aspects of coverage need attention.

Why the New Media Might Make for Better News

It is possible to imagine several reasons that new media coverage of politics might be more issue-focused and less inclined to marginalize non-traditional sources, thus demonstrating more independence from government. First, differences in the production and dissemination of news in the new and traditional media might lead to differences in content. One of the reasons that the news media traditionally have failed to cover political debates in-depth, especially on broadcast television, is time constraints. The typical network newscast is roughly 22 minutes long (excluding commercials), and just a portion of that time is devoted to politics and public affairs. As a result, most broadcast news reports are less than one minute, and many can be as short as just a sentence or two.[20] That isn't that much time to tell a story about a complicated change to, say, the nation's welfare system. And while print outlets have more space— lengthy stories in the prestige press can occasionally run to several thousand words—they are still constrained by the size of the "news hole," or the amount of editorial content in a newspaper left after advertising has been placed on the pages.

But cable news channels and Internet sites don't face the same limitations. With 24 hours of news to fill, cable outlets possess more flexibility in devoting time to stories. Articles on web sites can be as long as editors want them to be; theoretically, there are no page limits, unlike in the print media (although readers' attention spans may impose a practical limit). These structural differences suggest that political coverage in the new media might be lengthier and more substantive than in traditional news outlets. If one of the factors that has limited the depth with which journalists cover politics has been time and space constraints,[21] then we might find new media more likely to provide meatier discussions and analyses of public policy.

Second, because new media outlets are also not tied as closely to traditional journalistic conventions and routines, such as beat reporting, they may be less reliant on government officials and perspectives. The "bottom-up" model of many blogs, in which readers are encouraged to offer feedback and critique news stories, may also lead to more attention to non-traditional sources.[22] There is some evidence that this is happening. In a comparison of "citizen journalism" web sites and local daily newspapers, Serena Carpenter finds that web outlets were more likely to include non-official sources than newspaper journalists.[23] Madanmohan Rao argues that news coverage of the Iraq War debate was much less reliant than mainstream outlets on U.S. government sources, who mostly articulated pro-invasion views.[24] As a result, these outlets appear less likely to "index" their coverage to the parameters of debate within the government than traditional outlets. That may lead news coverage in new media outlets to offer perspectives that diverge from the range of views being expressed inside the government.

Why the New Media May Look a Lot like the Old Media

At the same time, several factors suggest that new media content may in fact look very much like its traditional predecessors. First, cable news channels and political blogs remain reliant on advertising to stay in business. And that means they have to attract viewers and readers. While the media environment has changed, it's not clear that citizens' taste in news has. Research on audience preferences shows that most Americans are not particularly interested in meaty policy discourse, instead preferring more superficial, entertaining fare, such as a focus on the "horse race" during election time.[25] This is not to mention the spike in news attention when a celebrity, like Michael Jackson or Anna Nicole Smith, dies.[26] The news focuses on the non-substantive aspects of politics, such as the legislative process and political maneuvering, in part because that's what media executives believe their audiences will tune in to.

New media outlets are subject to the same realities. If American news consumers continue to prefer coverage of process and political implications rather than in-depth analyses of policy substance, new media outlets will have an incentive to provide the same kind of coverage that traditional outlets typically have. While there is very little empirical research that has examined new media content in these terms, one study found that online and print news outlets had very similar amounts of "mobilizing information," that is, information that would encourage citizens to get involved in politics, suggesting that the new media were no more attentive to the substantive implications of political developments.[27]

Second, cable outlets and the most popular political blogs are in many ways an extension of the mainstream media.[28] Some of the most popular new media venues are run by former mainstream journalists (e.g., Andrew Sullivan). And while the structure of the new media may be different and new media journalists may have more freedom to take political positions, they are still likely to be attentive to the institutional actors who possess political power. Journalists, regardless of the venue, are still interested in "shedding light on future developments" and will be disproportionately interested in the political actors they believe will affect political debate.[29] Whatever the differences in the cultures of new and traditional media, it is hard to imagine bloggers not devoting significant attention to the Supreme Court's March 2012 hearing on the Patient Protection and Affordable Care Act, as the nine robed justices held the fate of the Obama Administration's major domestic policy achievement in their hands. Indeed, traditional and online journalists see many aspects of their jobs in similar ways.[30] This suggests that new media outlets will have an incentive to pay particular attention to the contours of debate within the mainstream of the government, since these debates will set the terms by which a policy debate is likely to be resolved. Moreover, much of the content in the "blogosphere" is derived from news that originated in mainstream news outlets.[31] As a result, new media content may be similarly likely to be "indexed" to the range of views articulated within the mainstream of government debate.

These competing expectations and the scant empirical evidence suggest the need to examine quality of news coverage in traditional and new media along these important dimensions. In the next section, I describe the results of a small study of news coverage of the 2011 debate over U.S. involvement in the civil war in Libya that will help illuminate the similarities and differences in news coverage of policy debates.

Case Study: The 2011 Debate over U.S. Intervention in Libya

In February 2011, the "Arab Spring" uprisings in Tunisia, Egypt, and other Middle Eastern and North African nations spread to Libya. After the military forces of longtime dictator Muammar Gaddafi fired on a group of protestors in the coastal city of Benghazi, the protests quickly escalated into a full-scale rebellion. With the Libyan government under siege, Gaddafi's military forces began striking back, killing rebel fighters and terrorizing civilians who were alleged to be supportive of the insurgency. By early March, a civil war was under way.

With the prospect of a humanitarian disaster looming, international officials in late February began deliberating over whether and how to intervene in Libya. There was sporadic talk of sending in ground troops to stop the bloodshed, but the main focus was the implementation of a no-fly zone by an international coalition to give protection to Libyan civilians who might otherwise be targeted by the threatened Gaddafi regime. In the United States, the political debate focused on the extent to which the country should participate in an international action, and whether it should take a leadership role in doing so. In the end, the Obama Administration ended up providing military support to a NATO-led no-fly zone created late in March.

The United States' possible involvement in Libya provides an opportunity to examine whether the traditional and new media covered this political debate differently. In particular, did the new media provide more high quality news, in terms of the substantive focus of coverage, a less heavy reliance on government officials, and a wider range of perspectives? Or have the hopes for reconstituting the news anew been too optimistic?

To answer these questions, a research assistant and I conducted a content analysis of news coverage of the Libya debate in six popular media outlets.[32] We analyzed coverage on the CBS Evening News and in *The Washington Post*, two traditional news outlets. We also examined the coverage from MSNBC, Fox News, the liberal political blog Daily Kos, and the conservative political blog Hot Air, four new media venues.[33] We randomly selected 10 Libya-related news stories from each outlet between February 15 and March 31, the six-week period during which discussion of possible U.S. military intervention in Libya was at its peak. Stories in the *Post* were drawn from the front section of the newspaper, and the CBS stories came from the network's half-hour nightly newscasts. On Fox, we coded transcripts from the 6 p.m. show *Special Report*, the network's closest approximation of a typical news broadcast. On MSNBC, our transcripts were drawn from *Hardball with Chris Matthews*, a program that uses a talk show format but that regularly features news reporting and analysis from the network's correspondents. Stories from Daily Kos and Hot Air were drawn from the sites' archives.

Substantive Coverage

The first question is about the substance of coverage. The stories in the sample were analyzed to determine whether they focused primarily on (1) non-substantive aspects of the story, such as the political "game" (e.g., the effect of Libya action on Barack Obama's popularity), off-hand remarks about the situation by political officials, or minor legislative actions that communicated little about the issues at hand, or (2) the substance of the debate, such as the difficulty of implementing a no-fly zone, the positions of the White House or Republican leaders, or the implications for U.S. foreign policy. By standards of democratic theory, most observers would argue that substantive stories are more useful for citizens trying to discern what the correct course of action should be than stories about the possible electoral implications or other more trivial topics.

Overall, coverage of the Libya episode was more substantive than tends to be the case in most policy debates. Sixty-eight percent of the all the stories in our sample were focused on substance, while just 32 percent emphasized non-substantive themes. But Figure 13.1 shows that the traditional outlets were more likely to cover the issue in substantive terms than their new media counterparts. All of the CBS News stories we analyzed were substantive, while 70 percent of the *Post*'s coverage focused on substantive themes.

Fox News and the conservative blog Hot Air were similarly substantive, but MSNBC and Daily Kos took a different approach. Seventy percent of MSNBC's transcripts and 60 percent of Daily Kos' articles were coded as non-substantive. On Daily Kos, for instance, one article was simply a snarky dispatch that pointed out that U.S. Rep. Tom Marino (R-Pennsylvania) seemed not to know that Libya was in Africa. Although perhaps entertaining—especially when Daily Kos writer Barbara Morrill suggested that the congressional representative "go to a remedial geography class"— such a story does not provide much useful information for citizens trying to discern whether the United States should participate in an international military action. Several of the MSNBC segments were focused on the political and electoral implications for President Obama of participating in enforcing the no-fly zone.

There is too much variation across the new media outlets to conclude that on this dimension—the relative emphasis on policy substance—the new media are any "worse" than traditional media. But they certainly aren't any better, and some of the newer outlets clearly framed their coverage of the debate in less than helpful terms. If we judge news content by how much citizens might have learned about the substance of the Libya debate, it doesn't appear that they

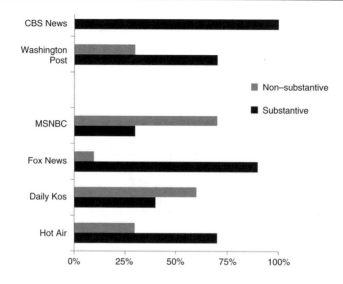

Figure 13.1 Substantive and non-substantive stories in coverage of the Libya debate

Note: Figure depicts the percentage of stories coded as substantive and non-substantive. Analysis is based on 10 randomly selected stories about the Libya episode in each news outlet from February 15 through March 31, 2011.

would have been better served by turning to cable news outlets and web sites than to newspapers or network news.

The Diversity of Sources and Perspectives in the News

What about the diversity of voices and viewpoints included in the news? And in particular, are there differences in the tendency of traditional and new media to rely on the perspectives of government officials, the very people that the Fourth Estate is expected to be calling to account? In the parlance of the political communication literature, how reliant are news outlets on "official" sources? Our coding scheme analyzed every statement from an individual that appeared in our news stories or segments that advocated or opposed U.S. involvement in Libya. We recorded the direction of the statement—whether it supported U.S. involvement or opposed it—the identity of the speaker, and noted whether the speaker was a government official.

The top two pairs of bars in Figure 13.2 confirm what research has found repeatedly: Traditional news outlets like CBS News and the *Post* rely heavily on the perspectives of government officials. Ninety percent of the statements on CBS News were attributed to government officials—Obama, other White House officials, Republicans in Congress, and the like—as were 71 percent in

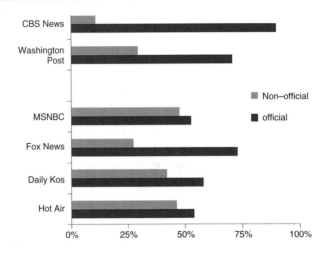

Figure 13.2 Official and non-official sources in coverage of the Libya debate

Note: Figure depicts the percentage of source statements attributed to official and non-official sources. Analysis is based on 10 randomly selected stories about the Libya episode in each news outlet from February 15 through March 31, 2011.

the *Post*. A small minority came from citizens, interest groups, the Libyan rebels themselves, or other voices outside the halls of government.

And while Fox News quoted official sources at a high rate—72 percent of the time—the other new media outlets had more source diversity. Official sources made up 58 percent of statements in Daily Kos dispatches, 54 percent in Hot Air stories, and 53 percent on MSNBC. This appears to be the product of two factors. First, these outlets relied more heavily on analysis of the Libyan crisis from independent experts from outside government officialdom. This was especially true on MSNBC, where "Hardball" roundtables included guests like Middle East expert Shibley Telhami, intelligence analyst Bob Baer, and other figures from think tanks and organizations in Washington.

Second, all of the new media outlets gave their anchors, reporters, and writers leeway to offer their own opinions, something that typically occurs only in op-ed pieces in traditional media. For instance, in a February 26 post, the Daily Kos blogger Meteor Blades passionately advocated for military intervention, writing that "the cause is just" and that "standing by while protesters armed only with rocks and cellphone cameras are gunned down by machine gun-toting loyalists and mercenaries is simply unacceptable." The new media's greater reliance on opinionated journalism gave readers and viewers more arguments for and against intervention from outside the halls of government. From the perspective of the value of an independent press, this may be an argument in favor of the kind of journalism that has emerged in the new media.

We can peel back one layer more by looking at the extent to which President Obama and White House officials dominated the news—perhaps what we can call the extent of "Obaminance" in the Libya debate. Traditionally, the media have a tendency to rely heavily on the executive branch as sources in foreign policy debates, owing to the influence that presidents wield over military matters. Consistent with Figure 13.2, Figure 13.3 shows that the new media were less likely to rely on the Obama administration than were the traditional media. Seventy-two percent of CBS News source statements came from White House officials, as did 42 percent in the *Post.* Fox News also relied on the administration for about half of its quotes, but the other new media outlets were considerably less focused on the president and his underlings.

While government and White House sources were less prominent in the new media, this did not, however, lead to more diversity in the perspectives available to news consumers about possible U.S. involvement in Libya. In all the news outlets, as shown in Figure 13.4, more than half of the source statements were supportive of U.S. intervention, with MSNBC's 59 percent being the lowest. And in fact, the distributions for Fox News, Daily Kos, and Hot Air were all more pro-intervention than in the traditional media. This suggests that while the traditional media relied on officials within government more heavily, this actually led to slightly more variation in the arguments about whether the United States should get involved. The overall picture, however,

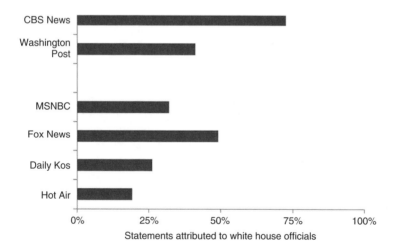

Figure 13.3 Prevalence of White House officials in coverage of the Libya debate

Note: Figure depicts the percentage of source statements attributed to White House officials, including President Barack Obama. Analysis is based on 10 randomly selected stories about the Libya episode in each news outlet from February 15 through March 31, 2011.

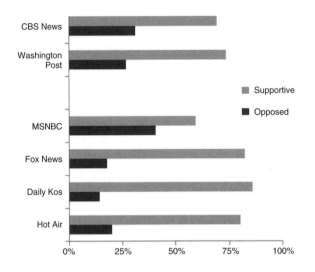

Figure 13.4 Statements in coverage supportive of and opposed to U.S. intervention in Libya

Note: Figure depicts the percentage of source statements coded as supportive of and opposed to U.S. intervention in Libya. Analysis is based on 10 randomly selected stories about the Libya episode in each news outlet from February 15 through March 31, 2011.

is one of similarity—the differences between the traditional and new media were not large.

In summary, the analysis of coverage of potential U.S. involvement in the 2011 Libyan civil war suggests that the content of the news in traditional and new media outlets is not dramatically different. There was no clear difference in the amount of substantive and non-substantive coverage of the debate, as the various new media outlets treated the story in different ways. New media outlets did turn less frequently to official and White House sources, replacing their perspectives with those of independent experts and often the writers and reporters themselves. But in the end, the viewpoints that traditional and new media consumers were exposed to—with respect to whether the United States should get involved in the Libyan crisis—were nearly identical.

Conclusion

On April 8, 2012, Patrick B. Pexton, writing in the *Washington Post,* lamented the newspaper's relatively scant coverage of the issue concerns of the D.C. Metropolitan area's Members of Congress. While the newspaper covers politics with gusto, reporters often ignore some of the more mundane legislative activities of the region's politicians. This, Pexton said, puts local voters in a bind. "If newspapers don't cover the substantive work of these officials . . . how can the people judge if they're doing their jobs or not?" he wrote. "How can they hold their representatives accountable?"

According to many observers, this is the central charge of the media: to provide citizens with the information they need to hold the government accountable for its actions. Because the media serve as the public's window into politics, whether the press offers high-quality public affairs coverage can affect whether citizens have the chance to carry out their democratic responsibilities effectively. While scholars typically have been critical of the media's coverage of politics—noting their tendency to focus on non-substantive aspects of policy debates and to report on a narrow range of perspectives, most of them emanating from within the government—the rise of the new media has raised hopes that the quality of the news might improve.

As this chapter has suggested, however, there appear to be few reasons for optimism about the quality of the information being provided to citizens in the new media environment. The evidence that scholars have accumulated thus far suggests that because new media outlets are subject to many of the same forces as their mainstream counterparts, the content of political news has not changed in ways that help citizens make "better" judgments. New media outlets do not tend to be systematically more likely than the traditional media to focus on policy information rather than non-substantive themes. And while new media may be less dependent on government sources, this does not necessarily translate into a wider diversity of perspectives in the news. When it comes to news quality in the early decades of the 21st century, it seems as if everything new is old again.

Notes

1 W. Lance Bennett, *News: The Politics of Illusion*, 8th ed. (New York: Pearson Longman, 2009); Regina G. Lawrence, "Game-Framing the Issues: Tracking the Strategy Frame in Public Policy News," *Political Communication* 17 (2000): 93–114; Thomas E. Patterson, *Out of Order* (New York: Vintage, 1994); Joseph N. Cappella and Kathleen Hall Jamieson, *Spiral of Cynicism: The Press and the Public Good* (New York: Oxford University Press, 1997).
2 Lawrence, "Game-Framing the Issues."
3 Matt Guardino, "Taxes, Welfare and Democratic Discourse: Mainstream Media Coverage and the Rise of the American New Right." (Ph.D. diss., Syracuse University, 2011).
4 Guardino, "Taxes, Welfare and Democratic Discourse."
5 Gadi Wolfsfeld, *Making Sense of Media and Politics: Five Principles in Political Communication* (New York: Routledge, 2011).
6 W. Lance Bennett, "Toward a Theory of Press-State Relations in the United States," *Journal of Communication* 40 (1990): 103–125; Scott L. Althaus, Jill A. Edy, Robert M. Entman and Patricia Phalen, "Revising the Indexing Hypothesis: Officials, Media, and the Libya Crisis," *Political Communication* 13 (1996): 407–421.
7 Todd Gitlin, *The Whole World is Watching: Mass Media in the Making and Unmaking of the New Left* (Berkeley: University of California Press, 1980).
8 Leon V. Sigal, *Reporters and Officials* (Lexington: Heath and Company, 1973).

9   Guardino, " Taxes, Welfare and Democratic Discourse."

10 Althaus et al., "Revising the Indexing Hypothesis"; Danny Hayes and Matt Guardino, "Whose Views Made the News? Media Coverage and the March to War in Iraq," *Political Communication* 27 (2010): 59–87.

11 John Zaller, *The Nature and Origins of Mass Opinion* (New York: Cambridge University Press, 1992).

12 John Zaller, "A Theory of Media Politics." (unpublished manuscript, University of California, Los Angeles, 1999).

13 Robert M. Entman, *Projections of Power: Framing News, Public Opinion, and U.S. Foreign Policy* (Chicago: University of Chicago Press, 2004); Robert M. Entman and Benjamin I. Page, "The News before the Storm: The Iraq War Debate and the Limits to Media Independence," in *Taken by Storm: The Media, Public Opinion, and U.S. Foreign Policy in the Gulf War*, ed. W. Lance Bennett and David L. Paletz. (Chicago and London: University of Chicago Press, 1994), 82–101.; Danny Hayes and Matt Guardino. N.d. *Influence from Abroad: How Foreign Voices in the Media Shape U.S. Public Opinion*, Unpublished manuscript, American University.

14 Hayes and Guardino, "Whose Views Made the News?"

15 By new media, I refer to cable television channels and Internet sites. But I do not include under the heading of "new media" online outlets that are primarily vehicles for mainstream news content in this new venue. For instance, the liberal blog "Talking Points Memo" is a new media outlet, but nyt.com, the *New York Times'* website, is not. The *Times'* website primarily reproduces its print content, and thus is not sufficiently different from the print version to be considered a new media source.

16 Zoe M. Oxley, "More Sources, Better Informed Public? New Media and Political Knowledge." in *iPolitics: Citizens, Elections, and Governing in the New Media Era*, ed. Richard L. Fox and Jennifer M. Ramos (New York: Cambridge University Press, 2011).

17 Max McCombs, R. Lance Holbert, Spiro Kiousis, and Wayne Wanta, *The News and Public Opinion: Media Effects on Civic Life* (Cambridge, UK: Polity Press, 2011).

18 Natalie Jomini Stroud, *Niche News: The Politics of News Choice* (New York: Oxford University Press, 2011).

19 Shanto Iyengar and Kyu S. Hahn, "Red Media, Blue Media: Evidence of Ideological Selectivity in Media Use," *Journal of Communication* 59 (2009): 19–39; Eric Lawrence, John Sides, and Henry Farrell, "Self-Segregation or Deliberation? Blog Readership, Participation, and Polarization in American Politics," *Perspectives on Politics* 8 (2010): 141–157.

20 Doris A. Graber, *Processing Politics.* (Chicago: University of Chicago Press, 2001).

21 James N. Druckman, "Media Matter: How Newspapers and Television News Cover Campaigns and Influence Voters," *Political Communication* 22 (2005): 463–481.

22 Ray Maratea, "The e-Rise and Fall of Social Problems: The Blogosphere as a Public Arena," *Social Problems* 55 (2008): 139–160.

23 Serena Carpenter, "How Online Citizen Journalism Publications and Online Newspapers Utilize the Objectivity Standard and Rely on External Sources," *Journalism and Mass Communication Quarterly* 85 (2008): 531–548.

24 Madanmohan Rao, "New Media: Countering US Mainstream Media Views in Iraq War I and Iraq War II," *Media Asia* 30 (2003): 133–137.

25 Shanto Iyengar, Helmut Norpoth and Kyu Hahn, "Consumer Demand for Election News: The Horserace Sells," *Journal of Politics* 66 (2004): 157–175.

26 http://pewresearch.org/pubs/413/too-much-anna-nicole-but-the-saga-attracts-an-audience and http://pewresearch.org/pubs/1271/news-interest-too-much-michael-jackson.

27 Lindsay Hoffman, "Is Internet Content Different After All? A Content Analysis of Mobilizing Information in Online and Print Newspapers," *Journalism and Mass Communication Quarterly* 83 (2006): 58–76.

28 Richard Davis, "Interplay: Political Blogging and Journalism," in *iPolitics: Citizens, Elections, and Governing in the New Media Era*, ed. Richard L. Fox and Jennifer M. Ramos (New York: Cambridge University Press, 2011).

29 Zaller, "A Theory of Media Politics."

30 William Cassidy, "Variations on a Theme: The Professional Role Conceptions of Print and Online Newspaper Journalists," *Journalism and Mass Communication Quarterly* 82 (2005): 264–280.

31 Jure Leskovec, Lars Backstrom, and Jon Kleinberg, "Meme-Tracking and Dynamics of the News Cycle," Proceedings of the 15th ACM SIGKDD International Conference on Knowledge Discovery and Data Mining, 2009.

32 I thank Jon Weakley for assistance.

33 *The Washington Post* and CBS Evening News were chosen because research has shown that these outlets offer a fair representation of the way other national news organizations cover politics. MSNBC and Fox News represent the kind of ideologically driven news programming that has become more common on cable news and in the new media environment. Daily Kos and Hot Air constitute the most "centrally linked" sites in the liberal and conservative "blogosphere," according to the Blogosphere Authority Index compiled by communication scholar David Karpf (http://www.blogosphereauthorityindex.com/). See David Karpf, "Measuring Influence in the Political Blogosphere: Who's Winning and How Can We Tell?" *Politics and Technology Review* (2008): 33–41.

Chapter 14

Politics in the Digital Age
A Scary Prospect?

Roderick P. Hart

The age of digital media finds us living in a New Oz. Yelp tells us where to eat, Groupon saves us money, Foursquare finds our friends at the corner bar, and Facebook keeps our identities intact. And there is more: Smart phones help us download music, digital commons make people briskly convivial, and Wikipedia renders thinking easy. Everything digital, a digital everything, is ours for the taking: E-learning at cut-rate prices, shopping on a thousand websites, J-dates on your laptop, Web-MD at the ready. The road to the Emerald City is now paved in silicon chips, not gold, and the only witches one must worry about are those cozying up to Nintendo's vampires. To be sure, the dangers of cyber-bullying, phishing attacks, and malware must be reckoned with, as must the more complex challenges of disintermediation, time-shifting, the design economy, and the transnational imaginary. Things have changed so profoundly that the qualities Dorothy and her three friends depended upon—love, courage, wisdom—are now antique.

That is, until it comes to politics, and then they come roaring back, for politics is an ancient thing focusing on ancient needs—land and ethnic sovereignty, scarce resources and group solidarity. Politics fights new battles each day but, as the Middle East continually reminds us, it fights old battles again and again. Sins committed in the name of politics are also ancient: murder, lust, avarice, conquest, despotism. Read any political history from any era and it is as if time has stood still, which is why so many people reject politics out of hand.

Dorothy was one such person. She loved all things, Munchkins and small dogs included, and only came into possession of her prized ruby slippers because of a certain meteorological disturbance. The Wizard of Oz, in contrast, was a proto-political fellow, a canny practitioner of the arts of legerdemain whose logic of control was to pit good witches against bad witches and to keep everyone else clad in a sparkling shade of green. The Wizard ultimately overplayed his hand but, as he wafted out of sight in his balloon, one had the distinct impression he would find another people to lead since everyone, everywhere, needs an Emerald City.

And where lies our Oz? What flags fly aloft in the Land of New Media? What is one to make of the Obama campaign in 2008, the Arab Spring in 2010, and the Occupy movement in 2011, events that were especially powerful because they were digitally based? What happens to politics when old methodologies like the newspaper endorsement, the speech from the Oval Office, the town hall on the village square, and the telephone poll become antediluvian? Where is politics headed when Independents outnumber both Republicans and Democrats, when Fox News and MSNBC let you choose your news based on your politics, and when one's religious susceptibilities are commodified by nationwide super-PACS? How can Dorothy cope in such an age? My answer: She can rediscover three old friends—journalists who love democracy, citizens who prize enlightened decision-making, and scholars brave enough to ask new questions. Contemporary politics has its problems but its solutions lie within each of us, as they once did for Dorothy and her erstwhile companions.

Journalists and the Need for Devotion

When it comes to journalism today, even a plucky lass like Dorothy would have reason to worry for a great many forces now threaten it. Fine newspapers are being dismantled, good people are losing their jobs, and all media-inflected industries—including advertising, public relations, radio, movies and television—are desperately seeking a profitable way forward. Newspaper publishers often joke that their problems could be solved by the resuscitation of the American automobile industry and the cornucopia of space ads it formerly purchased, but they make such observations in jest, knowing full well that we are living in an age of disruption. Authorities like Leonard Downie and Michael Schudson[1] have imaginatively proposed how the news media might sustain themselves during such times, but they do not underestimate the challenges facing the industry.

Here, though, I will concentrate on a single set of facts and explain why I think journalism will thrive in the future. By trade, I am a content analyst, one who systematically inspects political texts to uncover their latent meanings. One tool I use is a computer program called DICTION (www.dictionsoftware.com) that passes over a text with the assistance of some 10,000 search words assigned to forty lexical categories—motion words, familiar terms, passive language, embellishment, and so on. The signal value of the program is that it provides an "overall" understanding of a text by featuring five Master Variables: (1) *Certainty*: Language indicating resoluteness, inflexibility, and completeness and a tendency to speak *ex cathedra*; (2) *Optimism*: Language endorsing some person, group, concept or event or highlighting their positive entailments; (3) *Activity*: Language featuring movement, change, the implementation of ideas and the avoidance of inertia; (4) *Commonality*: Language highlighting the agreed-upon values of a group and rejecting idiosyncratic modes of engagement; and (5) *Realism*: Language describing tangible, immediate, recognizable matters that affect people's everyday lives.

The notion here is that if one could know only a few things about a verbal text, these five variables—how strong vs. tentative it is, how upbeat vs. pessimistic it is, and so on—would capture its overall tone. Over the years, I have used these techniques to examine contemporary political affairs[2] and, when doing so, have hit upon a curious fact: News reports are inevitably lower on *Realism* than politicians' speeches, ads, or debates.

I fought against this fact when first discovering it. It made no sense to me that political pandering would be more "grounded" than the sober facts reported each day in the nation's press. Had I mistakenly labeled my content variables? Were the texts I sampled weirdly idiosyncratic or encoded improperly? I also had to consider the worst possibility of all: Was my formula for calculating *Realism* faulty? Ultimately, I answered no to all these questions. After passing over some thirty thousand texts with these tools, the trends were clear and consistent, even if perplexing. Figure 14.1 shows how stubborn the trend lines have been over time.

As with all surprises, these data prompted basic questions: If news reports do not exclusively trot out facts, what do they do? If readers do not pick up the local paper to see what is going on, why do they pick it up? If the press is not producing "the first draft of history," what is its purpose? If reporters are not watchdogs or detectives, what are they?

Reporters, I have come to understand, are not really in the fact business at all or, at least, not exclusively so. Mostly, reporters are in the meaning business. Readers do not pick up the paper just to see what is going on. They do so

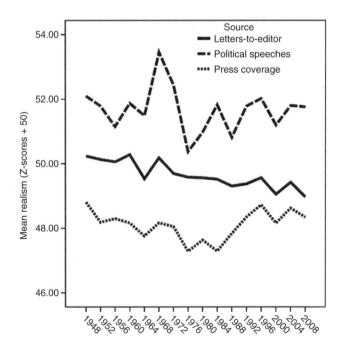

Figure 14.1 Realism scores for message types

because they want to know what it means that something is going on. LBJ rightfully mourned when CBS's Walter Cronkite *judged* the Vietnam war unwinnable. He did so because he knew that Cronkite's *interpretations* held sway for the nation's citizens. A 1972 burglary in the District of Columbia was not interesting because of the tell-tale tape left on an office door but because of the *motives* and *intentions* of those who staged the Watergate break-in. As of this writing, the nation is wondering about the President's take on the war in Afghanistan, but mostly they want to know the *reasons* for our having entered the fray, the *explanation* for our continued presence, and the *logic* to be followed when extricating ourselves. Meanings, judgments, interpretations, motives, intentions, reasons, explanations, logics—this is the stuff of journalism; these are the forces that make readers turn the page.

These are also the forces that will sustain journalism in the future. News organizations will struggle for a time but journalism will survive because meanings and judgments and interpretations and motives and intentions and reasons and explanations and logics will continue to fascinate people. We humans *will* wring an understanding out of life; that is our fate. As the French philosopher Maurice Merleau-Ponty explains, we are "condemned to meaning,"[3] which is why reporters will always have jobs in some kind of organization in some kind of future. The world is too large, its facts too plentiful, and our lives too busy for us to take on such duties ourselves. We will always need interpreters; we will always demand them.

Some people disagree. Some say that the information-rich Web will make each of us our own reporters, that we will no longer need a middleperson. Not so. The more information that storms into our lives, the more we will be cast adrift. In an Internet world, knowing a great many things quickly becomes a case of knowing too many things. And that, in turn, becomes a kind of living death—we know we exist but we don't know where we live and we don't know why. So Jay Adelson, CEO of Digg, got things backwards when declaring: "Increasingly, over time, I think information is ubiquitous. I think that I will be able to get a lot of that data—sometimes not even assembled by an individual— to give me the answer that I want. And for that, I will not pay."[4] Mr. Adelson may be correct that mere information will become increasingly cheap as the cost of an online presence diminishes, but it is precisely because of those diminishing costs that the felt need for meaning will skyrocket. That is, having moment-to-moment access to a stock-ticker produces as much anxiety as satisfaction unless one also has the ability to *interpret* its various curves and squiggles. Information, ultimately, is but a smidgen of what is needed to live a life.

And so we must be careful when speculating about the future of journalism. To focus exclusively on its digital challenges is to forget why journalism became a craft in the first place—because journalists loved meaning, because they were devoted to truth-telling. To be sure, journalism also came about because people also wanted to know what was going on, but it became an institution because people wanted to know *why* as well as what. No doubt, it will take some time for

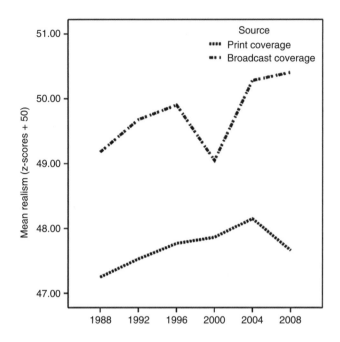

Figure 14.2 Realism scores for print vs. broadcast coverage

the media industries to work out new pricing models and there will be dislocations in the meantime. But Figure 14.2 shows what is at stake. Consistently over the last twenty years, newspapers have outpaced television news in the meaning business, which is to say that, compared to broadcasters, print reporters have delivered more ideas than facts per unit time. People read things—in print and online—because moving images often confuse them. Television stations have their heralds, but newspapers have their guides. We need both, but especially the former.

In short, we must reexamine why journalism became such a valued institution in the first place. Good journalism is what economists call a "credence good," something that has tangible value because of its authoritativeness and social attractiveness. It is hard to put an exact price tag on a credence good but somehow the market manages—Cancun rather than Asbury Park for vacation, chocolate ice cream rather than plain vanilla. Because journalism is a credence good, it will survive because it helps humans aim better.

To be sure, the crisis in journalism is real. Proud news organizations have been humbled and nobody has yet discovered how to price reportage in a disruptive age, although many are trying. As we wait for the news industry to right-size itself, we must ask six questions of those who have sounded journalism's death knell:

- The Educational Question: Why would the need to learn for its own sake, the impulse to go beyond superficial understandings, the desire to comprehend complex issues in greater depth, suddenly be erased from the human gene pool?
- The Political Question: Why would the forces that gave birth to the press—distrust of unseemly forms of influence, curiosity about those in power, a passion to contest contestable ideas—suddenly give way to mass quiescence?
- The Economic Question: Why should age-old financial principles—that information access creates market opportunities, that in-depth knowledge has mercantile value, and that you ultimately get what you pay for—be suddenly renounced?
- The Credibility Question: Why would we suddenly take cues from people we do not know, from anonymous passersby on the Internet Road, rather than place our faith in persons and institutions that have proved trustworthy in the past?
- The Taste Question: Why would our abilities to distinguish between valuable and valueless writing, between the authoritative and the servile, between the elegant and the pedestrian, suddenly be extinguished?
- The Competitiveness Question: Why would ancient forms of contestation—to be smarter than others, to achieve more by knowing more, to imagine richer possibilities than our rivals—suddenly surrender to mere dithering?

Clearly, all six of these questions must be answered in the negative. I do not know what economic model will save journalism, but I am confident it will be found. My suspicion is that online aggregators will ultimately develop efficient subscription services that let readers become one-stop shoppers. So, for example, a Texan will pay a vendor for the *Dallas Morning News*, *Sports Illustrated*, and *Texas Monthly*, while his expatriate cousin in Manhattan will pay a different vendor for all three publications plus *The Atlantic* and the *New York Times*. Once a functional pricing model is found for such services, we may pay a bit more for the news but readers will still read—and writers will still write—because both are matters of survival.

No doubt, some people will continue to exempt themselves from democracy's discussions and that might mean we will have news-for-somebodies (the *Wall Street Journal*) and news-for-nobodies (*Entertainment Tonight*). That would be a dangerous condition but it is already a dangerous condition. Of one thing I am sure: There will always be a market for authoritative interpretations. People will pay for news that helps them navigate their ways in the world. A democratic citizenry has no other choice, which is why journalism will survive, even thrive, in the years ahead. All that is needed are journalists—Tin Woodsmen who love meaning.

Citizens and the Need for Wisdom

The most extraordinary thing about the age of New Media is not the inventions themselves—for example, being able to maintain moment-to-moment contact with friends via Twitter. No, of special note are (1) the speed with which these marvels have entered our lives and (2) the sense of control they provide us. So, for example, GPS devices have made maps obsolete and digital radio has brought country music to Albany as well as Amarillo. Despite the novelty of these inventions, it has become hard to imagine life without them. Equally, customers no longer feel squeamish when setting foot in a new car showroom because the Web has given them every price-point for every option on every car. All of these new-found powers are now embedded in our engines of desire.

But there is danger too. The Digital Age makes us feel in charge even when we are not in charge, something that television does as well.[5] Digitized information lies at our fingertips constantly, but what kind of information is it and what is its value? True, we can select from a bewildering array of websites including singing dogs on YouTube, but how does that profit us? We can discover how aloe vera is being used in Thailand and we can Photoshop our girlfriend's head onto the body of a gorilla. There is power in that but what kind of power? Who, really, is in charge when we surf-and-click in our bedrooms at 2 a.m.? Who built Yahoo's site menu for us and what were their motives when doing so? Consumer choices are wonderful, but what kind of wonderful? Might digital power be its very opposite: the ceding of power to others and, thereby, our obligation to act in the real world? The Web makes us smart, but does it make us discerning? These are the questions confronting the New Scarecrow, today's digital citizen. Being a citizen has never been easy because politics itself is so often disappointing. Taxes increase, the roads do not get paved, the mayor is caught with a prostitute, and taxes increase again. Somehow, miraculously, a sufficient number of voters continue to queue up at the ballot box, vote the bums out of office, and start anew. Despite the frustrations of democracy, digital tools offer new possibilities: (1) ordinary citizens can now present counter-narratives to received orthodoxies and thereby propel social change; (2) journalists can interact with readers directly and that makes them more accountable; (3) complete strangers can find common cause after discovering one another on list-servs; (4) entirely new constituencies can erupt via the Web (the Tea Party comes to mind, as do environmental activists); (5) micro-targeting lets politicians deliver precisely the right message to precisely the right citizens; (6) crowdsourcing makes traditional, hierarchical structures passé.

So it would be foolish to issue a broadside against all things digital for they can indeed be adjuncts to democracy. But they can also be deceptive, making us feel smarter than we are. Accordingly, a discerning citizen must be able to spot the seven deadly sins of the digital era:

- Distantiation: The *New York Times* recently ran a story describing how young New Yorkers now socialize—sitting with one another in a bar, each person on his or her own cell phone, apparently oblivious to one another. "'It's a generational thing,' said one of the bar patrons. 'I could be out with my friends and we're all on our phones, still carrying on the conversation, and it's not weird to anyone.'"[6] Digital interaction as a proxy for direct social involvement? Can this be healthy? One wonders. And one wonders especially when it comes to politics.

Distantiation, the deliberate or inadvertent attempt to create social distance, is a constant possibility today. And the greatest of all dangers occurs when distantiation masquerades as connectedness, making an asynchronous aggregate appear to be an extended family. Real families, in contrast, eat together, shoot hoops together, mow the lawn together, laugh and cry together. World Wide Webbers, in contrast, just click and click. A democracy needs more than clickers; it needs neighborhood activists, city council members, political functionaries, door knockers, playground volunteers, and more. Feeling political, in short, is not being political, no matter how intriguing a given website might be or how fulfilled one may feel after completing an online poll. Real politics requires one to get out of the house.

- Presentism: Today lasts for twenty-four hours, but politics lasts forever and that is both a blessing and a curse. It is a blessing when a polity derives its meaning from those who have gone before, who have fought the good fight. The Lincoln Memorial in Washington and the Martin Luther King Jr. Museum in Atlanta attest to democracy's struggles and thus speak to the ages. But the past can also be a curse, encouraging a group to harbor old grudges about old fights, encouraging them to have another go at what has gone before.

Living in the moment is an alternative to living in the past and that has become easier in the digital age. Psychologists now talk about decay theory, our capacity to forget even important matters because of our constant distractions. The Web is a cornucopia of distractions and that fosters time displacement, the tendency to defer substantive action to some later time because we are so busy clicking. Real political problems, alas, abhor time displacement. Poor people must eat, soldiers need supplies, cops and firefighters expect a paycheck. To become lost in the present is to be blind to the lessons of the past and to tomorrow's demands as well.

- Impulsivity: At its best, politics is a thoughtful business, encouraging deep discussion and careful study to keep a polity from being precipitous. As Max Weber says, politics is the strong and slow boring of hard boards. Practical polls phrase it this way: don't watch the sausage being made unless you want to observe hard-won compromises. If a democracy did not require common assent, if that assent were easily achieved, and if collective endeavors (the space shuttle, cancer research) were cost-free, voters' frustrations would vanish in a fortnight. Want things done faster? Try autocracy.

Or try the Internet. There, things move with lightning speed, resulting in Internet addiction for some people. Do you keep thinking about your next online activity? Do you feel restless, moody, or irritable when trying to cut down on Internet use? Did you stay online longer than you had intended? These are the Web's psychological dangers. It has its political shortcomings as well: Have you sent an email too quickly, out of anger? Did you join an online group whose motives you did not fully understand? Have you grown tired of reflective enterprises like philosophy and religion? Do you sing paeans to online voting because it keeps you from standing in the rain? The Web's "demand flow"– to see more, to have more, to do things right away—is now constant for us. These are hardly conditions supporting enlightened decision-making.

•   Incidentalism: The Web amounts to nothing, really. It is, instead, a collection of all that exists and, hence, not a collection at all. The Web is an assemblage: The Giraffe Lovers Association, the Al Qaeda Training Manual, the Kappa Sigma Reunion, the Mickey Mantle Memorial in Grand Lake, Oklahoma. The Web has no rhyme, no reason. It is a library with a poor card catalog system, a smorgasbord brunch ten football fields long. It welcomes you with open arms each day no matter what your current mood. Jesus? Pornography? A dim sum recipe? Look no further; all awaits.

The Web is anti-philosophical. It stands for nothing because it cannot stand still, so obsessed is it with gathering more streaming videos. Politics, in contrast, deals with central tendencies. Politicians may be intrigued by the odd voice or the bizarre social theory, but they cannot really take them seriously lest they lose that precious fifty-one percent of the people. So, for example, during the 2012 Republican primary, Mitt Romney called himself a conservative and Newt Gingrich referred to himself as a Washington outsider. Both claims were palpably false but they were made nonetheless, thereby indicating where the Republican base stood during that election. The World Wide Web is a bit of this and that but practical politics is far, far tidier.

•   Fabulism: All of the foregoing can be seen as the thoughts of an author too old and too uptight to appreciate the sumptuous potential of the Digital Age. That may be true but I think not. Admittedly, there is something magical, something liberating, about the Web's capacity to erase the line between fact and fiction. The World of Warcraft, fantasy football, pirated websites, doctored photographs, parodied rock groups, fake webcam downloads—joyous creations, harmless baubles. The Web helps us experience an alternate reality whenever we wish. Surely that is therapeutic in a harried world where so many real-life dangers await.

But here is another viewpoint: "The World Wide Web—where one finds a URL for every lie." Each day, the Web announces its claims: *Hidden U.S.–Israeli Pact Uncovered. Sarah Palin, Notorious Lesbian. End-time Awaits Nebraska Republicans. JFK Still Alive. Illegal Immigrants Control Arizona Senate.* To the best of my knowledge, all of these headlines are false but surely someone on the Web has thought such thoughts, perhaps a thousand someones. And what of us? How will we judge what is real and what is unreal? Will we turn to the establishment press, to vaunted academic authorities or, instead, to the strangers among us? At first these seem like questions a research librarian might ask but, in reality, they are questions all citizens must ask in an age of aggressive dissimulation.

- Objectification: If the Web actually does mix fact and fantasy, distance and intimacy, two questions await: (1) Who is really real? and (2) What are our obligations to people who have been virtually transmogrified? Cyberbullying brings these matters to mind. As of this writing, Dharun Ravi, a Rutgers University student, has been convicted of a hate crime for putting online a hidden video of his roommate, Tyler Clementi, engaged in a homoerotic act. From all appearances, Mr. Ravi was not an irredeemably evil person but he failed to differentiate between person and persona. And the consequences were immediate: The flesh-and-blood Mr. Clementi killed himself when his encounter was shared with *everyone in the world* via the Web. If such a crime can be perpetrated by a bright, fairly normal college student, what can we expect in the future from those less thoughtful than Mr. Ravi?

  Lauren Pierce, another college student, brings us back to politics. In November of 2011, Ms. Pierce, the head of the College Republicans on the University of Texas campus, sent out a Tweet urging her cohorts not to assassinate Barack Obama ("tempting though it might be") so he would go down in history "as the worst president" ever. The Tweet made its way around the world, exposing Ms. Pierce as crass and thoughtless. Does this incident attest merely to the idiocies of youth or to the Web as a handmaiden of incivility? Shouldn't a bright college senior have assumed that her remarks would go viral? Shouldn't she have remembered that all actions have consequences? Where did Ms. Pierce learn her digital manners? These are the questions of our age.

- Statelessness: Many of the foregoing remarks apply to all things digital, but the Web makes things particularly hard on governance. That is a good thing except when it is a bad thing. So, for example, the Web has welcomed the Animal Liberation Front, Earth First!, the Kurdish Workers Party, Hizbollah, the White Aryan Resistance and, according to one source, some 2,200 other extremist sites.[7] In addition, research shows that heavy online users have starkly libertarian tendencies, attracted as they are to the Web's openness and anomie.[8] Anyone loving a free and open democracy can appreciate such developments, but they surely do put pressure on the State.

  Given the openness of democratic processes and how responsive elected officials must be to their constituents, political leaders now engage in a war of words with all manner of individuals. Given, too, the plethora of information now available about everything—some true, some false, some irredeemably false—one must take great pains to sort the wheat from the chaff. As economists would say, the "cost of entry" on the Web is remarkably low. A distinctive political worldview and a bit of time with Dreamweaver immediately puts one in the deconstruction business. But what about the poor voter? Which alleged governmental conspiracy, if any, should be considered true? Which hacked website produces reliable evidence about an elected official? Which rumor about the judicial system is true and which a red herring? Even if the Web does not produce anarchy, it makes monitoring governmental affairs harder—and more important—than ever before.

As wonderful as the digital revolution might be, today's voter is being severely challenged. If Dorothy's friend, the Scarecrow, needed a brain to get by in Oz, he would need two or three brains today. The seven deadly sins of the Digital Age have made folly attractive and politics seem easy. But politics is never easy. Human enmity and bad luck continue to conspire against us, so it takes discernment to guard against the silliness and malevolence the world so amply provides. Online bounties exist but politics is, ultimately, a brick-and-mortar business where real people with real problems work things out. There is nothing virtual about any of that.

Scholars and the Need for Courage

In many ways, scholars were not ready for the Digital Age when it suddenly dawned. Computer-based advances became a whirlwind in the late twentieth century and things have only gotten (1) faster, (2) tinier, (3) more powerful, and (4) more ubiquitous since then. We now live in an era of Big Data, an era that lets scholars process massive amounts of information. So, for example, researchers have found spikes in Google searches for "flu symptoms" a few weeks before patients begin flooding into hospital emergency rooms; other studies show that similar searches for "house sales" predicts the market better than do real estate economists.[9] With Web-based data now growing at 50 percent a year, everything demands to be studied. "Unstructured" data or what Lohr (2012) calls "data in the wild"—words, images, video streams—are especially inviting to students of politics, but so too are "network" analyses—who is talking to whom—and GPS tracks—what is happening where, when, and how often. The age of Big Data admits no cowardly lions to the academy.

But scholars cannot be foolish either. More data does not mean more important data. Google searches for "Tea Party" may turn up something interesting, or it can turn up nothing. Grimmer and Stewart note that even though computer-based searches reduce the costs of data collection, they introduce knotty epistemological problems.[10] Why? Because (1) words are multi-meaningful (e.g., a "cool" temperature or a "cool" tune); (2) words change their meaning when nested among other words (e.g., "liberal politicians" vs. "liberal arts"); (3) texts provide different answers when asked different questions (e.g., looking specifically for "conservative" references in a text vs. just asking what words were used with high frequency); (4) analyzing a text with off-the-shelf software (thereby letting you compare your results to that of others) vs. operating intuitively, on your own, and seeing what you see.

The Web is a treasure trove because it contains so much user-generated content. E-government websites (and discussion-boards) abound. The latest political event generates thousands of Tweets. Political attitudes are laid bare on websites of all political persuasions. Heretofore "undiscussable" topics (e.g., candidates' sex lives, matters of racial hegemony, etc.) are now avidly discussed and often cloaked by anonymity. Anyone with a beef, anyone with an attitude, can get online, thereby giving scholars unique access to the "tectonic plates," the deep structures, of politics. One can look at Internet chatter to discover which attitudes are fading and which are picking up steam, what new facts are making the rounds. Other questions beckon: Do voters feel close to or distant from their elected officials? Which national events excite the popular imagination and which fade away quickly? Which political discussions migrate from one platform to another (e.g., from late-night TV to YouTube to email to RSS feeds)? What distinguishes the political complexion of Linked-in vs. Facebook users? Which Wikipedia sites are being constantly edited (i.e., fought-over)?

One of the great advantages of the Web is that it lets us "zoom out," in Steven Pinker's terms, to see *patterns* of attitude and behavior that cannot be seen by observing things one-at-a-time. It also lets us see *epochal* developments, slow-and-steady changes that are too subtle to notice at any one point-in-time. Says Pinker:

> No historian with a long view could miss the fact that we are living in a period of extraordinary intellectual accomplishment… It's easy to focus on the idiocies of the present and forget those of the past. But a century ago our greatest writers extolled the beauty and holiness of war. Heroes like Theodore Roosevelt, Winston Churchill and Woodrow Wilson avowed racist beliefs that today would make people's flesh crawl. Women were barred from juries in rape trials because supposedly they would be embarrassed by the testimony. Homosexuality was a felony. At various times, contraception, anesthesia, vaccination, life insurance and blood transfusion were considered immoral.[11]

To embrace the full potential of the political web, however, scholars must overcome certain phobias:

- Isolophobia: fear of being alone. Traditionally, political scholars have used such data-gathering techniques as opinion polls, laboratory experiments, and econometric analysis. These procedures lend themselves easily to quantification and seem more trustworthy than data "infected" by human biases. But human biases lie at the heart of politics, so scholars must strike out on their own and study voter irrationalities directly. It will take courage and some new research techniques to do so. In-depth interviewing and online polling, for example, permit greater interaction between researcher and subject than do traditional surveys. Engaging voters in sustained, perhaps even psychotherapeutic, dialogue can add depth of insight not permitted by traditional methods.

- Logophobia: fear of words. The Web is awash in words, words having color, subtlety, humanity, intensity. Voters often use words half-thinkingly and thus open themselves up to researchers in inviting ways. Fortunately, a number of methods let scholars study words empirically.[12] But turning words into numbers has its pitfalls, so scholars must be astute when examining (1) what words mean and (2) how they function. Words can be nettlesome, especially when attended by emotion (as they often are in politics), so scholars must reach across the disciplines (combining Political Science with Communication with Sociology with Psychology with Linguistics) and treat words with all the complexity they deserve.

- Anthrophobia: fear of people. Heretofore, scholars have mostly featured the "one-way" messages of politics, those headed from president to Congress, from government agencies to citizens, from the networks to their viewers. As Eveland, Morey and Hutchens recommend, we need to understand what happens when people talk back to one another, when they truly interact.[13] Although they did not study online behavior, scholars like Katherine Cramer Walsh, Julie Lindquist, and Frank Bryan show us how to study voters in their own spaces.[14] For Walsh it was a group of Ann Arbor retirees, for Lindquist the denizens of a working-class bar, for Bryan the crusty residents of small towns in Vermont. There is a richness to their studies, a willingness to fully engage the mindsets of those being studied. As a preeminently interactional medium, the Web offers ample research opportunities of this sort.

- Bathophobia: fear of low places. Politics is about power, so it is natural that scholars have featured its most powerful practitioners in the past—presidents, monarchs, ambassadors. Too, the elite press—especially the *New York Times*, the *Washington Post*, the four major networks—have provided grist for scholars' mills. With the advent of the Web, however, we can now study everyday voices, what people say when standing around the digital water cooler.[15] Instead of just studying moments of high drama such as political campaigns, we must listen to voters during their off-hours. These everyday discussions will shed light on the micro-cultures of politics, telling us, for example, what teenagers are saying to one another on MySpace, allegedly the 11th most populated country in the world. The Web provides vernacular depth and vernacular breadth. We need to understand both dimensions.

So there is still much to learn about politics in the Digital Age. Each day, the Web hosts thousands of new sites but not all are created equally. Some have "digital authority" (credibility, or at least believability), while others are politically inert even if popular. Which is which? Too, some sites become engines of cynicism, preaching that politics is worthless, something to be derided. Who sponsors such sites? What motivates them? Across the Web, a wide range of opinions abounds and that is glorious in a robust democracy. But which opinions are on the rise, which are falling off, and what predicts which outcome? On the pro-politics side, a number of good-government organizations are working assiduously to get people to vote on Election Day. How successful have they been and what did they do to overcome voter lethargy? And what of young voters? We know they are especially susceptible to celebrities' opinions but which celebrities and which opinions? Angelina Jolie (on the Left) and Lee Greenwood (on the Right) have performed such functions in the past, but what galvanizes the youth vote today? There is much to study on the World Wide Web.

The Web is more than words, of course. Pictures have a special way of reaching to the sinews of our beings and we need to understand them better.[16] That will require new ways of (1) capturing and (2) cataloguing images, especially since the Web provides such a torrent of them. This will be hard work since pictures are "multi-layered" in meaning. Consider a picture of Barack Obama: a male, a powerful male, a powerful American male. Which of these features arrests our attention as we prowl about WhiteHouse.gov? Which one is emphasized when Mr. Obama is parodied on *Saturday Night Live*? Which feature predominates when the president is rendered through animation? When he becomes an avatar in a video game? When he becomes something entirely new via a video mashup? Ordinary people take-in these visual data and make exquisitely subtle discriminations based on them. But how do they do so and how can scholars build search engines smart enough to understand these images? Answers to such questions lie on the horizon and researchers are only now beginning to grapple with them.[17] To sort through this complexity it will take courage, the courage of a lion.

Conclusion

The Digital Age is not leaving us anytime soon. Each day brings new aps, new downloads, all of which can be turned to political ends. Are these digital wonders really shaping politics in powerful ways? That, too, is a research question. It seems plausible that they are since the Web is shaping everything else—how we shop, how we learn, how we conduct our family lives. But politics is an old thing and also stubborn: force bends to greater force, less money loses out to more money. These are not digital matters. These are brute, primitive matters and they determine who will live and who will die, war being the continuation of politics by other means. So it remains to be seen how politics is changing. Students of political communication must pursue that question.

And that brings us back to Dorothy. When she returned to Kansas, Dorothy seemed a different young woman. She had had a grand adventure, met strange new people, and imagined wondrous things. But the lessons she learned about love, wisdom, and courage translated easily to Kansas for that is where she had been raised on such truths. Her experiences in Oz only whetted an appetite she already possessed. So must it be with us. Politics is said to be an entertainment industry for ugly people, which is to say it is an industry that asks everyday people to rise up and solve great problems. Because we live in Kansas, not Oz or Hollywood, we must rise up as well. To fail to do so would be to forego the lessons Dorothy teaches so well.

Notes

1 Leonard Downie and Michael Schudson, "The Reconstruction of American Journalism," *Columbia Journalism Review.* October 19, 2009. Accessed on March 19, 2012 at http://www.cjr.org/reconstruction/the_reconstruction of_american.php

2 Roderick P. Hart, *Campaign Talk: Why Elections are Good for Us* (Princeton: Princeton University Press, 2000); Roderick P. Hart, Jay P. Childers and Colene Lind, *Political Tone: How Leaders Talk and Why* (Chicago: University of Chicago Press, in press).

3 Maurice Merleau-Ponty, *The Phenomenology of Perception* (London: Routledge, 2002).

4 Jay Adelson, "Technology Roundtable," *Time*, November 23, 2009, 96.

5 Roderick P. Hart, *Seducing America: How Television Charms the Modern Voter* (New York: Oxford University Press, 1994).

6 John Leland, "Out on the Town, Always Online," *New York Times*, November 21, 2011, 32.

7 Simon Wiesenthal Center. *Digital Hate 2001.* [CD] Los Angeles, CA.

8 Eric M. Uslaner, "Trust, Civic Engagement, and the Internet," *Political Communication* 21 (2004): 223–242.

9 Steve Lohr, "The Age of Big Data," *New York Times*, February 12, 2012. Accessed on March 19, 2012 at http://www.nytimes.com/2012/02/12/sunday-review/big-datas-impact-in-the-world.html?pagewanted=all

10 Justin Grimmer and Brandon M. Stewart, "Text as Data: The Promise and Pitfalls of Automatic Content Analysis Methods for Political Texts," Unpublished paper accessed on March 19, 2012 at http://stanford.edu/~jgrimmer/tad2.pdf.

11 Steven Pinker, "To See Humans' Progress, Zoom Out," *New York Times.* February 26, 2012, ¶3. Accessed on March 28, 2011 at http://www.nytimes.com/roomfordebate/2012/02/26/are-people-getting-dumber/zoom-out-and-youll-see-people-are-improving

12 Roderick P. Hart, *Diction 5.0: The Text-analysis Program* (Thousand Oaks, CA: Sage-Scolari, 2000); Daniel J. Hopkins and Gary King, "A Method of Automated Nonparametric Content Analysis for Social Science," *American Journal of Political Science* 54 (2010), 229–247; James W. Pennebaker, Martha E. Francis, and Roger J. Booth, *Linguistic Inquiry and Word Count: LIWC* (Mahway, NJ: Erlbaum Publishers, 2001); Michael Laver, Kenneth Benoit and John Garry, "Extracting Policy Positions from Political Texts Using Words as Data," *American Political Science Review* 97 (2003), 311–331.

13 William P. Eveland, Alyssa C. Morey, and Myiah J. Hutchens, "Beyond Deliberation: New Directions for the Study of Informal Political Conversation from a Communication Perspective," *Journal of Communication* 61 (2011), 1082–1103.

14 Katherine Cramer Walsh, *Talking about Politics: Informal Groups and Social Identity in American Life* (Chicago: University of Chicago Press, 2003); Julie Lindquist, *A*

Place to Stand: Politics and Persuasion in a Working-class Bar (New York: Oxford University Press, 2002); Frank Bryan, *Real Democracy: The New England Town Meeting and How it Works* (Chicago: University of Chicago Press, 2003).

15 Two fine examples of this kind of work include Gerald A. Hauser, *Vernacular Voices: The Rhetoric of Publics and Public Spheres* (Columbia: University of South Carolina Press, 1999) and Karen Tracy, *Challenges of Ordinary Democracy: A Case Study in Deliberation and Dissent* (University Park, PA: Pennsylvania State University Press, 2010).

16 See, for example, Robert Hariman and John L. Lucaites, *No Caption Needed: Iconic Photographs, Public Culture, and Liberal Democracy* (Chicago: University of Chicago Press, 2007).

17 Ja-Hwung Su, Yu-Ting Huang, Hsin-Ho Yeh and Vincent S. Tseng, "Effective Content-based Video Retrieval using Pattern-indexing and Matching Techniques," *Expert Systems Applications* 37 (2010): 5068–5085; Tsung-Hung Tsai, Wen-Huang Cheng and Yung-Huan Hsieh, "Dynamic Social Network for Narrative Video Analysis," *Proceedings of the 19th ACM International Conference on Multimedia*, New York City, 2011.

Bibliography

Aarøe, Lene. "Investigating Frame Strength: The Case of Episodic and Thematic Frames." *Political Communication* 28 (2011): 207–226.

Aberbach, Joel D., and Bert A. Rockman. "Hard Times for Presidential Leadership? (And How Would We Know?)." *Presidential Studies Quarterly* 29 (1999): 757–778.

Aday, Sean, and James Devitt. "Style over Substance: Newspaper Coverage of Elizabeth Dole's Presidential Bid." *Harvard International Journal of Press and Politics* 6 (2001): 52–73.

Adelson, Jay. "Technology Roundtable." *Time*, November 23, 2009.

Agnew, Spiro. "Speeches on the Media." In *Killing the Messenger: 100 Years of Media Criticism*, edited by Tom Goldstein, 67–69. New York, NY: Columbia University Press, 1989.

Alexander, Deborah, and Kristi Andersen. "Gender as a Factor in the Attribution of Leadership Traits." *Political Research Quarterly* 46 (1993): 527–545.

Allen, Mike. "Fox 'Not Really News,' Says Axelrod." *Politico*, http://www.politico.com/news/stories/1009/28417.html.

Althaus, Scott. "When News Norms Collide, Follow the Lead: New Evidence for Press Independence." *Political Communication* 20 (2003): 386.

Althaus, Scott L., Jill A. Edy, Robert M. Entman and Patricia Phalen. "Revising the Indexing Hypothesis: Officials, Media, and the Libya Crisis." *Political Communication* 13 (1996): 407–421.

Ansolabehere, Stephen, and Shanto Iyengar. *Going Negative: How Attack Ads Shrink and Polarize the Public.*New York: The Free Press, 1995.

Ansolabehere, Stephen, Shanto Iyengar, Adam Simon and Nicholas Valentino, "Does Attack Advertising Demobilize the Electorate?" *American Political Science Review* 88 (1994): 829–838.

Ansolabehere, Stephen and James M. Snyder, Jr. "Using Term Limits to Estimate Incumbency Advantages When Officeholders Retire Strategically." *Legislative Studies Quarterly* 29 (2004): 487–515.

Arceneaux, Kevin. "Cognitive Bias and Strength of Political Arguments." *American Journal of Political Science* 56 (2009): 271–285.

Arceneaux, Kevin, Martin Johnson and Chad Murphy. "Polarized Political Communication, Oppositional Media Hostility, and Selective Exposure." *Journal of Politics* 74 (2011): 174–186.

Arnold, R. Douglas. *The Logic of Congressional Action.* New Haven, CT: Yale University Press, 1990.

Arnold, R. Douglas. *Congress, the Press, and Political Accountability.* New York: Russell Sage Foundation and Princeton University Press, 2004.

Bagdikian, Ben H. "Congress and the Media: Partners in Propaganda," *Columbia Journalism Review.* (January/February 1974): 3–10.

Bai, Matt. "The Framing Wars." *New York Times Magazine,* July 17, 2005.

Barrett, Andrew W. "Gone Public: The Impact of Going Public on Presidential Legislative Success." *American Politics Research* 32 (2004): 338–370.

Barrett, Andrew W., and Jeffrey S. Peake. "When the President Comes to Town: Examining Local Newspaper Coverage of Domestic Presidential Travel." *American Politics Research* 35 (2007): 3–31.

Bartels, Larry M. *Presidential Primaries and the Dynamics of Public Choice.* Princeton, N.J.: Princeton University Press, 1998.

Bartels, Larry M. "Partisanship and Voting Behavior, 1952–1996." *American Journal of Political Science* 44 (2000): 35–50.

Bartels, Larry M. "Beyond the Running Tally: Partisan Bias in Political Perceptions." *Political Behavior* 24 (2002): 117–150.

Basil, Michael, Caroline Schooler and Byron Reeves. "Positive and Negative Political Advertising: Effectiveness of Advertisements and Perceptions of Candidates." In *Television and Political Advertising,* edited by Frank Biocca, 245–262. Hillsdale, New Jersey: Earlbaum, 1991.

Baum, Matthew, and Tim Groeling. *War Stories: The Causes and Consequences of Public Views of War.* Princeton: Princeton University Press, 2010.

Baum, Matthew A., and Samuel Kernell. "How Cable Ended the Golden Age of Presidential Television: From 1969 to 2006." In *Principles and Practice of American Politics: Classic and Contemporary Readings,* edited by Samuel Kernell and Steven S. Smith, 311–326. Washington, DC: CQ Press, 2010.

Baumeister, Roy F., Ellen Bratslavsky, Catrin Finkenauer and Kathleen D. Vohs. "Bad Is Stronger Than Good." *Review of General Psychology* 5 (2001): 323–370.

Baumgartner, Frank, Suzanna L. De Boef, and Amber E. Boydstun. *The Decline of the Death Penalty and the Discovery of Innocence.* Cambridge: Cambridge University Press, 2008.

Baumgartner, Frank R., and Bryan D. Jones. *Agendas and Instability in American Politics.* Chicago: University of Chicago Press, 1993.

Baumgartner, Jody C., and Peter L. Francia. *Conventional Wisdom and American Elections: Exploding Myths, Exploring Misconceptions.* New York: Rowman & Littlefield Publishers, 2008.

Baumgartner, Jody C., and Jonathan S. Morris. "My Face Tube Politics: Social Networking Websites and Political Engagement of Young Adults." *Social Science Computer Review* 28 (2011): 24–44.

Benford, Robert D., and David A. Snow. "Framing Processes and Social Movements: An Overview and Assessment." *Annual Review of Sociology* 26 (2000): 611–639.

Bennett, W. Lance. "Toward a Theory of Press-State Relations in the United States." *Journal of Communication* 40 (1990): 103–127.

Bennett, W. Lance. *News: The Politics of Illusion,* 8th ed. New York: Pearson Longman, 2009.

Bennett, W. Lance, and David L. Paletz, ed. *Taken by Storm: The Media, Public Opinion, and U.S. Foreign Policy in the Gulf War.* Chicago, IL: University of Chicago Press, 1994.

Bennett, W. Lance, Steven Livingston and Regina Lawrence. *When the Press Fails: Political Power and the News Media From Katrina to Iraq.* Chicago: Chicago University Press, 2007.

Bimber, Bruce A. and Richard Davis. *Campaigning Online: The Internet in U.S. Elections.* New York: Oxford University Press, 2003.

Bishop, Bill. *The Big Sort: Why the Clustering of Like-Minded America Is Tearing Us Apart.* New York: Houghton Mifflin Harcourt, 2008.

Blake, Aaron, "Newt Gingrich's War on Republican Debate Moderators," Washingtonpost.com, http://www.washingtonpost.com/blogs/the-fix/post/newt-gingrichs-war-on-republican-debate-moderators/2011/11/10/gIQAiy558M_blog.html.

Blumler, Jay G., and Michael Gurevitch. "The New Media and Our Political Communication Discontents: Democratizing Cyberspace." *Information, Communication & Society* 4 (2001): 1–13.

Bode, Leticia. "Facebooking it to the Polls: A Study in Online Social Networking and Political Behavior." *Journal of Information, Technology, and* Politics (forthcoming).

Bode, Leticia. "Political Information 2.0: A Study in Political Learning Via Social Media." Ph.D. diss., University of Wisconsin, 2012.

Bode, Leticia, David Lassen, Young Mie Kim, Travis N. Ridout, Erika Franklin Fowler, Michael Franz, and Dhavan Shah. "Putting New Media in Old Strategies: Candidate Use of Twitter during the 2010 Midterm Elections." paper presented at the annual meeting of the American Political Science Association, Seattle, September 1–4, 2011.

Bode, Leticia, Emily K. Vraga, Porismita Borah and Dhavan V. Shah. "A New Space for Political Behavior: Political Social Networking and Its Democratic Consequences." *Journal of Computer-Mediated Communication* (forthcoming).

Booth, Robert. "Downing Street 'Did Not Record Who Knew' about Andy Coulson." *The Guardian,* October 5, 2011.

Brader, Ted. *Campaigning for Hearts and Minds.* Chicago: University of Chicago Press, 2006.

Bradley, Amy M. and Robert H. Wicks. "A Gendered Blogosphere? Portrayal of Sarah Palin on Political Blogs during the 2008 Presidential Campaign." *Journalism and Mass Communication Quarterly* 88 (2011): 807–820.

Braestrup, Peter. *Big Story: How the American Press and Televison Reported and Interpreted the Crisis of Tet 1968 in Vietnam and Washington.* Novato, CA: Presidio, 1994.

Brewer, Paul R., Joseph Graf, and Lars Willnat. "Priming or Framing: Media Influence on Attitudes Toward Foreign Countries." *International Journal of Communication Studies* 65 (2003): 493–508.

Brewer, Paul R., and Kimberly Gross. "Values, Framing, and Citizens' Thoughts about Policy Issues: Effects on Content and Quantity." *Political Psychology* 26 (2005): 929–948.

Brody, Richard A. "Is the Honeymoon Over? The American People and President Bush." *The Polling Report* 17 (2001): 5–7.

Brooks, Deborah J., and John G. Geer. "Beyond Negativity: The Effects of Incivility on the Electorate." *American Journal of Political Science* 51 (2007): 1–16.

Bryan, Frank. *Real Democracy: The New England Town Meeting and How it Works.* Chicago: University of Chicago Press, 2003.

Buchanan, Bruce. *The Citizen's Presidency: Standards of Choice and Judgment.* Washington, D.C.: CQ Press, 1987.

Burrell, Barbara C. *A Woman's Place is in the House: Campaigning for Congress in the Feminist Era.* Ann Arbor: University of Michigan Press, 1994.

Byers, Dylan, and Keach Hagey, "CNN's John King Puts Himself on Firing Line." Politico, http://www.politico.com/news/stories/0112/71705.html.

Bystrom, Dianne G. "Advertising, Web Sites, and Media Coverage: Gender and Communication along the Campaign Trail." In *Gender and Elections*, 2nd ed., edited by Susan J. Carroll and Richard L. Fox, 239–262. Cambridge: Cambridge University Press, 2010,

Bystrom, Dianne G., Terry A. Robertson and Mary Christine Banwart. "Framing the Fight: An Analysis of Media Coverage of Female and Male Candidates in Primary Races for Governor and US Senate in 2000." *American Behavioral Scientist* 44 (2001): 1999–2012.

Bystrom, Dianne G., Mary Christine Banwart, Lynda Lee Kaid, and Terry A. Robertson. *Gender and Candidate Communication: Video Style, Web Style, and News Style*. New York: Routledge, 2004.

Campbell, James E. *The American Campaign: U.S. Presidential Campaigns and the National Vote*. College Station, TX: Texas A & M University Press, 1996.

Canes-Wrone, Brandice. "The President's Legislative Influence from Public Appeals." *American Journal of Political Science* 45 (2001): 313–329.

Canes-Wrone, Brandice. *Who Leads Whom? Presidents, Policy, and the Public*. Chicago: University of Chicago Press, 2006.

Cappella, Joseph N., and Kathleen Hall Jamieson. *Spiral of Cynicism: The Press and the Public Good*. New York: Oxford University Press, 1997.

Carpenter, Serena. "How Online Citizen Journalism Publications and Online Newspapers Utilize the Objectivity Standard and Rely on External Sources." *Journalism and Mass Communication Quarterly* 85 (2008): 531–548.

Carter, Sue, Frederick Fico and Jocelyn A. McCabe. "Partisan and Structural Balance in Local Television Election Coverage." *Journalism and Mass Communication Quarterly* 79 (2002): 41–53.

Cassidy, William. "Variations on a Theme: The Professional Role Conceptions of Print and Online Newspaper Journalists." *Journalism and Mass Communication Quarterly* 82 (2005): 264–280.

Castells, Manuel. *Information Power*. Oxford: Oxford University Press, 2009.

Center for American Women in Politics. "Facts on Women Office holders, Candidates and Voters." Accessed April 10, 2012. http://www.cawp.rutgers.edu/fast_facts/index.php.

Chandler, David. *From Kosovo to Kabul and Beyond: Human Rights and International Intervention*. London: Pluto Press, 2005.

Chong, Dennis. "How People Think, Reason, and Feel about Rights and Liberties." *American Journal of Political Science* 37 (1993): 867–899.

Chong, Dennis, and James N. Druckman, "Framing Public Opinion in Competitive Democracies." *American Political Science Review* 101 (2007): 637–655.

Chong, Dennis, and James N. Druckman. "Framing Theory." *Annual Review of Political Science* 10 (2007): 103–126.

Chong, Dennis, and James N. Druckman, "Dynamic Public Opinion: Communication Effects Over Time." *American Political Science Review* 104 (2010): 663–680.

Chong, Dennis, and James N. Druckman. "Identifying Frames in Political News." In *Sourcebook for Political Communication Research: Methods, Measures, and Analytical Techniques*, edited by Erik P. Bucy, and R. Lance Holbert, 238–67. New York: Routledge, 2011.

Christensen, Henrik S. "Political Activities on the Internet: Slacktivism or Political Participation by Other Means?" *First Monday* 16 (2011).

Church, Scott H. "YouTube Politics: YouChoose and Leadership Rhetoric during the 2008 Election." *Journal of Information Technology & Politics* 7 (2010): 124–142.

CIRCLE. "Youth Voting." Center for Information and Research on Civic Learning and Engagement. Accessed on July 1, 2012, http://www.civicyouth.org/quick-facts/youth-voting/.

Coe, Kevin, David Tewksbury, Bradley J. Bond, Kristin L. Drogos, et al. "Hostile News: Partisan Use and Perceptions of Cable News Programming." *Journal of Communication* 58 (2008): 201–219.

Clayman, Steven E., Marc N. Elliott, John Heritage and Laurie L. MacDonald. "Historical Trends in Questioning Presidents, 1953–2000." *Presidential Studies Quarterly* 36 (2006): 561–583.

Clinton, Joshua, and John Lapinski. "'Targeted' Advertising and Voter Turnout: An Experimental Study of the 2000 Presidential Election." *Journal of Politics* 66 (2004): 69–96.

Cohen, Jeffrey E. *The Presidency in the Era of 24-Hour News*. Princeton: Princeton University Press, 2008.

Cohen, Jeffrey E. *Going Local*. New York: Cambridge University Press, 2010.

Cohen, Jeffrey E. and Ken Collier. "Public Opinion: Reconceptualizing Going Public." In *Presidential Policymaking*, edited by Steven A. Shull. Armonk, NY: M.E. Sharpe, 1999.

Cohen, Jeffrey E., and John A. Hamman. "The Polls: Can Presidential Rhetoric Affect the Public's Economic Perceptions?" *Presidential Studies Quarterly* 33 (2003): 408–422.

Cohen, Jeffrey E. and Richard J. Powell. "Building Public Support from the Grassroots Up: The Impact of Presidential Travel on State-Level Approval." *Presidential Studies Quarterly* 35 (2005): 11–27.

Congress on Facebook. "The Social Congress: Key Findings." http://www.facebook.com/note.php?note_id=10150328408545071. Accessed April 26, 2012.

Cook, Timothy E. *Making Laws and Making News: Media Strategies in the U.S. House of Representatives*. Washington: Brookings Institution, 1989.

Cook, Timothy E. *Governing With The News: The News Media as a Political Institution*, 2nd ed. Chicago: University of Chicago Press, 2005, 102–109.

Copson, Raymond W. *Congressional Black Caucus and Foreign Policy: 1971–2002*. New York: Novinka Books, 2003.

Cortese, Juliann, and Jennifer M. Proffitt. "Political Messages in the First Presidential YouTube Election: A Content Analysis of the 2008 Presidential Candidates' YouTube Sites." Paper presented at the annual conference of the Association for Education in Journalism and Mass Communication, Boston, August 5–8, 2009.

Coyne, John R., Jr. *The Impudent Snobs: Agnew vs. the Intellectual Establishment*. New Rochelle, NY: Arlington House, 1972.

Crawford, Craig. *Attack the Messenger: How Politicians Turn You Against the Media*. Lanham, MD: Rowman and Littlefield, 2006.

Davey, Monica. "On Eve of Prison, Blagojevich Keeps Talking, But Some Tune Out." *New York Times*, March 14, 2012.

Davis, Richard. "Interplay: Political Blogging and Journalism." In *iPolitics: Citizens, Elections, and Governing in the New Media Era*, edited by Richard L. Fox and Jennifer M. Ramos. New York: Cambridge University Press, 2011.

Davis, Richard, Jody C. Baumgartner, Peter L. Francia, and Jonathan S. Morris. "The Internet in U.S. Election Campaigns." In *The Routledge Handbook of Internet Politics*, edited by Andrew Chadwick and Philip N. Howard, 13–24. New York: Routledge Taylor and Francis Group, 2009.

Delli Carpini, Michael, and Scott Keeter, *What Americans Know About Politics and Why It Matters*. New Haven, CT: Yale University Press, 1996.

Devitt, James. "Framing Gender on the Campaign Trail: Female Gubernatorial Candidates and the Press." *Journalism and Mass Communication Quarterly* 79 (2002): 445–463.

de Vreese, Claes H. "The Effects of Strategic News on Political Cynicism, Issue Evaluations, and Policy Support." *Mass Communication and Society* 7 (2004): 191–214.

Dickerson, John. "The Good News from Iraq: We Can't Hear It—The Bombs are Too Loud." Slate.com, http://www.slate.com/id/2138622/.

Dilliplane, Susanna. "All the News You Want to Hear: The Impact of Partisan News Exposure on Political Participation." *Public Opinion Quarterly* 75 (2011): 287–316.

Dilulio, John J. "The Hyper-Rhetorical Presidency." *Critical Review* 19 (2007): 315–324.

Disch, Lisa. "The Impurity of Representation and the Vitality of Democracy." *Cultural Studies* 26 (2012): 207–222.

Doherty, Brendan. "Elections: The Politics of Permanent Campaign: Presidential Travel and the Electoral College, 1977–2004." *Presidential Studies Quarterly* 37 (2007): 749–773.

Dolan, Kathleen A. "Is There a 'Gender Affinity Effect' in American Politics?" *Political Research Quarterly* 61 (2008): 79–89.

Dolan, Kathleen A. *Voting for Women: How the Public Evaluates Women Candidates*. Boulder: Westview Press, 2004.

Domke, David. *God Willing? Political Fundamentalism in the White House, the "War on Terror" and the Echoing Press*. London: Pluto Press, 2004.

Downie, Leonard, and Michael Schudson. "The Reconstruction of American Journalism," *Columbia Journalism Review*. October 19, 2009. Accessed March 19, 2012, http://www.cjr.org/reconstruction/the_reconstruction of_american.php.

Druckman, James N. "The Implications of Framing Effects for Citizen Competence." *Political Behavior* 23 (2001): 225–256.

Druckman, James N. "Political Preference Formation: Competition, Deliberation, and the (Ir)relevance of Framing Effects." *American Political Science Review* 98 (2004): 671–686.

Druckman, James N. "Media Matter: How Newspapers and Television News Cover Campaigns and Influence Voters." *Political Communication* 22 (2005): 463–481.

Druckman, James N. "Competing Frames in the Political Campaign." In *Winning with Words: The Origins and Impact of Political Framing*, edited by Brian F. Schaffner and Patrick J. Sellers, 101–116. New York: Routledge, 2010.

Druckman, James N. "What's It All About? Framing in Political Science." In *Perspectives on Framing*, edited by Gideon Keren, 279–302. New York: Psychology Press, 2011.

Druckman, James N. "Media Effects in Politics." In *Oxford Bibliographies Online: Political Science*, edited by Rick Valelly. New York: Oxford University Press, 2012.

Druckman, James N. and Toby Bolson. "Framing, Motivated Reasoning, and Opinions about Emerging Technologies." *Journal of Communication* 61 (2011): 659–688.

Druckman, James and Dennis Chong. "A Theory of Framing and Opinion Formation in Competitive Elite Environments." *Journal of Communication* 57 (2007): 99–118.

Druckman, James N., Jordan Fein and Thomas Leeper. "A Source of Bias within Public Opinion Stability." *American Political Science Review* (forthcoming).

Druckman, James N., and Justin W. Holmes, "Does Presidential Rhetoric Matter? Priming and Presidential Approval." *Presidential Studies Quarterly* 34 (2004): 755–778.

Druckman, James N., Martin J. Kifer and Michael Parkin. "Campaign Communications in U.S. Congressional Elections." American Political Science Review 103 (2009): 343–366.

Druckman, James N. and Lawrence Jacobs. "Presidential Responsiveness to Public Opinion." In *The Oxford Handbook of the American Presidency*, edited by George Edwards, 160–181. Oxford: Oxford University Press, 2010.

Druckman, James N., Lawrence Jacobs, and Eric Ostermeier. "Candidate Strategies to Prime Issue and Image." *Journal of Politics* 66 (2004): 1180–1202.

Druckman, James N., Martin J. Kifer and Michael Parkin. "Timeless Strategy Meets New Medium: Going Negative on Congressional Campaign Web Sites, 2002–2006." *Political Communication* 27 (2010): 88–103.

Druckman, James N., James H. Kluklinski and Lee Sigelman. "The Unmet Potential of Interdisciplinary Research." *Political Behavior* 31 (2009): 485–510.

Druckman, James N., and Kjersten Nelson. "Framing and Deliberation: How Citizens' Conversations Limit Elite Influence." *American Journal of Political Science* 47 (2003): 729–745.

Druckman, James N., Erik Peterson, Rune Slothuus. "How Elite Partisan Polarization Affects Public Opinion Formation." Paper presented at the annual meeting of the Midwest Political Science Association, Chicago, April 12–15, 2012.

Duerst-Lahti, Georgia. "Masculinity on the Campaign Trail." In *Rethinking Madam President: Are We Ready for a Woman in the White House*, edited by Lori Cox Han and Caroline Heldman, 87–112. Boulder, CO: Lynne Rienner Publishers, 2007.

Dunaway, Johanna. "Markets, Ownership, and the Quality of Campaign News Coverage." *Journal of Politics* 70 (2008): 1193–1202.

Dunaway, Johanna, Regina G. Lawrence, Melody Rose, and Christopher Weber. "Media Coverage of Female Political Candidates across Electoral and Institutional Contexts." Paper presented at the annual meeting of the Western Political Science Association, San Antonio, TX, April 22, 2011.

Edwards III, George C. *Governing by Campaigning: The Politics of the Bush Presidency.* New York: Pearson Longman, 2007.

Edwards III, George C. *On Deaf Ears: The Limits of the Bully Pulpit.* New Haven: Yale University Press, 2003.

Edwards III, George C. *The Strategic Presidency: Persuasion and Opportunity in Presidential Leadership.* Princeton: Princeton University Press, 2009.

Edy, Jill. *News and the Collective Memory of Social Unrest.* Philadelphia: Temple University Press, 2006.

Entman, Robert M. "Framing: Toward Clarification of a Fractured Paradigm." *Journal of Communication* 43 (1993): 51–58.

Entman, Robert M. *Projections of Power: Framing News, Public Opinion, and U.S. Foreign Policy.* Chicago: University of Chicago Press, 2004.

Entman, Robert M., and Benjamin I. Page. "The News before the Storm: The Iraq War Debate and the Limits to Media Independence." In *Taken by Storm: The Media, Public Opinion, and U.S. Foreign Policy in the Gulf War*, edited by W. Lance Bennett and David L. Palet, 82–101. Chicago and London: University of Chicago Press, 1994.

Enelow, James N. and Melvin J. Hinich. *The Spatial Theory of Voting*. Boston: Cambridge University Press, 1984.

Eshbaugh-Soha, Matthew. "Local Newspaper Coverage of the Presidency." *International Journal of Politics/Press* 13 (2008): 103–119.

Eshbaugh-Soha, Matthew. "Presidential Signaling in a Market Economy." *Presidential Studies Quarterly* 35 (2005): 718–735.

Eshbaugh-Soha, Matthew, and Jeffrey S. Peake. *Breaking Through the Noise: Presidential Leadership, Public Opinion and the News Media*. Palo Alto: Stanford University Press, 2011.

Eshbaugh-Soha, Matthew, and Jeffrey S. Peake, "'Going Local' to Reform Social Security." *Presidential Studies Quarterly* 36 (2006): 689–704.

Evans, C. Lawrence. "Committees, Leaders, and Message Politics." In *Congress Reconsidered*, 7th ed., edited by Lawrence Dodd and Bruce Oppenheimer. Washington, DC: Congressional Quarterly Press, 2001.

Eveland, William P., Alyssa C. Morey, and Myiah J. Hutchens. "Beyond Deliberation: New Directions for the Study of Informal Political Conversation from a Communication Perspective." *Journal of Communication* 61 (2011), 1082–1103.

"Facebook Gets a Facelift." The Facebook Blog. Accessed February 26, 2012, https://blog.facebook.com/blog.php?post=2207967130.

Falk, Erika. *Women for President: Media Bias in Eight Campaigns*, 2nd ed. Urbana, IL: University of Illinois Press, 2010.

Farabaugh, Karen. "Jimmy Carter: Negative Political Ads are Dividing the Nation." *Voices of America*, January 25, 2012.

Farnsworth, Stephen J., and Robert Lichter. *The Mediated Presidency: Television News and Presidential Governance*. Lanham, MD: Rowan and Littlefield, 2006.

Farnsworth, Stephen J., and S. Robert Lichter. *The Nightly News Nightmare: Television's Coverage of U.S. Presidential Elections, 1988–2004*, 2nd ed. Lanham, MD: Rowman & Littlefield, 2008.

Feldman, Lauren. "Partisan Differences in Opinionated News Perceptions: A Test of the Hostile Media Effect." *Political Behavior* 33 (2011): 407–432.

Fernandes, Juliana, Magda Giurcanu, Kevin W. Bowers and Jeffrey C. Neely. "The Writing on the Wall: A Content Analysis of College Students' Facebook Groups for the 2008 Election." *Mass Communication and Society* 13 (2010): 65–675.

Festinger, Leon. *A Theory of Cognitive Dissonance*. Stanford: Stanford University Press, 1957.

Finbow, Robert. "Presidential Leadership or Structural Constraints? The Failure of President Carter's Health Insurance Proposals." *Presidential Studies Quarterly* 28 (1998): 169–187.

Finkel, Steven, and John G. Geer. "A Spot Check: Casting Doubt on the Demobilizing Effect of Attack Advertising." *American Journal of Political Science* 42 (1998): 573–595.

Fiorina, Morris P., and Samuel Abrams. "Political Polarization in the American Public." *Annual Review of Political Science* 11 (2008): 563–588.

Fiorina, Morris, with Samual Abrams and Jeremy Pope. *Culture War? The Myth of a Polarized America*, 3rd ed. New York: Longman, 2011.

Fischer, Peter, Stefan Schulz-Hardt and Dieter Frey. "Selective Exposure and Information Quantity: How Different Information Quantities Moderate Decision Makers' Preference for Consistent and Inconsistent Information." *Journal of Personality and Social Psychology* 94 (2008): 231–244.

Fischer, Peter, Eva Jonas, Dieter Frey, and Stefan Schulz-Hardt. "Selective Exposure to Information: The Impact of Information Limits." *European Journal of Social Psychology* 35 (2005): 469–492.

Foot, Kristen A., and Steven M. Schneider. *Web Campaigning.* Cambridge, MA: The MIT Press, 2006.

Fowler, Erika Franklin, and Travis N. Ridout. "Advertising Trends in 2010." *The Forum* 8 (2010): 1–15.

Fowler, Erika Franklin, Ken Goldstein and Dhavan Shah. "The Challenge of Measuring News Consumption." *Political Communication Report* (2008). Accessed on April 30, 2012, http://www.jour.unr.edu/pcr/1801_2008_winter/roundtable_fowler.html.

Fowler, Linda L. and Jennifer L. Lawless. "Looking for Sex in All the Wrong Places: Press Coverage and the Electoral Fortunes of Gubernatorial Candidates." *Perspectives on Politics* 7 (2009), 519–536.

Fox, Richard L. "Congressional Elections: Where Are We on the Road to Gender Parity?" In *Gender and Elections: Shaping the Future of American Politics,* edited by Susan Carroll and Richard Fox, 97–116. New York: Cambridge University Press, 2006.

Franz, Michael M., Paul B. Freedman, Kenneth M. Goldstein, and Travis N. Ridout. *Campaign Advertising and American Democracy.* Philadelphia, PA: Temple University Press, 2007.

Fraser, Matthew, and Soumitra Dutta. "Barack Obama and the Facebook Election." *US News and World Report,* November 19, 2008. Accessed March 4, 2012, http://www.usnews.com/opinion/articles/2008/11/19/barack-obama-and-the-facebook-election

Freedman, Jonathan L. "Preference for Dissonant Information." *Journal of Personality and Social Psychology* 2 (1965): 287–289.

Freedman, Paul, and Ken Goldstein. "Measuring Media Exposure and the Effects of Negative Campaign Ads." *American Journal of Political Science* 43 (1999): 1189–1208.

Freedman, Paul, William Wood, and Dale Lawton. "Do's and Don'ts of Negative Ads: What Voters Say." *Campaigns & Elections* 20 (1999): 20–25.

Fridkin, Kim L., and Patrick Kenney. "Variability in Citizen Reactions to Different Types of Negative Campaigns." *American Journal of Political Science* 55 (2011): 307–325.

Fridkin, Kim L., Patrick J. Kenney and Gina Serignese Woodall. "Bad for Men, Better for Women: The Impact of Stereotypes during Political Campaigns." *Political Behavior* 31 (2009): 53–77.

Froomkin, Dan. "Bush, Deep Throat and the Press." *The Washington Post,* June 3, 2005, accessed April 30, 2012, http://www.washingtonpost.com/wp-dyn/content/blog/2005/06/03/BL2005060300818.html.

Gaines, Brian J. and Jeffery J. Mondak. "Typing Together? Clustering of Ideological Types in Online Social Networks." *Journal of Information Technology & Politics* 6 (2009): 216–231.

Gamson, William A. *Talking Politics.* Cambridge: Cambridge University Press, 1992.

Gamson, William A., and Andre Modigliani. "The Changing Culture of Affirmative Action." In *Research In Political Sociology,* edited by Richard G. Braungart, 137–177. Greenwich: JAI, 1987.

Garramone, Gina. "Voter Response to Negative Political Ads." *Journalism Quarterly* 61 (1984): 250–259.

Garrett, R. Kelly. "Politically Motivated Reinforcement Seeking: Reframing the Selective Exposure Debate." *Journal of Communication* 59 (2009): 676–699.

Garrett, R. Kelly. "Echo Chambers Online?: Politically Motivated Selective Exposure among Internet News Users." *Journal of Computer-Mediated Communication* 14 (2009): 265–285.

Geer, John. *In Defense of Negativity: Attack Ads in Presidential Campaigns.* Chicago: University of Chicago Press, 2006.

Geer, John, and Richard Lau. "A New Approach for Estimating Campaign Effects." *British Journal of Political Science* 35 (2006): 269–290.

Gelber, Alexis. "Digital Divas: Women, Politics and the Social Network." Joan Shorenstein Center on the Press, Politics, and Public Policy, June 2011: 1–39.

Gentzkow, Matthew and Jesse M. Shapiro. "Ideological Segregation Online and Offline." *The Quarterly Journal of Economics* 126 (2011): 1799–1839.

Gerber, Alan S., James G. Gimpel, Donald P. Green, and Daron R. Shaw, "How Large and Long Lasting are the Persuasive Effects of Televised Campaign Ads?" *American Political Science Review* 105 (2011): 135–150.

Gerber, Alan, and Donald Green. "The Effects of Canvassing, Telephone Calls, and Direct Mail on Voter Turnout: A Field Experiment." *American Political Science Review* 94 (2000): 653–663.

Gerber, Alan S., and Gregory A. Huber. "Partisanship and Economic Behavior: Do Partisan Differences in Economic Forecasts Predict Real Economic Behavior?" *American Political Science Review* 103 (2009): 407–426.

Gerber, Alan S., and Gregory A. Huber. "Partisanship, Political Control, and Economic Assessments." *American Journal of Political Science* 54 (2010): 153–173.

Gershkoff, Amy. "Memo to Democratic Campaign Managers: Times are a 'Changin' and So Should Your Paid Media Strategy." *Roll Call*, June 8, 2010. Accessed March 29, 2012, http://thehill.com/opinion/op-ed/102023-memo-to-democratic-campaign-managers- times-are-achangin-and-so-should-your-paid-media-strategy-

Ghonim, Wael. *Revolution 2.0: The Power of the People is Greater Than the People in Power: A Memoir.* New York: Houghton Mifflin Harcourt, 2012.

Gidengil, Elisabeth, and Joanna Everitt. "Talking Tough: Gender and Reported Speech in Campaign News Coverage." *Political Communication* 20 (2003): 209–232.

Gilbert, Eric, Tony Bergstrom, and Karrie Karahalios. Blogs Are Echo Chambers." Paper presented at the Hawaii International Conference on System Sciences, January 5–8, 2009.

Gilens, Martin. "Political Ignorance and Collective Policy Preferences." *American Political Science Review* 95 (2001): 379–396.

Gill, Rosalind. "Postfeminist Media Culture: Elements of a Sensibility," *European Journal of Cultural Studies* 10 (2000): 147–166.

Gillmor, Dan. *We the Media: Grassroots Journalism, By the People, for the People.* Cambridge: O'Reilly, 2004.

"Gingrich Slams Moderators, Media for Trying to Create Infighting." Real Clear Politics, September 7, 2001, http://www.realclearpolitics.com/video/2011/09/07/gingrich_slams_moderators_media_for_trying_to_create_infighting.html.

Gitlin, Todd. *The Whole World is Watching: Mass Media in the Making and Unmaking of the New Left.* Berkeley: University of California Press, 1980.

Glasgow University Media Group. *War and Peace News.* Milton Keynes: Open University Press, 1985.

Glassman, Matthew Eric, Jacob R. Straus, and Colleen J. Shogan. "Social Networking and Constituent Communication: Member Use of Twitter during a Two-Week Period in the 111th Congress." *Congressional Research Service Report* 7-5700 R40823. February 3, 2010. www.crs.gov.

Goffman, Erving. *Frame Analysis: An Essay on the Organization of Experience.* Cambridge: Harvard University Press, 1974.

Goldberg, Bernard. *Bias: A C.B.S. Insider Exposes How the Media Distort the News.* Washington, DC: Regnery Publishing, 2002.

Goldstein, Ken, and Paul Freedman. "Campaign Advertising and Voter Turnout: New Evidence for a Stimulation Effect." *Journal of Politics* 64 (2002): 721–740.

Gowing, Nik. "Time to Move On: New Media Realities, New Vulnerabilities of Power." *Media, War and Conflict* 4 (2011): 13–19.

Graber, Doris A. *Processing the News: How People Tame the Information Tide,* 2nd ed. New York: Longman Group, 1988.

Graber, Doris A. *Processing Politics.* Chicago: University of Chicago Press, 2001.

Graber, Doris A. *Mass Media and American Politics,* 6th ed. Washington, D.C.: CQ Press, 2002.

Graber, Doris A. *Mass Media and American Politics,* 8th ed. Washington, D.C.: CQ Press, 2010.

Grant, Tobin J., and Thomas J. Rudolph. "Value Conflict, Group Affect, and the Issue of Campaign Finance." *American Journal of Political Science* 47 (2003): 453–469.

Grimmer, Justin, and Brandon M. Stewart. "Text as Data: The Promise and Pitfalls of Automatic Content Analysis Methods for Political Texts." Unpublished paper accessed March 19, 2012. http://stanford.edu/~jgrimmer/tad2.pdf.

Groeling, Tim. *When Politicians Attack: Party Cohesion in the Media.* New York: Cambridge University Press, 2010.

Groeling, Tim, and Samuel Kernell. "Congress, the President, and Party Competition via Network News." In *Polarized Politics: Congress and the President in a Partisan Era,* edited by Jon R. Bond and Richard Fleisher, 73–93. Washington, DC: CQ Press, 2000.

Gross, Doug. "Survey: More Americans Get News from Internet than Newspapers or Radio." CNN, March 1, 2010. http://articles.cnn.com/2010-03-01/tech/social.network.news_1_social-networking-sites-social-media-social-experience?_s=PM:TECH

Grossman, Michael Baruch and Martha Joynt Kumar. *Portraying the President: The White House and the News Media.* Baltimore: Johns Hopkins University Press, 1981.

Guardino, Matt. "Taxes, Welfare and Democratic Discourse: Mainstream Media Coverage and the Rise of the American New Right." Ph.D. diss., Syracuse University, 2011.

Gueorguieva, Vassia. "Voters, MySpace, and YouTube: The Impact of Alternative Communication Channels on the 2006 Election Cycle and Beyond." *Social Science Computer Review* 26 (2008): 288–300.

Gulati, Girish J., and Christine B. Williams. "Closing the Gap, Raising the Bar: Candidate Web Sites Communication in the 2006 Campaigns for Congress." *Social Science Computer Review* 24 (2007): 443–465.

Gunther, Albert C., and Kathleen Schmitt. "Mapping Boundaries of the Hostile Media Effect." *Journal of Communication* 54 (2004): 55–70.

Hagan, Joe. "The Coming Tsunami of Slime." *New York Magazine,* January 22, 2012.

Hale, Matthew, Erika Franklin Fowler and Kenneth M. Goldstein. "Capturing Multiple Markets: A New Method for Analyzing Local Television News." *Electronic News* 1 (2007): 227–243.

Hallin, Daniel. *The Uncensored War: The Media and Vietnam*.Berkeley, CA: University of California Press, 1989.

Hallin, Daniel. *The Uncensored War: The Media and Vietnam*. Oxford: Oxford University Press, 1986.

Hammond, Philip. *Framing Post-Cold War Conflicts: The Media and International Intervention*. Manchester: Manchester University Press, 2007.

Hampton, Keith, and Barry Wellman. "Neighboring in Netville: How the Internet Supports Community and Social Capital in a Wired Suburb." *City & Community* 2 (2003): 277–311.

Hänggli, Regula. "Key Factors in Frame Building How Strategic Political Actors Shape News Media Coverage." *American Behavioral Scientist* 56 (2012): 300–317.

Hänggli, Regula, and Hanspeter Kriesi. "Frame Construction and Frame Promotion (Strategic Framing Choices)." *American Behavioral Scientist* 56 (2012): 260–278.

Hanson, Gary, Paul Michael Haridakis, Audrey Wagstaff Cunningham, Rekha Sharma and J. D. Ponder. "The 2008 Presidential Campaign: Political Cynicism in the Age of Facebook, MySpace and YouTube." *Mass Communication & Society* 13 (2010): 584–607.

Hansen, Glenn J., and Hyunjung Kim. "Is the Media Biased against Me? A Meta-Analysis of the Hostile Media Effect Research." *Communication Research Reports* 28 (2011): 169–179.

Hansen, Kasper M. "The Sophisticated Public: The Effect of Competing Frames on Public Opinion." *Scandinavian Political Studies* 30 (2007): 377–396.

Hargrove, Edwin C. *The President as Leader: Appealing to the Better Angels of Our Nature*. Lawrence: University of Kansas Press, 1998.

Hariman, Robert and John L. Lucaites. *No Caption Needed: Iconic Photographs, Public Culture, and Liberal Democracy*. Chicago: University of Chicago Press, 2007.

Harris, Douglas B. "Partisan Framing in Legislative Debates." In *Winning with Words: The Origins and Impact of Political Framing*, edited by Brian F. Schaffner and Patrick J. Sellers, 45–47. New York: Routledge, 2010.

Hart, Roderick P. *Campaign Talk: Why Elections are Good for Us*. Princeton: Princeton University Press, 2000.

Hart, Roderick P. *Diction 5.0: The Text-analysis Program*. Thousand Oaks, CA: Sage-Scolari, 2000.

Hart, Roderick P. *Seducing America: How Television Charms the Modern Voter*. New York: Oxford University Press, 1994.

Hart, Roderick P., Jay P. Childers and Colene Lind. *Political Tone: How Leaders Talk and Why*. Chicago: University of Chicago Press, in press.

Hart, William, Dolores Albarracín, Alice Eagly, Inge Brechan, Matthew J. Lindberg, and Lisa Merrill. "Feeling Validated Versus Being Correct: A Meta-Analysis of Selective Exposure to Information." *Psychological Bulletin* 135 (2009): 555–588.

Hauser, Gerald A. *Vernacular Voices: The Rhetoric of Publics and Public Spheres*. Columbia: University of South Carolina Press, 1999.

Hayes, Danny. "Candidate Qualities through a Partisan Lens: A Theory of Trait Ownership." *American Journal of Political Science* 49 (2005): 908–923.

Hayes, Danny. "The Dynamics of Agenda Convergence and the Paradox of Competitiveness in Presidential Campaigns." *Political Research Quarterly* 63 (2010): 594–611.

Hayes, Danny, and Matt Guardino. "Whose Views Made the News? Media Coverage and the March to War in Iraq." *Political Communication* 27 (2010): 59–87.

Hayes, Danny, and Matt Guardino. Forthcoming. *Influence from Abroad: Foreign Voices, the Media, and U.S. Public Opinion.* New York: Cambridge University Press.

Heath, Thomas. "Value Added: A Political Junkie's Foray Into the Ad Wars." *Washington Post,* August 24, 2009. Accessed March 9, 2012, www.washingtonpost.com/wp-dyn/content/article/2009/08/23/AR2009082302445.html.

Heith, Diane. "The Lipstick Watch: Media Coverage, Gender, and Presidential Campaigns." In *Anticipating Madam President,* edited by Robert P. Watson and Ann Gordon, 123–130. Boulder: Lynne Rienner Publishers, 2003.

Heldman, Caroline, Susan Carroll, and Stephanie Olson. "'She Brought Only a Skirt': Print Media Coverage of Elizabeth Dole's Bid for the Republican Presidential Nomination." *Political Communication* 22 (2005): 315–335.

Herbst, Susan. "The Rhetorical Presidency and the Contemporary Media Environment." *Critical Review* 19 (2007), 335–343.

Herman, Edward, and Noam Chomsky. *Manufacturing Consent: The Political Economy of the Mass Media.* New York: Pantheon, 1988.

Hess, Stephen. *Live! From Capitol Hill: Studies of Congress and the Media.* Washington, DC: The Brookings Institution, 1991.

Hess, Stephen, and Sandy Northrop. *Drawn & Quartered: The History of American Political Cartoons.* Montgomery, AL: River City Publishing, 1996.

Hess, Stephen. *The Ultimate Insiders.* Washington: Brookings Institution, 1986.

Hetherington, Marc J. "Resurgent Mass Partisanship: The Role of Elite Polarization." *American Political Science Review* 95 (2001): 619–631.

Hilbig, Benjamin E. "Sad, Thus True: Negativity Bias in Judgments of Truth." *Journal of Experimental Social Psychology* 45 (2009): 983–986.

Hill, Seth, James Lo, Lynn Vavreck and John Zaller. "The Duration of Advertising Effects in the 2000 Presidential Campaign." Paper presented at the annual meeting of the American Political Science Association, Boston, August 28–31, 2008.

Hillygus, D. Sunshine, and Todd Shields. *The Persuadable Voter: Wedge Issues in Presidential Campaigns.* Princeton: Princeton University Press, 2008.

Hoffman, Lindsay. "Is Internet Content Different After All? A Content Analysis of Mobilizing Information in Online and Print Newspapers." *Journalism and Mass Communication Quarterly* 83 (2006): 58–76.

Hofstetter, C. Richard, David Barker, James T. Smith, Gina M. Zari, and Thomas A. Ingrassia. "Information, Misinformation, and Political Talk Radio" *Political Research Quarterly* 52 (1999): 353–369.

Holbrook, Thomas M. "Did the Whistle-Stop Campaign Matter?" *PS: Political Science* 35 (2002): 59–66.

Hollander, Barry A. "Persistence in the Perception of Barack Obama as a Muslim in the 2008 Presidential Campaign." *Journal of Media & Religion* 9 (2010): 55–66.

Holm, Else Marie. *Emotions as Mediators of Framing Effects.* Arhaus: Politica, 2012.

Holtz-Bacha, Christina. "Professionalization of Political Communication." *Journal of Political Marketing* 1 (2002): 23–37.

Hopkins, Daniel J., and Gary King. "A Method of Automated Nonparametric Content Analysis for Social Science." *American Journal of Political Science* 54 (2010): 229–247.

Hoskins, Andrew, and Ben O'Loughlin. *Media and War: The Emergence of Diffused War.* Cambridge: Polity, 2010.

Howard, Philip N. *New Media Campaigns and the Managed Citizen.* New York: Cambridge University Press, 2005.

Huddy, Leonie, and Nayda Terkildsen. "Gender Stereotypes and the Perception of Male and Female Candidates." *American Journal of Political Science* 37 (1993): 119–147.

Hurley, Particia, and Kim Quaile Hill. "Beyond the Demand Input Model: A Theory of Representation Linkages." *The Journal of Politics* 65 (2003): 304–326.

Ito, Tiffany A., Jeff T. Larsen, N. Kyle Smith, and John T. Cacioppo. "Negative Information Weighs More Heavily on the Brain: The Negativity Bias in Evaluative Categorizations." *Journal of Personality and Social Psychology* 75 (1998): 887–900.

Iyengar, Shanto. *Is Anyone Responsible? How Television Frames Political Issues.* Chicago: University of Chicago Press, 1991.

Iyengar, Shanto, Helmut Norpoth and Kyu S. Hahn. "Consumer Demand for Election News: The Horserace Sells." *The Journal of Politics* 66 (2002): 157–175.

Iyengar, Shanto, Kyu S. Hahn, Jon A. Krosnick and John Walker. "Selective Exposure to Campaign Communication: The Role of Anticipated Agreement and Issue Public Membership." *Journal of Politics* 70 (2008): 186–200.

Iyengar, Shanto and Kyu S. Hahn. "Red Media, Blue Media: Evidence of Ideological Selectivity in Media Use." *Journal of Communication* 59 (2009): 19–39.

Iyengar, Shanto and Donald Kinder. *News That Matters.* Chicago: University of Chicago Press, 1987.

Iyengar, Sahnto, Helmut Norpoth and Kyu Hahn, "Consumer Demand for Election News: The Horse Race Sells." *Journal of Politics* 66 (2004): 157–175.

Iyengar, Shanto, Nicholas A. Valentino, Stephen Ansolabehere, and Adam F. Simon. "Running as a Woman: Gender Stereotyping in Women's Campaigns." In *Women, Media, and Politics,* edited by Pippa Norris, 77–98. Oxford: Oxford University Press, 1997.

Jackson, Richard. *Writing the War on Terrorism: Language, Politics and Counter-Terrorism.* Manchester: Manchester University Press, 2006.

Jacobs, Lawrence R., and Robert Y. Shapiro. "The Rise of Presidential Polling: The Nixon White House in Historical Perspective." *Public Opinion Quarterly* 59 (1995): 163–195.

Jacobson, Gary. *The Politics of Congressional Elections.* New York: Longman, 2004.

Jacoby, William G. "Issue Framing and Public Opinion on Government Spending." *American Journal of Political Science* 44 (2000): 750–767.

James, Karen E., and Paul J. Hensel. "Negative Advertising: The Malicious Strain of Comparative Advertising." *Journal of Advertising* 20 (1991): 53–69.

Jamieson, Kathleen Hall. *Everything You Think You Know about Politics and Why You are Wrong.* New York: Basic Books, 2000.

Jamieson, Kathleen Hall, and Joseph N. Cappella. *Echo Chamber: Rush Limbaugh and the Conservative Media Establishment.* New York: Oxford University Press, 2008.

Jamieson, Kathleen Hall, and Jacqueline Dunn. "The 'B' Word in Traditional News and on the Web." *Nieman Reports,* Summer 2008.

Jones, Brian. *Failing Intelligence: The True Story of How We Were Fooled into Going to War in Iraq.* London: Biteback, 2010.

Just, Marion, et al., *Crosstalk: Citizens, Candidates, and the Media in a Presidential Campaign.* Chicago: University of Chicago Press, 1996.

Kahn, Kim Fridkin. *The Political Consequences of Being a Woman: How Stereotypes Influence the Conduct and Consequences of Political Campaigns.* New York: Columbia University Press, 1996.

Kahn, Kim F. and Patrick J. Kenney. "Do Negative Campaigns Mobilize or Suppress Turnout? Clarifying the Relationship between Negativity and Participation." *American Political Science Review* 93 (1999): 877–889.

Kahn, Kim, and Patrick Kenney. *No Holds Barred: Negativity in U.S. Senate Campaigns.* Upper Saddle River, NJ: Pearson Prentice Hall, 2004.

Kaid, Lynda Lee. "Political Advertising and Information Seeking: Comparing Exposure via Traditional and Internet Channels," *Journal of Advertising* 31 (2002): 27–35.

Kaid, Lynda Lee. "Political Web Wars: The Use of the Internet for Political Advertising." In *The Internet Election*, edited by Andrew Paul Williams and John C. Tedesco, 67–82. Lanham, MD: Rowman & Littlefield, 2006.

Kaid, Lynda Lee, and Monica Postelnicu. "Political Advertising in the 2004 Election: Comparison of Traditional Television and Internet Message." *American Behavioral Scientist* 49 (2005): 265–278.

Kaplan, Noah, David K. Park and Travis N. Ridout. "Dialogue in American Political Campaigns? An Examination of Issue Engagement in Candidate Television Advertising." *American Journal of Political Science* 50 (2006): 724–736.

Karpf, David. "Measuring Influence in the Political Blogosphere: Who's Winning and How Can We Tell?" *Politics and Technology Review* (2008): 33–41.

Kedrowski, Karen. *Media Entrepreneurs and the Media Enterprise in the U.S. Congress.* Cresskill, NJ: Hampton Press, 1996.

Kellerman, Barbara. *The Political Presidency: Practice of Presidential Leadership from Kennedy through Reagan.* New York: Oxford University Press, 1986.

Kerbel, Matthew R., and Joel D. Bloom. "Blog for America and Civic Involvement." *Harvard International Journal of Press/Politics* 10 (2005): 3–27.

Kernell, Samuel. *Going Public: New Strategies of Presidential Leadership*, 4th ed. Washington, DC: CQ Press, 2007.

Kernell, Samuel, and Laurie L. Rice. "Cable and the Partisan Polarization of the President's Audience." *Presidential Studies Quarterly* 41 (2011): 693–711.

Kim, Young Mie. "How Intrinsic and Extrinsic Motivations Interact in Selectivity: Investigating the Moderating Effects of Situational Information Processing Goals in Issue Publics' Web Behavior." *Communication Research* 34 (2007): 185–211.

Kim, Young Mie. "Where Is My Issue? The Influence of News Coverage on Subsequent Information Selection on the Web." *Journal of Broadcasting and Electronic Media* 52 (2008): 600–621.

Kim, Young Mie. "Issue Publics in the New Information Environment: Selectivity, Domain-specificity, and Extremity." *Communication Research* 36 (2009): 254–284.

Kim, Young Mie, Fei Shen, and Ivan Dylko. "Now Going into the Public: Development of Presidential Candidates' Leadership Strategies from 1980 to 2008." Paper presented at the annual meeting of the American Political Science Association, Boston, August 28–31, 2008.

Kim, Young Mie, Bryan Wang, Melissa Gotlieb, Itay Gabay, and Stephanie Edgerly. "Ambivalence Reduction and Polarization in the Campaign Information Environment: The Interaction between Individual-level and Contextual-level Influences." *Communication Research* (Forthcoming).

Kinder, Donald. "Communication and Opinion." *Annual Review of Political Science* 1 (1998): 167–197.

Kinder, Donald, and Lynn Sanders. *Divided by Color: Racial Politics and Democratic Ideals.* Chicago: University of Chicago Press, 1996.

King, James, and Jason McConnell. "The Effect of Negative Campaign Advertising on Vote Choice: The Mediating Influence of Gender." *Social Science Quarterly* 84 (2003): 843–857.

Klar, Samara. "Partisanship and Preference Formation in a Social Context." Working paper, 2012.

Klar, Samara. "The Influence of Competing Identity Primes on Preference." Paper presented at the Annual Meeting of the Midwest Political Science Association, Chicago, March 12–15, 2012.

Klite, Paul, Robert A. Bardwell, and Jason Salzman. "Local TV News: Getting Away with Murder." *The International Journal of Press/Politics* 2 (1997): 102–112.

Klotz, Robert. "Virtual Criticism: Negative Advertising on the Internet in the 1996 Senate Races." *Political Communication* 15 (1998): 347–365.

Klotz, Robert. *The Politics of Internet Communication.* Lanham, MD: Rowman & Littlefield, 2003.

Knobloch-Westerwick, Silvia and Jingbo Meng. "Looking the Other Way: Selective Exposure to Attitude-Consistent and Counterattitudinal Political Information." *Communication Research* 36 (2009): 426–448.

Knobloch-Westerwick, Silvia, and Jingbo Meng. "Reinforcement of the Political Self through Selective Exposure to Political Messages." *Journal of Communication* 61 (2011): 349–368.

Koch, Jeffrey W. "Do Citizens Apply Gender Stereotypes to Infer Candidates' Ideological Orientations?" *Journal of Politics* 62 (2000), 414–429.

Koch, Jeffrey. "Campaign Advertisements' Impact on Voter Certainty and Knowledge of House Candidates' Ideological Positions." *Political Research Quarterly* 61 (2008): 609–621.

Krugman, Paul. "Fighting off Depression." *New York Times,* January 4, 2009.

Krupnikov, Yanna. "When Does Negativity Demobilize? Tracing the Conditional Effect of Negative Campaigning on Voter Turnout." *American Journal of Political Science* 55 (2011): 796–812.

Krupnikov, Yanna. "Negative Advertising and Voter Choice: The Role of Ads in Candidate Selection." *Political Communication* (forthcoming).

Kuklinski, James H., and Gary M. Segura. "Endogeneity, Exogeneity, Time, and Space in Political Representation." *Legislative Studies Quarterly* 20 (1995): 3–21.

Kuklinski, James H., Paul J. Quirk, Jennifer Jerit, David Schwieder, and Robert F. Rich. "Misinformation and the Currency of Democratic Citizenship." *Journal of Politics* 62 (2000): 790–816.

Kull, Steven, Clay Ramsay and Evan Lewis. "Misperceptions, the Media, and the Iraq War." *Political Science Quarterly* 118 (2003): 569–598.

Kumar, Martha Joynt. *Managing the President's Message: The White House Communications Operation.* Baltimore: Johns Hopkins University Press, 2007.

Kushin, Matthew J., and Masahiro Yamamoto. "Did Social Media Really Matter? College Students' Use of Online Media and Political Decision Making in the 2008 Election." *Mass Communication and Society* 13 (2010): 608–630.

Ladd, Jonathan M. *Why Americans Hate the Media and How it Matters.* Princeton, NJ: Princeton University Press, 2012.

Lakoff, George. *Don't Think of an Elephant!: Know Your Values and Frame the Debate: The Essential Guide for Progressives.* White River Junction: Chelsea Green, 2004.

Laracey, Melvin. *Presidents and the People: The Partisan Story of Going Public.* College Station: Texas A&M University Press, 2002.

Larson, Stephanie Greco, and Lydia M. Andrade. "Determinants of National Television News Coverage of Women in the House of Representatives, 1987–1998." *Congress & the Presidency* 32 (2005).

Lassen, David S., and Adam R. Brown. "Twitter: The Electoral Connection?" *Social Science Computer Review* 29 (2010): 419–436.

Latimer, Christopher P. "Utilizing the Internet as a Campaign Tool: The Relationship between Incumbency, Political Party Affiliation, Election Outcomes, and the Quality of Campaign Web Sites in the United States." *Journal of Information Technology & Politics* 4 (2008): 81–95.

Lau, Richard. "Negativity in Political Perception." *Political Behavior* 4 (1982): 353–77.

Lau, Richard, Lee Sigelman and Ivy Brown Rovner. "The Effects of Negative Political Campaigns: A Meta-Analytic Reassessment." *Journal of Politics* 69 (2007): 1176–1209.

Laver, Michael, Kenneth Benoit and John Garry. "Extracting Policy Positions from Political Texts Using Words as Data." *American Political Science Review* 97 (2003), 311–331.

Lawrence, Eric, John Sides, and Henry Farrell. "Self-Segregation or Deliberation? Blog Readership, Participation, and Polarization in American Politics." *Perspectives on Politics* 8 (2010): 141–157.

Lawrence, Regina G. "Game-Framing the Issues: Tracking the Strategy Frame in Public Policy News." *Political Communication* 17 (2000): 93–114.

Lawrence, Regina G., and Melody Rose. *Hillary Clinton's Race for the White House: Gender Politics and the Media on the Campaign Trail.* Boulder, CO: Lynne Reinner Publishers, 2009.

Leary, Mary Ellen. *Phantom Politics: Campaigning in California.* Washington, D.C.: Public Affairs Press, 1977.

Lee, Aileen. "Why Women Rule the Internet." *TechCrunch*, March 20, 2011.

Lee, Nam-jin, Dhavan V. Shah and Jack M. McLeod. "Processes of Political Socialization: A Communication Mediation Approach to Youth Civic Engagement." *Communication Research* (forthcoming).

Leibovich, Mark. "Vexing Issue for the Clinton Campaign: What to Make of Bill?" *New York Times,* April 29, 2008, A15.

Leland, John. "Out on the Town, Always Online." *New York Times,* November 21, 2011, 32.

Leskovec, Jure, Lars Backstrom, and Jon Kleinberg. "Meme-Tracking and Dynamics of the News Cycle." Proceedings of the 15th ACM SIGKDD International Conference on Knowledge Discovery and Data Mining, 2009.

Liasson, Mara. "Obama Grants 4 Local TV Stations Interviews." *National Public Radio,* April 19, 2011, accessed April 30, 2012, http://www.npr.org/2011/04/19/135533892/obama-goes-on-local-tv-with-his-take-on-the-budget.

Lichter, S. Robert, and Daniel R. Amundson. "Less News is Worse News: Television News Coverage of Congress, 1972–1992." In *Congress, the Press, and the Public,* edited by Thomas E. Mann and Norman J. Ornstein, 131–140. Washington, DC: The American Enterprise Institute and The Brookings Institution, 1994.

Liebes, Tamar. *Reporting the Arab-Israeli Conflict: How Hegemony Works.* London: Routledge, 1994.

Lightman, David. "Congressional Budget Office Compares Downturn to Great Depression." McClatchy Newspapers, http://www.mcclatchydc.com/2009/01/27/60822/congressional-budget-office-compares.html.

Lindquist, Julie. *A Place to Stand: Politics and Persuasion in a Working-class Bar*. New York: Oxford University Press, 2002.

Livingston, Steven. "Clarifying the CNN Effect: An Examination of Media Effects According to Type of Military Intervention." *Research Paper R-18*. Cambridge, MA: The Joan Shorenstein Center, 1997.

Livingston, Steven, and Todd Eachus. "Humanitarian Crises and U.S. Foreign Policy." *Political Communication* 12 (1995): 413–429.

Lohr, Steve. "The Age of Big Data." *New York Times*, February 12, 2012. Accessed March 19, 2012, http://www.nytimes.com/2012/02/12/sunday-review/big-datas-impact-in-the-world.html?pagewanted=all.

Lovett, Mitchell J., and Michael Peress. "Targeting Political Advertising on Television." Unpublished manuscript, Rochester, NY: University of Rochester, 2010.

Lowi, Theodore. *The Personal Presidency: Power Invested Promise Unfulfilled*. Ithaca, NY: Cornell University Press, 1985.

Lyons, Richard D. "Howard Henry Baker Jr." *New York Times*, January 5, 1977, A14.

Macedo, Stephen. *Democracy at Risk: How Political Choices Undermine Citizen Participation, and What We Can Do About It*. Washington, DC: Brookings Institution Press, 2005.

Madden, Mike. "Barack Obama's Super Marketing Machine." *Salon*, July 16, 2008. Accessed March 4, 2012, http://www.salon.com/2008/07/16/obama_data/

Malecha, Gary Lee, and Daniel J. Reagan, *The Public Congress: Congressional Deliberation in a New Media Age*. New York: Routledge, 2012.

Mancini, Paolo. "Leader, President, Person: Lexical Ambiguities and Interpretive Implications." *European Journal of Communication* 26 (2011): 48–63.

Maratea, Ray. "The e-Rise and Fall of Social Problems: The Blogosphere as a Public Arena." *Social Problems* 55 (2008): 139–160.

Margolis, Michael, and Gary A. Mauser, eds. *Manipulating Public Opinion*. Belmont CA: Brooks Cole, 1989.

Margolis, Michael, and David Resnick. *Politics as Usual: The Cyberspace "Revolution."* Thousand Oaks, CA: Sage, 2000.

Mascaro, Christopher M., and Sean P. Goggins. "Brewing up Citizen Engagement: The Coffee Party on Facebook." *Proceedings of the 5th International Conference on Communities and Technologies* (2011).

Matei, Soren, and Sandra Ball-Rokeach. "Real and Virtual Social Ties: Connections in the Everyday Lives of Seven Ethnic Neighborhoods." *American Behavioral Scientist* 45 (2001): 550–564.

Mattes, Kyle, and David Redlawsk. "Negative about Negativity: Public Opinion and the Framing of Negative Campaigning." Paper presented at the annual meeting of the American Political Science Association, Seattle, September 1–4, 2011.

Matthews, Douglas, and Beth Dietz-Uhler. "The Black-Sheep Effect: How Positive and Negative Advertisements Affect Voters' Perceptions of the Sponsor of the Advertisement." *Journal of Applied Social Psychology* 28 (1998): 1903–1915.

Mayer, Jeremy D. and Michael Cornfield, "The Internet and the Future of Media Politics." In *Media Power, Media Politics*, 2nd ed., edited by Mark J. Rozell and Jeremy D. Mayer, 319–338. Lanham, Md.: Rowman and Littlefield, 2008.

McCarty, Nolan. "The Policy Consequences of Partisan Polarization in the United States." Unpublished paper (2012).

McCarty, Nolan, Keith T. Poole, and Howard Rosenthal. *Polarized America: The Dance of Ideology and Unequal Riches.* Cambridge, MA: MIT Press, 2006.

McCombs, Maxwell E., and Donald L. Shaw. "The Agenda-Setting Function of Mass Media." *Public Opinion Quarterly* 36 (1972): 176–187.

McCombs, Max, R. Lance Holbert, Spiro Kiousis, and Wayne Wanta. *The News and Public Opinion: Media Effects on Civic Life.* Cambridge, UK: Polity Press, 2011.

McGill, Kevin. "Times-Picayune Cuts Half of Newsroom Staff." *Bloomberg Businessweek,* June 12, 2012. http://www.businessweek.com/ap/2012-06-12/times-picayune-cutting-half-of-newsroom-staff

Meffert, Michael F., Sungeun Chung, Amber J. Joiner, Leah Waks and Jennifer Garst. "The Effects of Negativity and Motivated Information Processing During a Political Campaign." *Journal of Communication* 56 (2006): 27–51.

Merleau-Ponty, Maurice. *The Phenomenology of Perception.* London: Routledge, 2002.

Miller, David, and Rizwaan Sabir. "Propaganda and Terrorism." In *Media and Terrorism: Global Perspectives,* edited by Daya Thussu and Des Freedman. Thousand Oaks: Sage Publications, 2011.

Morozov, Evgeny. "The Brave New World of Slacktivism." *Foreign Policy,* May 19, 2009.

Morris, Jonathan S., and Rosalee A. Clawson. "Media Coverage of Congress in the 1990s: Scandals, Personalities, and the Prevalence of Policy and Process." *Political Communication* 22 (2005): 297–313.

Muddiman, Ashley. "Something about Incivility: Impact of Uncivil Mediated Messages on Political Trust and Perceived Entertainment Value." Paper presented at the International Communication Association annual conference, Boston, May 26–30, 2011.

Mueller, John. *War, Presidents and Public Opinion.* New York: John Wiley, 1978.

Murrow, Edward R. October 15, 1958, RTNDA Convention, Chicago. Available online at www. Turnoffyourtv.com/commentary/hiddenagenda/nurrow.html: Download date March 14, 2012.

Mutz, Diana C., and Byron Reeves. "The New Videomalaise: Effects of Televised Incivility on Political Trust." *American Political Science Review* 99 (2005): 1–15.

Nabi, Robin L. "Exploring the Framing Effects of Emotion: Do Discrete Emotions Differentially Influence Information Accessibility, Information Seeking and Policy Preference?" *Communication Research* 30 (2003): 224–247.

National Public Radio. "Sen. Grassley's Twitter Broadside at Obama." *All Things Considered.* June 8, 2009, http://www.npr.org/templates/story/story.php?storyId=105128505.

Nelson, Thomas E., Sarah M. Bryner, and Dustin M. Carnahan. "Media and Politics." In *Cambridge Handbook of Experimental Political Science,* edited by James N. Druckman, Donald P. Green, James H. Kuklinski and Arthur Lupia, 201–213. New York: Cambridge University Press, 2011.

Nelson, Thomas E., Rosalee A. Clawson and Zoe M. Oxley. "Media Framing of a Civil Liberties Conflct and Its Effect on Tolerance." *The American Political Science Review* 91 (1997): 567–583.

Neumayer, Christina, and Judith Schossboeck. "Political Lurkers? Young People in Austria and Their Political Life Worlds Online." Proceedings of the International Conference for E-Democracy and Open Government. Krems, Austria, May 2011.

Neustadt, Richard E. *Presidential Power and the Modern Presidents: The Politics of Leadership from Roosevelt to Reagan.* New York: The Free Press, 1990.

Neustadt, Richard E. "The Weakening White House." *British Journal of Political Science* 31 (2001): 1–11.

"Newt Gingrich Blasts Chris Wallace for His 'Gotcha' Questions at IA Debate," YouTube, http://www.youtube.com/watch?v=KxQTp07KS_k.

Nicholson, Stephen P., and Robert M. Howard. "Framing Support for the Supreme Court in the Aftermath of Bush v. Gore." *Journal of Politics* 65 (2003): 676–695.

Nie, Norman. "Sociability, Interpersonal Relations, and the Internet: Reconciling Conflicting Findings." *American Behavioral Scientist* 45 (2001): 420–435.

Nixon, Richard. *Memoirs.* New York: Grossett and Dunlop, 1978.

Noel, Hans. "The Coalition Merchants: The Ideological Roots of the Civil Rights Realignment." *The Journal of Politics* 74 (2012): 156–173.

Nyhan, Brendan, and Jason Reifler. "When Corrections Fail: The Persistence of Political Misperceptions." *Political Behavior* 32 (2010): 303–330.

"NYT Reporter: Santorum Outburst Was for Cameras." CBS News. http://www.cbsnews.com/8301-505267_162-57404351/nyt-reporter-santorum-outburst-was-for-cameras/.

O'Connor, Brendan, Ramnath Balasubramanyan, Bryan R. Routledge, and Noah A. Smith. "From Tweets to Polls: Linking Text Sentiment to Public Opinion Time Series." Tepper School of Business, Paper 559, 2010. http://repository.cmu.edu/tepper/559

O'Keefe, Daniel. *Persuasion: Theory of Research.* Thousand Oaks: Sage Publications, 2002.

Ostrom, Jr., Charles W., and Dennis M. Simon. "The Man in the Teflon Suit? The Environmental Political Drama and Popular Support in the Reagan Presidency." *Public Opinion Quarterly* 53 (1989): 58–82.

Oxley, Zoe M. "More Sources, Better Informed Public? New Media and Political Knowledge." In *iPolitics: Citizens, Elections, and Governing in the New Media Era,* edited by Richard L. Fox and Jennifer M. Ramos. New York: Cambridge University Press, 2011.

Page, Benjamin I., Robert Y. Shapiro and Glenn Dempsey. "What Moves Public Opinion?" *American Political Science Review* 81 (1987): 23–44.

Panagiotopoulos, Panagiotis, Steven Sams, Tony Elliman and Guy Fitzgerald. "Do Social Networking Groups Support Online Petitions?" *Transforming Government: People, Process and Policy* 5 (2010): 20–31.

Papacharissi, Zizi. "The Virtual Sphere: The Internet as a Public Sphere." *New Media and Society* 1 (2002): 9–27.

Pariser, Eli. *The Filer Bubble: What the Internet is Hiding from You.* New York: The Penguin Press, 2011.

Pasek, Josh, Eian More and Daniel Romer. "Realizing the Social Internet: Online Social Networking Meets Offline Civic Engagement." *Journal of Information Technology and Politics* 6 (2009): 197–215.

Patterson, Thomas. *Out of Order.* New York, Knopf, 1993.

Patterson, Thomas E. *Out of Order.* New York: Vintage, 1994.

Paul, David, and Jessi L. Smith. "Subtle Sexism? Examining Vote Preferences When Women Run Against Men for the Presidency." *Journal of Women, Politics, and Policy* 29 (2008): 451–476.

Pearson, Rick. "Topinka Gambling on Casino." *Chicago Tribune,* August 24, 2006.

Pearson, Rick, and John Chase. "Election Shrouded by Levine Guilty Plea." *Chicago Tribune*, October 29, 2006.

Pennebaker, James W., Martha E. Francis, and Roger J. Booth. *Linguistic Inquiry and Word Count: LIWC.* Mahway, NJ: Erlbaum Publishers, 2001.

Peters, Jeremy. "As TV Viewing Habits Change, Political Ads Follow Would-Be Voters Online." *New York Times*, April 2, 2012, A10.

Peterson, Mark Allen. "Making Global News: 'Freedom of Speech' and 'Muslim Rage' in U.S. Journalism." *Contemporary Islam* 1 (2007): 247–264.

Pew Research Center. "Americans Spending More Time Following the News," September 12, 2010. Accessed March 15, 2012, www.people-press.org/files/legacy-pdf/652.pdf.

Pew Research Center, "Cable Leads the Pack as Campaign News Source," February 7, 2012. Accessed July 1, 2012, www.people-press.org/files/legacy-pdf/2012%20Communicating%20Release.pdf, 4.

Pew Research Center. "Social Networking Sites and Politics," March 12, 2012. Accessed July 1, 2012, www. pewinternet.org/~/media//Files/Reports/2012/PIP_SNS_and_politics.pdf.

Pew Research Center. "Too Much Anna Nicole, But the Saga Attracts an Audience." Last modified February 16, 2007. http://pewresearch.org/pubs/413/too-much-anna-nicole-but-the-saga-attracts-an-audience.

Pew Research Center. "Too Much Michael?" Last modified July 1, 2009. http://pewresearch.org/pubs/1271/news-interest-too-much-michael-jackson.

Peyser, Marc. "Red, White & Funny." *Newsweek*, January 5, 2004.

Pilkington, Ed, and Amanda Michel. "Obama, Facebook and the Power of Friendship: The 2012 Data Election." *The Guardian*, February 17, 2012. Accessed February 17, 2012, http://www.guardian.co.uk/world/2012/feb/17/obama-digital-data-machine-facebook-election

Pillar, Paul. *Intelligence and U.S. Foreign Policy; Iraq, 9/11 and Misguided Reform.* New York: Columbia University Press, 2010.

Pinker, Steven. "To See Humans' Progress, Zoom Out." *New York Times*. February 26, 2012, 3. Accessed March 28, 2011. http://www.nytimes.com/roomfordebate/2012/02/26/are-people-getting-dumber/zoom-out-and-youll-see-people-are-improving.

Piston, Spencer. "How Explicit Racial Prejudice Hurt Obama in the 2008 Election." *Political Behavior* 32 (2010): 431–451.

Pope, John. "Times-Picayune to Cut Back to Publishing Three Days a Week." *Washington Post*, May 26, 2012. http://www.washingtonpost.com/politics/times-picayune-to-cut-back-to-publishing-three-days-a-week/2012/05/26/gJQAyltisU_story.html

Pribble, James M., et al. "Medical News for the Public to Use: What's on Local TV News?" *The American Journal of Managed Care* 12 (2006): 170–176.

Prior, Markus. "Any Good News in Soft News? The Impact of Soft News Preference on Political Knowledge." *Political Communication* 20 (2003): 164.

Prior, Markus. "News vs. Entertainment: How Increasing Media Choice Widens Gap in Political Knowledge and Turnout." *American Journal of Political Science* 49 (2005): 577–592.

Prior, Markus. *Post-Broadcast Democracy: How Media Choice Increases Inequality in Political Involvement and Polarizes Elections.* Cambridge and New York: Cambridge University Press, 2007.

Rae, Nicol C. "Republican Congressional Leadership in Historical Context." *Extensions* (Spring 2005): 5–9.

Raju, Manu. "GOP Leaders Fear Anti-Obama Tone." *Politico*, July 23, 2009. Accessed April 26, 2012. http://www.politico.com/news/stories/0709/25302.html.

Rao, Madanmohan. "New Media: Countering US Mainstream Media Views in Iraq War I and Iraq War II." *Media Asia* 30 (2003): 133–137.

Rasiej, Andrew, and Micah L. Sifry. "The Web: 2008's Winning Ticket." *Politico*, November 12, 2008. Accessed March 4, 2012 http://www.politico.com/news/stories/1108/15520.html

Ridout, Travis N., and Michael Franz. *The Persuasive Power of Campaign Advertising.* Philadelphia: Temple University Press, 2011.

Ridout, Travis N., Michael M. Franz and Erika Franklin Fowler. "Advances in the Study of Political Advertising." *Journal of Political Marketing* (forthcoming).

Ridout, Travis N., Michael Franz, Kenneth Goldstein and William Feltus. "Separation by Television Program: Understanding the Targeting of Political Advertising in Presidential Elections." *Political Communication* 29 (2012): 1–23.

Ridout, Travis N., Michael Franz, Kenneth Goldstein and Will Feltus, "Microtargeting Through Political Advertising," *Political Communication* 29 (2012): 1–23.

Riker, William H. *The Strategy of Rhetoric: Campaigning for the American Constitution.* New Haven: Yale University Press, 1996.

Robinson, Piers. "The CNN Effect: Can the News Media Drive Foreign Policy." *Review of International Studies* 25 (1999): 301–309.

Robinson, Piers. *The CNN Effect: The Myth of News, Foreign Policy and Intervention.* London and New York: Routledge, 2002.

Robinson, Piers, Peter Goddard, Katy Parry and Craig Murray. "Testing Models of Media Performance in War: U.K. TV News and the 2003 Invasion of Iraq." *Journal of Communication* 52 (2009): 678–688.

Robinson, Piers, Peter Goddard, Katy Parry, Craig Murray and Phil Taylor. *Pockets of Resistance: British News Media, War and Theory in the 2003 Invasion of Iraq.* Manchester: Manchester University Press, 2010.

Robinson-Riegler, Gregory L., and Ward M. Winton. "The Role of Conscious Recollection in Recognition of Affective Material: Evidence for Positive-Negative Asymmetry." *Journal of General Psychology* 123 (1996): 93–104.

Rockman, Bert A. "When it Comes to Presidential Leadership, Accentuate the Positive, but Don't Forget the Normative." In *Presidential Leadership: The Vortex of Power*, edited by Bert A. Rockman and Richard W. Waterman, 311–330. New York: Oxford University Press, 2008.

Rockman, Bert A., and Richard W. Waterman. "Two Normative Models of Presidential Leadership." In *Presidential Leadership: The Vortex of Power*, edited by Bert A. Rockman and Richard W. Waterman, 331–347. New York: Oxford University Press, 2008.

Roselle, Laura. "Local Coverage of the 2000 Election in North Carolina: Does Civic Journalism Make a Difference?" *American Behavioral Scientist* 46 (2003): 600—616.

Rosenblatt, Alan J. "Aggressive Foreign Policy Marketing: Public Response to Reagan's 1983 Address on Lebanon and Grenada." *Political Behavior* 20 (1998): 225–240.

Rosenstiel, Tom, et al., *We Interrupt This Newscast: How to Improve Local News and Win Ratings, Too.* Cambridge: Cambridge University Press, 2007.

Rosenstone, Stephen J. and John Mark Hansen. *Mobilization, Participation, and Democracy in America.* New York: Pearson Education, 2003.

Rotman, Dana, Sarah Vieweg, Sarita Yardi, Ed Chi, Jenny Preece, Ben Shneiderman, Peter Pirolli, and Tom Glaisyer. "From Slacktivism to Activism: Participatory Culture in the Age of Social Media." Paper presented at the conference on Human Factors in Computing Systems, Vancouver, British Columbia, May 7–12, 2011.

Rottinghaus, Brandon. "Strategic Leaders: Identifying Successful Momentary Presidential Leadership of Public Opinion." *Political Communication* 26 (2009): 296–316.

Rottinghaus, Brandon. *The Provisional Pulpit: Modern Presidential Leadership.* College Station: Texas A&M University Press, 2010.

Rozell, Mark J. *In Contempt of Congress: Postwar Press Coverage on Capitol Hill.* Westport, CT: Praeger, 1996.

Rutenberg, Jim. "Nearing Record, Obama's Ad Effort Swamps McCain." *New York Times,* October 17, 2008.

Saad, Lydia. "Bush Soars into State of the Union with Exceptional Public Backing." *The Gallup Organization, Poll Analyses,* January 29, 2002.

Sanbonmatsu, Kira. "Gender Stereotypes and Vote Choice." *American Journal of Political Science* 46 (2002): 20–34.

Sanbonmatsu, Kira. *Where Women Run: Gender and Party in the American States.* Ann Arbor: University of Michigan Press, 2006.

Sanbonmatsu, Kira and Kathleen Dolan, "Do Gender Stereotypes Transcend Party?" *Political Research Quarterly* 62 (2009): 485–494.

Sands, Geneva. "Gingrich: News Media Reporting on Economy is 'Sad'." The Hill, http://thehill.com/video/campaign/192793-gingrich-news-media-reporting-on-economy-is-sad.

Sanger, David E. "Bush, Focusing on Terrorism, Says Secure U.S. Top Priority." *The New York Times,* January 29, 2002.

Sapiro, Virginia. "If U.S. Senator Baker Were a Woman: An Experimental Study of Candidate Images." *Political Psychology* 3 (1982): 61–83.

Schaefer, Todd M. "Persuading the Persuaders." *Political Communication* 14 (1997): 97–111.

Schaffner, Brian F. "Priming Gender: Campaigning on Women's Issues in U.S. Senate Elections." *American Journal of Political Science* 49 (2005), 803–817.

Schaffner, Brian F., and Mary Layton Atkinson. "Taxing Death or Estates? When Frames Influence Citizens' Issue Beliefs." In *Winning with Words: The Origins and Impact of Political Framing,* edited by Brian F. Schaffner and Patrick J. Sellers, 121–135. New York: Routledge, 2010.

Schattschneider, E. E. *The Semisovereign People: A Realist's View of Democracy in America.* New York: Holt, Rhineart and Winston, 1960.

Scheufele, Dietram. "Framing as a Theory of Media Effects," *Journal of Communication* 49 (1999): 103–122.

Schudson, Michael. *The Good Citizen: A History of American Civic Life.* New York: The Free Press, 1998.

Schweitzer, Eva Johanna. "Innovation or Normalization in E-campaigning." *European Journal of Communication* 23 (2008): 449–470.

Sears, David O., and Jonathan L. Freedman. "Selective Exposure to Information: A Critical Review," *Public Opinion Quarterly* 31 (1967): 194–213.

Sellers, Patrick. *Cycles of Spin: Strategic Communication in the U.S. Congress.* New York: Cambridge University Press, 2010.

Shah, Dhavan V., Jaeho Cho, Seungahn Nah, Melissa R. Gotlieb, Hyunseo Hwang,

Nam-Jin Lee, Rosanne M. Scholl and Douglas M. McLeod. "Campaign Ads, Online Messaging, and Participation: Extending the Communication Mediation Model." *Journal of Communication* 57 (2007): 676–703.

Shah, Dhavan V., Nojin Kwak and R. Lance Holbert. "'Connecting' and 'Disconnecting' with Civic Life: Patterns of Internet Use and the Production of Social Capital." *Political Communication* 18 (2001): 141–162.

Shah, Dhavan V., Jack M. McLeod and So-Hyang Yoon. "Communication, Context, and Community: An Exploration of Print, Broadcast, and Internet Influences." *Communication Research* 28 (2001): 464–506.

Shales, Tom, and James Andrew Miller. *Live from New York: An Uncensored History of Saturday Night Live.* Boston, MA: Little Brown, 2002.

Shaw, Daron. "A Study of Presidential Campaign Event Effects from 1952 to 1992." *Journal of Politics* 61 (1999): 387–422.

Sides, John, and Jake Haselswerdt. "Campaigns and Elections." In *New Directions in Public Opinion*, edited by Adam Berinsky, 241–257. New York: Routledge, 2012.

Sigal, Leon V. *Reporters and Officials.* Lexington: Heath and Company, 1973.

Sigelman, Lee. "Disarming the Opposition: The President, the Public, and the INF Treaty." *Public Opinion Quarterly* 54 (1990): 37–47.

Sigelman, Lee and Mark Kugler. "Why Is Research on the Effects of Negative Campaigning So Inconclusive? Understanding Citizens' Perceptions of Negativity." *Journal of Politics* 65 (2003): 142–160.

Simon Wiesenthal Center. *Digital Hate 2001.* [CD] Los Angeles, CA.

Sinclair, Barbara. "Hostile Partners: The President, Congress, and Lawmaking in the Partisan 1990s." In *Polarized Politics: Congress and the President in a Partisan Era*, edited by Jon R. Bond and Richard Fleisher, 134–153. Washington, DC: CQ Press, 2000.

Sinclair, Barbara. *Party Wars: Polarization and the Politics of National Policy Making.* Norman, OK: University of Oklahoma Press, 2006.

Sinclair, Barbara. *Unorthodox Lawmaking: New Legislative Processes in the U.S. Congress.* 4th ed. Washington, DC: CQ Press, 2011.

Singel, Ryan. "Net Politics Down but Not Out." *Wired.* February 2, 2004. Accessed March 22, 2012 http://www.wired.com/politics/law/news/2004/02/62123?currentPage=all

Sloan, John W. *The Reagan Effect: Economics and Presidential Leadership.* Lawrence: University of Kansas Press, 1999.

Slothuus, Rune. "When Can Political Parties Lead Public Opinion? Evidence from a Natural Experiment." *Political Communication* 27 (2010): 158–177.

Slothuus, Rune, and Claes H. de Vreese. "Political Parties, Motivated Reasoning, and Issue Framing Effects." *The Journal of Politics* 72 (2010): 630–645.

Smith, Aaron. "The Internet and Campaign 2010." Pew Research Center. 2011. http://www.pewinternet.org/~/media//Files/Reports/2011/Internet%20and%20Campaign%202010.pdf

Smith, Aaron. "The Internet's Role in Campaign 2008." Pew Internet Reports, April 15, 2009.

Sniderman, Paul and Sean M. Theriault. "The Structure of Political Argument and the Logic of Issue Framing." In *Studies in Public Opinion*, edited by Willem E. Saris and Paul M. Sniderman, 133–165. Princeton: Princeton University Press, 2004.

Soroka, Stuart and Stephen McAdams. "An Experimental Study of the Differential Effects of Positive Versus Negative News Content." Paper presented at the Elections,

Public Opinion and Parties Annual Conference, Colchester, United Kingdom, September 10–12, 2010.

Sosnik, Douglas, Matthew Dowd and Ron Fournier. *Applebee's America: How Successful Political, Business, and Religious Leaders Connect with the New American Community*. New York: Simon and Schuster, 2006.

Souley, Boubacar, and Robert H. Wicks. "Tracking the 2004 Presidential Campaign Web Sites: Similarities and Differences." *American Behavioral Scientist* 49 (2005): 535–547.

Special Issue "The CNN Effect Revisited," *Media, War and Conflict* 4 (2011): 3–95.

Stein, Sam. "Anita Dunn: Fox News an Outlet for GOP Propaganda." Huffington Post, http://www.huffingtonpost.com/2009/10/11/anita-dunn-fox-news-an-ou_n_316691.html.

Stelter, Brian. "Finding Political News Online, the Young Pass It On." *New York Times*, March 27, 2008. Accessed March 23, 2012, http://www.nytimes.com/2008/03/27/us/politics/27voters.html

Stetler, Brian. "Local TV Newscasts Expanding." *New York Times*, August 21, 2011, B1.

Stevens, Daniel P., et al. "Local News in a Social Capital Capital: Election 2000 on Minnesota's Local News Stations." *Political Communication* 23 (2006): 61–83.

Stevens, Daniel. "Elements of Negativity: Volume and Proportion in Exposure to Negative Advertising." *Political Behavior* 31 (2009): 429–454.

Stokes, Donald E. "Spatial Models of Party Competition." In *Elections and the Political Order*, edited by Angus Campbell, et al., 161–179. New York, NY: Wiley, 1966.

Streissguth, Thomas. *Media Bias*. New York, NY: Benchmark Books, 2006.

Stromer-Galley, Jennifer. "On-line Interaction and Why Candidates Avoid It." *Journal of Communication* 50 (2000): 111–132.

Stromer-Galley, Jennifer. "Diversity of Political Conversation on the Internet." *Journal of Computer-Mediated Communication* 8 (2003): 0.

Stromer-Galley, Jennifer, and Andrea B. Baker. "Joy and Sorrow of Interactivity on the Campaign Trail: Blogs in the Primary Campaign of Howard Dean." In *The Internet Election: Perspectives on the Web in Campaign 2004*, edited by Andrew Paul Williams and John C. Tedesco, 111–131. Lanham, Maryland: Rowman & Littlefield, 2006.

Stroud, Natalie Jomini. "Media Effects, Selective Exposure, and Fahrenheit 9/11." *Political Communication* 24 (2007): 415–432.

Stroud, Natalie Jomini. "Media Use and Political Predispositions: Revisiting the Concept of Selective Exposure." *Political Behavior* 30 (2008): 341–366.

Stroud, Natalie Jomini. *Niche News: The Politics of News Choice*. New York: Oxford University Press, 2011.

Su, Ja-Hwung, Yu-Ting Huang, Hsin-Ho Yeh and Vincent S. Tseng. "Effective Content-based Video Retrieval using Pattern-indexing and Matching Techniques." *Expert Systems Applications* 37 (2010): 5068–5085.

Sulkin, Tracy. *The Legislative Legacy of Congressional Campaigns*. Cambridge: Cambridge University Press, 2011.

Sunstein, Cass R. *Republic.com 2.0*. Princeton: Princeton University Press, 2007.

Taber, Charles S., and Milton Lodge. "Motivated Skepticism in the Evaluation of Political Beliefs." *American Journal of Political Science* 50 (2006): 755–769.

Taintor, David. "Santorum: Real Conservatives Curse out the New York Times."

Talkingpointsmemo.com, http://2012.talkingpointsmemo.com/2012/03/santorum-real-conservatives-criticize-new-york-times.php.

Tam-Cho, Wendy, James Gimpel and Iris Hui. "Voter Migration and the Geographic Sorting of the American Electorate." Working Paper.

Taylor, Philip M. "Perception Management and the 'War' Against Terror." *Journal of Information Warfare* 1 (2002): 16–29.

Tedin, Kent, Brandon Rottinghaus and Harrell Rodgers. "When the President Goes Public: The Consequences of Communication Mode for Opinion Change Across Issue Types and Groups." *Political Research Quarterly* 64 (2010): 506–519.

Tewksbury, David and Scott Althaus. "Differences in Knowledge Acquisition among Readers of the Paper and Online Versions of a National Newspaper." *Journalism & Mass Communication Quarterly* 77 (2000): 457–479.

Tewksbury, David, Jennifer Jones, Matthew W. Peske, Ashlea Raymond, and William Vig. "The Interaction of News and Advocate Frames." *Journalism and Mass Communication Quarterly* 77 (2000): 804–829.

"The Low Road to Victory." *New York Times*, editorial. April 23, 2008.

Thorson, Kjerstin, Brian Ekdale, Porismita Borah, Kang Namkoong and Chirag Shah. "YouTube and Proposition 8: A Case Study in Video Activism." *Information, Communication & Society* 13 (2010): 325–349.

Thussu, Daya. *News as Entertainment: The Rise of Global Infotainment*, 2nd ed. London: Sage, 1997.

Tirman, John. *The Deaths of Others: The Fate of Civilians in America's Wars*. Oxford: Oxford University Press, 2011.

"Tony Blair Godfather to Rupert Murdoch's Daughter." British Broadcasting Corporation, September 5, 2011. Accessed March 29, 2012, www.bbc.co.uk/news/uk-politics-14785501.

Towner, Terri L., and David Dulio. "The Web 2.0 Election: Does the Online Medium Matter?" *The Journal of Political Marketing* 10 (2011): 165–188.

Tracy, Karen. *Challenges of Ordinary Democracy: A Case Study in Deliberation and Dissent*. University Park, PA: Pennsylvania State University Press, 2010.

Trippi, Joe. *The Revolution Will Not Be Televised: Democracy, the Internet, and the Overthrow of Everything*. New York: William Morrow, 2004.

Tsai, Tsung-Hung, Wen-Huang Cheng and Yung-Huan Hsieh. "Dynamic Social Network for Narrative Video Analysis." *Proceedings of the 19th ACM International Conference on Multimedia*, New York City, 2011.

United States Census Bureau, *Statistical Abstract of the United States*. Washington, DC: United States Government Printing Office, 2002,

United States Census Bureau, *Statistical Abstract of the United States*. Washington, DC: United States Government Printing Office, 2006.

United States Census Bureau, *Statistical Abstract of the United States*. Washington, DC: United States Government Printing Office, 2012.

Uslaner, Eric M. "Trust, Civic Engagement, and the Internet." *Political Communication* 21 (2004): 223–242.

Utz, Sonja. "The (Potential) Benefits of Campaigning Via Social Network Sites." *Journal of Computer-Mediated Communication* 14 (2009): 221–243.

Vallone, Robert P., Lee Ross and Mark R. Lepper. "The Hostile Media Phenomenon: Biased Perception and Perceptions of Media Bias in Coverage of the Beirut Massacre." *Journal of Personality and Social Psychology* 49 (1985): 577–585.

Vargas, Jose Antonio. "Barack Obama, Social Networking King." *The Washington Post*, October 6, 2007. Accessed March 23, 2012, http://voices.washingtonpost.com/44/2007/10/barack-obama-social-networking.html

Vargas, Jose Antonio, "Obama Raised Half a Billion Online," *The Washington Post*, November 20, 2008. Accessed March 4, 2012, http://voices.washingtonpost.com/44/2008/11/obama-raised-half-a-billion-on.html

Vinson, C. Danielle. *Local Media Coverage of Congress and its Members: Through Local Eyes*. Cresskill, N.J.: Hampton Press, 2003.

Vinson, C. Danielle. "The Congressional Black Caucus Goes Public: How the CBC Uses the Media to Influence Policymaking." Paper presented at the annual meeting of the Midwest Political Science Association, Chicago, Illinois, April 22–24, 2010.

Vitak, Jessica, Paul Zube, Andrew Smock, Caleb T. Carr, Nicole Ellison, and Cliff Lampe. "It's Complicated: Facebook Users' Political Participation in the 2008 Election." *Cyberpsychology, Behavior, and Social Networking* 14 (2011): 107–114.

Waismel-Manor, Israel, and Yariv Tsfati. "Why Do Better-Looking Members of Congress Receive More Television Coverage?" *Political Communication* 28 (2011): 440–463.

Wallsten, Kevin. ""Yes We Can': How Online Viewership, Blog Discussion, Campaign Statements, and Mainstream Media Coverage Produced a Viral Video Phenomenon." *Journal of Information Technology & Politics* 7 (2010): 163–181.

Walsh, Katherine Cramer. *Talking about Politics: Informal Groups and Social Identity in American Life*. Chicago: University of Chicago Press, 2003.

Wattenberg, Martin. *Where Have All the Voters Gone?* Cambridge: Harvard University Press, 2002, 90–91.

Weisman, Jonathan. "GOP Backers Offer Immigration Bill Change; Provision Would Require Illegal Residents to Return Home to Gain Legal Status." *Washington Post*, June 26, 2007.

Welch, Reed L. "Presidential Success in Communicating with the Public Through Televised Addresses." *Presidential Studies Quarterly* 33 (2003): 347–365.

Welch, Reed L. "Was Reagan Really a Great Communicator? The Influence of Televised Addresses on Public Opinion," *Presidential Studies Quarterly* 33 (2003): 853–876.

Wells, Chris, Justin Reedy, John Gastil, and Carolyn Lee. "Information Distortion and Voting Choices: The Origins and Effects of Factual Beliefs in Initiative Elections." *Political Psychology* 30 (2009): 953–969.

Wenger, Andreas, and Marcel Gerber. "John F. Kennedy and the Limited Test Ban Treaty: A Case Study of Presidential Leadership." *Presidential Studies Quarterly* 29 (1999): 460–487.

Wesleyan Media Project. "Outside Group Involvement in GOP Contest Skyrockets Compared to 2008," January 30, 2012. Accessed on July 1, 2012, http://mediaproject.wesleyan.edu/2012/01/30/group-involvement-skyrockets/

West, Darrell M. *The Rise and Fall of the Media Establishment*. Boston: Bedford/St. Martin's, 2001.

Westmoreland, William C. "Vietnam in Perspective." *Military Review* 59 (1979): 34–43.

Wicks, Robert H., and Boubacar Souley. "Going Negative: Candidate Usage of Internet Web Sites during the 2000 Presidential Campaign." *Journalism and Mass Communication Quarterly* 80 (2003): 128–144.

Williams, Christine B., and Girish J. Gulati. "Social Networks in Political Campaigns: Facebook and the 2006 Midterm Election." Paper presented at the annual meeting of the American Political Science Association, Chicago, Illinois, August 30–September 2, 2007.

Williams, Christine B., and Girish J. Gulati. "Communicating with Constituents in 140 Characters or Less: Twitter and the Diffusion of Technology Innovation in the United States Congress." *Social Science Research Network Working Paper Series*, Paper 43 (2010).

Williams, Christine B., and Girish J. Gulati. "Social Networks in Political Campaigns: Facebook and the Congressional Elections of 2006 and 2008." *New Media & Society* (forthcoming).

Wilson-Smith, Anthony. "Making Fun of the News." *Maclean's*, February 15, 2004.

Witt, Linda, Karen M. Paget, and Glenna Matthews. *Running as a Woman: Gender and Power in American Politics*. New York: The Free Press, 1994.

Wojcieszak, Magdalena E., and Diana C. Mutz. "Online Groups and Political Discourse: Do Online Discussion Spaces Facilitate Exposure to Political Disagreement?" *Journal of Communication* 59 (2009): 40–56.

Wolf, Gary. "How the Internet Invented Howard Dean," *Wired*, January 2004. Accessed March 22, 2012, http://www.wired.com/wired/archive/12.01/dean.html

Wolfsfield, Gadi. *The Media and Political Conflict: News from the Middle East*. Cambridge and New York: Cambridge University Press, 1987.

Wolfsfeld, Gadi. *The Media and Political Conflict*. Cambridge: Cambridge University Press, 1997.

Wolfsfeld, Gadi. *Making Sense of Media and Politics: Five Principles in Political Communication*. New York: Routledge, 2011.

Wood, Dan B. *The Politics of Economic Leadership: The Causes and Consequences of Presidential Rhetoric*. Princeton: Princeton University Press, 2007.

Wood, Dan B.. *The Myth of Presidential Representation*. Cambridge: Cambridge University Press, 2010.

Wood, Dan B., Chris T. Owens and Brandy M. Durham. "Presidential Rhetoric and the Economy." *Journal of Politics* 67 (2005): 627–645.

Wood, Dan B. and Arnold Vedlitz. "Issue Definition, Information Processing, and the Politics of Global Warming." *American Journal of Political Science* 51 (2007): 552–568.

Woodall, Gina Serignese, and Kim L. Fridkin. "Shaping Women's Chances: Stereotypes and the Media." In *Anticipating Madam President*, edited by Robert P. Watson and Ann Gordon, 69–86. Boulder, CO: Lynne Rienner Publishers, 2003.

Wu, H. Denis, and Nicole S. Dahmen. "Web Sponsorship and Campaign Effects: Assessing the Difference between Positive and Negative Web Sites." *Journal of Political Marketing* 9 (2010): 314–329.

Wyckoff, Gene. *The Image Candidates: American Politics in the Age of Television*. New York: The MacMillan Company, 1968.

Young, Garry, and William B. Perkins. "Presidential Rhetoric, the Public Agenda, and the End of Presidential Television's 'Golden Age.'" *Journal of Politics* 67 (2005): 1190–1205.

Zaller, John. *The Nature and Origins of Mass Opinion*. Cambridge and New York: Cambridge University Press, 1992.

Zaller, John. "The Myth of Massive Media Impact Revived." In *Political Persuasion and*

Attitude Change, edited by Diana C. Mutz, Paul M. Sniderman, and Richard A. Brody, 17–78. Ann Arbor: University of Michigan Press, 1996.

Zaller, John R. *A Theory of Media Politics*. Unpublished manuscript, University of California, Los Angeles, 1999. Accessed April 15, 2012, http://www.sscnet.ucla.edu/polisci/faculty/zaller/media%20politics%20book%20.pdf.

Zhang, Weiwu, Thomas J. Johnson, Trent Seltzer, and Shannon L. Bichard. "The Revolution Will Be Networked: The Influence of Social Networking Sites on Political Attitudes and Behavior." *Social Science Computer Review* 28 (2010): 75–92.

Ziemke, Dean A. "Selective Exposure in a Presidential Campaign Contingent on Certainty and Salience." In *Communication Yearbook 4*, edited by Dan Nimmo, 497–511. New Brunswick, NJ: Transaction Books, 1980.

Index